Plato's Theory of
Education

Plato's Theory of Education

by

R. C. LODGE

Professor of Logic and History of Philosophy in the University of Manitoba
Author of "Plato's Theory of Ethics."

With an Appendix on

THE EDUCATION OF WOMEN ACCORDING TO PLATO

by Rabbi Solomon Frank, Ph.D.

NEW YORK / RUSSELL & RUSSELL

International Library of Psychology
Philosophy and Scientific Method

FIRST PUBLISHED BY KEGAN PAUL, TRENCH, TRUBNER & CO. LTD.

IN THE INTERNATIONAL LIBRARY OF PSYCHOLOGY, PHILOSOPHY,

AND SCIENTIFIC METHOD IN 1947

REISSUED, 1970, BY RUSSELL & RUSSELL

A DIVISION OF ATHENEUM PUBLISHERS, INC.

BY ARRANGEMENT WITH ROUTLEDGE & KEGAN PAUL, LTD., LONDON

L. C. CATALOG CARD NO: 77-81486

ISBN 0-8462-1395-8

PRINTED IN THE UNITED STATES OF AMERICA

CONTENTS

PREFACE

This book is written primarily for students of educational theory ; that is to say, for men and women engaged in the practice of education partly as pupils—do we ever cease to be pupils ? —and partly as teachers, i.e., as citizens who have adopted the teaching profession as their lifework. In the second place it is written for students who are interested in Plato as a thinker, and who find in his writings, not merely literary fascination, but a standing challenge to their powers of thought and a certain leadership which assists them to develop a philosophy of their own. In the third place, it is hoped that the work will be of use to that wider group of readers who are interested in the life of the mind and are seeking stimulation toward renewing and deepening their visions of what might be and what, with goodwill and intelligent co-operation, may yet come to be.

Such students will look for the actual evidence of Plato's educational theories, presented clearly and without ambiguity. They will look also for completeness, and for such an arrangement as will enable them to appreciate the nature of Plato's educational vision and the depth of his philosophic insight. Finally they will expect guidance in choosing wisely between the conflicting interpretations of scholars, and in applying to present-day problems, so far as such application is possible, those doctrines of Plato which have perennial value.

In attempting to satisfy such expectations, it is incumbent upon a present-day writer to explain briefly his own bias. The reason for this is that Plato's *Dialogues* are dramatic, not systematic presentations of doctrine ; and the evidence indicates beyond the possibility of doubt that what scholars, however scholarly, publish as " *Plato's* theories," are usually a full-length portrait of the interpreter. Plato does something to his readers. They find themselves taking sides. The *Dialogues* have consequently always constituted a kind of philosopher's mirror in which, turn and twist as he may, the reader succeeds in the end in discovering —idealized, perhaps, and converted by Platonic Love into something deeper and more sincere than before, essentially—himself.

Thus : to Grote Plato represents Victorian democracy and the utilitarian theory. To Natorp the *Dialogues* are *eine Einfuhrung in den Idealismus :* an introduction to Neokantian idealism of the Marburg School. To Wilamowitz Plato is a distinguished professor (*nur noch Lehrer*), disillusioned by the failure of his Motherland's great war of aggression and dedicating himself to stimulating his students to appreciate the inner life of the spirit.

To the present interpreter Plato is a writer, teacher, and thinker, reflecting the life of his own times and working toward the establishment of an ideal community. Technically he is a comparative philosopher, comparing dialectically the chief varieties of philosophic belief : with a bias in favour of idealism, as contrasted with a simple realism and an equally simple pragmatism, but presenting his views dramatically and leaving it to the reader to reach decisions of his own. Confident above all things that in the balanced philosophic life, as it is more and more brought to bear upon the space-time world, is to be found the solution of all human problems, he sets himself to release the sources of that life, wherever possible, and calls upon all friends of ideas to join him in this co-operative quest.

My obligations are obvious : primarily to Plato himself, as edited by John Burnet ; secondarily to commentators and writers on Plato, both past and present ; and in the third place to philosophers and present-day writers on Education. From these sources I have drawn what my educational background and experience have enabled me to draw ; and I present the result in the hope that it will be found useful, primarily, by students of educational theory.

To the authorities of the Oxford University Press I owe especial thanks for their permission to quote from Jowett's Translation of the Dialogues. I should add that my citations are almost always slightly condensed, and are sometimes slightly revised, so as to bring out more clearly for my purposes what I take to be the meaning of the Greek text. Translations from the *Epistles* (which were not translated by Jowett) are my own.

Winnipeg, 1947.

Plato's Theory of
Education

INTRODUCTION

Plato's Theory of Education is developed formally and with some approach to systematic constructiveness in two Dialogues only : the *Republic* and the *Laws*. In the *Republic* the ideal outline is clear and distinct, unhampered by the concrete limitations of actual human experience. In the *Laws* the ideal is still there ; but its outline is somewhat blurred by the attempt to apply it to the fluctuating actualities of life, as envisaged by the disillusioned experience of Plato's old age. However, while these two Dialogues alone treat the subject formally, there is no writing of Plato's which is not " protreptic," an invitation to philosophize, to join the chosen band who are trying, by pooling their experiences in academic discussion, to clarify their ideas and win their way to some principle which will enable them to recognize true value, wherever found. This principle of ideality and value, definitely accepted as Platonic and definitely stated to be of central significance and transcendental import, appears only once upon the Platonic stage, and even then, with its radiance veiled from mortal eyes.[1] But what reader can doubt that this " idea of good " is behind the scenes of each and every Platonic drama, an off-stage *deus ex machina* : guiding the discussions even when the results seem negative, and constituting in each of the *dramatis personae*, the *nisus* or unseen impulse which urges him onward, in quest of his ultimate self ?

Who are the persons of the Platonic drama ? It is very easy to realize that the spotlight is usually focussed upon the character of *Socrates*, and that even when Socrates is silent or almost silent his presence is tremendously felt.[2] But Socrates is not the only *persona*, and his thoughts are never soliloquies. Even when the soul is conversing with itself, its thoughts are always in the form of discussion or dialogue. There is a convergence of more minds than one ; and each of these minds makes a positive contribution to the discussion.

Which are these other minds, the non-socratic phases of Plato's soul when it converses with itself? There is (1) a Timaeus, a Simmias or Cebes, a representative, specified or unspecified, of " the Pythagoreans," mathematicians and mystics, with whom

Socrates feels a certain affinity. There is (2) a Parmenides, a
Zeno, or an Eleatic visitor, otherwise unnamed, who represents
the " Eleatic School " of pure logic with which, it is thought,
Plato himself admits spiritual affiliation.[3] There is (3) a Cratylus,
a Protagoras or other representative of the Heraclitean " philosophy
of the flux," which views experience, as well as objective reality,
as a tissue of physical motions and nothing more, and whose
account of sense-perception is perhaps accepted by Plato himself.[4]
There is (4) a Gorgias, or some one of his many admirers and
pupils such as Meno, Pausanias, Phaedrus, Protarchus, and Polus,
or Protagoras in another of his many phases, that is to say, some
representative of " rhetoric " in its pretension to the throne of
wisdom ; and we have also (5) a Hippias, Prodicus, or Thrasymachus, a Euthydemus, Dionysodorus, or other representative
of the minor teachers of public speaking and political psychology
called " sophists " or " retailers of sham wisdom."

In addition to these, we meet with representative Athenians
such as Callicles, Ctesiphon, Laches, Nicias, and the Athenian
Stranger,[5] and their counterparts from the other cities of Hellas,
such as Cleinias, Euclid, Ion, and Megillus ; and there are great
numbers of young Athenians. Of these, some are friends of
Socrates : men like Adeimantus, Agathon, Alcibiades, Glaucon,
Phaedo, and Polemarchus. Others are representative of some
" virtue " such as modesty, friendship, or the search for knowledge : men like Charmides, Lysis, Menexenus, and Theaetetus.
Still others are present mainly *in statu pupillari* : youths like
Hippocrates, young Cleinias, young Critias, and some of
" Philebus' Boys." Finally, we have a number of lay figures,
mere interlocutors who represent the pupils of Plato's Academy :
characters like Meno's slave, *young* Socrates, and the Theaetetus
of the " dialectical " Dialogues.

The characters mentioned all have speaking parts, however
slight : although it is true that some of them shade off into what
may be called the Chorus of the drama. The rest of the Chorus
is composed of a considerable group, partly named and partly
unnamed, who lend their attention, and sometimes murmur
approval or entreaty. Some of these preserve, to retail to their
friends, it may be years afterwards, a memorized account of the
great discussions at which they were privileged to be present. In
these discussions, it is always upon Socrates, or upon some two or
three other speakers who represent the varieties of philosophic
theory, that the spotlight is focused. Around the central figures,

we glimpse in the half-light the citizens and foreign visitors, the academic youngsters and distinguished educators, the sport-club professionals, attendants, flute-girls and other " profane persons," characters who give the drama its stage setting and local colour. Beyond these, above and around and behind, unseen but present in idea and sometimes reeiving honourable mention, are the poets and other writers, with Homer at their head, the legendary gods, demi-gods, and heroes, the priests and interpreters, the artists, scientists, and philosophers, and the multitudinous devotees of the cult of pleasure, wealth, and power.

All these are upon the stage itself, or at least form part of the local setting and lend to the Platonic drama a universal-Hellenic atmosphere. As thus presented, the *dramatis personae* belong for the most part, as has recently been observed, to the past. They represent the Socratic Age, a generation which had passed away before Plato's *Republic*, for instance, was written.[6] But our picture is incomplete unless we remember that in front of the stage, in the vast auditorium before which the *personae* play their parts, are the spectators, the countless readers of Plato's Dialogues. And these include, not merely Plato's contemporaries, but especially the rising generations which represent the future. Of this Plato is well aware.[7] If then, the we are to do justice to the intention of the Dialogues, we must not regard his work as outdated, fixated in a past which is gone. We should rather compare him with Homer's Nestor, who had outlived two generations, associating always with great men, and with the third generation was still every inch a king. Plato too is one of those " whose view The past, the present, and the future knew " ; and we should regard him as transcending the limitations of time : writing, like Thucydides, for eternity.

The vast array of Platonic *personae* falls roughly into three groups. In the first and largest group we have representatives of the conventional, commonsense Athenian judgment of values : expressing not very articulately, the views of the ruling class. Like the " First, Second, and Third Citizen " in a Shakespearean drama, and the " Lords, Ladies, etc." at the end of the Elizabethan list of characters. such *personae* are there for mass-effect. They reinforce what is said and done. They amplify the general civic point of view. They perform, in short, the functions of a Chorus : shading off imperceptibly into the audience and so extending the range of participants who sit in judgment upon the dramatic action. Or rather, while seeming to sit in judgment, such persons, together with the audience into which they melt, are really carried out of themselves by the dramatic action. The spectators become participators and are swept along in the current of events, so that at the end they are no longer where they were at the beginning. They have been educated.

In the second group of *personae*, which is smaller but more vocal than the first, we have the representatives of popular thought whose formulations are not merely highly articulate but claim to be authoritative, as popular proverbs claim to be authoritative. This group includes the poets, both epic and gnomic, who with the Greeks seem to have taken the place in popular thinking once held among us by the Bible, i.e., as furnishing authoritative guidance for the conduct of life. The group includes further popular modern teachers like Gorgias, Protagoras, and Thrasymachus : humanists or pragmatists who formulate and inculcate the importance and self-sufficiency of individual and social desire. It includes, finally, citizens like Callicles, who accept and carry out in practice the new teaching that "*man* is the measure of all things."

Convinced that their judgment is sound, such authoritative life-guides prove highly critical of other views, and are prepared, for their friends or for a definite consideration, to communicate the magic formulas—such as "Justice is the interest of the stronger," and "Pleasure is the true standard of value"—which provide the keys to happiness, leadership, and social success.[8] Poets, sophists, and statesmen alike manufacture slogans and formulas which, used with discretion, enable the practical believer in direct action to mould popular opinion almost at will,[9] or at least sufficiently to keep ahead of the direction in which it is most likely to move.[10] Mob-psychology is a little uncertain, and such leadership is precarious ;[11] but still, representatives of this group are convinced that this way, and this way alone, safety lies.[12]

The third group of *personae* is very small : consisting indeed only of Socrates and a few "friends of ideas" or students of philosophy, whether Pythagorean, Eleatic, or Academic, whose ideals point beyond biosocial manipulation to the co-operative search for truth. Such philosophers or seekers after wisdom are attempting to discover and formulate the principle and main features of a purely ideal world, in the hope that eventually the ideal standards thus found will be capable of application to the concrete problems of life, and that it will be possible for especially selected and educated leaders to imitate or participate in ideal reality, and to guide the rest of us in the same general direction.[13]

The action of a Platonic drama is not external but internal. The dramatic conflict is not so much between persons, as between what the persons stand for : their philosophies, i.e., speculative theories or hypotheses whose consequences—all ultimately of practical and vital import—are elaborated in the *Dialogues* and compared in idea. Plato's own philosophic attitude is thus essentially comparative. He projects artistically upon his central stage plans of action and principles of explanation which are fundamentally alternatives.[14]

The formulas propounded by the *personae* of Plato's second group, reveal to the characters of the first group their own inherent aims and ideals. In proportion as these aims receive more articulate expression, certain lurking inconsistencies and oppositions are brought out, which prove irreconcilable. In the lengthy speeches of this or that professor of rhetoric, or in the question-and-answer discussions which Socrates succeeds in stripping to essentials, the issues become sharply defined. These alternatives constitute, for the members of the first group of *personae*, who seem to be sitting in judgment, a challenge which has to be met. The importance of the issue for actual life is recognized, and a definite choice has to be made. Sometimes in the heat of the discussion, the protagonists and their followers change sides and appear as maintaining the reverse of the thesis with which they began.[15] Sometimes they discover that they are in the impossible position of trying to say both yes and no to the same thesis. They are like children saying " give us both ! " Sometimes they recognize the exclusiveness of the alternatives brought out by the discussion, but remain in a state of Socratic ignorance, unable to make and defend a definite choice.[16] Very rarely, a speaker succeeds, it is thought, in converting an antagonist to his own way of thinking.[17] But as a rule, like Ben Jonson's *Everyman in His Humour*, the Platonic drama presents characters who maintain and express only their own position. Critical comparison, in the form of discussion, merely brings out and emphasizes the essential differences, and indeed the mutual exclusiveness, of the alternatives involved, and leaves it to the audience to come to its own conclusion.

In a word, in the Platonic drama, the action definitely includes the audience. Plato's readers start, presumably, from membership in the first group, and by participating in the discussions, project themselves into all sides and end, either as convinced adherents of some one of the views characteristic of members of the second group,[18] or else as seekers gradually acquiring membership in the third group, the friends of ideas who constitute Plato's spiritual academy. If they beome members of this small band of wisdom-lovers who are seeking after a truth which they have not yet found,[19] they do not assert this or that position to be categorically true. They treat all theories hypothetically, comparing their theoretical and practical values so as to use for the purposes of life whatever views, accepted hypothetically, seem most assured and most nearly in accord with the demands of truth as an absolute ideal.[20]

It has been supposed by many editors of individual Dialogues, and indeed by very distinguished expositors of the inner meaning of whole groups of Dialogues, that Plato, even where the results are admittedly negative, i.e., even where, after discussion of both sides, the summary is deliberately inconclusive, provides for the attentive reader hints which, followed up intelligently, will guide him to a solution of the problem which Plato regards as " right." Plato is regarded as a writer of elementary textbooks *in usum scholarum :* textbooks which, like the medieval masterpieces of the Scholastics, raise questions, give (a) the " right " answer, and (b) a number of " wrong " answers, and proceed to substantiate the " right " answer and to refute the " wrong " answers. This well-meaning effort on the part of schoolmasters has led to a tremendous expenditure of ingenuity, especially in the case of Dialogues which do not fit easily into the scheme.[21] But scholarly ingenuity has seemed equal to the occasion, and has seldom failed to point out which of the alternatives discussed represents Plato's " own " view, the side which he himself takes and wishès his reader to take. From this standpoint, Plato is regarded, not as a comparative philosopher, but as an " idealist," engaged in refuting the position of " realism " or " materialism," or the position of " humanism " or " pragmatism."

Widespread, however, as this mode of interpretation seems to be, the unbiassed reader will doubt whether it is substantiated by the evidence of the Dialogues. In the Dialogues, it is not positions, abstract philosophical theses, which are substantiated or refuted. It is persons. The persons who hold this position or that, are refuted and convinced of their ignorance. But the position, considered in itself, remains neither substantiated nor refuted. It can be taken up again, in the same or in some other Dialogue ; and the person who maintains it can pass through the salutary process of refutation, For refutation, as Plato understands it, is an educative process. It affects not positions but individuals, and effects in their souls a process of purification. It does not substitute a " right " view for a " wrong " answer to some philosophic question. It induces rather a state of mind, a subjective attitude favourable to the search for truth, the conviction of ignorance which is the beginning of wisdom.[22]

In the *Gorgias*, Gorgias himself is refuted. His position is not refuted. It is taken up by Polus. Polus is then refuted, and the position is maintained by Callicles. Callicles is refuted. But even Callicles is not convinced that the position is refuted. He cannot " answer " Socrates ; but he still thinks that Socrates' position is all wrong, and that the position he has failed to maintain is really sound.[23] Substantially the same position is maintained in the *Republic*, first by Polemarchus and then by Thrasymachus. Thrasymachus is refuted. But so far is his position from being refuted, that it is taken up again by Glaucon and Adeimantus ; and it is still taken seriously in the latest of Plato's works, the *Laws*.[24]

So too in the *Parmenides*, Socrates is refuted. But the position of idealism, which he has failed to maintain, is not itself refuted, in spite of the commentators.[25] In the *Theaetetus*, Protagoras, or rather his representative, is refuted. But so far is *his position* from being refuted, that Socrates himself takes it up and re-states it.[26] The conflict between positions is in fact regarded by Plato as unending. The ideal patterns, whether positive or negative, belong in a realm which transcends human affirmation or human refutation. They remain untouched ; and to suppose that Plato is trying, by dialectical arguments, to eliminate one side of the conflcit, or even that he has the slightest hope that one side will ever be eliminated, is simply not in accordance with the evidence.[27] Refutation is subjective, not objective. It is an educational, not a metaphysical weapon ; and its function is, not to solve problems, but to stimulate persons.

As the writer sees it, Plato's philosophy may be regarded as "reasoned truth,"[28] not in the sense of the logical demonstration of the correctness of this or that position, but in the sense of the reasoned, dialectical exposition of both this and that position as speculative alternatives. For Plato, as for Socrates, no single alternative is " final." It is left to the audience, the readers who sit in judgment and are stimulated to join the academic band of wisdom-lovers, to decide for themselves " in friendly rivalry "[29] where they will make their stand. Plato's position is essentially

comparative, dramatic, protreptic. As the well-known letter
states : in the Dialogues we find, not opinions of Plato, but
Socrates made young and handsome.[30] It should be added that
we find also Protagoras, Parmenides, and the rest, all flourishing
in the timeless and spaceless realms of the spirit, in eternal youth
and beauty, like the figures on some Grecian urn : forever pursuing and pursued, forever evading and renewing the conflict.
The conflict between ideals is unending,[31] and this indicates that,
while it behoves a man, as a man, to take sides in the conflict or
possibly to take a stand *audessus de la mêlée*,[32] final proof and final
disproof are out of the question. Comparison, objective yet sympathetic, doing full justice to all sides of each proposed solution,
is the only theoretic attitude worthy of the philosopher. And
this is the position taken by Plato himself. As a man, he has a
bias and does not conceal it. But as a philosopher, he does not
permit his bias to induce him to treat as closed, issues which he
knows remain forever open.[33] Biassed in favour of idealism,[34] he
still does not close his eyes to the facts of life, but presents idealism
as one alternative view, in perpetual conflict with crude realism
and crude humanism or pragmatism.

In studying *Plato's Theory of Education* we shall therefore try to
be just to all sides of each question, as they are expounded and
compared by Plato : to the commonsense beliefs set forth in the
various Dialogues ; to the alternative theories and formulations
brought to grips in the various discussions ; and we shall not
regard as absolutely final the idealistic views propounded in the
Republic. If we are to be just to the evidence of the Dialogues as a
whole, we shall look for truth in the comparison of all sides and
the one-sided victory of none. It is precisely in such comparison
and discussion that, unless we are mistaken, *Plato's Theory of
Education* itself consists. For only thus does the reflective, balanced
judgment which depends upon itself in matters of practice, come
into being.[35]

---

[1] *Rep.* 508e f. Cf. Fouillée, *La philosophie de Platon*, p. 353 ; Natorp, *Platos Ideenlehre*
pp. 172, 173 ; Taylor, *Plato, The Man and his Work*, pp. 230–231 ; Wilamowitz-
Moellendorff, *Platon*,[2] Vol. I pp. 388, 391, Vol. II, p. 209.
[2] Cf. Friedländer, *Platon*, Vol. I, pp. 152 ff. [3] *Theaet.* 183e f., *Soph.* 241d, 242a.
[4] *Theaet.* 156a–157b, 159c–160e, 167d, 168b, 182. Cf. Aristot., *Met.* 987a 32 ff.
[5] Other members of this general class are Anytus, Apollororus, Aristophanes,
Cephalus, Chaerephon, Cleitophon, Critias, Crito, Euthyphro, Hermocrates, Hermo-
genes, Hippothales, Lysimachus, Philebus.
[6] Burnet, *E.Gr.Phil.* [7] *Phaedo* 102a, *Rep.* 497c–d, *Laws*, 811c f., 817b f., cf.
765d f., 769e, 858c f, 88od f., 957d, 964 d f.
[8] *Prtg.* 354b–c, 357a, 358a f., *Rep.* 337d, 338a–c, e–339a, 344c, *Phileb.* 11b, *Laws*
732 e f., cf. 714 c–d.

[9]*Gorg.* 452d–435a, 454 a–b, 455, d–456 c, *Rep.* 336a, 365d. [10]*Rep.* 492–493.
[11]*Gorg.* 515a–520d, *Rep.* 496c–d. [12]*Gorg.* 521a–b.
[13]*Gorg.* 506e, *Meno* 88 b–d, *Rep.* 472c f., 484c d., 490b, 500b ff., 518c f., 527b ff.,
534 b f., 540a–b, cf. 441e f., *Phaedr.* 247c f., Sym. 211e f., *Parm.* 132 d, *Polit.* 295a f.,
300c f., *Phileb.* 40b–c, 58a, *Laws*, 709, 770, 898 f., 903b f.
[14]Cf. *Gorg.* 487e f., *Tim.* 51c f., *Soph.* 243d, 245e ff., *Phileb.* 19c–d, cf. 11, 28d–e,
60a f. [15]*Prtg.* 361.
[16]*Rep.* 538c, *Theaet.* 200c, cf. 155b–c, 158e, 162c–d, 196c–d, *Parm.* 131e, 135c
Phileb. 33d, 58a–b.
[17]This is thought to be the case, e.g., with Thrasymachus (*Rep.* 354a, 498c) and,
Theodorus (*Theaet.* 183b–c, 179b), as well as with youthful interlocutors.
[18]*Prtg.* 336–338, cf. 358a, Euthyd *Rep.* 339e f.
[19]Cf. *Rep.* 357, 506b f., *Theaet.* 200e f.
[20]*Phaedo* 99d ff., *Meno* 86d f., *Sym.* 211e f., *Rep.* 505e f., *Theaet.* 157c–d, *Tim.* 29c, 44d,
48d, *Parm.* 135e f.
[21]E.g., *Parmenides*, and *Theaetetus*. H. Bonitz, *Platonische Studien*, Berlin, 1875, is
representative of the older group of scholars ; but the tendency is still with us.
[22]*Gorg.* 458a, *Soph.* 230 f. On the other side, cf. *Rep.* 538c, *Theaet.* 161d.
[23]*Gorg.* 513c, cf. 461a f., 481b f., 505c f., 511a–b. [24]*Rep.* 357a, 358b f., *Laws* 714c f.
[25]Cf. *Parm.* 135b f., *Soph.* 253e f., 254b f., 259e f. [26]*Theaet.* 165e ff.
[27]Cf. *Rep.* 472b f., 508e f., 517b–c, *Theaet.* 176a, e, *Parm.* 133b f., *Laws* 906a.
[28]Cf. Nettleship, *Lectures on the Republic.* [29]*Prtg.* 338e, *Tim.* 51b–d, 54b.
[30]*Epist.* 314c. Cf. Friedländer, *op. cit.*, Vol. I, pp 152, 156–159.
[31]*Theaet.* 176a, *Polit.* 273b, *Laws* 906a. [32]*Phaedo*, 65 ff ; *Laws*, 727 f.
[33]Cf. *Lysis* 218a–c, *Charm.* 165c, *Rep.* 506c f., 509c, 537d f., *Tim.* 29c, 48d, 53d,
Soph. 243 ff., 246b–c.
[34]*Phaedo* 74a f., 78d, 99e f., 102b, 105b–e, *Tim.* 51d f., *Theaet.* 185d–e, *Parm.*
135b–c, *Soph.* 246c f.
[35]*Lach.* 188a f., 200a f. ; *Meno* 84a f. ; *Euthyd.* 288c–291a ; *Rep.* 590e f., cf. 540ab ;
Phaedr. 276 f., 278ab ; *Epist.* 341–344c.

CHAPTER I

EDUCATION DEFINED

Modern students approach the subject of educational theory with a definite distinction in mind. The term " education " is understood in two senses, one very wide, and one somewhat narrow. In the wider or more generic sense, education is used as equivalent to " experience," the experience of a living organism interacting with its normal environment.[1] An insect such as a bee, an animal such as a horse or dog, can learn from experience. When the environment stimulates, the organism, with its inherited action-tendencies, responds. If the consequences are satisfactory to the organism, the response may be repeated or continued until it has worked itself out. If unpleasant or painful, the primary reaction-tendency may be modified until satisfaction is attained.

So also with human organisms. Falling in love, being stung by mosquitoes, losing money on the Stock Exchange, are experiences which are, in this wider or generic sense, highly " educative." Various action-tendencies are stimulated and the natural responses modified until satisfaction is attained. In this way we regard a mother as " educated " by her baby, a teacher by his pupils, a dictator by his subjects.

In almost all contacts with our environment, we do more than merely react to stimulation. We modify our reactions until a satisfactory result is reached. In such cases, i.e., wherever our responses are more than mere reflexes or pure routine, we are being " educated." Nature is the great teacher. Experience is a process of learning ; and we all, as long as our experience lasts, may be regarded as learners. Education in the generic sense is thus equated with " experience " understood as interaction with nature. In nature, stimuli occur as they happen to occur : without guidance, design, or plan ; and in our interaction with such chance stimuli, we learn or modify our inherited action-patterns and so become " educated."

The term " education " is also understood in a narrower sense. Experience or nature is still the teacher ; but, in the specific social institution known as " schooling," it is *guided* experience, *nurture* rather than *mere* nature, which is said to be especially educative. Here the stimulation is under social control, and the pupil's reaction is under social direction. In our schools, experience is not left to itself, but is selected and amplified in accordance with the community value-judgment. Highly specialized techniques are brought to bear. The traditional background and outlook of the social group are imparted to the rising generation in accordance with an approved plan ; and the natural reaction-tendencies of the youthful organisms are modified until they take on the patterns regarded by the community as desirable. In the narrower sense, .then " Education " is understood as *socially controlled experience.*

When we turn from modern educational theory to the ancients in general, and to Plato in particular, we still find a distinction between " education " and " schooling." But the lines are drawn differently ; so differently, that the ancient picture can hardly be superimposed upon the modern canvas. In the first place, the Greeks seldom think of " nature " as a teacher, or of the school as doing in a specific way what experience, left to itself, already does in a generic way. In fact, nature and nurture are sharply opposed. Education is thought of as a specifically human institution : a social technique or art not found *in rerum naturae,* but invented by man. As a technical art, education represents, not nature, but a human improvement upon nature.

Left to himself, natural man no doubt falls in love, dislikes mosquitoes, and objects to losing money or anything else which he cherishes as valuable. But a Greek philosopher does not regard such experiences as " educative." Unguided experience is " chaotic," and chance is the direct antithesis of the ordered cosmos produced by the inspired artificer. The Greek regards it as his mission to co-operate, not with nature but with God : humanizing and Hellenizing the world of nature.[2] Education, as he understands it, is a definite art : an art which guides, re-shapes, and controls human experience in accordance with an intelligible principle of value ; improving upon nature at every step of the game.

In the second place, while education might conceivably, even for a writer like Plato, be described as " socially controlled experience," the control, for a Greek, is very different from what it is for a modern. It is community control ; but it is emphatically not localized within the school. It is diffused through the community as a whole, and is a function of all social institutions with-

out exception Such social institutions as the family and clan, the
army, the church and the stage, the business firm and courts of
law, the political assembly and other forms of human association,
are found in modern, as in ancient times. But with us the educational emphasis, originally concentrated upon the family, school
and church, has in recent generations become concentrated almost
exclusively upon the school. With us the business of education
is entrusted almost exclusively to highly trained professionals.
These are not only permitted but expected to do, in the way of
education, what the other social institutions nowadays leave
undone.

With the Greeks, however, the school is only one of the social
institutions concerned with educating the rising generation. It is
not a public, but a private institution. Its teachers are not public
officials, but cheap hirelings. They are qualified to train the
children in elementary techniques : to play games, to read and
write, to make a little music. But that is all.[3] For educating the
children so that they become full members of the community, the
typical Greek looks to community institutions proper ; and the
true educators are not the school-teachers, but the adult free-born
citizens. It is not merely in their capacity as parents or uncles,
but as representatives of the community ways of living in all their
aspects, organized and unorganized, that the citizens are regarded
as educational authorities. They are qualified, not only in common opinion, but in Plato's mature judgment, to act as authorities
to supervise and direct the behaviour of the rising generation,
and to correct without hesitation whatever they consider amiss in
the behaviour of the school-teachers. For the development of
true manliness, public spirit, and any sort of idealism, the children
look, not to the school and its imported professionals, but to the
older generations who belong.[4]

Thus we realize that with the Greeks " education " normally
signifies, not following nature, but directing human nature to
socially approved ends ; and that in such education the place
allotted to schools and the work of the schoolteacher is necessarily
humble and technical. And further : with the Greeks the
adult civic standpoint is final. There is no question of respect for
anything but adult civic standards. The child is not entitled to a
child's life, an existence in which he is assisted to think, speak,
and act as a child. On the contrary : from the beginning he is
to be trained in the civic virtues of self-control, manliness, and the
like.[6] Like the sons and apprentices in artisan families, the

young citizen is educated almost entirely by extra-curricular methods. He looks on at the parental activities which will one day be his activities, and in the meantime he acts as a helper : fitting himself gradually for the performance of civic duties. He cannot as yet handle the spear and heavy armour of the adult ; but he can play with mimic weapons and can take part in field sports whose aim is undisguised preparation for adult warfare.[7] And when he has learnt to ride he can be conducted with the other children of the community, in troup-formation, to look on while his parents take part in hand-to-hand combat with the enemy. His officers will play the part of tutors, explaining the whys and wherefores of each military evolution ; but the fighting is not academic. It is desperately real. Adult life is an unremitting struggle for existence, and the nursery is not the goal.[8]

So too there is no question of education for education's sake. Modern authorities sometimes write as though Rousseau's alleged " discovery of childhood " had changed the facts of life ; as though what is taught to children should have no immediately practical end, but should primarily be educative, stimulating the child to develop his own, largely playful interests, This would make life within the school very different from life in the adult world, and the graduate of many a modern glorified kindergarten must find the transition to actual life difficult.[9] But to the Greeks it is unquestionable that education is for the sake of life, adult civic life, and not *vice versa*. Every Greek child is, by right of birth, a recruit in the army of Hellenism. All his life he must play his part in the unending conflict between Hellenism and Barbarism, between the life of reason and the chaos of mere nature ; and it is education which develops the eye of his soul and turns him into an exponent and defender of the Hellenic way of life.

All this is true, not merely of Plato's countrymen, but of Plato himself. His philosophy does not question, but formulates, expands, and deepens the Hellenic point of view. He does not philosophize for the sake of philosophizing, but accepts the background and outlook of the Greek city-state. He merely endeavours to give to the city-state an ideal formulation, to construct a pattern which the Greek educator and administrator can keep always before his eyes ;[10] and his educational theories have always the practical aim of training for citizenship, or it may be for leadership, in an idealized Hellenic community. While it is true that incidentally he has something to say of vocational and technical

training, it is beyond doubt that his chief interest is in education
for character, education for citizenship, and education for leadership in a small community of freemen co-operating in realizing the
ideal which we know as the Hellenic way of life.

[1]Cf. Lodge : *Philosophy of Education*, 1937, pp. 23–26.
[2]*Rep.* 472d f., 500c f., 508e f., 540ab, 590e ff. ; *Tim.* 30a, 44a–c, 48a, 52d f., 69b–d,
87 ff. ; *Parm.* 133b f. ; *Polit.* 273b f. ; *Phil.* 26b ; *Laws*, 857d, 903b ff.
[3]cf. Demosthenes, *De Corona*, sect. 258.
[4]*Apol.* 24c f. ; *Prtg.* 325c f. ; *Meno.* 91–93a ; *Laws* 664b f. , 804cd, 808e f., 964bc.
[5]*Laws* 659c. This passage is typical.
[6]*Prtg.* 325c f. ; *Rep.* 412b, 425b, 465a ; *Laws* 791–794b.
[7]*Rep.* 537a ; *Laws* 643a f., 813 ff.   [8]*Rep.* 466e f. ; cf. *Laws* 625e f., 805d f.
[9]Cf. Dewey : *Democracy and Education*, Ch. XV, pp. 416–417.
[10]*Rep.* 395b f., 472b f., 517bc, 540ab, 590e—592 ; *Laws* 739, 811b f. ; 967d f.

CHAPTER II

VOCATIONAL AND TECHNICAL EDUCATION

Vocational and technical education belong to that side of life which the average freeborn Greek citizen regarded as " banausic " and unworthy of his serious attention ; and to some extent Plato's aristocratic upbringing induced in him a tendency to share this general prejudice. But his association with Socrates, the sculptor's son who never wearied of bringing the analogy of the arts and crafts into his reasonings, seems to have enabled him to outgrow this class feeling, and we know that in his later years, as head of a great educational institution, he trained his students deliberately in applying the techniques of dialectical analysis to such pursuits as angling, hunting, and weaving.[1]

This fact indicates beyond possible doubt that Plato saw in such pursuits something worthy of a philosopher's attention. His interest in them is not merely incidental. They are not introduced as mere background effects, picturing the life of his time. They have a definite place in his ideal city, and when we look more closely at what Plato has to say about them, we find that they contain, in themselves, certain ideal elements which enable their practitioners to participate in the good life. We have thus a treatment which goes beyond the typical Greek citizens point of view and presents something characteristically Platonic ; and when we realize further that the discussion of the arts and crafts frequently has an explicitly educational reference, we can see that, if we collect and put together all that Plato has to say in this field, we shall have evidence which at least assists in enabling us to understand the more specialised views of education (for character, citizenship, and leadership) usually associated by scholars with his name.

The vocations or techniques in which a man may be trained to some sort of professional proficiency are nowhere either fully classified or fully listed in the *Dialogues*. Most of the references are incidental and illustrative of wide fields of which the boundaries are not very clearly marked. In particular, the discussion is sometimes far from precise as to whether the actual

practice of some skill is under consideration, or the teaching of
that practical skill. It is not always clear whether a teacher like
Protagoras is a teacher of subject-matter or a teacher of pedagogy :
whether he trains his pupils to be public speakers or merely
sophists, teachers of the subject.[2] So too the qualifications for
teaching are either practical or pedagogic achievements.[3] And
it is frequently assumed that the practitioner of an art is somehow
not completely competent unless he can reason philosophically
about his art, defining it with technical accuracy and being able
to defend his definition against dialectical criticisms.[4] Thus it is
not always the art itself which is under consideration, but rather
the concept of the art, its " idea " ; and in many of the references
it is not so much the vocational as the dialectical significance of
the art upon which attention is focussed. For a writer with Plato's
philosophic interests this is perhaps inevitable, and for the moment
we shall content ourselves with drawing up, for purposes of discussion, a roughly classified list of all the techniques and vocations
of which he treats.

These may be presented as follows :

(1) The arts and crafts. These fall into two divisions :
    (a) The crafts or technical activities of artisans, such as
        building, carpentering, pottery, weaving, etc., in which
        something concrete and useful, such as a house or boat, a
        table or bed, a cup or a piece of dress-goods, is produced.[5]
    (b) The arts or technical activities of artists, such as music,
        painting, poetry, prose writing (forensic or political), etc.,
        in which something concrete and beautiful (as well as
        useful) is produced.[6]

(2) The sciences, understood by Plato as mathematical in their
    methodology, and as partly concrete-physical (Pytha-
    gorean), partly abstract-philosophical (Platonic) in their
    reference.
    These include :
    (a) Arithmetic.[7]
    (b) Geometry (both plane and solid).[8]
    (c) Physics (also at times called astronomy), the study of solids
        in motion.[9]
    (d) Harmonics, the study of tones, scales, rhythms, consonance
        and dissonance, with reference to their principles.[10]

(3) The social sciences, especially ethics and politics.[11]

(4) The vocations. Under this term are included :

(a) Farming, whose function is to provide the community with food, by tending plants and animals, where nature gives the increase. Human reason does little, as compared with nature. Under this term Plato includes the apiarist, the cattle-man, etc.[12]

(b) Angling and hunting, with a similar function. The objects sold for food are, however, not cultivated but grow wild, and have to be captured in an activity involving skill and sometimes courage.[13]

(c) Innkeeping.[14]

(d) The shipmaster's calling, which involves knowledge as well as courage.[15]

(e) Retail trading, which markets (for profit) the produce of others, but itself produces nothing.[16]

(f) Wholesale merchandizing, involving export and import activities,[17]

(g) Banking and finance, the activity which makes money make money.[18]

(h) Civil engineering.[19]

(i) Teaching, i.e., training in elementary techniques. This includes nurses, playground games mistresses, sports-club professionals, teachers of reading, writing, arithmetic and the bare essentials of song-and-dance music.[20]

(j) Military vocations, including archery, equitation, the use of chariots, javelins, slings, spears, and defensive armour, both light and heavy.[21] Possibly boxing and wrestling should also be included.[22]

Under these four heads are grouped all the professional techniques discussed in the *Dialogues*. They represent activities for which there is a social need, activities by the practice of which members of the typical Hellenic community earn their living and for which they receive some sort of training. It is in the training received that we are at present interested ; and we shall inquire, taking one group at a time, precisely how the individual acquires the training which develops his proficiency to the professional level.

(1a). In the crafts, according to the universal Hellenic practice, vocational training was what we should call extra-curricular. There was no school or technical institute, public or private, where the future smith, carpenter, potter, or weaver could, for a

fee, receive instruction. Craftsmanship in the trades was heredi-
tary and its techniques were passed on from father to son.

The son learned his trade by growing up in his father's family
and participating in the family activities, imitating what he saw
his father doing. At first the imitation would be playful and
childish, carried out with such toy tools as a child could handle.
Later it would be more deliberately purposive. Practice produced
technical proficiency in details and the growing boy would act,
first as his father's " helper," then as his associate, and would
eventually himself become the head of a family, and the centre from
which further training in the family craft would radiate.[23] As we are
informed in the Laws[24] :

> To be good at anything, it is first necessary to practice that thing
> from youth up, both in play and in earnest, with the particular move-
> ments which the work requires. The boy who is to be a good builder
> must play at building children's houses. The boy who is to be a
> carpenter learns to measure and apply the line in play. They use
> mimic tools, learning while they are young the knowledge which they
> will require for professional practice when they are grown up. The
> child is trained in acquiring the excellence which the man will possess
> to perfection.

Vocational training of this kind was not, in Greek usage, confined to actual sons. There might be, and frequently were, adopted
sons or other members of the family who lived with the family
and grew up participating in its activities as apprentices, and thus
acquired the family trade.[25] The family provided the tools of the
trade and the apprentices doubtless repaid by service the full
value of what training they received. They looked on, helped, and
learned by doing, doing what they saw the family doing.

The principles involved in such vocational training in the
crafts are formulated by Plato as (1) association (the regular Greek
word), i.e., participating in the activities of the family and receiving some sort of direction from its head, (2) imitation or direct
copying of the movements by which skill with tools is demonstrated, and (3) continued practice until manipulative dexterity
has been thoroughly acquired. Such training was informal and
biosocial rather than institutional, i.e. resembled the cookery
and needlework in which girls became proficient, in that it took
place within the family.[26]

(1b). In the arts, vocational training in Ancient Greece was
somewhat similarly extra-curricular. There was no Art Institute,
College of Music, or School of Architecture in our modern sense.

The professional flautist was almost always the son or daughter of a professional flautist, and in general the professional artist learned the techniques of his art in much the same way as the carpenter or potter learned the techniques of his trade. Both were chiefly matters of manipulative dexterity, and were developed by living and growing up in the family of a professional, doing what the professional did and so, by association, imitation, and long practice, acquiring professional proficiency with the instruments and techniques of the painter, architect, musician, poet, or prose-writer.[27]

In fact, in most of the references, Plato makes very little distinction between the vocational training of the artist and the vocational training of the craftsman. There are, indeed, contexts in which he seems to recognize an important distinction between a *great* poet or other artist and a mere hand-worker. But for the most part he thinks of poets as craftsmen, hired for a particular job, somewhat as a modern studio executive thinks of authors as script-writers, hired to put together, under direction, the words required by this or that scenario.[28] They provide technical assistance in producing a revised version of the national literature, in composing hymns for public occasions, and the like ; but always subject to the approval of the community authorities.

When we consider the arts and crafts as vocations, however, we notice certain differences. While in both arts and crafts, generally speaking, professional *expertise* is passed on from father to son, in the case of the arts it is also possible for youths who are neither members of an artists' family nor apprentices in the usual sense, to " associate " with the family for a definite fee and thus to pick up the techniques of this or that artist. Such persons, unless unusually gifted, would of course seldom become as expert as the artist's sons, as can readily be understood ; and artistic families might thus expect to take fees for turning out, not professionals, but amateurs.[29] In fact they might even go further and by taking pupils from families which were willing to pay fees, pupils whose powers were appreciative rather than creative, might provide general education rather than impart productive skill.[30]

In spite, however, of these differences, which made the artistic family pass over imperceptibly into a sort of trade-school and even educational institute to an extent not attained in the craftsman's family, it must be recognized that vocational education in the arts, as in the crafts, remained informal, within the family. It should further be recognized that this type of vocational education has remained, in the arts, the standard pattern in Europe until very recent times.

So far, we have treated both arts and crafts as activities in which vocational education, by association, imitation, and practice, develops manipulative dexterity. If, however, we are to follow Plato further, into a realm more especially his own, we must proceed from a distinction which he makes more than once. Certain of the arts and crafts are as we have hitherto described them : radically empirical, following a rule of thumb, dependent upon the senses and a trial-and-error method which may be described as " conjecture " or happy guess-work. Others, however, have what may be called a definitely intellectual feature : namely, a mathematical structure, which can be apprehended, not by the senses, but by the reason.

For instance, we read in the *Philebus*[31] that

If arithmetic, mensuration, and weighing be taken away from any technique, the rest will be only conjecture and the better use of the senses which comes from experience and practice, in addition to a certain power of guessing which is perfected by attention and pains. Music is empirical in this sense ; for in music sounds are harmonized, not by exact measure, but by skilful conjecture. Flute music is perpetually guessing at the pitch of each vibrating note, and is thus doubtful and inexact.

Builders, on the other hand, use a number of measuring instruments, and so attain to greater accuracy. The builder has a rule, a lathe, a compass, a line, and an ingenious instrument for straightening wood. Such arts and crafts are more exact.

The art of exact measurement, when applied in the arts and crafts, does away with the merely manipulative techniques and the guess-work which depends upon sensation. Thus, in architecture, if the pillars upon which a pediment rests are to *look* straight to the eye, the artist will design pillars which *look* straight, but are really a little thicker in the middle than at the ends ; or in the statuary's art, if the proportions of a more than life-size statue are to *look* right, certain parts will have to be out of exact proportion. Plato refers frequently to these techniques which base themselves upon sensuous satisfaction, and contrasts them with exact mathematical measurement. The artists of his time clearly based their work upon this appeal to appearance and opinion[32] ; and if Plato deliberately prefers exact measurement (as he undoubtedly does), this is because he is not, from an educational standpoint, interested in the perfection of the arts and crafts as techniques. He admits that the mechanical, useful, and popular arts and crafts have their own aims and technical methods and he does not propose to interfere with those methods, as far as the training of artists and craftsmen is concerned. He understands perfectly that mathematical studies have a value in their application to artistic production, as well as for the philosophic purposes in which he himself is especially interested.[33] From the vocational standpoint, then, the study of arithmetic, geometry, and mensuration requires to be added, as a vitally important discipline for the carpenter, weaver, musician, and poet, which will place those who are proficient in intellectual studies in a position of superiority to all merely manipulative technicians. As we read in the *Laws*,[34]

No single instrument of education in youth has such mighty power in the arts and crafts, as the study of arithmetic. Above all, arithmetic stirs up the youth who is naturally sleepy and dull, and makes him quick to learn, retentive, shrewd and he makes progress quite beyond his natural powers.

This line of thought connects the arts and crafts, as mental disciplines, with the sciences, i.e., is a first step along the road of studies which terminates in dialectic and the philosophic vision of the realm of transcendental ideas. The craftsman's definite knowledge and intelligent grasp of efficient techniques,[35] and the artist's vision of ideals that never were on sea or land point in the same general direction. The work of mind, in these as in other fields, represents the concrete operation of value-judgments and of their principle, the idea of good or principle of value.[37] But, when all is said and done, the first step remains only a first step. The concreteness of the arts and crafts has to be overcome by the abstracting power of reason, before further steps can be taken. The craftsman and the artist are no philosophers, just as the philosopher is no artist.[38] The education which fits a man for a life of craftsmanship or for creative artistry is and remains, not philosophical, but vocational.

A further line of thought defines the arts and crafts in relation to community needs. In the ideal republic craftsmen belong to the largest section of the community, namely, the workers who minister to the needs of the governing classes, as well as of their own group. They build the houses, ships, and other conveyances; they create the furnishings, clothe the citizens, and in general do the work which raises the standard of living above the most primitive level.[39] In so functioning, they represent the principle of the division of labour, each man concentrating upon the task for which his own gifts fit him, and thus illustrate the idea of good or principle of development of maximal value in concrete operation.[40]

So also in the model city of the *Laws*, where it is further laid down explicitly that the numbers and location of the craftsmen are determined in all cases by the magistrates.[41] As to the artists, their function is always to create, in accordance with their own inherent principle, but under the direction of the governing classes. Their creations are accepted in so far as they provide a sort of sensuous amplifier of the social ideals approved by the group ; and they may also be called in to advise the authorities in revising the productions of pre-censorship generations of artists such as Homer.[42] Their business is to create (or revise) the songs and dances, the prayers, praises, and thanksgivings, suitable both for private education in the family, and for public ceremonials of all sorts.[43]

The training which fits craftsmen and artists for playing this part does not differ in essentials from the vocational education already discussed. For this further use of their trained gifts does not demand self-direction on the part of either artist or craftsman. The experts create and revise to order ; and the order comes, not from themselves, but from their superiors, the community authorities. There is no art for art's sake in Plato.[44] Artists like craftsmen, are and remain what their training has made them : useful technicians whose function is to execute orders, and also, when commanded, to provide for the children of the higher classes rudimentary training of an educational rather than technical nature in the elements of their respective arts and crafts.[45] They make a useful contribution to the higher life, but themselves hardly pass beyond its threshold.

2. The sciences, when pursued vocationally, are treated by Plato as analogous to the arts and crafts, although it is admitted that their intellectual structure is so much more developed that they ought to be regarded as a step higher upon the cognitive ladder. Both reach the level of *doxa* or opinion, but the sciences reach the level of *right* opinion, falling just short of what a philosopher would regard as the level of *knowledge*.[46] The most distinguished professional exponents of science are the so-called Pythagoreans, the devotees of mathematical methodology.[47] Less distinguished, but widespread, are the scientists who rest upon

sensuous observation and experimentation, subordinating their reason to their senses, as in the notorious case of musical acoustics :[48]

> The teachers of harmony compare tones and consonances, restricting their studies to what can be heard with the ear. They talk of " condensed " notes, and put their ears close to the vibrating strings, as if they were catching sounds from them. Some maintain that they can distinguish an intermediate note and so have discovered the least discernible interval, and that this should be the unit of measurement. Others insist that the two tones have passed into a single tone. Both sides thus set their ears before their understanding, as they tease and torture the strings and rack them upon the pegs of the instrument.

Even the Pythagoreans, however, confine their attention to the harmonies which can be heard by the ear. " They investigate the numbers of the harmonies which are heard, and never attain to the harmonies which are natural to number as such. They never reflect why some numbers are harmonious and others not."[49] That is to say, all the sciences, in spite of their mathematical methodology, contain a great deal which rests upon sensuous observation and opinions which cannot justify themselves at the bar of reason. The techniques of exploration and verification are carried on in so-called " schools " such as the Pythagorean fraternity. But this is a sort of family affair guided, not so much by rigidly objective methods as by the *ipse dixits* of the Master. Empirical routine, happy guess-work, and adherence to the explanatory patterns accepted by such a school without further investigation, sometimes hit the mark and so attain to the stage of right opinion. An Empedocles founds a " school " of popular science, resting upon a number of somewhat fanciful analogies and so providing a somewhat mythological background for his more specialized explanations of phenomena.[50] A Heraclitus develops a " school " which interprets all phenomena, both natural and social, as phases of a certain " flux " which obeys the universal " law " of a pendulum swinging backwards and forwards from one extreme to the other.[51] A Pythagoras sees everywhere analogies (largely fanciful) with mathematics.[52] Each school thus has its own mythology or uncritical acceptance of certain explanatory patterns assumed as authoritative, and thus depends, not merely upon sensuous observation, but also upon a good deal of half-rationalized, half-primitive, naive belief.

The education of a young man for the profession of scientist thus involved disciple-ship. Such a student would enroll himself under a given Master, accepting (or at least not challenging) the techniques and shibboleths characteristic of the particular school, and thus absorbing its background and outlook. Such vocational training as he received was analogous to the technical training he would receive if associating with the family of an artist, except in so far as the technical methods of the scientist were less a matter of manipulating instruments or objects, and more a matter of mathematical calculation.

Let us now consider the sciences discussed by Plato *seriatim.* Arithmetic, vocationally considered, is studied not abstractly, but always in its concrete applications. The elements should be taught, as Plato himself insists, in the Egyptian manner, i.e., as problems involved in playing some game :

> In Egypt arithmetical games have been invented for the use of children, which they learn as a pleasure and amusement They have to distribute apples and garlands among groups of varying sizes ; and they arrange pugilists and wrestlers as they pair together by lot or remain over, showing how their turns come in natural order. They distribute vessels of different metals mingled, or of a single metal, and adapt to their amusement the numbers in common use ; in this way making more intelligible to the pupils domestic and military arrangements.[53]

As the child grows older, his play passes over into purposive co-operation with his parents and later into the serious work of earning a living for himself and a family of his own. So the concrete play-arithmetic of his childhood passes over into a concrete work-arithmetic in which he first helps his parents in their activities of buying and selling and eventually sets up in business for himself. Most arithmetic is commerical arithmetic.[54]

It is doubtless true that calculation can be applied to many if not all aspects of human association, e.g., to all the arts and sciences ; and it is doubtless true that the inter-relations of numbers to one another can be investigated in abstraction from such concrete applications. In fact, they even lend themselves to advanced philosophical consideration.[55] But such highly abstract studies are, from a biosocial standpoint, "useless." They are not vocational, and it is vocational arithmetic, arithmetic in the concrete applications needed in the biosocial activities of everyday community living, that we are at present considering. The arithmetic actually used " by merchants and retail tradesmen " in their business is always concrete. It is learnt, like the arithmetic of a more playful childhood, by doing it in concrete social surroundings, and its technical insights are driven home by repeated practice, by intensity, recency, and frequency.[56] Studied with a vocational aim, it is carried, as a rule, no further than is required for practical success.[57]

That is to say, vocational arithmetic represents a technique parallel in its associations and objectives to the vocational arts and crafts investigated above. Like these it has also a secondary use, namely, as an instrument, not of professional proficiency, but of liberal education. Its elements can be taught, for a fee, to the children of the ruling classes, not for utilitarian purposes, but merely to brighten their intelligences ; for which purpose a little learning can be very effective.[58]

In one respect, the mathematical sciences differ seriously from the arts. The arts, in their non-intellectual aspect, lean very heavily, not only upon habit, but upon guesswork and manipulative imitation. In mathematical studies, while drill plays a certain part, guesswork is reduced to a minimum, and manipulative imitation has no place whatever. These studies presuppose an " eye of the soul," i.e., a power of intellectual discrimination which can be developed but not created by education.[59] It is perhaps identical with what lies at the root of the arts too, on their intellectual side ; but insight is so different from manipulative proficiency that it can only be taught, even for vocational purposes, by a distinctive method. In fact, in the mathematical sciences the pupil is self-taught. All that his instructor can really do is to help the pupil by directing his attention to this or that aspect of a problem. The pupil has to understand for himself. The source of his knowledge comes from within.[60]

Geometry, vocationally considered, is studied in two ways. The first is concrete, the second abstract. Studied concretely, the measurement of length, breadth, and depth has practical applications, not only in the games which amuse children and some men, but also in most of the arts and sciences which attempt to deal with the actual world. It is ordinarily pursued with reference to direct biosocial, community needs.[61] In its more elementary reaches this sort of concrete geometry is very widely studied. First, of course, in a spirit of play which is not devoid of utilitarian consequences. " The future carpenter should learn to measure concretely, in play,"[62] and problem-games on the Egyptian model provide lots of fun for those who play them. In fact, the quality and quantity of direct amusement is something like what you get from playing draughts ; but, while draughts has no usefulness whatever, geometrical games make their participants more likely to be useful citizens.[63] Solid geometry is not generally considered to be as " practical " as plane geometry. " Its studies are charming, but none of its votaries can suggest any practical use for them " ; and the community neglects to give it any encouragement. Solid geometry thus remains somewhat undeveloped in its more advanced reaches, and is likely to remain so, unless direct government encouragement is forthcoming.[64]

Abstract geometry is studied especially by the so-called Pythagoreans, and to some extent in Plato's Academy.[65] The usual method is to investigate the relations of lines and surfaces in plane and solid figures of regular type, but to investigate them under certain assumptions or " hypotheses." Lines, angles, diagonals, etc., are assumed hypothetically as data whose inter-relations are to be investigated abstractly. The treatment is strictly scientific, but does not go, Plato thinks, far enough. As long as the assumptions remain unquestioned, the study is without a sound philosophical basis. Vocational students, however, *leave such assumptions* unchallenged and unexplained.[66] As long as their interest remains vocational only, and is not philosophical, Plato does not suggest that their method is not adequate for its purposes. His own endeavour is not to turn out geometricians, but something else, namely, philosophers.[67]

The methods observed by the student of geometry resemble closely the methods observed by the students of arithmetic. The concrete techniques which are studied only with reference to their applications appeal to concrete biosocial interests. These interests are stimulated by association and by the community feeling which comes from association. But the intellectual insight employed in abstract geometry, and also in these concrete techniques, depends on the " eye of the soul," and is essentially self-taught. The instructor merely poses problems and indicates the direction in which the disciple should look to find for himself the answers and to satisfy himself that the answers are correct. Such experiments are not manipulative but intellectual.[68]

From the vocational point of view, the geometrical expert thus developed, will not only be of service in practical affairs, i.e., in solving concrete problems in the arts and sciences in fields where community need is obvious. He will also be in demand in a secondary way, as a teacher of elements to the children of the governing classes in such a way as to awaken their minds in general. " In all departments of knowledge, as experience proves, any one who has studied geometry is infinitely quicker of apprehension than one who has not." For this purpose, as in the case of arithmetic, a little learning will be sufficient.[69]

Astronomy, the physical science which deals with solids in motion,[70] is also studied in two ways. In the first place, it is studied in the concrete, by means of gross sensuous observation of the starry heavens. Men look up at the sun and moon, at the morning and evening star, and direct sensuous experience seems to show them that these and other celestial bodies have no absolutely fixed courses but " wander out of their path in all manner of ways " and are thus properly called planets or wanderers.[71] Repeated observation of the movements of a select few of these bodies, enables the scientist who knows how to apply a few simple mathematical techniques to understand and explain such phenomena as the succession of " day " and " night," the phases of the moon, eclipses of sun and moon, and solstices and changes of the seasons, and to arrange the results of his investigations in the form of a rough calendar which will be of great practical use to farmers, sailors, and indeed to most members of the community who are interested in the weather and in the measure of time.[72]

Useful, however, as such rough generalizations are in their practical applications, the skilled technician of the so called Pythagorean stamp finds them inadequate and seeks a more refined and mathematically exact kind of systematic knowledge. While he still expects his new mathematical physics to apply to the actual phenomena which can be observed,[73] his mathematical techniques take him into a region where intellectual insight rather than the crude observation of the senses is the criterion of truth. He constructs a patterned world made up of mathematical solids, tetrahedra, octohedra, eikosihedra, and cubes, thought of as contained within a single sphere, whose purely circular motion compresses them, and from these hypotheses as data draws inferences as to the behaviour of these solids in motion.[74] Between his calculated results and the actual behaviour of observed phenomena he discovers interesting analogies which seem to verify his hypotheses[75] ; and he does not hesitate to construct physical models which represent the celestial bodies and at the same time move in accordance with his calculations.[76] He is of course perfectly aware that these models and these calculations refer to an actual cosmos which is not mathematically exact and permanent in its motions ; but he studies the actual deviations as well, and takes infinite pains in investigating the precise motions of the celestial bodies, in so far as such investigation is of any use to the community.[77] He is, in fact, only a more refined development of the concrete astronomer ; for not only does he refer to the actual phenomena, but he also never questions his own mathematical hypotheses, as a speculative philosopher would do.[78]

On the subject of education in astromony, Plato's attention is directed to the problem of how to train a man to be *not* an astronomer, but a philosopher. For this higher purpose, he is enjoined " to leave the starry heavens alone " and to confine his attention to abstract problems referring to strictly mathematical hypotheses themselves, and to regard even the higher kind of (Pythagorean) astronomy as secondary, an occupation for the philosopher's leisure hours only.[79] Plato does not, however, in any sense challenge the propriety of the usual scientific methods, for a man who is intending to become a professional astronomer[80] ; and from what he says, we can infer with reasonable certainty what vocational education in this field would do.

In the first place, the would-be astronomer would always pay the closest possible attention to the apparent behaviour of the physically observable heavenly bodies. At first, no doubt, in play, but later with all the interests of a grown man.[81] He would endeavour to understand the heavenly motions, cataloguing them, systematizing them with the help of appropriate mathematical techniques, and constructing experimental models. He would be particularly interested in the socially useful applications of his investigations, but would also develop, on the intellectual side, an interest in technical problems. His problems, however, would always have ultimate reference to the observed phenomena, and would never become too remote from the actual facts.[82] A mind like that of Sir James Jeans, rather than of Plato's philosopher-king, would be his ideal.

So far we have considered the scientific study of (1) points (2) lines and surfaces, and (3) solids in motions, in a motion, that is, which is perceptible to the eye. We now pass to consider (4) a sister physical science which studies solids in motion, but in a motion perceptible not so much to the eye as to the ear. " Harmonics " or physical acoustics, like the preceding sciences, is studied by would-be professionals in two ways, the one concrete, the other abstract.

The concrete " harmonist " investigates the musical properties of vibrating chords of varying lengths and degrees of tension. He listens for full tones, half-tones, " enharmonic " tones, etc., as used in Greek music, and tightens or loosens his chords on the instrument until his ear assures him that the tone produced by his plectrum is neither too tense nor too relaxed, but just right.[83] He also studies consonances and dissonances, listening carefully for interference notes and for the least audible unit of tone-discrimination. In every case the criterion of what is musical or unmusical is provided by the trained ear.[84] His investigations have a practical bent. They are definitely useful, not merely to artistic performers upon musical instruments such as the lyre and harp, but to the manufacturers of such instruments, and may even suggest the invention of novel instruments of greater range.[85]

The more abstract student of " harmonics " is the so-called Pythagorean, who reduces experimentally to standardized mathematical formulation the proportions of the octave ($\frac{1}{2}$), the fourth, and the fifth, and investigates the proportions of the other notes recognized in the Greek musical scales. He depends less upon the ear, and more upon intellectual insight into mathematical techniques. But his data are, and remain to the end, the tones which can be heard by the ear ; and these, which come as nature's gift to man, he never questions, any more than he challenges the presuppositions of his mathematical techniques.[86]

A further step taken by some Pythagoreans and quite definitely by Plato himself leads into philosophical speculation. It was supposed that the intervals between the planetary orbits of the physical cosmos corresponded to the intervals between the notes of one of the standardized Greek scales and were based upon the same numerical proportions : so that human music (which could be heard) corresponded, in principle, to an alleged cosmic music (which could not be heard by the human ear).[87] It would readily be supposed that the " perfect system of scales " erected upon this speculative basis would have no interest for practising musicians. But in actual fact, for three centuries or so after Plato's death these speculations provided a standard system accepted by professionals; so that even this philosophizing had a certain vocational interest.[88] It should however be added, that this vocational reference was accidental. Plato's aim was to develop, not scientists, but philosophers ; and his interest in the work of practising musicians was even more remote.

This philosophic interest is not however intended to interfere with the vocational education which turns a man into a scientific expert in the field of physical acoustics. *That* education proceeds, at first in play, and later with growing professional interest, by keeping always in close touch with primary data which (for the scientist) remain beyond question. These are (1) the musical tones differentiated by the human ear and (2) the presuppositions of the mathematical techniques, in terms of which the relations of the tones to one another are experimentally systematized. Once an expert in this field, the scientist can, as a secondary activity, purvey elementary instruction to the children of the governing classes, an instruction designed, not to turn them into scientists, but to provide them with part of the basis and part of the stimulus which can be used to advantage in the higher (dialectical) education which turns them into philosophers.[89]

3. The social sciences, with Plato as with us, are in a somewhat ambiguous position. They are more like arts than sciences. They make use of as much scientific method as they can, especially in the way of mathematical techniques ; but their subject-matter viz., man in his social value relations, is so vague and general that it is difficult for the social scientist to escape pretentious trivialities and to attain to exactitude. *Ethics*, e.g., easily becomes little more than general preaching : the expression of group experience in the form of proverbs or of imperatives—formulations which fail, either to justify their encapseled wordly-wisdom or to apply to individual cases.[90] Such formulations and their interpretations constitute the especial field of poets and rhetoricians, whose inconsistencies and disagreements are almost a byword.[91] If you insist upon treating ethics as an exact mathematical science, it turns into something like pure hedonism : a view which appealed to the professors of Socrates' day much as to Jeremy Bentham and his modern followers.[92] But who does not see that the professors are translating the normative value-judgment which discriminates goods and evils into something quite different : viz., the factual judgment of social psychology or the formal conclusion of inferential logic or the addition and substraction of elementary mathematics ?[93]

Or consider *politics*, the " royal science " of government which discusses especially leadership and social administration. This is even more evidently in an inexact position. Social leadership, in Plato's time as in ours, seems to be an art rather than a science. A leader is a gifted individual co-operating with chance in guiding the human herd in a desirable direction. His concrete empiricism coupled with a few technical tricks borrowed from the social psychologists, enables a bold and unscrupulous ruler to achieve his ends. But in truth neither ends nor means have been reduced by intellectual analysis to any kind of strict science. Plato tells us that its professors

> Do in fact teach nothing but the opinion of the many. This is their whole wisdom. It is as if a man should study the tempers and desires of a great beast which he feeds. He would learn how to approach and handle the beast, at what times and from what causes the beast is dangerous or mild, what is the significance of his various cries, and by what sounds he can be infuriated or soothed. After the man, by constant attendance, has become perfect in all this, he calls his knowledge wisdom and makes of it a system which he proceeds to teach—although he has no sound conception of the principles and passions of which he speaks ; " honourable " " just " and " good " and their opposites are settled for him by the degree of their accord with the tastes and tempers of the great brute. Good and evil are equated with what the beast likes or dislikes ; and he accounts for them only by calling them " necessary."[94]

The vocation of social scientist, that is to say, of an " authority " in this field, is shared by two distinct types ; (1) the intellectuals such as the poets and the professors of public speaking and political science. These are spiritually akin, since poetry is merely a particular species of rhetoric,[95] and the professors always treat poetry and its interpretations as the most essential part of their curriculum. Thus the great Protagoras :

> I am of the opinion that skill in poetry is the principal part of education. By this I understand the power of knowing which of the compositions of the poets are correct, and which incorrect. I include also the ability to distinguish the correct from the incorrect, and to explain the reason for making this distinction.

Such intellectuals always assume, not merely that they can string phrases together effectively, but also that they understand fully the subject-matter of which oratory, whether in verse or in prose, treats.[97]

The second type is, not the intellectual, but the man of action, the dictator or statesman who uses the techniques of oratory to influence men to the actions he considers desirable, but does not hesitate, if persuasion fails, to appeal to direct action, i.e., to force.[98] Both types play into each other's hands, the men of action patronising literature and the intellectuals associating themselves with the men of power.[99] The alliance is usually overbalanced on the side of power. It is not wisdom which directs action, but action which is supported by a kind of parasitic wisdom.

Those who make politics their professional occupation are thus concerned with fees and the other rewards which constitute the sweets of power.[100] They are highly concrete in their interests, and study for their vocation by associating with persons like themselves, strengthening their inner conviction that they are somehow born to rule.[101] Their intellectual equipment consists of psychological tricks learnt from the professors of oratory and political science and applied without scruple in what they take to be their own interest as rulers.[102]

Plato, in this as in other fields, is interested, not in educating scientists as such, but in developing a few chosen spirits into philosophers. But whereas, in other fields, he is content to leave these who choose to devote themselves to science—e.g., the Pythagoreans—to continue using their own methods and retaining their own ideals, in the field of social science he regards the actual practitioners as " the enemy " and is resolved to banish them from his ideal community. The poets of power, the professors of the right of might, and practising dictators are regarded as dangerous rivals of his own views, and, as such, are definitely excluded from the chosen land.[103] In their place he demands an alliance of wisdom and power, preferably in a single hand, but with wisdom directing action, rather than action dragging wisdom in its train. His *philosopher*-kings are at the opposite pole from the power-devotees of human history, and represent, not a new deal—a reshuffle of the loaves and fishes—but a new ideal altogether with the alleged sweets of power placed in a definitely subordinate position. Mankind, with its vocational power-seekers, seems to him in a topsy-turvy condition ; a condition which he does not propose to leave as it is, but to overturn and destroy : setting up in its place his new idealism.[104]

Model the form of a vast, many-headed beast. Make a second form, smaller, of a lion ; and a third, yet smaller, of a man. Join them and let the three grow into one. Fashion the outside into a single image, as of a man, so that, seen from the outside, the creature will look like a single human being.

To maintain that it is profitable for a human being to be unjust means (in terms of this imaginary model) that it is profitable for this creature to feast the many-headed beast and strengthen the lion within him, but to starve and weaken the man, who is liable to be dragged about at the mercy of the other two ; and he is not to harmonize them, but to allow them to fight with each other.

The champion of justice replies that a human being should always so speak and act as to give to the man within him the most complete mastery over the entire creature. He should watch over the many-headed beast like a good farmer, fostering and cultivating the gentle qualities and preventing the wild qualities from growing. He should make the lion-heart his ally, and caring for them all in common should unite the several parts with one another and with himself.[105]

4. We now turn from the techniques of the arts and sciences which are used for vocational purposes to the vocations proper, in which men devote their lives to some activity which is socially useful, in order to earn a living. Such cases as farming, and other methods of providing the community with food, furnish rather obvious examples. What are sometimes called the primary industries all come under this head. The pecuniary rewards are not, as a rule, high, because, while the results are useful to the community, they are not very hard to produce and market, the really valuable part of the work of production being done by nature rather than by man. The methods of agriculture, for instance, are primitive and traditional. They are simple, and call for brawn rather than brain. Farming is learnt on the farm, by farming : i.e., by association with farmers, imitating what they do and acquiring the dexterity in farming operations which comes of itself in such associations. Keeping cows, hens, pigs, and goats follows the same simple rules. Nature gives the increase and sets the tempo ; man waits upon nature, and plays the part of servant rather than of master : protecting and feeding the domestic animals and cultivated plants, until the time comes for marketing the harvest.[106]

Commercial fishing with nets, like the trapping of wild animals by laying snares, is a similarly primitive and traditional way of securing food and other social utilities. Here there is not, as a rule, much protection or feeding. Fisherman and huntsmen for the most part do not so much-co-operate with nature as leave it alone until they are ready. Then, they interfere with it, converting its products, without service, to their own ends. The techniques of fishing and hunting are also simple and traditional. They are learned by youths associating with experienced huntsmen and doing what they see their elders do. As much food (or other social utility) for as little work as possible seems to be the vocational huntsman's aim.[107]

Trading, from the higgling of retailers to the export and import activities of wholesalers, together with such associated activities

as those of ships' captains, harbour masters, and hotel keepers on
the one hand, and bankers, underwriters, and financiers on the
other, provides another obvious example of a vocation. The
exchange of products and services is essential to the community,
and distribution and production have always gone hand in hand.[108]
Such commercial activities are also acquired by association and
imitation of elders. Not only families, but whole races are ad-
dicted to such pursuits, and Plato is quite prepared to leave most
trading to the races among whom such activities are traditional.
He does not interfere with either their methods or their results,
but permits them to carry on their traditional vocations in his
model community, because of their recognized usefulness, as long
as the authorities permit.[109]

No one of the 5,040 citizen families shall engage in trade, either retail
or wholesale. Such tradesmen must be either foreigners or resident
aliens. Anyone who likes can become a resident alien on certain
conditions. He pays no sojourner's tax or sales tax or business tax.
But he must practice a definite art, and may not stay longer than
twenty years from the date of his resignation (unless the magistrates
grant an extension.).

In respect of the various retail occupations, which are allowed because they seem necessary to the community, the magistrates shall take
counsel with the experts, and shall consider what amount of receipts,
after deducting expenses, will produce a moderate profit to these occupations. They shall fix in writing and maintain strictly what they
decide upon as the right percentage of profit.

So far as commercial vocations require the use of arithmetic
and calculation,[110] they have an intellectual side which is technical
and is acquired by insight rather than by association, imitation,
and practice. But commerical associations tend to prevent this
insight developing along its own line into pure thought and
philosophy. Commercial associations remain and tend to develop
business men rather than philosophers.[111]

Certain occupations, such as civil engineering or the direction
of a merchant or passenger ship, involve a great deal of technical
knowledge. The engineering expert is taken into consultation
when it is a question of constructing roads, docks and other
harbour works, walls and fortifications, and various types of
machinery, and his advice is of considerable value to the community.[112] And the ship's captain, in his own line of work, can
also be of great use.[113] But such occupations do not properly fit
a man for carrying out the duties of citizenship, and such experts
are treated as belonging to a lower class in the community :[114]

The engineer is sometimes of the greatest use to the community. And if he were to talk in your grandiose style, Callicles, he would bury you under a mountain of words, insisting that we ought all to be engineers, and that no other profession is worth thinking about. Nevertheless, you despise him and his techniques. You sneer and call him a mechanic. You will not permit your daughter to marry his son, or your son to marry his daughter. Yet what justice or reason is there in your superior attitude? Your censure of engineering and similar technical vocations is ridiculous.

In fact, such occupations would seem to be ranked somewhere midway between the activities of artisans and hand-labourers on the one hand, and of civic superintendents on the other. For such vocations youth is educated by going through the mill : associating with the workers in the particular field and beginning on the artisan level. As experience brings familiarity and skill, they gradually work their way up to positions of relative authority and become experts in their own right. So far as mathematics is involved, their development depends upon the attainment of concrete insight. So far as the rest of their training is concerned, association, imitation, and practice are the dominant principles.

Teaching, in Ancient Greece, ranked as one of the menial arts of service. You could earn your living at it ; but it was a poor living and was definitely looked down upon, The nurse and " tutor " were domestic servants, and for the most part servants who were of no particular use in other respects ; and the teacher of the three R's was in little better case, except that he did not live directly in a Greek family, but lived by himself, sometimes in a teacherage of his own. The teachers of games, sports, and music were a little more like our modern club professionals, but their civic status remained definitely inferior.[115]

The question is, how do domestic slaves and " foreigners attracted by pay " fit themselves for this vocation of teaching ? There were no teacher-training institutions in antiquity, and some of the teachers were dreadfully incompetent.[116] The domestic slaves presumably learned their business by association with the members of the family, and by imitating what such associations impressed upon them as valuable.[117] But the foreigners attracted by pay seem to have been in another class altogether. They consisted of the semi-independent artisans or workers who taught as a side-line the arts which they practised (or had practised) professionally.[118] Such men passed on to their pupils the elements of what they themselves knew ; and what they knew they had learned by doing. This means that they had themselves associated with masters and had picked up by association, imitation, and practice something of the techniques which made their original masters successful practitioners of some art. Reading in Ancient Greece meant recitation, dramatic performance of some prose or verse work which had been committed to memory.[119] It rested upon previous training in the elements of grammar and was taught by men who had been rhapsodes or reciters themselves. It corresponds roughly to what we call "elocution," and was taught in the teens.[120] The content of the "readers" used by such teachers was patriotic material, usually from the approved poets, which would (it was supposed) have an edifying effect upon the pupils and would develop in them the urge to acquire and practise the virtues of their ancestors.[121]

Plato follows the Hellenic usage, except that he makes education compulsory instead of optional, and that his board of philosophic censors prescribe the content of the approved textbooks in every field of study. Education is so all-important that it cannot be left to "chance persons," however expert in practical techniques, to decide such matters.[122] Thus to the methods of learning already mentioned, namely, association, imitation, and practice under acknowledged masters, he adds conformity to the ideals and rules insisted upon by the community authorities.[123]

The military vocations are taken very seriously, by Plato no less than other Greeks. Warfare is the natural and inevitable inter-civic relationship in the case of communities which are ambitious to raise their standard of living above the primitive level of Arcadian simplicity ; and where this is the case, preparedness is a necessity for the governing classes.[124] Men, women, and children must be thoroughly prepared to do their duty on the battlefield.[125] Such preparation is partly physical, partly a matter of *morale ;*[7] and both sides must be developed by suitable training.

On the physical side, health and strength are developed partly by diet, and partly by a variety of gymnastic exercises : but never for their own sake, as ends-in-themselves. They are developed always for the community, and are intended to be used for military purposes. Wiriness rather than strength, and speed because of its usefulness in war, are especially stressed.[126] Dancing and field sports are engaged in, partly for the same general purpose, partly to familiarize the growing children of both sexes with the movements and the weapons used in warfare. The Pyrrhic dance is a war-dance. It

imitates the modes of avoiding blows and missiles by dropping **or**

giving way, or springing aside, or rising up or falling down ; also the
opposite postures which are those of action, e.g., the imitation of
archery and the hurling of javelins, and of all sorts of blows. The
action is direct and muscular, giving a straight movement to the
limbs.[127]

The training of children in horsemanship, archery, and the use
of the sling and javelin commences early, at the age of six ; and
the monthly sports-meets, when the whole community engages in
competitions and mimic contests, both on foot and on horseback,
and always using the appropriate military weapons, keeps the
members of the ruling classes in training.[128] Military evolutions,
the movements of armies, and encampings also come under the
head of community gymnastics :

> Of all these things there ought to be public teachers, receiving pay
> from the state, and their pupils should be the men and boys in the
> state, and also the girls and women. All citizens, male and female
> alike, shall attend to military matters. There is a very great difference
> between one who has been trained in gymnastic exercises and one who
> has not been. Our citizens are to be trained to be ambidextrous. He
> who has the double powers of attack and defence must not leave them
> untrained.[129]

Association, imitation of techniques, and constant practice
under competitive conditions, are the methods by which pupils,
who are the sons and daughters of the governing classes, acquire
proficiency in community gymnastics. But there is a great difference between what they learn from artists and scientists on the
one hand, and from the military trainers on the other. In the
arts and sciences there is no intention of turning them into
professionals. They learn a little, for the sake of its educational
value in a general education. From the military trainers they
learn to be as expert themselves as possible ; because the techniques so acquired will be used in earnest in the inevitable
inter-civic warfare.

Their teachers, however, are experts in a higher sense. They
are, for the most part, foreigners attracted by pay, like the other
teachers in the model city of the *Laws*.[130] But certain of them are
themselves citizens, officers put in charge of the children who are
learning the art of war from looking on at actual battles. These
officers act as lecturer-demonstrators on the actual field of battle[131]
and it is implied in the *Laws* that the " public teachers receiving
pay from the state " to teach " archery, weapon-hurling, the use
of the light shield, heavy-armed fighting, and military evolutions

and movements of armies and encampings " may be selected by the director of education as his assistants from " the citizens, male or female."[132] But whether citizens or foreigners, these teachers are professionals because of their proven merit, appointed because of their ability.

Such teachers, then, practice the military vocations in an especial sense ; partly because they are of outstanding excellence, like Xanthias and Eudorus " who were reputed the most celebrated wrestlers of their day" and were employed by Thucydides to train his sons[133] ; and partly because they earn their living by teaching the military arts. The military trainers are thus comparable to the trainers in the arts and sciences ; although it is true that the community insists upon their pupils attaining to a greater degree of proficiency, because of the immense practical importance of success in warfare to the group as a whole.

On the side of *morale*, training is partly given by the teachers of gymnastics ; but far more is given by the teachers of " music," i.e., by the literature of a patriotic nature which is learned by heart and by the marches and dances which develop the spirited part of the soul.[134] As we are told in the *Republic* :

> In selecting our soldiers and educating them in music and gymastic we were contriving influences which would prepare them to take the dye of the laws to perfection ; and the colour of their opinion about dangers and of every other opinion was to be fixed indelibly by their nurture and training—not to be washed away by such potent lyes as pleasure, sorrow, fear, and desire. I exclude uninstructed pugnacity, such as that of a wild beast or slave, and mean the courage which characterizes a citizen-soldier.[135]

---

¹*Soph.* 219 ff. ; *Polit.* 279 ff. ; *Laws* 823 f.
²*Prtg.* 312ab, cf. 315a, 318 ; *Gorg.* 459b ff.   The problem is not confined to Ancient Greece. ³Cf. *Lach.* 185c ff. ; *Rep.* 600, 606e f.
⁴*Rep.* 533–534e ; *Phaedr.* 275de ; cf. *Apol.* 21 ff. ; and the " confessions of ignorance " in the various Socratic *Dialogues.*
⁵*Prtg.* 319bc, 328a ; *Rep.* 421cd, 533b, 597b, d ; *Gorg.* 449c ; *Polit.* 283a ; *Laws* 643a–c. ⁶*Prtg.* 312, 318 ; *Lach.* 180c ; *Rep.* 400b, 424c ; *Phaedr.* 257c f,, 277b ff. ; *Laws* 668 ff., 799 ff.
⁷*Rep.* 522c–526c ; *Tim.* 47a ; *Phil.* 55d f., *Laws* 747, 809c, 818c f. ; cf. *Gorg.* 451ab.
⁸*Rep.* 526c–527c, 528bc ; *Laws* 817e, 819c f.
⁹*Rep.* 527d f., 528d f. ; *Tim.* 38 ff. ; *Laws* 821 f., 967a f. ; cı. *Gorg.* 451c.
¹⁰*Rep.* 530d f. ; *Tim.* 47cd ; cf. *Laws* 657b.
¹¹*Charm.* 174b f. ; *Prtg.* 323 f. ; *Rep.* 402c, 528c f., 504b ff. ; *Polit.* 259b f., 292b f., 297, 309 ff. ; *Laws* 846d f.
¹²*Rep.* 369c f., 370d, 420d f. ; *Soph.* 219b ; *Phil.* 56a ; *Laws* 643b, 743d, cf. 949c.
¹³*Soph.* 219 ff. ; cf. *Rep.* 373b ; *Laws* 823 f.
¹⁴*Laws* 842cd, 918c f. ¹⁵*Rep.* 488de ; *Laws* 643d.
¹⁶*Rep.* 371c f. ; *Soph.* 219c, 223d ; *Laws* 643d, 842d, 847a, d, 849, 918b f.
¹⁷*Rep.* 370e f. ; *Laws* 705a f. ¹⁸*Rep.* 330b, 550c ff. ; *Laws* 741b ff., 842cd.
¹⁹*Gorg.* 512b f. ²⁰*Lach.* 184d f. ; *Prtg.* 312b, 326c ; *Meno* 93e f. ; *Rep.* 376d f., 381d, 383b, 406b, 410c ; *Laws* 794a f., 804d, 808c, 811d ff. ; cf. Lys. 209bc.

[21]*Lach.* 179e, 181c ff. ; *Rep.* 466e f. ; *Laws* 794c ff. [22]*Rep.* 422bc ; *Laws* 796a–d, 814c. [23]*Rep.* 466e f. [24]*Laws* 643bc, condensed. [25]*Rep.* 421d ; cf. 537a.

[26]Cf. *Rep.* 455c. [27]*Prtg.* 318bc.

[28]*Laws* 802a f. In general, Plato subordinates creative authorship to a state censorship (cf. *Rep.* 377, 386 ff., 401, 395 ; *Laws* 801, 817de).

[29]*Prtg.* 326a–c, 327a–c. [30]*Prtg.* 312b. [31]*Phil.* 55d f., 57cd, condensed. Cf. *Rep.* 531.

[32]*Soph.* 235d f. ; *Phil.* 55d f., 56, 59a.

[33]*Prtg.* 356cd (condensed) : " The art of measurement does away with the effect of appearances and, showing the truth, would fain teach the soul at last to find rest in the truth, and would thus save our life." (Cf. *Rep.* 524c ff.).

[34]*Laws* 747b, cf. *Rep.* 526b, 527c. The method of studying mathematics differs *toto caelo* from the methods hitherto discussed : namely, association, imitation, and practice. It is discussed *infra*, in connection with the study of the sciences (see pp. 32 ff.). [35]*Apol.* 22cd. [36]*Rep.* 472d. [37]*Rep.* 504e ff.

[38]*Ion, passim* ; *Rep.* 475d, 476a, 495e f., 596d f. ; *Phaedr.* 245a.

[39]*Rep.* 369d ff., 372e f. [40]*Rep.* 394e f. [41]*Laws* 846d.

[42]*Laws* 802a f. ; cf. 811, 817, 852e f. [43]*Prtg.* 326a f. ; *Laws* 656 f., 810c, 811a.

[44]*Rep.* 377, 386 ff., 401, 595 ff. ; *Laws* 801, 817d, 829d.

[45]*Prtg.* 312ab ; *Laws* 846d f. [46]*Rep.* 533b, d.

[47]*Rep.* 530d f. Cf. E. Frank : *Plato u.d.s–g. Pythagoreer*, 1923, *passim*. The great contemporary school of Democritus, at Abdera, is never mentioned, either explicitly or implicitly, in the *Dialogues* ; and its omission constitutes something of a problem for the Plato student.

[48]*Rep.* 531ab, condensed. A similar story is told in modern times of the tone-psychologist Carl Stumpf in his disagreement with Wilhelm Wundt as to how far it was possible to go in actually hearing the remoter difference-tones (whose presence is indicated by mathematical calculation).

[49]*Rep.* 531d. [50]For a Platonic example, cf. *Sym.* 185e ff.

[51]Cf. *Crat.* 439c ff. ; *Theaet.* 156 ff. (Plato was himself a pupil of Cratylus.)

[52]*Tim.* 31d ff. [53]*Laws* 819bc, condensed. [54]*Rep.* 498a, 525c, 565a.

[55]*Rep.* 510c f., 522c ff. ; *Phil.* 55e, 56d. [56]*Meno* 85c ; *Laws* 643b. [57]*Rep.* 498ab.

[58]*Rep.* 526 ; *Laws* 747, 804cd, 809c, 819c. Overmuch learning produces the expert mathematician, of whom Plato has no very high opinion (cf. *Rep.* 531e, and the *persona* Theodorus in the *Theaetetus*). [59]*Rep.* 511c, 521c ff. ; *Theaet.* 185d. [60]*Meno* 85b f.

[61]*Rep.* 526d, 527a, cd, 536e f. [62]*Laws* 643c. [63]*Laws* 817e f., 819c, 820c.

[64]*Rep.* 528c f. [65]*Tim.* 53cd, etc. ; *Theaet.* 147c f. [66]*Rep.* 510c f. [67]*Rep.* 511b f., 533cd.

[68]*Meno* 82 ff., *Rep.* 511c, 527d f. ; *Theaet.* 185c f. [69]*Rep.* 527c ; *Laws* 747, 804cd, 809c, 819c. [70]*Rep.* 528b, 530c ; cf. *Tim.* 53b ff. [71]*Gorg.* 451c ; *Laws* 821bc.

[72]*Rep.* 527cd, 530ab ; cf. *Tim.* 37d, 39b f.

[73]*Rep.* 531a, c. Whether the philosophy of the *Timaeus* is Pythagorean or Platonic is disputed. Cf. A. E. Taylor : *A Commentary on Plato's Timaeus*, 1928, *passim*.

[74]*Tim.* 37c ff., 48 ff., 57d ff. [75]*Tim.* 59c ff. [76]*Tim.* 40cd. [77]*Rep.* 530ab.

[78]*Rep.* 510c ff., 529c f., 533c f. ; *Tim.* 53c.

[79]*Rep.* 529b–531a ; *Tim.* 59cd. [80]*Tim.* 53bc. [81]*Rep.* 536d f. ; *Laws* 821bc.

[82]*Rep.* 527e f. [83]*Rep.* 349de, 530c f. [84]*Rep.* 531ab ; *Laws* 812c f.

[85]Whether the " Panharmonion " of *Rep.* 399cd is intended as a novel instrument on which more than one scale could be played, or whether it represents merely a chromatic way of composing music, without regard to the specific scales, is disputed.

[86]*Rep.* 510c f., 531c ; cf. *Tim.* 47.

[87]*Tim.* 35 f. Cf. E. Frank : *Plato u.d.s–g. Pythagoreer*, pp. 13–15.

[88]Cf. H. E. Wooldridge : *Oxford History of Music*, 1901, Vol. I, pp. 9–13. Cf. Frank : *Op. Cit.*, pp. 181–184.

[89]For this purpose, as in the case of the material drawn from other sciences, no very prolonged or strictly scientific training is required. *Laws* 810a suggests three years as entirely suitable.

[90]*Prtg.* 320c ff. ; *Rep.* 331d f., Bks. II–III and X ; *Phaedr.* 275d.

[91]*Prtg.* 338e ff., 347b f. ; *Phaedr.* 277e ; *Laws* 670e, 719.

[92]*Prtg.* 348a. With the notable exception of Grote, scholars draw technical distinctions between the Hedonism of the *Protagoras* and modern hedonistic " science." (Cf., e.g., T. D. Goodell : Plato's Hedonism, in *Am. Jour. Philol.*, Vol. XLII, 1921).

[93]Examples abound in the reasoning attributed to Socrates himself. E.g., the arguments with Thrasymachus (*Rep.* I) are censured, not only by modern scholars, but by Socrates and Glaucon in the *Dialogue* itself (*Rep.* 354, 357–8).

⁹⁴*Rep.* 493a f., slighty condensed. ⁹⁵*Gorg.* 502. ⁹⁶*Prtg.* 338e f., slightly condensed·
⁹⁷*Ion* 540b ff. ; *Gorg.* 459d f. ; *Phaedr.* 260 ff. ; *Laws* 810d f.
⁹⁸*Rep.* 338d f., 565c ff. ; *Laws* 709e ff. ⁹⁹*Rep.* 568a f.
¹⁰⁰*Rep.* 343 f., 345c ff., 362ab. ¹⁰¹*Alc.I* 104 ff. ; *Rep.* 494 f. ; cf. 492 f. ; *Gorg.* 510c f.
¹⁰²*Gorg.* 463a f., 466b ff. ¹⁰³*Rep.* 398a, 568b, 595 ff., 605a, 807a ; *Laws* 817.
¹⁰⁴*Gorg.* 492e f., 521cd ; *Rep.* 587d f. ; *Polit.* 300c ff., 304 ff. But cf. also *Laws* 709 ff.
¹⁰⁵*Gorg.* 588c f., condensed. ¹⁰⁶*Rep.* 369cd, 370cd ; *Soph.* 219b ; *Laws* 743d, 889d,
949e.
¹⁰⁷*Soph.* 219c ff. ; *Laws* 823c f. There were certain fish preserves in Iran and
Egypt (*Polit.* 264c).
¹⁰⁸*Rep.* 370e f. ; *Soph.* 223b f. ; *Laws* 705a, 842d, 849de, 918bc, 920bc.
¹⁰⁹" Egyptians, Phoenicians, and many other races " are mentioned in *Laws* 747c.
So too in more modern times : Jews were given privileged positions because of their
usefulness as traders (Werner Sombart : *The Jews and Modern Capitalism*, 1913,
Chs. II–VII). The quotation in the text is from *Laws* 850 and 918 ff., condensed.
¹¹⁰*Rep.* 525c ; *Laws* 747a, 819c. ¹¹¹*Rep.* 498ab. ¹¹²*Prtg.* 319, 322de ; *Gorg.* 514.
¹¹³*Gorg.* 511c f. ¹¹⁴*Gorg.* 512b–d, condensed.
¹¹⁵*Prtg.* 312b, 326c ; *Meno* 94bc ; *Rep.* 377c, 381d, 383b ; *Laws* 794 f., 804d f.,
808c f., 811d ff. ¹¹⁶*Meno* 94c.
¹¹⁷*Rep.* 377a ff., 381d, 383b, etc. indicate clearly enough that local traditions passed
on by domestic servants carried with them undesirable associations.
¹¹⁸*Meno* 94d ; *Prtg.* 326bc ; *Lach.* 180c ; *Rep.* 400b.
¹¹⁹*Prtg.* 326ab ; *Phaedr.* 228. ¹²⁰*Prtg.* 325e f. ; *Laws* 809e f.
¹²¹*Prtg.* 326a ; *Laws* 810c, e f. ¹²²*Laws* 804cd ; cf. *Lach.* 185 f. ; *Rep.* 377b f.
¹²³*Laws* 811d f., 817d f. For further treatment, see *infra*, Ch. VII.
¹²⁴*Rep.* 372d–373e, 374b ff. ; *Laws* 795b f.
¹²⁵*Rep.* 452a, 456a, 457a, 466d ff. ; *Laws* 813e f., 830.
¹²⁶*Rep.* 404, 410b f., 422a–c.
¹²⁷*Laws* 815a f., condensed. Cf. *Laws* 796b, 942c f.
¹²⁸ *Laws* 829–831a ; cf. 794c. The monthly sports-meets are Platonic. They were
not regular Hellenic practice (*Laws* 829).
¹²⁹*Laws* 794d f., 813 f., condensed. The inclusion of women is Platonic, not
Hellenic.
¹³⁰*Laws* 804d is explicit on this point. Stesilaus in the *Laches* is a foreigner.
¹³¹*Rep.* 467c f. is explicit. ¹³²*Laws* 813b f. ¹³⁷*Meno* 94cd.
¹³⁴*Rep.* 386 ff., 410 ; *Laws* 633 f. indicates the Spartan standpoint : from which,
gymnastic seems to have provided most of the *morale*. (But Spartans did also sing the
patriotic songs ascribed to Tyrtaeus).
¹³⁵*Rep.* 429e f., condensed. Cf. also *Laws* 810e f.

CHAPTER III

EDUCATION FOR THE PROFESSIONS

The professions were much the same in Ancient Greece as they are in present-day civilization ; and in fact some of them, such as the medical profession, can still claim to exhibit a certain continuity of tradition with their ancient origins. Although methods have altered, professional ideals, as shown in the Hippocratean oath, remain in general much the same. Out of the mass of material in the *Dialogues* we select for especial study such passages as deal with :

1. The medical profession.[1]
2. The legal profession.[2]
3. The professor's profession.[3]
4. The theological profession.[4]
5. The military profession.[5]

Medicine, as practised in Hellas, resembles the sciences discussed. It has two levels, the one a matter of experience and close attention to facts, the other a matter of insight and reasoning which rises to the interpretation of facts. Corresponding to these two fairly distinct aspects, we find two fairly distinct types of physician, (1) the doctor's assistants, and (2) the physicians proper.

(1) The assistant or " inferior type of practitioner " might be what we should call a dietician who would not venture to prescribe medicines, but would put the patient under a regimen. For certain kinds of disease such treatment would be entirely adequate, and might indeed be prescribed by a professional gymnastic trainer.[6]

For certain other kinds of disease, medicines would be necessary: a pill or potion with an emetic or cathartic effect, producing a rough and ready cure and requiring for its administration no very high degree of scientific attainment. For such maladies also the assistant's services would be adequate. The use of such assistants would leave the physician free to attend to the more difficult cases, and especially to his more lucrative patients.[7]

Finally the assistant's services would be offered to the poorer class of patients, especially to those of inferior social rank. It is implied that the practitioner who devoted his full time to sick slaves would himself be a slave :

> The slave-doctors run about and cure the slaves or wait for them in the dispensaries. Practitioners of this sort never let their patients discuss their individual ailments. They prescribe what mere experience suggests, as though they had exact knowledge ; and when they have given their orders like a tyrant, they rush off with equal assurance to other slave-invalids. [8]

Professionals of this inferior sort are educated for their profession by association, imitation, and rule-of-thumb experience :

> They acquire their knowledge of medicine by observing and obeying their masters : empirically, and not according to the way of learning natural to freemen, who have learned scientifically the art which they impart scientifically to their pupils. They are empirical physicians, who practise medicine without science. [9]

There is yet a further sort of inferior physician, the quack, who has not even the experience of the empirical assistants, and has no real insight into the laws and theoretical principles of health and disease, but has picked up a few prescriptions, either from a book or from hearsay. He knows the effects of certain drugs, and can identify the drugs ; but when it comes to relating this superficial knowledge to actual patients, he proves unable to identify the concrete diseases. He does not know to whom, at what times, and in what quantities his drugs should be administered in order to effect a cure. [10]

Contrasted with all these we have (2) the physician proper, illustrated in the *Dialogues* by the *personae* of Eryximachus and his father Acumenus. According to the evidence the physician proper, in the first place, has experience. From observation upon themselves as well as upon others, and upon a very great number of others as well as upon themselves, such practitioners are thoroughly acquainted with the nature and processes of the chief diseases to which the human body is liable. That is to say, their experience is not less, but more than that of the assistant doctors considered above. As we are told in the *Republic* : [11]

> The best physicians are those who have treated the greatest number of constitutions good and bad. From youth up they have combined with the knowledge of their art the greatest experience of disease. It is better for them not to be robust of health themselves, but to have had all manner of diseases in their own persons. For it is not with the

body, but with the mind, that they cure the body. And thus they infer the bodily diseases of others from the knowledge of what has taken place in their own bodies.

In the second place, genuine physicians have scientific knowledge, of the kind associated with the Pythagoreans. Experimentation joined to observation of consequences has enabled them to build up a system of rules which can fairly safely be applied in practice. It is not a perfect system, for medicine, at its best, is a highly empirical art and requires, at every stage, a master's judgment. It is only when the master-physician is unable to keep an eye on his patients that he leaves written prescriptions (such as are found in medical treatises) to be applied without modification. But his scientific knowledge enables him to do what the mere empiric, however successful his practice, can never do : namely, to discuss his cases, to explain the nature of diseases, and to say why he prescribes this or that treatment. His is a *rational* art, i.e., a science in the Pythagorean sense.[12]

In the third place, genuine physicians are practical philosophers. They regard the human being as a microcosm exhibiting the same laws as the macrocosm, and can relate questions of specific health and disease to the general laws of motion in the physical universe. Man, like the cosmos, is made up of the four elements, earth, water, fire, and air, mingled in certain proportions. His health is the balanced unity of these elements, so that they function harmoniously : a balance which would, if left to itself, continue.[13] It is when the balance is upset, so that there is too much of this or that element, interfering with the orderly processes of change within the body, that the pathological processes called diseases occur. Too much fire results in fevers. Too much water, in dropsies.[14]

With this philosophical insight into the world, as well as experience of his patients, the skilful practitioner avoids the crude use of specific drugs, and of the surgeon's knife. These specifics remedy, indeed, the balance ; but they do so crudely and violently, irritating the tissues and overtaxing the system as a whole. He prefers to proceed gently, prescribing gradual changes of regimen, and thus curing his patient as a whole : bringing him from an unwise, to a wise and prudent manner of living,[15] in accordance with his philosophic, no less than of his scientific, insight :

Of all motions, self-motion is best ; for it is most akin to the motion of the universe and the motion of thought. Motion caused by others

is less good. Worst of all is when parts of the body are moved by external agencies, when the body as a whole is at rest.
Therefore the best mode of purifying and re-uniting the body is gymnastic. Next best is a surging motion, as in sailing. The third, I mean the purgative treatment of certain physicians, is to be adopted only in extreme cases. Diseases as a rule should not be irritated by such medicines. Drugs only aggravate and multiply the evil.[16]

How does the physician become educated for his profession ? In the first place, by studying under masters of repute in medicine. Secondly, by observation and experience. Thirdly, by experimentation upon himself and others.[17] Fourthly, by systematizing his results into a theory : and finally, by generalizing his views by the application of philosophy. This may make him a little pedantic, as in the case of Eryximachus.[18] But the philosopher-practitioner is intended as a worthy parallel to the philosopher-king.[19]

The treatment of *the legal profession* in the *Dialogues* is somewhat parallel to the treatment of the medical profession. As the one is concerned with governing men in their eating, drinking, exercising and resting so as to ensure their physical health : so the other is concerned with governing men in their social relations so as to ensure the moral and political health of the community. Both govern by rules, based upon technical knowledge and insight, prescribing certain ways of living ; and in both cases these rules may be verbal directions, exhortations, or what are called decrees —or they may be given in a form which is undeviating, as in the case of written prescriptions or written laws, toward which unquestioning obedience is expected.[21]

The parallel extends almost down to details. As there are two sorts of doctor, the slavish assistant and the genuine physican, so there are two levels in the legal profession. The lower level is that of the advocate who passes his whole time in and about courts of law and similar places. He does not belong socially to the slave class ; but *spiritually speaking*, Plato does not hestitate to call his mind slavish. He is unfree, first, because he is tied down to considerations of place and time ; secondly, because (like the doctor's assistant) he cannot question the letter of the prescriptions which he follows, but has to accept them as absolute standards ; thirdly, because he can decide nothing of himself but has to direct his whole efforts to flatter, cajole, and persuade others (the

judges or jury), thus putting his fate in their hands. All the
associations of his kind of work combine to keep him below the
level of real manhood :

> Knocking about the courts from youth up, he has become keen and
> shrewd ; but his soul is small and uprighteous. His condition, which
> has been that of a slave from youth, has deprived him of true growth
> into uprightness and independence. By dangers and fears which have
> proved too much for his tender honesty, he has been driven into
> crooked ways, practising deception and retaliation, and becoming
> stunted and warped. And so he has passed from youth into manhood,
> becoming a keen but narrow, little, legal, mind, fighting about the
> images and shadows of justice—a justice which he has never seen in
> itself.[22]

This means that the advocate whose professional training is a
matter of concrete experience based upon association, imitation,
and practice without insight into principle, is living in the kingdom of shadows which represents the lowest stage of intelligence. In " fighting with other men about shadows, distracted in
the struggle for power," such a man never rises above the stage
of opinion, and has no genuine conception of the higher ideals of
his profession.[23] His whole life is spent among men like himself,
clever rogues who seem smart in the company of their fellows, but
are entirely lost in the company of men of liberal education.[24]
    The higher type of legal luminary has been trained as a freeman
is trained. That is to say, the whip of necessity has been laid aside,
and he has not been subjected to the debasing constraints of time
and place, of hope and fear, which have made of the inferior
lawyer the thing that he is. His experience has not been confined
to the narrow usages of local courts, but he has travelled and has
studied the laws and usages of many communities. He can cite
the practice of the Scythians in favour of ambidexterity, of the
Cretans in favour of dancing in armour, of the Lacedaemonians in
favour of military gymnastics for women, of the Egyptians in
favour of teaching mathematics by games.[25] In general, he is
full, not only of wise maxims, but of relevant instances : ready on
all constitutional points to discuss parallel institutions elsewhere.
In the ancient world he is the social equivalent of the Pythagorean
scientist, and in the modern world he corresponds to the authority
who holds the degree Doctor of Civil Law. In the *Dialogues* he
is personified in the character of the Athenian Stranger who is
requested to serve on a constitutional commission in the *Laws*,[26]
and clearly belongs to the class which is qualified to tender expert

advice to administrative authorities. Neither the ideal city of the *Republic* nor the model city of the *Laws* is ever to be without such legal experts ; and it is clearly recognized that a few such persons are to be found in the actual communities of the Hellenic world.[27]

To experience and science, i.e., to knowledge of actual social usages and the consequences of the different types of social institution, the legal expert (as Plato develops him) adds a touch of philosophy :

> He who has not contemplated the mind of nature which is said to exist in the stars, and gone through the previous training, and seen the connection of music with these things, and harmonized them all with laws and institutions, is not able to give a reason of such things as have a reason. He who is unable to acquire this in addition to the ordinary virtues of a citizen, must be a subordinate, one of the mass who only follow the voice of the laws.[28]

Plato's picture of the legal profession thus terminates in de-lineating a philosopher-lawyer who is the counterpart of the philosopher-physician already discussed.

For the profession of the law-lord and legal expert, the education suggested by Plato depends upon wide experience of men and affairs, a thorough training in habits of law,[29] further education in scientific habits of thought, culminating in philosophic insight into the ideal principle of value.[30] Further discussion of these factors is postponed, as coming more properly under the heading " Education for Leadership."

Under the head of " professor " we can understand the teaching personnel in the field of higher education ; men who perform a very important function in developing to full manhood select adolescents of the governing classes—a function indispensable in any civilized community, whether actual or ideal. What they pass on to their pupils is not so much the concrete techniques of the arts and sciences as training in critical reflection upon human values. They may select for study the values found in actual life, in striking cases like those of Archelaus, Aristides, Cambyses, Cimon, Cyrus, Pericles, Themistocles, etc. ;[31] or they may prefer to study the values enshrined in the formulations of authoritative literature, [32] thus teaching their pupils to reflect upon the traditional criticisms of life current in the Hellenic world.

The worthwhileness to the community of this function is beyond question. In ancient as in modern times professors of literature, government, public speaking, and philosophy were sought after and induced to place their talents at the service of this or that community by the offer of pecuniary rewards and other honours. Like the other teachers considered above, they were for the most part "foreigners attracted by pay." It is implied that the fees were pretty high, and that the services of the more eminent professors were considered worthy of the fees paid. Young men of good family are represented as eager to study under acknowledged masters ; and the situation generally was something like " going to college " in our times. [33]

Men who pursued the career of teaching in the field of higher education professionally, i.e., as a way of earning their living, were a phenomenon of the generation immediately preceding Plato. [34] By his own time they had become something of a commonplace. They are frequently discussed in the *Dialogues*, usually in a slightly satirical, and sometimes in a bitter spirit. The best-known picture of professors in action is to be found in the *Protagoras*, and the keenest analysis of their nature and function in the *Sophist*, but they form part of the background of almost all of the *Dialogues* and frequently step forward into the limelight, if only for a moment.

Like doctors and lawyers, professors fall into two groups, (1) an inferior group of assistants, imitators, and pretenders to personal ability in this lucrative field. Among assistants are men like Antimoerus and Polus. [35] Among pretenders are men like Euthydemus and Dionysodorus. [36] And as to imitators, almost all of the younger professors imitate the older and more venerable men like Gorgias and Protagoras. In this group belong also the inferior sort of philosophers, " puny creatures who jump out of the trades into philosophy," men clever at their own crafts but narrow-minded, warped and maimed in their souls, " unworthy of education," generating " sophisms captivating to the ear, but without genuine wisdom." [37]

This inferior group study for their profession by association with a master, and by imitating his mannerisms and concrete techniques, but without his insight into principle. [38] Moreover, like the inferior members of the legal profession, they are intimidated by the social environment and fail to develop independence of judgment. It is easy to praise the Athenians among the Athenians, and they develop the habit of flattering their audience and pay-masters and formulating for their benefit their own views :

When men meet together and the world sits down at an assembly of any sort and there is a great uproar, praising some things which are said and done and blaming others, exaggerating both praise and blame with shouting and clapping of hands, so that the echo of the place of assembly redoubles the noise—at such a time will not a young man's heart leap within him ? Will any private training enable him to stand firm against the overwhelming flood of popular opinion ? Will he not have the notions of good and evil which the public in general have, doing what they do, and being like them ?[39]

Practically all such professors thus become amplifiers of their master's voice and inculcate the traditional conservatism of the possessing classes. They tell the public what the public wants to be told and thus fail to develop either in themselves or in their pupils a genuinely critical standpoint which will rise above the level of mass opinion. And this tends to be true, not merely of the inferior professors, but even of their leaders, men like the great professionals, Protagoras and Gorgias.[40]

Let us now consider the superior group of professional teachers in the field of higher education. Failing to develop a genuinely critical standard of values, they tend to specialize and devote themselves to work of secondary importance : to erudition, to expansion of work done by the classical writers, to pretentious analyses which fail to pass beyond the barest elements, to limited aspects of limited fields of study. As Protagoras himself says, " most professors tend to fall back again into the arts from which they profess to emancipate their pupils," as we see happen in the case of many of the specialists in our Arts Colleges today. This gives them a sense of mastery in a field which they have made their own, however secondary, and provides them with an excuse for not really educating their pupils.[41]

Thus Hippias of Elis, the distinguished polymath, who was " willing to answer any questions anyone has to ask, whether at Olympia, where all the Hellenes were assembled," or at Athens in the home of Callias the " millionaire and patron of professors." He would answer ex cathedra questions of a scientific nature, of a literary nature, of a technical nature, and, as he himself said, " had never found any man who was his superior in anything."[42]

When he went to the Olympic games, all he had on was made by himself. He had a ring of his own workmanship, and another seal, and a strigil and an oil flask, all of which he had himself made. He had made the shoes on his feet, the cloak and tunic he wore, and, in particular, the finely woven girdle of his tunic. And he carried with him poems and prose compositions of every recognized type, and referred to his own art of memory, as well as the other arts, in all of which he was proficient.[43]

On the other hand " the excellent Prodicus " of Ceos confined his ideas of " a complete education," even in his fifty-drachma course, to " grammar and language," and in the one demonstration lecture which Socrates attended confined his attention to the study of synonyms and dialectical variants. Apart from this, he wrote a set composition in prose on *The Virtue of Heracles*, elaborating upon a classical theme.[44]

Examples of pretentious analyses resulting in little more than high-sounding names for obvious elements are furnished by reference to the authorities on rhetoric, such as Polus, with his " treasuries of diplasiology, gnomolgy, eikonology, in which he teaches the names of which Licymnius made him a present," and the great Protagoras himself. Such authorities " suppose that they have found the art in its preliminary conditions, and imagine that to apply it in practice, with Periclean effectiveness, is something which their pupils can easily do for themselves."[45]

Thus we see that the actual professionals in the field of higher education tend to devote themselves to something analogous to Pythagorean science : cataloguing the phenomena in their special fields and confining themselves to the building up of fact into theory, but without developing the kind of insight which is characteristic of philosophy.[46]

Faced with this professional higher education, which trains in techniques but does not really educate, Plato insists upon the necessity of going further. The truest and best teachers in this field should have developed the especial insight characteristic of philosophers. They will then be able to do what they profess, namely, to educate their pupils beyond repeating and cataloguing their masters' words. It was association with the philosopher Anaxagoras, and not poring over the elementary analyses of the rhetorical manuals, which made Pericles the great speaker that he was :—

All the great arts require discussion and high speculation about the truths of nature. It is from this that sublimity of thought and perfection of execution come. This was the quality which (in addition to

his natural gifts) Pericles acquired from his intercourse with Anaxagoras. He was thus imbued with the higher philosophy and attained
to the knowledge of Mind and the negative of Mind (the favourite
themes of Anaxagoras) ; and he applied what suited his purpose to
the art of speaking.[47]

That is to say, Plato's account of education for the profession
of " professor " starts with association and imitation, accepts the
necessity of broad experience and scientific analyses, and cul-
minates with a touch of the philosopher's vision. As he sees the
matter, it is only the *philosopher*-teacher who is competent to direct
and expound the higher education. He is analogous to the philosopher-physician and the philosopher-lawyer discussed above.

When they have reached fifty years of age and have distinguished
themselves in every branch of knowledge, they must raise their eyes to
the universal light which lightens all things, and behold the absolute
good. That is the pattern according to which they are to order the
lives of individuals and their own lives too : making philosophy their
chief pursuit. When they have brought up in each generation others
like themselves and left them in their place, they will depart to the
Islands of the Blest.[48]

The *theological profession*, in Ancient Greece, was in the hands of
three kinds of practitioner : (1) the soothsayer, (2) the interpreter,
and (3) the priest. Hellenic religion had two main sources. There
was (a) the animism natural to humanity in its primitive and early
cultural levels. Men feel themselves surrounded by forces like
themselves, capricious but far more powerful : operating through
such agencies as light and darkness, wind and tempest, and indeed
through everything that moves and has life and growth. " All
things are full of gods," as Thales taught. In as much as man's
weal and woe obviously depend upon the beneficence or mal-
eficence of this environment, clemency or inclemency of the
seasons, moderation or fury of the winds and waves, fruitfulness
or stubbornness on the part of mother earth, it seems natural and
inevitable that human dependence upon the goodwill of such forces
should express itself in attitudes of prayer and worship. And
further : such feelings associate themselves very readily with
objects of large size, perceptible to the senses, such as the sun,
moon, and stars, greater rivers like the Nile, and the larger lakes
and oceans. But since the life of early man is predominantly
local, bounded by a very narrow horizon, it is natural that

rudimentary rituals of propitiation and worship should attempt to link human destiny with environmental agencies near at hand.[49] Hence the worship of local deities of all sorts : a worship assisted by finding here and there stones (of meteoric origin as a rule) which bore some resemblance to the human form divine, and could be regarded as images of this or that power, sent by no human hand as a guide to the erection of local temples with local rituals.

The other source (b) of Hellenic religion was the intuitions of the poets, who created or formulated and popularized local and national legends dealing with such things. The poems of Hesiod and the Homeric Hymns were recognized as the most authoritative of these literary sources. In this way, out of local traditions[50] and poetic formulation of myths, was contrived the content of Hellenic religion. It was of no very great antiquity and pretended to no very great authority in matters of detail. But its inclusion of the great nature-myths satisfied the religious feelings of a people whose nature called for some reflective projection of its biosocial struggles, its history, and its ideals.

Against this background, there developed (1) the soothsayer or prophet : a character corresponding somewhat to the fortune-teller, tea-cup reader, and horoscope-giver of modern times, with tendencies partly in the direction of orthodox religion, partly in the direction of unauthorized magic.[51] Such persons are regarded as interpreters of God's ways to men, and as a sort of go-between through whose mediumship men may approach divinity and receive inspired messages.[52] Following non-logical "hunches" or intuitions, as in the case of the "diviners" whose rods dip when passing over places where treasure can be found,[53] or deliberately inducing an unconscious phase by drugs, self-hypnotism, or sleep under conditions favourable to the reception of visions,[54] such persons put themselves *en rapport* with the god who uses them as his channel of communication :

God takes away the minds of prophets and uses them as His ministers, in order that we who hear them may know them to be speaking not of themselves who utter these priceless words in a state of unconsciousness, but that God is Himself the speaker, and through them is conversing with us.[55]

The definitely infra-rational nature of this inspiration is brought out, not merely in the passages which show the soothsayer and prophet, as contrasted with the augur and interpreter, to be obscure and comparatively unintelligent,[56] but especially in the attempt, in Plato's physiological psychology, to explain the mechanism of apparitions, dreams, and prophetic visions. They come as mental images, pictured before the mind, but definitely devoid of rational interpretation :

> Knowing that the lower principle in man would not comprehend reason, and even if attaining to some degree of perception would be led by phantoms and visions, God contrived the liver in such a form that the power of thought might be reflected back as in a mirror, giving images. Some gentle inspiration of the understanding makes use of the natural sweetness of the liver, rendering the portion of the soul which resides about the liver happy, enabling it to pass the night in sleep and to practise divination in sleep, inasmuch as it has no share of mind and reason. The authors of our being placed in the liver the seat of divination. And herein we see that God has given the art of divination not to the wisdom, but to the foolishness of man. No man in his wits attains prophetic truth and inspiration ; but when he receives the inspired word, either his intelligence is enthralled in sleep, or he is demented by some distemper or possession.[57]

The soothsayer is thus a comparatively uneducated person, belonging definitely to the lower ranks of the theological profession. His advice is sought in a number of obscure cases such as unusual homicides, burial customs, life in the next world, especially where pollution is suspected, or queer happenings which look like omens. His prophetic visions may also give indications as to the future.[58] But they are so obscure as to stand in need of interpretation by a man of trained intelligence who is no visionary ; and in general we are given to understand that the soothsayer or prophet is the lowest kind of theological authority.[59]

How does a man train himself for the position of soothsayer ? The discussions of the *Dialogues* leave this point a little obscure. In a sense, visionaries are born, not made. The would-be prophet has to have the animistic point of view rather well developed. That is to say, he has to have a certain feeling for the kinship of man with nature and with the powers behind nature : for the messages whispered by sacred oak trees, for the veridical nature of dream-phantoms and vivid mental imagery, for signs and portents of all kinds, and for the magical forces released and directed by spells and incantations. This sort of thing is a matter of infra-rational feeling, and so hardly calls for anything which could be termed education. A certain encouragement for the development of such feelings would come from association with other psychic and mediumistic persons, such as were found at centres like Dodona, Trophonium, and Delphi ; but apart from this indication, it is hinted that such persons are not so much educated, as ignorant and superstitious :

A more daring group are persuaded that they can do injury by sorceries, incantations, and " magic knots ; " and they make others believe that they are injured by the powers of the magician. It is not easy to know the nature of these things ; and when men are disturbed in their minds at the sight of waxen images fixed at their doors, or at the meeting of three roads or on the sepulchres of parents, it is futile to tell them they should despise such practices because their knowledge is uncertain. Such practices scare the multitude out of their wits as if they were children. The legislator and the judge must tell them that such would-be enchanters do not know what they are doing, unless they happen to be prophets or diviners—in which case they must be condemned to death.[60]

On the intellectual side, such persons educate themselves by studying certain kinds of poetry : the Orphic poems, and the passages in Homer which depict life in the underworld and give thrilling accounts of dreams and omens.[61] Furthermore, they accept and interpret certain usages and traditions which express folklore in the form of taboos and mysteries,[62] especially such as profess to purify individuals and cities from the stain of blood-guiltiness, and are passed on from generation to generation as " most true tales " because of their supposedly edifying character.[63]

Let us now consider the more important members of the theological profession. That prophetic messages are obscure and require interpretation, has already been indicated. These interpreters are sober-minded persons of trained intelligence. But a great deal more is said about them than that. Plato is determined to make the interpretation of prophecies and the direction of sacred rites as official as possible, and to keep it well under community control. There are thus no private persons posing as interpreters. All interpreters are public officials : acceptable to the central authority of Delphi and appointed for life. They function as a committee : sitting as experts along with the soothsayers and assisting the legislative bodies to frame detailed regulations respecting sacred matters. The legislative bodies act upon their expert advice ; and the final regulation thus receives the sanction of community law.[64]

Like the law-lords, these community experts are persons of the highest character : exemplary patterns of all the civic virtues. They are elected as follows : The twelve tribes (in the model city) sit in four divisions (each consisting of three tribes). Each

division selects one from among those of its members who are
sixty years or more and are of the highest reputation. This
gives a group of four candidates. The procedure is repeated, so
as to give a second group of four, and yet again, so as to give a
third group of four candidates. From each group of four, the
three receiving the highest vote, i.e., nine in all, are sent (after
inspection, to determine that they are " sound of body, of legitimate birth, and of a perfectly pure family, unstained by homicide
or other impiety for two generations ") to Delphi. Out of each
group of three, one is finally selected by " the God " (Apollo,
acting through his ministers at Delphi) ; and these three final
choices are declared official interpreters *ad vitam*[65]

The duties of these three interpreters, acting as a committee
in connection with the legislative authorities,[66] are declared to be
as follows : They receive from Delphi the general rules relating
to sacred matters, and apply them in detailed cases. In particular, they decide upon the rites and other sacred acts performed
in connection with marriage, birth, and death. Cemeteries are
under their absolute authority ; and homicides, suicides, and the
official rites of purification in connection with blood-pollution,
and with other forms of pollution, are referred to them for
decision. In general all sacred festivals and ceremonies are decided by committees upon which they have representation ; and
it is declared that all details left undiscussed by the protagonists
in the *Laws* may safely be committed to their charge.[67]

How is a man educated for such a position ? In general, his
education follows the lines fixed for the higher group of lawyers,
the law-lords whose experience is enlightened by scientific training
and a touch of philosophy. The interpreters are treated as parallel
to the law-lords, dealing with sacred matters where the law-lords
confine their attention to profane legislation. Their education
is thus a matter of wide experience, close study of sacred laws and
institutions, enlightened by philosophic insight into principle.
The philosopher-interpreter is a worthy companion to the
philosopher-lawyer considered above.[68]

Priests also belong to the higher ranks of the theological profession. They differ from interpreters in that their duties are for
the most part formal and ceremonial. They are public magistrates who carry out temple sacrifices and offer prayers on behalf

of the people in a solemn and appropriate manner. These duties, although highly important, are not particularly difficult. Almost any of the older citizens whose character is beyond reproach can be entrusted with the office, which is in most cases held only for a year, and the candidates are accordingly selected by lot. The candidates have to be sixty years of age, of good character, and of families whose purity is established for two generations. The reason for using the lot as a method of choice is that their selection will then depend upon no human meddling, but will be left to " the God."[69] No particular education is necessary in order to qualify a man for the office of temple-priest, other than the general education for citizenship (music, gymnastic, and life in eager obedience to the laws of the community). As there is to be, in the model city, at least one public festival in honour of some civic deity on each day of the year, it will take a good number of these elderly priests and priestesses to look after the services which come under their jurisdiction.[70] Many of the services involve the use of choirs, sometimes of several at once. These chant ceremonial hymns and prayers and perform processional dances, all of which have to be performed with proper regard for the prescribed ritual. [71]The prescription of ritual and the choice of hymns and dance-movements is, however, too complicated a matter to be left to priests appointed by lot ; it is therefore handled by experts appointed by properly qualified groups of citizens, and the advice of these experts is followed by the law-making committees.[72] Once prescribed and given the sanction of community law, these hymns and dances are preserved without change in principle ; and the priests are given representation on the controlling committee.[73]

In addition to these temple-priests, whose annual tenure and purely formal duties invest them with a merely ceremonial importance, there is a higher group, outranking in importance most of the magistrates, for whom indeed they furnish an examining body. Three citizens, of fifty years and upwards, selected by the whole body of citizens as the very best, appoint twelve examiners, known as the priests of Apollo and Helios. The three and their twelve appointees hold office for life. They not only examine the qualifications and behaviour of magistrates, and occupy various ceremonial positions of great importance, but also sit with the ten senior law-lords, and the director of education, the community visitor (or visitors), and selected younger men, constituting a revision council of the constitution.[74] It is possible, even, that they are to be identified with the " nocturnal council," although this point is left in obscurity.[75] In any case, these twelve (or possibly fifteen) higher priests are in a different class from the temple-priests, and approximate to the philosopher-law-lords, with whom they act as colleagues ; and they have the same education in philosophy as the colleagues with whom they are associated as superior magistrates.[76]

The military profession, like its predecessors in our investigation, has its lower and its higher ranks. The function of all ranks is to guard and preserve the community in war ; and the usefulness of this function is beyond question. It is second in importance only to that habitual intelligent law-abidingness which elevates a citizen into the group from which the very highest officials are selected.[77]

About the lower ranks, comparatively little is said in the *Dialogues*, the chief emphasis being upon the development of that specialized technique and skill for which much time is required if the warriors are to be trained adequately for leadership.[78] The implication is that the lower ranks exhibit less highly developed skill in military evolutions and are fitted for disciplined followership. They are strong, swift, and spirited, but not especially philosophical,[79] and are trained to carry out orders and act as auxiliaries,[80] behaving as described in the *Laws* :

No one should be without a commander, nor should his mind be accustomed to do anything of his own motion. Both in war and in peace he should look to and follow his leader, even in matters of detail. His standing, moving, exercising, eating, washing, standing guard at night, and delivering messages should be under command. He should not pursue or retreat except in obedience to orders, and should not teach or accustom his soul to know or understand how to do anything apart from others. Military life should always and in all things be in common and together, and the habit should be practised even in peace, from youth up. Anarchy should have no place in human life.[81]

Education for the lower ranks of the military profession follows the same lines as education for the higher ranks, up to a certain point. That is to say, the music and gymnastic are the same, and the participation in tests of character and of intelligence, as in the competitive military sports, is the same. But the lower ranks are recruited from those who display no outstanding excellence on these occasions.[82] That is to say, their education is a matter of association with masters and officials who train them, as well as with their contemporaries and equals. [83] But they are not found among the prize winners ; belonging rather to those steady but slow natures from whom loyal service, but no unusual genius is to be expected. [84]

The higher ranks are selected from the prize-winners, i.e., the outstanding characters in gymnastic and intellectual tests and labours. Once selected, they are given a more specialized training suited to their superior intelligences, and are also given opportunities of command which are denied the others :

> At the age of thirty-five, our selected candidates are compelled to hold any military or other office which young men are qualified to hold ; in this way they will get their experience of life, and there will be a further opportunity to try whether they will stand firm against temptation. This stage of their lives will last fifteen years ; and at the age of fifty those who have distinguished themselves in every action and every branch of knowledge at last raise their eyes to the absolute good, the pattern in accordance with which they are to order the State and the lives of individuals hereafter. [85]

The study of the specialized intellectual training which is given to these persons selected from the ranks, is postponed for the present, as it coincides with the intellectual side of the education for leadership, which will be investigated later.

So far we have studied vocational and technical education in the arts and sciences, the social sciences, the vocations, and the professions. We have found in all a lower phase of achievement, concrete, practical, and dependent upon association, imitation, and practice rather than upon insight into principle. In the sciences, vocations, and especially in the professions, we have found also a higher phase of achievement, resting partly upon experience and training, but requiring, for its full development, the kind of insight which comes from the serious systematic study of philosophy. Plato's own interest throughout is demonstrably less in the lower phase, which he tends to regard as unfree, and more in the higher phase which he regards as characterizing especially the type of humanity which is, in his opinion, suited for full citizenship and even more for leadership. In what follows, we shall consider education for citizenship and education for leadership.

[1]*Rep.* 373c, 405 ff., 459c ; *Laws* 720 f., 857de.

[2]*Rep.* 405a–c. 409 ; *Theaet.* 173–175 ; *Laws* 743.

[3]*Prtg.* and *Soph.*, *passim* ; cf. *Gorg.* 519b f. ; *Euthyd.* 303a, 304a ; *Rep.* 492 f. ; *Theaet.* 167a.

[4]*Lach.* 198e ; *Rep.* 379c, 386c ; *Laws* 759, 774e, 799 f., 800b, 828b, 845e, 865d, 871c, 873d, 916c, 958d, 964c, 966c.

[5]*Rep.* 374b ff., 522e, 525b, 526d, 527b ; *Polit.* 304e f. ; *Phil.* 56a ; *Laws* 643c, 755, 818c, 921e.

[6]*Rep.* 332c, 459c ; cf. 404a ; *Polit.* 294d ; cf. *Laws* 646d, 659e f., 839e f.

[7]*Rep.* 405ab, 406de, 407b f. ; *Laws* 720c.

[8]*Laws* 720bc, condensed. Cf. 857cd. The context implies that assistants who did not devote their *full* time to slaves were not themselves necessarily slaves (" whether they are slaves or freemen. . . ." 720a).

[9]*Laws* 720ab, 857d, condensed.

[10]*Phaedr.* 268 f.   [11]*Rep.* 408c f., condensed.

[12]*Gorg.* 465a ; *Polit.* 293ab, 295c f. ; *Phil.* 55e f. ; *Laws* 720.

[13]*Tim.* 81e ff. ; cf. *Rep.* 424a.   [14]*Tim.* 86a f. ; cf. *Soph.* 228a.

[15]*Theaet.* 167 ; *Tim.* 69b, 88b f. Cf. *Phaedr.* 269cd ; *Laws* 659e f.

[16]*Charm.* 156 f. ; *Tim.* 89a–c, condensed ; cf. *Laws* 903d.

[17]*Lach.* 185c ff. ; *Rep.* 408de.   [18]*Sym.* 176b f., 185d ff.   [19]*Polit.* 292c ff.

[21]*Rep.* 405a f. ; *Polit.* 293b ff. ; cf. *Laws* 769d, 772, 846c, 890d f.

[22]*Theaet.* 172c f. ; *Rep.* 517de, cf. 425e f., 520cd.

[23]*Rep.* 405bc, 516c f., 518e f.   [24]*Rep.* 409cd ; *Theaet.* 175c–177b.

[25]*Rep.* 409a f. ; *Laws* 795a, 796b, 806a, 819b, etc.   [26]*Laws* 702b, 753a, 969a f.

[27]*Rep.* 409 f. ; *Laws* 951–953d.   Solon and Lycurgus were traditionally regarded as authorities of this stamp (*Laws* 858c f.). The law-lords of the *Laws*, from whom the experts were selected, belong in general to this class.

[28]*Laws* 966c–967e, condensed. Cf. *Rep.* 531 ff.   [29]*Laws* 751c.

[30]*Rep.* 540a, 592 ; *Laws* 957 ; cf. *Sym.* 212a.

[31]*Lach.* 179c ; *Gorg.* 445e, 455e, 471a, 472b, d, 476d, 479a, e, 503, 515d f., 519a, 525d, 526b ; *Prtg.* 314e, 320a, 328c ; *Meno* 93f. ; *Menex.* 239e ; Laws 694a ff.

[32]*Prtg.* 338e ff. ; *Laws* 810b ff.

[33]*Prtg.* 310 ff., 328bc ; *Theaet.* 178d ff.

[34]*Prtg.* 316c f.   [35]*Prtg.* 315 a; *Gorg.* 448 f.   [36]*Euthyd.* 271c ff.

[37]*Rep.* 487c f., 489d, 490e ff., 492, 495c f. ; *Theaet.* 173c.

[38]As Ctesippus proves himself an apt pupil of teachers themselves inferior (*Euthyd.* 303e f.).   [39]*Rep.* 492b f., condensed.   [40]*Rep.* 492d–494a.   [41]*Prtg.* 318de.

[42]*Prtg.* 315bc ; *Hipp. Min.* 363d–364a.   [43]*Hipp. Min.* 368, condensed.

[44]*Crat.* 384b ; *Prtg.* 337a, 340e, f., 358a ; *Euthyd.* 277e ; *Meno* 75e ; *Sym.* 177b ; cf. *Charm.* 163d ; *Lach.* 197d ; *Theaet.* 151b.

[45]*Phaedr.* 266c–269d.

[46]*Phaedr.* 266d. Certain of the authoritative commentators on the *Protagoras* suppose that to bring out this distinction is the main point of the duel between Protagoras and Socrates.

[47]*Phaedr.* 269e f., condensed. The sequel gives Plato's account of the philosophical type of eloquence, together with its basis and divisions. But as this goes beyond the professional treatment of Plato's time (although it has become a part of our present-day manuals), it is not discussed further here.

[48]*Rep.* 537d–540b, condensed. Cf. *Laws* 964c, which explains that the higher teachers (no less than the higher law-lords) are patterns of the virtues. See also Ch. VII *infra*.

[49]*Laws* 886a ; cf. 898d–899d, 909e f.

[50]*Rep.* 363 ff. ; cf. *Laws* 713d f., 782b–d, 881a, 927a.

[51]For orthodox religion, cf. *Laws* 828a f. For magic, cf. *Rep.* 364a–c ; *Laws* 933a–d, 909b. For analogies to teacup reading, cf., *Ion* 3cd ; *Phaedr.* 244c ; *Phil.* 67b.

[52]*Sym.* 188b, 202d f. ; *Polit.* 290c f.   [53]*Laws* 913ab.   [54]*Tim.* 71a–c.

[55]*Ion* 534s, slightly condensed.   [56]*Phaedr.* 244 ; *Tim.* 72b.

[57]*Tim.* 71 f., condensed.   [58]*Ion* 538d f. ; *Phaedr.* 242c ; *Euthyph.* 4.

[59]*Tim.* 71e f. The chief example of a soothsayer in the *Dialogues* is Euthyphro. He is depicted not in his state of prophetic exaltation, but in his lucid moments. The quality of his intelligence stands out as ludicrously below the boundless claims he makes for himself as an authority upon all questions which fall within a soothsayer's province. (See *Euthyph.* 4e f., 11c ; cf. 3c, d).

⁶⁰*Laws* 933a f., condensed. ⁶¹*Rep.* 364b–365a ; *Ion* 538d f.
⁶²*Euthyph.* 6c ; *Laws* 713d f., 782bc. ⁶³Cf. *Laws* 865d f., 881a, 927a.
⁶⁴*Laws* 828ab, 964c.
⁶⁵*Laws* 759de. Jowett's translation of this section is not entirely correct.
⁶⁶*Laws* 828ab. ⁶⁷*Laws* 774e, 828b f., 845e, 865d, 871c, 873d, 916c, 958d ; cf.
770b f., *Rep.* 458c. Although it is not always so stated, it is to be understood that
prophets and priests would also, as a rule, co-operate on these committees. The
interpreters, however, were the really important officials. ⁶⁸Cf. *Laws.* 964bc. The
nearest thing to an example of this higher kind of " interpreter " in the *Dialogues* is
the Athenian Stranger of the *Laws*, when dealing with sacred matters (co-opted to
sit in committee with the official chairman of the controlling commission (Cleinias)
and his fellow-member (Megillus), and giving expert advice which is adopted as a
basis for legislation). The touch of philosophy in all these higher officials makes them a
little ready to " exhort, admonish, and educate " (the traditional method of educating,
Soph. 229e f.) by explaining the purpose of their prescriptions. The superior physician
discoursing about disease is " educating by his philosophizing,.' and so is the superior
law-lord with his " preambles " and the Athenian Stranger in his character as
interpreter (cf. *Laws* 719e f., 722e ff., 857d f., 879c f., 887 f.). As " interpreter " he
even goes so far as to give, not merely model " sermons," but the beginnings of
dogmatic theology (*Laws* 891d ff., 903b ff., cf. *Rep.* 377c ff.). ⁶⁹*Laws* 759, 800bc ;
cf. *Euthyph.* 14b f., *Polit.* 290c f. ⁷⁰*Laws* 828a. ⁷¹*Laws* 664 f., 670 f., 812b, 816bc.
⁷²*Laws* 765, 772a f. ⁷³*Laws* 799a f. The priests have the duty of excluding from the
services all nonconformists. ⁷⁴*Laws* 945b ff., 966d. ⁷⁵*Laws* 951e, 961a. The obscurity is supposed by scholars to be due to the " unfinished " state of the *Laws*.
⁷⁶*Laws* 962b f., 964. The ·reference is indicated in the context as applying to the
members of the " nocturnal council " which is the " anchor of the State." ⁷⁷*Rep.*
373e f., *Laws* 921d f. Cf. *Laws* 945e ff. ⁷⁸*Rep.* 374d ff. ⁷⁹*Rep.* 376bc. ⁸⁰*Rep.* 389de,
414b. ⁸¹*Laws* 942a f., condensed, cf. *Rep.* 466c ff. Cf. also *Laws* 808d f., *Lach.* 193ab,
Rep. 590d f., *Lysis* 207d f. ⁸²*Rep.* 412d ff. ⁸³*Rep.* 467d f., *Laws* 804c f., 813d f., 829 ff.
⁸⁴*Rep.* 503c f., 537b f., cf. *Theaet.* 144b. ⁸⁵*Rep.* 539d f., condensed.

CHAPTER IV

EDUCATION FOR CITIZENSHIP

The phrase " education for citizenship " has a vague sound in modern ears. Is not every one a " citizen " ? The butcher, the baker, the candlestick-maker are, surely, just as much citizens as the high-priests, the generals, and the philosophers—if not more so. That being the case, if you try to abstract from the education which qualifies a man for his especial function—as butcher, baker, military expert, poet, or what not—and ask what remains, it will not be much. The political aspect of his life, perhaps, attending meetings at which community policies of a general nature are decided, and voting for this or that policy, Of course, it is obvious that where policies depend on expert information, e.g., in expanding the navy, or equipping the army with the latest mechanized weapons, or deciding upon an official revision of the authorised hymnal for church services, or deciding what business taxes (if any) should be imposed, the assent of the " general citizen " will tend to be something of a rubber stamp, authorizing what the experts recommend.[1] A very little study of " civics " or " government " would seem to be sufficient to educate the members of the community for the exercise of their functions as " citizens." Anything more would be of the nature of general preaching : exhorting every citizen to " do his duty," to " deliberate prudently," to " vote honestly," and generally, to exhibit the approved " virtues."[2]

If there is some one quality, of which citizens *qua* citizens must be partakers—not the art of the carpenter or the smith or the potter, but—justice, self-control, holiness, in a word manly virtue : it is incredible that this should not be especially taught and cultivated. Education by admonition commences in childhood and continues throughout life. Parents and attendants try to improve children by setting forth that this is just, that unjust ; this is honourable, that dishonourable ; do this and abstain from that : enforcing obedience by threats and blows. Teachers carry on the good work : edifying poems are learnt by heart ; harmonies and rhythms inculcated ; bodies trained by gymnastics to fit them for civic life. The young adult is similarly guided by the laws and institutions of the city, admonishing and enforcing obedience. All have a mutual interest in teaching freely justice and the laws.[3]

The speech of Protagoras, from which this selection is taken, is in fact an excellent example of what at the present day we think of as " commencement day orations," containing general exhortation to the younger generation to be " good citizens "—whatever that may mean. Such admonition is " inspiring," but is emphatically not specific ; and to this day, when we think of " education for citzenship " images of after-dinner speakers float before the inner eye and echoes of moral platitudes ring in the inner ear.

But in Plato's theory of education, this vagueness is escorted politely to the frontiers and dismissed into the outer darkness where it belongs. If you are educating for citzenship, everything depends upon the kind of community of which your citizens are to be members. If you are in favour of a *Militärstaat* like Crete or Sparta, your gymnastic exercises, your school studies, and your social and civic institutions will all be directed to that one end, namely the practice of successful war. This will give the whole of your education for citizenship a specific twist ; and however efficient it may be in realizing its specific purpose, its results will be, humanely speaking, distinctly one-sided.[4] So too if you are in favour of a business man's community, or a democracy, or a dictatorship, you will find that the exercises, studies, and institutions all acquire a specific bent, adapting them to the specific principle which makes the constitution what it is.[5] It follows that in educating for citizenship, you cannot do such a thing " in general " without incurring the charge of futility. You have, first of all, to decide what kind of a city constitutes your ideal, and then proceed to construct social and educational institutions such as are required by that ideal.

In deciding what kind of a city will be the best for human beings, Plato insists upon starting with a clean sheet : pre-supposing only the general Hellenic aim of culture, i.e., of converting chaos into cosmos and of directing instinct by reason ; and avoiding local traditions and feuds, in so far as these would give a historical bias to his constructions and force them into their own channels.[6] With this aim he constructs the ideal city of the *Republic* and the model city of the *Laws*, paying more attention in the *Laws* to the human conditions under which his ideal is realizable.[7] But it is substantially the same ideal.

The abstract principle of the best is what Plato calls " the good " or " the idea (form) of good," i.e., the principle of so co-ordinating elements as to eliminate the futility of a conflict in which they would cancel one another's positive values (thus tending towards " chaos "). The elements are so rearranged as to harmonize and co-operate in bringing out each others' positive values, thus vitalizing the situation and bringing into existence the greatest possible quantity and quality of value—which would otherwise have remained slumbering in the bosom of not-being. [8]

Creation of value in accordance with this abstract pattern is the especial function of life, the vitality which we find animating plants, animals, human beings, and the yet higher beings in whom the Greeks believed. Found throughout nature, this animating principle is, at its best, identified with the creative artist who has fashioned the world, making out of a lawless, structureless, meaningless chaos a cosmic system of significance, beauty, and law. [9] The divine principle functions by creating a world in its own image, a world in which maximal value-vitalization shall be possible. [10] Hence the earth, sun and moon, and the rest of the celestial bodies : to the materialist, mere dead matter, to be catalogued by the scientist but not to be regarded as of any especial significance ; to the idealist, a symbol of God's plan for the universe, a stimulus and a guide to co-operative human endeavour. [11]

In man, the animating principle follows the same pattern : co-operating with God in realizing the maximal value inherent in human situations ; avoiding the futility of conflict tending toward chaos and any kind of one-sidedness, and striving by harmony and goodwill to humanize and rationalize the social situation as far as possible. [12]

This means that the best kind of city will not be the *Militärstaat* " so ordered as to conquer all other states in war." In a family distracted by feuds, it is best not to suppress and destroy one side, but " to reconcile and give laws which all will observe and so to keep them friends." In civil war it is best not to destroy one of the parties, but to reconcile all, and " re-establish peace and friendship." So in general, if we are making laws " for the sake of the best," we realize that

War, whether external or civil, is not the best ; but peace and good-will. No true statesman looks first of all to external warfare ; nor will he ever be a sound legislator who orders peace for the sake of war, and not war for the sake of peace. [13]

In the same way, the best kind of city will not be a typical monarchy or oligarchy or democracy. These abstract type-forms where government is in the hands of " the one, the few, or the many " are not real constitutions with a principle of vitality in them. They are " merely aggregations of men dwelling in cities " and are " the subjects and servants of a part of their own state." They have no genuine unity in them, such as we find in a mixed constitution in which there is a real balance of powers, as in Sparta or Cnossus.[14]

The ideal city will thus be like the celestial system : a group of elements of which each is completely a member of the group, with their activities all interwoven into a single pattern of rational law, directed from within in such a way as to animate and vitalize the greatest possible quantity and quality of value.[15] This means that the directing intelligence (akin to the Absolute Mind which has created the regular motions of the starry heavens and the mathematically calculable elements of the physical universe) of the city must be spread through the whole body of the citizens, so that each willingly co-operates with the rest in realizing, in the service of the whole, the best that is in him. Each " does his own work," i.e., performs the function for which his nature and his place in the community best fit him. The few highly trained individuals who are qualified to govern and direct, throw their whole souls into governing and directing ; and the comparatively large numbers whose qualifications do not reach so far co-operate willingly, and throw their whole souls into followership : so that there is complete unanimity and harmony as to who shall govern and who shall be governed.[16] All are thus animated by one and the same principle : the maintenance of the spirit of idealism.[17]

This means that what makes a citizen of the ideal city is public-spiritedness : the exact antithesis of private spirit, the spirit which looks to private gain in the shape of tangible goods such as wealth, pleasures, and power.[18] And this means that no citizen can possibly be a tradesman, artisan, or labourer, and that no sort of craftsman or business man can possibly be a citizen.[19] Members of most of the arts and crafts groups, and of those who pursue vocationally and professionally, i.e., in order to make money and earn largish incomes, most of the other activities found in cities, are absolutely alien in spirit to civic idealism, and such persons cannot possibly be admitted to citizenship. In so far as the products of the arts and crafts, the sciences and the usual vocations, are necessary in order to provide food, shelter, clothing, and tools for the community—and this necessity is not denied[20]—persons practising such arts for gain are admitted to the protection of the city. But not to its membership. Their activities are rigidly supervised by the magistrates, and the practitioners are and remain aliens, with only a limited residence permit.[21]

That is to say, citizenship is rigidly confined to the classes of " gold " and " silver " known as " guardians and auxiliaries," supposed in the *Republic* to be not less than one thousand in number, and to the lot-holders in the *Laws*, supposed to be precisely five thousand and forty in number.[22] The non-civic classes, if we include the bankers, merchants, and trades-people of all sorts, the workers, both rural and urban, and also most of the teachers, nurses, and household servants, would far outnumber the citizens : a situation notoriously present in Sparta, where an extremely small class of " Spartiates " were ministered to by a large group of Perioeci and a still larger group of Helots, and doubtless also in all Hellenic cities where trade was carried on by " metics " (resident aliens) and defence by mercenaries.[23]

Plato's account of education for citizenship is thus very properly (from his own standpoint) confined to potential full citizens ; the other classes are omitted, not from carelessness or lack of interest (as is sometimes thought), but by deliberate exclusion ; and since potential citizens, both in the *Republic* and in the *Laws*, fall into two groups (1) a group of docile and enthusiastic law-abiding men and women who require and accept direction and leadership from the governing classes, and (2) a small group of men and women selected and especially trained to provide precisely the leadership required, Plato's especial theory of education falls into two parts (1) education for citizenship, as such, an education described as " education in music and gymnastic," and (2) education for leadership, usually described as " higher education " or " intellectual education," and discussed by Plato with deliberate insistence upon its difference from the earlier education.[25] Roughly speaking, the distinction corresponds to the distinction in the modern world between primary and secondary education on the one hand, and university education on the other ; understanding under " university education " not only undergraduate or college instruction, but also the higher training given in graduate schools.

Let us study, then, under the head of " education for citizenship " the education of members of the silver class of auxiliaries in the *Republic*, and of the full citizen class in the *Laws*. The education of character which fits a child gradually for membership in the group of citizens, while beginning formally at birth, in fact commences still earlier, the pre-natal care going back to conception and indeed to marriage on the part of the parents.[26] Without denying or minimizing the biological, social, and indeed philosophical satisfactions associated with married life,[27] the constructor of cities in ideal outline emphasizes the racial function :

The bride and groom should realize that they are to produce for the state the best and fairest specimens of children that they can. Let both give their fullest attention to this, particularly at the time when their children are not yet born. And let the women overseers of such matters supervise those who are begetting children for ten years after marriage ; entering into the homes of the young parents, and applying admonitions and threats, and, if need be, reporting them to the law-guardians, who shall take action. If there are no children after ten years, let the couple take counsel with their kindred and with the women overseers, and be divorced for their mutual benefit.[28]

Personal and indeed family inclination induce persons who are socially, economically, and physically of the same type, to associate with one another. But in marriage such associations tend gradually toward introducing and accentuating differences within the community, whereas from the standpoint of the community it is vital that, so far as possible, extremes should marry, in order that their children may all centre around the community norm. The prelude to the marriage law thus admonishes as follows :

Every man shall follow, not after the marriage which is most pleasing to himself, but after that which is most beneficial to the state. Wise men advise you neither to avoid a poor marriage nor especially to desire a rich one. Other things being equal, always honour inferiors and form connexions with them. For the equable and symmetrical tends infinitely more to virtue than the unmixed. The headstrong should mate with the orderly, and the tame with the more aggressive ; the slower with the quicker, and the quicker with the slower. The city ought to be well mingled like a cup, in which the fiery wine is chastened by a soberer God, and becomes an excellent and temperate drink.[29]

Parenthood, that is to say, is a civic and patriotic duty, rather than a personal satisfaction to the individuals concerned, and Plato surrounds the phenomenon of birth with moral and social sanctions, with the idea that the children of such unions will inherit not merely the physical, but the moral and social features of their parents. Children of the " golden " class will as a rule exhibit all the characteristics, spiritual as well as physical, of that class. The same will be true of the " silver " class of auxiliary guardians. That is to say, the children when born, will already be of select quality, capable of receiving and benefiting by the formal education designed to fit them for full citizenship.[30]

Plato has observed that the rate of growth is most rapid in the early stages, and that " rapid growth without proper and abundant exercise is the source of endless evils in the body." He deduces that the body should have most exercise when it receives most nourishment, and hence insists upon the importance of motion, both in antenatal and post-natal care :

All bodies are benefited by shakings and movements, when they are moved without weariness, whether the motion proceeds from themselves, or is caused by a swing, or at sea, or on horseback, or by other bodies carrying them. This movement gives them mastery over food and drink, and so imparts to them beauty, health, and strength.[31]

Hence the advice, not merely that expectant mothers shall take daily walks, but that nurses shall rock the babies, carry them in their arms, and take them for daily walks for a couple of years or so, " taking care that their young limbs are not distorted by leaning on them, and continuing to carry them (when necessary) until the infant has completed its third year."[32] The reason for all this motion (" infants should live, if possible, as if always rocking at sea ") is partly to aid the central self-motion within the brain to control the processes of digestion, and partly to aid it to control such internal motions as fear, so that the child becomes cheerful and courageous. That is to say, this gymnastic assists in developing, not merely physique, but character.[33]

Pleasure and pain are the first perceptions of children, and furnish the subrational basis upon which character is developed by suitable training :

By education I mean that training which is given by suitable habits to the first instincts of virtue in children—when pleasure and pain are rightly implanted in non-rational souls. The particular training in respect of pleasure and pain, which leads you to hate and love what you ought to hate and love, is called " education."

The discipline of the pleasure-pain sense takes place *via* dancing and music. Young creatures are always wanting to move and cry out : leaping, skipping, overflowing with sportiveness, and uttering expressive cries. But while other animals are chaotic in these movements and cries, human beings are gifted with the pleasurable sense of harmony and rhythm ; so that in choric dances rhythm and harmony train human motility. This is a form of education, and the well-educated are those who are able to sing and dance well.[34]

The idea behind this attitude is that the pleasure-pain sense should not be left to itself, but should be controlled in such a way that children learn to avoid extremes and seek for the mean state :

The true life should neither seek pleasures nor entirely avoid pains, but should embrace the middle state, which is gentle and benign and rightly ascribed to God. Human beings who wish to be divine should pursue after this mean habit ; and we should allow no one to rush headlong into pleasures—especially the young ; for in infancy more than at any other time the character is engrained by habit. All men ought to avoid the life of unmingled pleasures or pains, and pursue always a middle course.[35]

The method by which this discipline of the pleasure-pain sense is developed is primarily by the control of movement (a) in dances, (b) in field sports. Let us consider dances first.

Choric movements are imitations of manners occurring in various actions, fortunes, dispositions. Each particular is imitated, and those to whom the words, songs, and dances are suited feel pleasure in them and call them beautiful. Good dances have a good effect, and vicious dances a bad effect. Consequently, poets cannot be allowed to teach in the dance (in the way of rhythm, melody, or words) to the children of well-conditioned parents anything they may happen to like, without reference to virtue or vice.[35]

To take a modern example, Plato would consider it highly improper to train schoolchildren in suggestive cabaret dances, so that they could take part in public performances of the " Maxim's " entertainment in *The Merry Widow*. Nor would he approve of a dancing mistress giving a spirited rendition of the " Rumba " on the same occasion. The dances of which he approves are the kind of dances in which citizens " pre-eminent in virtue and education " delight ; and the moral is, that " education is the constraining and directing of youth toward that right reason, which the law affirms, and which the experience of the eldest and best has agreed to be truly right."[37]

The dances approved by the community authorities fall into two main groups, (1) the dances of peace or order, and (2) the war-dances. Peace dances fall into two sub-groups, (a) dances expressive of escape from some danger into prosperity, under the guidance of come community deity, and (b) dances expressive of the continued preservation and possibily increase of a prosperity already enjoyed. The virtue inculcated by such dances is the virtue of temperance or self-control associated with piety toward the community deities, and with friendship toward fellow-citizens. Such dances are combined with suitable types of music, and are consecrated to the community deities, in whose honour (and as the Hellenes believed, in whose company) they are performed at the appropriate sacrificial feasts.[38]

The war-dances are direct imitations of warlike motions, e.g., of striking and parrying blows, charging and side-stepping, shooting and shield-work, and the like. The movements are strenuous, and suggest nobility and manliness, rather than dignity and grace. The virtue which they inculcate is courage in the service of the community, associated with piety toward the gods who guide to success in war, and comradeship toward the fellow-citizens who stand shoulder to shoulder with them on the battle-field. These dances are similarly combined with suitable types of music, and are consecrated to the appropriate deities and performed at the appropriate community festivals.[39]

Other types of dance, accepted in some Hellenic communities, but having no peaceful and no warlike character " or any meaning whatever," are the Bacchic dances consecrated to the Nymphs, Pan, the Silenuses, and the Satyrs, in which drunken men are imitated ; and the rather wild and frenzied Corybantic dances used in purification ceremonies and in the mysteries. These are not approved for citizen-participation, although it is quite understood that external observation, on rare occasions, will have a certain educative value.[40]

Why is it that dancing, in such community festivals, has an especially educative effect upon the non-rational part of our nature? Plato's answer is contained in his theory of the nature and function of art, and is partly expressed to Hellenic ears by his reference to the companionship of god and man in the consecrated festival-dance :

The gods have appointed holy festivals and have given to men the Muses and Apollo, the Muses' leader, and Dionysus, to be companions in such revels : that with the help of the gods men may improve their education. The gods stir us into life, and we follow them, our dance-companions, as we join hands together in choric dancing. Education is first given through Apollo and the Muses.[41]

This sense of companionship also links together the younger generation, which goes through the established dance-patterns, and the older generation, which does not dance, but participates vicariously :

In these choral festivities, we are unable to keep still. Our young men break forth in dancing and singing and we, who are their elders, deem that we are fulfilling our part in life when we look on. Having lost our agility, we delight in their sports and merry-making, because we love to think of our former selves ; and we gladly institute contests for those who are able to awaken in us the memory of our youth.[42]

This companionship is indeed a mystical thing, to be understood by initiates, but not capable of being reduced to strictly rational elements. The artistic use of dance-rhythms takes us altogether out of the every-day habit of understanding, and initiates us into some of the deeper mysteries of life, appealing to our sense of worship, in which there takes place a kind of merger of personality, the gods and heroes reaching down a helping hand to us, and we reaching up to a level altogether beyond our every-day personalities, and becoming inspired and rapt :

The " madness " which is superior to sanity is of divine origin. He who participates in this gift, by means of holy prayers and rites and by inspired utterances, so that he is truly possessed, is purified and made whole and exempt from evil. Next comes the " madness " of those who are possessed by the Muses : which, fastening upon a delicate and virgin soul and inspiring " frenzy " awakens lyrical numbers, adorning with these the myriad actions of ancient heroes for the instruction of posterity. Many noble deeds spring from this inspired " madness," and the " madness " of great love is the greatest of heaven's blessings.[43] The soul which attains any vision of truth in company with a god is preserved from harm until the next period and if always attaining is always unharmed.[44]

That is to say, these festival dances are a kind of earthly copy of the higher life of the gods, and suggest to some few of us reminiscences of that transcendental world :

There are a few who, going to the images, behold in them the realities, although with difficulty. Time was when with the rest of the beatified they saw beauty radiating brightness—we philosophers following in the train of Zeus, others in company with other gods. We beheld the beatific vision and were initiated into a most blessed mystery, celebrated in our state of innocency before we had experience of evil : when we were admitted to the sight of apparitions innocent and simple and serene and blessed, shining in pure radiance, pure ourselves and not yet enshrined in that living tomb of the human body which we now carry about with us.[45]

This inspiration appeals to the supra-rational element in man, and is renewed with considerable frequency. In the model city of the *Laws* there are no fewer than 365 church services, so arranged as to provide one for each day of the church year ; and of this number twelve, or one for each month, are great festivals of the kind described—so that man can enter into choral communion with God at regular intervals, and so keep his vision unsullied by everyday cares.[46]

So much for dancing as an instrument of education. Dancing is sometimes treated in connection with music, sometimes as a

subordinate form of gymnastic.[47] We pass on to consider field
sports, which undoubtedly come under the head of gymnastic.
As we are told in the *Laws*,

> At three, four, five, and even six years, the childish nature will re-
> quire sports. These will furnish an opportunity of getting rid of self-
> will in him by punishing him without disgracing him. Children of
> this age have certain natural modes of amusement which they invent
> for themselves when they meet. All children from three to six ought
> to meet at the village temples, with nurses to see that they behave
> properly, under the control of twelve playground matrons (one for each
> temple) selected from the women who have authority over marriage.[48]

That is to say, presumably, the community children play in
local groups, building sand-castles, playing " tag " and similar
games, and possibly playing " ball," under the general control
of the matron, who holds office for a year. The educative purpose
of such games is to develop the character of the children, making
them more co-operative and less egoistic, so that they will be able
to live and work together as fellow-citizens. Incidentally, such
games make their bodies healthy and strong, useful as instruments
for participating in civic life.

This supervised group play continues until the children reach
the age of six. At this age, a certain break occurs. The children
cease to play together informally, in the presence of their nurses,
and with a directing matron somewhere in the background. The
sexes are separated and are conducted to separate " schools,"
being accompanied as far as the school door by household attendants, the girls by their nurses, and the boys by their " tutors,"
i.e., the regular household servants who are aged and useless for
any more exacting kind of work. The chief duty of the attendants
is to see that no one interferes with their charges on their way to
and from " school," and that their behaviour on the street is
modest and decorous. No matron is in charge, but any citizen
is at all times concerned with the proper behaviour of children and
their attendants, and will correct with words, and indeed blows,
any unseemliness :

> At daybreak it is time for the youth to go to their schoolmasters. Of
> all animals the boy is the most unmanageable, since has the fountain
> of reason in him not yet regulated. He is the most insidious, sharp-
> witted, and insubordinate of animals. When he gets away from
> mothers and nurses, he must be under the management of tutors, on
> account of his childishness and foolishness ; and he must be controlled
> by the teachers under whom he studies. But he is not a free citizen, and
> any freeman who comes in his way may punish him and his tutor and

instructor, if they are doing anything amiss ; and this punishment is under the authority of the director of education, who keeps a sharp lookout and takes especial care of the children, directing their natures and turning them to good according to the law.[49]

At the school door, the child is turned over to the teacher, who is a public official appointed under the authority of the director of education. There are separate schools for the two sexes, with men teachers for the boys, and women teachers for the girls. But the subject matter of " school " education is approximately the same for both sexes from the age of six to the age of ten : namely, field sports considered important from the standpoint of the community. That is to say, the child learns, in a playful and informal manner, to ride on horseback, learning, of course, on especially safe and well-tamed horses, and to shoot accurately with bow and arrows, using weapons suited to his size and strength, and also to handle the javelin and slingshot. The training continues until the age of ten, by which time he is expected also to be able to handle the light shield and other defensive armour, and also to make some use of heavy armour: in preparation for the military duties of full citizenship.[50] Plato is especially concerned in having the children brought up to be ambidextrous, with both sides of the body equally well developed, so that they can shoot, hurl, and handle offensive and defensive weapons with either hand. They are also trained in running, jumping, and dancing, under suitable men and women teachers, and are even initiated into tactics and military evolutions, under officer lecturers.[51]

The " schools " attended from the age of six to the age of ten are obviously very different from modern schools. The curriculum is wholly a matter of " gymnastics " and field sports, and the method is by organized and directed " play." The exercises are of the nature which we nowadays consider *extra*curricular and teach, so far as we do teach them, in sports *clubs*. The instructor is precisely what we regard as a " club professional " who assists the children of well-conditioned parents to acquire, in a spirit of play, some degree of mastery over certain skilled movements, with the immediate aim of enjoyment and health, and with the intermediate aim of excelling in competitive field meets or " sports days," and perhaps in certain cases with the ultimate aim of making themselves efficient for some socially useful purpose. The association of the pupils with one another has, in our eyes, a certain social value, and the association during the adolescent and early adult period has a certain biologically selective function.

These characteristics of our modern sports clubs are all verifiable in the Platonic " schools," in spite of the fact that attendance in the sports-*schools* is compulsory for the children of citizens. Consider, first, the spirit of play. On this point Plato is very definite :

> A freeman ought not to be a slave in the acquisition of knowledge, knowledge so acquired obtains no hold on the mind. Let early education be a sort of amusement ; you will then be able to find out the natural bent. The teacher should endeavour to direct the children's inclinations and pleasures, by the help of amusements, to their final aim in life. The most important part of education is right training in the nursery, especially that tending to the acquisition of self-control.[52]

This does not mean, as is sometimes thought, that Plato bases his education upon the psychology of childhood, letting children develop with assisted spontaneity, following " the natural bent," in a kind of glorified sports kintergarten. Children, as Plato understands them, can never be left safely to themselves. They are " childish and foolish." That is to say, their action-tendencies, of themselves, are chaotic and without the power of rational self-direction. Childhood, if left to itself, is like a plant left to straggle and grow wild. For the best results, scientific cultivation is essential, until eventually reason develops and self-direction becomes possible.[53]

Just as primaeval chaos required a Divine Artist with an aesthetic value-judgment and mathematical techniques to turn it into an organized cosmos,[54] just as barbarism requires rational control if the social world is ever to be made safe for Hellenism, so the structureless and lawless tendencies of childhood require to be directed by mother, nurse, tutor, teacher, father, freeman,and civic institutions, if the child is ever to develop into the free self-determining citizen (Hellenic pattern).[55] It is the community standpoint, not the " natural bent " of childhood, which is the dominating factor. Education takes the play-tendencies of childhood, and directs and constrains them, until the growing child takes on the mould of the rational, co-operative, self-determining citizen. The gymnastic games at present under consideration develop the civic virtues of disciplined courage, self-control, friendly co-operation, and loyalty to the group and its ideals.[56]

Neither does Plato's insistence upon " play " mean that he is especially interested in developing the youthful mind to its full extent for its own sake. He does say that knowledge acquired by compulsion obtains no hold on the mind, and accordingly prescribes compulsory play as the method of instruction. But the emphasis is quite as much upon the " compulsion " which directs play-tendencies aright, as upon the playfulness of the child which responds to such treatment as a kitten responds to a rope drawn in front of it, or a fish to a skilfully wiggled artificial bait.[57] Organized games are pursued, not for their own sake, but because they develop physique and moral and mental habits which will one day be useful " with a view to war and the management of home and city," i.e., they are dominated by the ideal of education, not for education's sake, but for citizenship.[58]

There are two further points to be noted in connection with Plato's account of " play " in education. It is not confined to the playground children, or children in their sports schools, but continues in the later schools, and indeed throughout life. It is consistent with the freedom of the self-determining citizen that he should be a little careless, playful, amateurish, and wilfully independent of considerations of time and place. Meticulous accuracy in any respect, enforced hurry and absence of gentlemanly leisure, are inconsistent with the freedom and dignity of the citizen. Let slaves and hired professionals attend to details ! The citizen supervises, deliberates, and gives general directions. Let his subordinates execute his orders ! In educating for citizenship then, Plato allows full scope to this " gentlemanly interest " *motif*.[59]

In the second place, solemn talk about " rational self-determination " when applied to human beings, even when these are idealized as the full citizens of some model city, seems to Plato a little overdone. The Hellenic equivalents of Tom, Dick, and Harry, even when in convention assembled, tend to be all-too-human. Wisdom and rational self-determination are " attributes of the *gods*—and of very few men." The gods are, of course, idealized patterns of wisdom, entirely transcending the capacities of poor humanity. This means that, as compared with the gods, it is impossible to take Tom, Dick and Harry altogether seriously. In such a comparison they appear as puppets, playthings in the hands of the gods, little Pinochios drawn this way and that by the strings of irrational desire, and pushed in this direction and that like pieces in a game played by others. All we can do is, play the game of life as best we can, holding fast to " the golden cord of reason," and co-operating with our Divine Leader by occupying the place for which we seem to have been made. Such animated puppets easily take themselves too seriously in the scheme of things. "A sad necessity is laid upon them." But to the divine intelligence their antics, while viewed in a kindly and benevolent spirit, are never wholly tragic, never devoid of a touch of comedy. In playing the game which will make us good (human) citizens, there is thus always room for a laugh and the spirit of play. Childish ourselves, we never altogether put away childish things.[60]

In the model city of the *Laws*, the work of the sports schools is supplemented by regular sports meets, at which the whole community engages in competitive sports in the field, at least once a month :

> Every city should take the field at least for one day in every month, summer and winter, going out *en masse*, including the wives and child-dren. There should be games, tournaments, or sham battles, and prizes and encomia, preparing the whole city for war, making dancing and all gymastic tend to this end.[61]
>
> For boys we fix the length of the contest at half of the entire course, whether they contend as archers or as heavy-armed. As to girls, let those who are not grown up compete in the stadium and the double course, and the horse-course and the long course, running on the race-ground itself. Those who are thirteen and upwards shall be compelled to run up to eighteen, and may compete if not more than twenty. In the contests for single horse, mounted archers, and spearmen, women are not forced to compete by law ; but if from previous training they are strong enough and wish to compete, let them do so, girls as well as boys, and no blame to them[62].

This means that, just as the dancing is institutional preparation for the twelve great religious festivals, so the training in field-sports, from the sixth to the tenth year and possibly later, is institutional preparation for the twelve great military field days : so that (taking the two together) " gymnastics " constitutes state training for participation in these community festivals, and in the further great annual festivals in honour of those of the community's leaders who have departed this life.[63] It is also, of course, direct preparation for the military side of life, including not merely sham battles of many sorts, but actual warfare, when if, and as that occurs.[64] It keeps the citizens, both potential and actual, physically fit, and develops a number of civic virtues, of which courage, self-control, friendly co-operation, and disciplined obedience to community leaders, both human and divine, are the most conspicuous.[65]

We now pass to consider " music " and its place in the education which turns potential into actual citizens. This includes the spoken, as well as the sung, word, and also, in choric dancing, the danced word. That is to say, it is understood as including literature and the arts which are under the patronage of the Muses and their leader, Apollo. This is used as an instrument of character-education in two ways, the first informal, the second also informal, but institutional.

The first use of " music " in character-education commences at a very early period :

We begin education with music, including literature ; and we begin by telling children stories which, though not wholly destitute of truth, are in the main fictitious. These stories are told when they are not yet of an age to learn gymnastics. We thus teach music before gymnastics. The beginning, especially in the case of a young and tender thing, is the time at which the character is being formed, and the desired impression is more readily taken.

We shall therefore establish a censorship over writers of such stories and shall desire mothers and nurses to tell only the authorized fictions : moulding the mind with such tales even more fondly than they mould the body with their hands.[66]

This passage is thoroughly characteristic. It indicates (1) Plato's belief that education, to appeal to children, must be playful and amusing and must give direct pleasure. There is no "stern daughter of the voice of God " insisting that children should be seen but not heard and that Hellas expects that every boy each day will do his duty. On the contrary, just as Plato's own *Dialogues* are *literary* masterpieces, enjoyed as such, independently of their philosophic content and doing good as it were by stealth : so with these authorized children's readers. They contain more of the " Casabianca " and less of the " Do your best, Your very best, And do it every day " side of our modern writers for children : more of the interesting example, and less of the dry precept.[67]

The passage also foreshadows (2) Plato's preference of sincerity to veracity. There is no harm in Father Christmas stories, or Mother Goose tales, or Peter Pan. So long as " the tales which the young hear are models of virtuous thought," Plato is more than satisfied with them. Entertaining and edifying allegories are far better suited to the child-mind of the potential citizen than objective information about the facts of life and the truths of science.[68]

The passage also (3) suggests the importance, to Plato's way of thinking, of a somewhat rigid community control over the education of potential citizens. Their immature minds and characters are to be directly conditioned, from the very first, to take on the dye of the community laws, so that this shall be indelible. The words and melodies which they hear and repeat, the dance-movements which they see and learn, the whole of the social, moral, and intellectual environment with which they are surrounded, are all consistent with the system of values which the community is resolved to inculcate :

Let our artists be those gifted to discern the genuine nature of the beautiful and graceful ; then will our youth dwell in a land of health, amid fair sights and sounds, and receive the good in everything ; and beauty, the effluence of fair works, shall flow into eye and ear, like a salubrious breeze from a purer region, and insensibly draw the soul from earliest years into likeness and sympathy with the beauty of reason. Rhythm and harmony fasten upon the inward places of the soul, imparting grace, and he who has received this inner education will praise and rejoice over and receive into his soul the good and become noble and good, now in the days of his youth, before he is able to know the reason why ; and when reason comes he will salute the friend with whom his education has made him long familiar.[69]

" Music " thus familiarizes the children with stories about the gods, heroes, and men. Under the rigid community censorship, it presents a somewhat simplified picture of life, such as a child can understand, but is careful always to represent the gods as godlike, the heroes as heroic, and the men as human. The many thrilling passsages in great literature which depict the denizens of Olympus as behaving like the characters in a comic strip, and as anything but patterns of the accepted virtues, are ruthlessly expurgated ; and so are many stories about the great national heroes. As to actual men and women, they are depicted, for the most part, as behaving like good citizens, courageous, self-controlled, patriotic, religious-minded, co-operative, and disciplined[70]—although for contrast-effect a little comic depiction of the less beautiful side of life is permitted to creep in here and there. But poems depicting low life are not learnt by heart and recited with appropriate action by the future citizens. Children have to know about such things, but the knowledge is to come by way of observation, as external as possible.[71]

Let us consider this a little further. In the first place, everything presented to children is simplified. The stories told are purged of irrelevancies. Anything confusingly complex, especially anything suggestive of chaos, is eliminated. Only the broad general outlines are left. This means that, as in the case of Hellenic sculpture, the content and manner of the stories are idealized. Each man plays one part, and one part only. The shoemaker is a shoe-maker, and not a pilot as well. The farmer is a farmer, and not a member of a judge's court as well. Gods do not appear disguised as men and women ; but every character appears, as Ben Jonson would say, in his " humour."[72]

The musical accompaniments and dance-rhythms often ass-ciated with the poetic stories narrated to and acted by the children are similarly simplified. In fact, they are parallel in all respects : one note of the melody, one movement of the foot or body, rein-forces each syllable of the text. For all Plato's insistence upon the power of rhythm and harmony, the strictly musical side of this early training seems to modern readers excessively elementary. A modern composer constructs a tone-pattern and subordinates the words of the text to his musical aims : lengthening this syllable, shortening that, repeating here, omitting words altogether for a few bars, and so on. The Platonic composer for children allows himself no such liberties. The sense is the main thing ; the sound is strictly subordinate. The accents of the music follow the length and shortness of the syllables of the actual words, and the spirit of the music follows the spirit of the theme. Some idea of Hellenic music can be obtained from comparing it with certain Church chants (e.g., the " Gregorian " chants for certain psalms), which consist of a melody without accompaniment. All we have to do is to imagine the notes of the melodic chant strictly sub-ordinated to the syllables of the text (instead of *vice versa*), and we have an example of what is intended. An ancient example—with a good swing to it—is furnished by the marching-song attributed to Tyrtaeus, beginning :

Aget' Ō Spartās euāndrō

Korōi paterōn poliātān !

This is in anapaestic rhythm, and the marching foot comes down with a stamp on the accented syllables, as the Spartan youth swings along to battle.[73]

The " harmonies " of which Plato writes are what we should call scales, something like our major and minor diatonic scales. In Plato's time these had already become too complex for any but the experts, and to this day it is a little uncertain how they are to be understood in detail.[74] They were highly conven-tionalized, some being used for convivial occasions, others for war, some for praises offered to the gods, others for lamentations, some for men, others for women, etc. Plato, simplifying for educative purposes, retains only the Dorian and Phrygian scales, the one associated (conventionally) with the marching of young men to battle in courageous mood, the other with the ceremonial dances called *Emmeleiai*, expressive of self-control and gratitude to the gods for past and present benefits.[75]

What is meant by this " conventionalization " of certain scale-intervals as expressive of certain types of character, is easily intelligible.   It is like the way in which musical amateurs in modern times often assume that " C Major " is the proper scale in which to compose cheerful music, while funeral marches should always be in a " Minor " key ; whereas the professional is only too well aware that *any* mood can be expressed in *any* scale, and that the most celebrated of all funeral marches (Handel's March in *Saul*) is itself composed in " C Major." As Plato understands it, such musical " conventions " are established, on the advice of experts, by the authority of the legislature, *more Egyptiaco*.   He does not question, but indeed advocates a similar practice, being convinced that behind the conventions is the authority of nature itself.[76] That is to say, expert inspiration succeeds in discovering the ideal patterns which exist in nature, and legislative authority succeeds in establishing, for the guidance and education of citizens, moulds or patterns which have objective validity.

The censorship which, in association with the advice of experts, lays down certain patterns to which composers of songs and dances are to conform on pain of not being employed in the ideal or model city, is no mere rubber stamp, authority confirming anything which the expert practitioners of the arts think should be a matter of community regulation.   On the contrary, the censors, while not themselves creative artists, are persons of the highest degree of philosophical training, and have attained to genuine insight into the nature and function of the ideal realm.   They take the lead, informing the experts in general as to what they wish done, and permitting only the slightest of deviations in detail from the ideal principles which they lay down.   The community is to be a replica, in human form, of the ideal realm, and their insight represents the highest human court of appeal. The children are to be educated, in this early stage, so as to take on, in this non-rational way, as nearly as possible the ideal forms themselves.   Each potential citizen is to be becoming, by the approved artistic influences, day by day more nearly a pattern of courage, temperance, justice, piety, and co-operative friendliness.[77]

This early informal music in the home and at social gatherings is supplemented by attendance at the various church services and festivals, and continues throughout the life of the citizen. But at the age of ten, the potential citizen enters upon a course of school training in this field. From ten to thirteen, he learns his letters :

> The young ought to be occupied with their letters until they are able to read and write ; but the acquisition of perfect beauty or quickness in writing, if nature has not stimulated them to acquire these accomplishments in three years, they should let alone. As to the learning of compositions which are not set to the lyre, whether in prose or verse, the director of education shall advise teachers to learn and approve compositions like Plato's *Laws*(i.e., presumably, the *Dialogues*), and then commit to them the instruction of youth (i.e., the teachers will use texts which are consistent with Plato's regulations).[78]

In learning to read, the pupil is first taught by his teacher to identify and name the letters of the alphabet as written and spoken in short and easy syllables. He soons learns to distinguish them accurately enough, using both eye and ear in the process. It takes him a good deal longer to identify them accurately in longer and more difficult syllables ; and the teacher assists him by drawing attention to the simpler cases of their occurrence, which are already known to the child. By pointing back to these, and then taking up the long and difficult syllable again, he at last enables the child to overcome the difficulty and achieve the desired recognition :

> The best way is to refer the children first to cases where they judge correctly and then compare these with the cases in which they do not yet know the letters : i.e., to show them that the letters are the same and have the same character in both combinations—placing all cases in which they are right side by side with all cases in which they make mistakes. In this way they have examples and learn that each letter in every combination is always the same (and never different) and is called by the same name.[79]

Having thus succeeded in recognizing the letters of the alphabet as individual letters, identical with themselves whatever the combination in which they are found, the pupil is next taught to combine the letters in easy syllables. " This *S* (he is told) and this *O*, when put together thus, *S-O*, are pronounced *SO*, the first syllable of the name *SOCRATES*." In this way, first by being told and then being taught to identify what he has been told, by discriminating this or that syllable in a great variety of combinations (appealing always to both eye and ear), the pupil learns to recognize, first the simpler, and then the more complex syllables which are of frequent occurrence. From these he proceeds to simple words, nouns, verbs, etc., until he can recognize and read what is placed before him.[80]

Writing is taught somewhat similarly :

In learning to write, the writing-master first draws lines with a style for the use of the young beginner. He then gives the pupil the tablet, and makes him follow the impress of the lines (before he permits him to reproduce the copy freehand).[81]

Having thus learnt to read and write, the pupil copies out and commits to memory the standardized poems and prose compositions approved by the community for the purpose. The state-approved teacher[82]

puts into his hand, as he sits on the school bench, the works of great poets, containing admonitions, tales, praises, and encomia of the famous men of old. These he learns by heart, in order that he may imitate or emulate and desire to become like them.[83]

This seems to be about all that the child learns directly from the reading and writing teacher. The value of such instruction for good citizenship is obvious. But Plato tells us a good deal more about letters ; and this is presumably studied by the teachers themselves. As it has indirectly a good deal to do with the realization of the ideal realm, reproducing on earth the outlines of the ideal city which exists " in heaven," we shall follow up his further hints in this place.

The student whose mind is at all alert soon observes a number of interesting things about letters and syllables. In the first place, letters, while all equally letters, have certain groupings into which they naturally fall. They can be classified as (1) vowels, (2) semivowels, and (3) mutes (the remaining letters which are neither vowels nor semivowels), and indeed lend themselves to yet more minute sub-classifications.[84] And further : certain of these letters can be combined with others to form syllables and words, while others can not. A scientist of the Pythagorean type might be satisfied with investigating these facts and cataloguing the classified phenomena. He might even go further and observe a certain parallelism between the sounds which make up letters and the sounds which make up tones in music, and even a slightly remoter parallelism between the letter-sounds (and music sounds) and the colours which are the elements in painting, and admit of certain types of combination analogous to syllables.[85] It is to be presumed that professional students of letters are aware of these phenomena and of their apparent interrelation.

But it is possible to go further. The philosopher is not content with classifying phenomena. He wants to know why. Why do letters take the forms they do ? Why, out of the theoretically infinite possibilities of sound issuing through the lips, do such letters as R, S, L, and the various vowels, stand out and take form, even as Red, Green, and Blue stand out in the field of colour, or the notes of the standardized scale in music ? And why are some combinations possible and others not ? The philosopher's mind is not at rest until he has found some answer to these questions.

The answer attributed to Socrates in the *Cratylus* is that letters and their classes are copies or reproductive representations of elementary forces and their classes in *rerum natura*. A name is a verbal picture, an image in letters and syllables, of a reality existing in nature. In fact, just as Plato supposes that musical scales reproduce ideal intervals in accordance with which the physical universe has been constructed, and that musical experts can discover the " natural " scales, and that these can then be established by the legislature for ever, so Socrates suggests that language is a natural reproduction of the nature of objective forces, behind which (doubtless) ideal meaning is to be divined. He thus indicates an ideal language which reproduces in its nouns, verbs, syllables, and letters, the features of the physical cosmos (and so, indirectly, of the ideal realm of which the physical cosmos is a copy). He also indicates the various " corruptions " which have been operating to alter this ideal language, fixed by the original great legislator, into the somewhat debased Hellenic language used in his own time. [86]

The point of this is that the expert teacher of language, if philosophically minded, will realise that the use of language is to suggest, by art, the ideal forms of things, and so to prepare the mind of the young to accept these ideal forms, primarily as embodied in literature. In this way, he is preparing his pupils for citizenship in a community which is intended to be a human replica of the ideal realm itself. The pupil absorbs unconsciously what the teacher, if philosophically minded, communicates with conscious purpose.

At the age of thirteen, every citizen in the model city studies instrumental music for three years, " neither more nor less, and whether his father or he himself like or dislike the study." He learns, that is to say, to accompany his own voice on the lyre, playing the standard melodic patterns adopted by the community, note for note in unison with the vocalized syllables of the approved songs.

The teacher and the learner use the sounds of the lyre because its notes are pure (as contrasted with the notes of the flute). The performer who teaches and the pupil who learns render note for note in unison. Complexity and variation of notes, when the strings give one sound, and the poet or composer gives another in the melody—also when concords and harmonies are made in which lesser and greater intervals, slow and quick, high and low notes, are combined ; also when the composer makes complex variations of rhythms adapted to the notes of the lyre—all that sort of thing is not suited to pupils who are to acquire a speedy and useful knowledge of music in three years. For opposed principles are confusing and create difficulty in learning, and our young people should learn quickly, and their mere necessary acquirements are not few or trifling. As to the words of the songs which the chorus-masters are to teach, their character has been described above (*Laws* 799, 811), as those consecrated for the different festivals.[87]

The study of music is precisely analogous to the study of letters, described above. There is a certain analogy between the sounds which are standardized as letters of the alphabet, and sounds which are standardized as the tones of a recognized musical scale. The pupil is taught to identify the different tones, i.e., to acquire an absolute pitch, and to train himself to recognize and love the sequences characteristic of the " classical " music-patterns. Around these classical patterns his taste in tone, rhythm, and melodic sequence is methodically built up, so that he can detect and despise the meretricious innovations which destroy art by reintroducing chaos. His school studies in musical execution are reinforced, not only by singing the folk-music established for use in the home and in private circles, but by participating in the regular church services and (if more than usually musical) undergoing voluntary training for participation in these services and in the regular music festivals, which take place at least once a month and are competitive, with adjudications, prizes, and encomia.[88]

In all this music, the potential citizen follows only the established patterns approved for community use. These are simplified, i.e., idealized as far as possible. A committee of experts operating under the direction of a legislative committee of highly educated authorities, tries to discover the " natural " scales, i.e., the sequences and intervals which reproduce the intervals of the great scale in accordance with which the intervals of the planets in the cosmos have been arranged by the Creative Artist who framed that cosmos. The idea is that the standardized earthly music will then be a reproduction, following the guidance of inspiration, of this large-scale cosmic music, and will thus prepare the young to be citizens, not merely of an earthly community, but of a community which is based upon the cosmic and more-than-cosmic patterns of the ideal realm itself.[89]

We are now in a position to compare the education for citizenship in its three main forms : by dancing, by gymnastic, and by music and art generally. In all three, the educator starts with the unorganized pleasure-pain sense of children, and their unregulated tendency to seek expression in rhythmic movement.[90] In all three this is trained and developed partly by associations in the home and nursery, partly by direct school associations and imitations of patterned activities. In all three they pass from home and school, without a serious break, to the life around them, the life of the community itself, participating in a daily life in which dancing, military exercises, and singing are very much in evidence, and particularly so in the twelve monthly festivals, and in the extra annual festivals for which provision is made.[91] As we read in the *Laws*,

> In our city the youths and maidens are well nurtured, and have nothing to do, and are not undergoing excessive and servile toils. Their only cares during their whole life are sacrifices and festivals and dances. The right way of living is to live in sports always ; sacrificing, singing, and dancing, in honour of the established gods : propitiating the deities and living according to the appointment of nature—being for the most part puppets, but having some little share of reality.[92]

Thus we see how education in music and gymnastic is a preparation for good citizenship, It starts in the home, receives a slightly technical direction in the schools, and is continued in the life of the community, which consists precisely in community singing, community dancing, and community gymnastics and military exercises. In so living, the citizens keep their community spirit fresh and strong, and their sense of followership unimpaired. Like the citizens of Sparta, they are released from the cares of food, trade, and the provision of an income for their families, and devote themselves, *sans arrière pensée*, to the manifold joys and duties of citizenship, " being for the most part puppets " :

> Our pupils, setting aside every other business, are to dedicate themselves wholly to the maintenance of freedom in the state, making this

their craft, and engaging in no work which does not bear upon this end. They are not to practise anything else, or to imitate any but the characters suitable to their profession—the courageous, the temperate, the holy, the free, and the like. [93]

In this way, by taking up into their lives " the courageous, the temperate, and the like," young citizens participate directly in the transcendental " ideas " of courage, temperance, etc., and so " have some little share of reality," i.e., become self-directing individual and social expressions of the ideal realm, " the city which exists in idea only." [94] Beyond that, they are not expected to go. When

they know the ideal forms of temperance, courage, liberality, magnificence, and their kindred, as well as the contrary forms, in all their combinations, and can recognize them and their images wherever found ; and the beautiful soul harmonizes with the beautiful form, and the two are cast in one mould, so that music ends in the love of beauty,

their education for citizenship is complete. [95]

One further point remains to be discussed. How far does Plato provide for the possibility of progress ? As far as the citizens who are not being educated for leadership are concerned, the answer is, clearly, that they are to follow their leaders. Of themselves, they initiate nothing. Their supreme virtue is to obey their leaders, their gods, and the laws of the community. They have no severe intellectual problems to face. All that sort of thing is settled for them by the best brains of the group. Theirs not to reason why. The young citizen never dreams of questioning the wisdom enshrined in the constitution. He does what his elders and betters tell him, and they tell always the same story, so that he is completely conditioned to docility. The games of childhood, the dances and music-patterns of his youth and manhood, vary only in detail. The ideal forms, once discovered, are maintained without change in principle. Any change would be, in his eyes, a step away from the ideal ; and innovation, when presented before him, is always given a ludicrous and unworthy twist, so that he will never seek it or regard it with any sentiment but contempt. [96]

If innovations are made in sports, and the young never speak of having established notions of good and bad taste, no greater evil can happen in a state. Children who make innovations in their games, when they grow up to be men will be different from the last generation of children and will desire a different sort of life, with other institutions and laws. And this is evil.

We must try in every possible way to prevent our youth from even desiring to imitate new modes either in dance or song. Music and gymnastic must be preserved in their original form, and no innovations made. [97]

The only way in which change or innovation of any sort will be permitted, is if such change is prescribed by the leaders. We therefore answer this question provisionally by saying that, as far as citizenship, as such, is concerned, considered apart from education for leadership, no *direct* provision is made for progress. On the contrary, from the standpoint of the average citizen, change in games, gymnastic, music, or the laws is an idea which never even occurs to him, except in so far as it is directed by the authorities. How far the possibility of progress in community usuages is at all provided for, is therefore to be discussed further, when we are considering education for leadership. [98]

[1]Cf. *Prtg.* 319, 322 f., *Rep.* 332d–333d ; *Laws* 799 f., 802, 811, 817, 858e f.   [2]*Sophs* 230a, *Laws* 729b. The Athenian Stranger in the *Laws* is not above this, cf. *Law.* 903b f.   [3]*Prtg.* 324d ff., highly condensed.   [4]*Laws* 625d f., 630b ff.   [5]For the business man's community, cf. *Rep.* 550c–557a ; for democracy, *Rep.* 557a–565c ; for dictatorship, *Rep.* 564a ff. On the general question, cf. *Rep.* 338d f.   [6]*Rep.* 501a f., 540d. *Laws* 737ab.   [7]*Rep.* 472b f., *Laws* 739, 746.   [8]Cf. *Phaedo* 97c, 99a, d, *Rep.* 507 ff. [9]*Tim.* 28 ff., 48e f., 53b.   [10]*Tim.* 29e f., cf. *Rep.* 379b f.   [11]*Tim.* 40a f., 47b, cf. 37–39, *Laws* 821 f., 886 ff., 903b f.   [12]*Euthyd.* 292c, *Gorg.* 503a, 513e f., *Rep.* 421bc, 428cd, 505a, 508 ff., 517b, 526d, 532a, 540, *Phaedr.* 237d.   [13]*Laws* 626b, 627c f., 628d, condensed. Cf. *Laws* 803d f., 829a.   [14]*Laws* 712b f., cf. 693d, 756e. Cf. also *Rep.* 422d f., 449a, 544 ff., *Polit.* 292 f., *Phil.* 61 ff.   [15]*Rep.* 463e f., *Laws* 964–968a.   [16]*Rep.* 431–435a, cf. 428–430, 474bc.   [17]*Rep.* 394d–395c, 414d ff.   [18]For a full discussion of the evidence, cf. R.C. Lodge : *Plato's Theory of Ethics*, 1928, ch. IX.   [19]*Soph.* 219, 223d, *Laws* 842d, 846c, 847a, 919, cf. 705a.   [20]*Rep.* 369c ff.   [21]*Laws* 850, 919c f. [22]*Rep.* 423a. *Laws* 737d f., 771, 877d.   [23]*Rep.* 428d f., 431c, 588e f., cf. 578c f.   [24]*Rep.* 412–415c, 540ab, *Laws* 963 ff.   [25]*Rep.* 518d, f., 520d ff., *Laws* 967d f.   [26]*Laws* 789, 792e. [27]*Rep.* 402ef., 458cd, *Phaedr.* 248d ff. *Laws* 776, 930a. *Symp.* 206 ff.   [28]*Laws* 783d– 784c, condensed. Cf. *Rep.* 459 ff., where the point of view is specifically eugenic. [29]*Laws* 773, condensed. Cf. *Polit.* 310. In the *Republic*, mating is made to look like pure chance. A system of lots is introduced, but these (as in a modern sports club " draw " for tennis or Badminton tournaments) are secretly arranged by the central committee of experts to produce the best possible results for the group as a whole. Cf. *Rep.* 459 f.   [30]*Rep.* 463c f., cf. 461a, 415ab, cf. 416e f.   [31]*Laws* 788d f., condensed. [32]*Laws* 789c f.   [33]*Laws* 790c f., *Tim.* 88b f.   [34]*Laws* 653 f., highly condensed. Habit is not the mechanical product of external " conditioning," but originates in the " self-motion " within the soul. [35]*Laws* 792c f., condensed. Cf. *Rep.* 619a, where this pursuit of the mean is said to be the " way of happiness."   [36]*Laws* 655d f., condensed.   [37]*Laws* 658e f. Frivolous and indeed vicious exhibitions are sometimes attended, for their educative effect. They enable the young to appreciate by contrast the value of their own more serious institutions. But such attendance is a matter of external observation. The performers are non-civic professionals upon whom they look down, never " children of well-conditioned parents." (*Laws* 816c f., cf. *Rep.* 395b f., 409).   [38]*Laws* 814d ff., cf. Rep. 399a f. Cf. also *Laws* 653c f.   [39]*Laws* 815a, 816b f., cf. *Rep.* 399a f.   [40]*Laws* 815c, 816c f., cf. note 37 *supra*. Cf. also *Laws* 790d, for the possibly remedial effect of such dances. Cf. also *Rep.* 378a. *Phaedr.* 244e.   [41]*Laws* 653c f., condensed.   [42]*Laws* 657d. [43]*Phaedr.* 244d f., condensed.   [44]*Phaedr.* 248c, cf. 249cd. For the " merger of personality " cf. *Phaedr.* 252c f.   [45]*Phaedr.* 250bc, condensed. The whole context is very much to the point.   [46]*Laws* 828a f. Cf. also *Rep.* 498c, 520d. The non-rational vision is a kind of dream, of which the philosopher-guardian's vision of truth is the reality, *Rep.* 520bc, *Symp.* 212a.   [47]*Laws* 795de.   [48]*Laws* 793d f., condensed. Although, in

the *Republic*, children are removed from their mothers at birth, and brought up in state *crèches* by state experts (like the Dionne quintuplets), while in the *Laws* the parents are left in charge : less difference appears in detail than might be expected ; for the state expert, rather than the individual parent, is actually charged with the work of education for the community. [49]Condensed from *Laws* 808d f., Cf. also *Laws* 794c f., and 765d f. Cf. also *Prtg.* 325d f., *Lysis* 207d ff., *Rep.* 590e f. [50]*Laws* 794d. 813d f. The girls too " if they do not object " receive the same training in the *Mädchenschulen*. [51]*Rep.* 466d f., *Laws* 813d f. [52]Condensed from *Rep.* 536e, *Laws* 643c ; cf. also *Rep.* 425a, *Laws* 793d f. [53]*Rep.* 441ab, 590e f., *Laws* 765e f., 808d, cf. *Tim.* 77a f. [54]*Tim.* 53a f., 69b f., cf. 28–30c. [55]*Prtg.* 325c f., *Rep.* 376d ff., *Laws* 808c f., 963e, cf. also 942a. [56]*Rep.* 424e f., *Laws* 643b f., 797b f. [57]*Rep.* 537a, *Laws* 804d, cf. 811c f. [58]*Laws* 809b f., cf. 797a f. [59]*Gorg.* 484d f., *Theaet.* 172c f., *Laws* 803d f., 806d f., 810b f., 812de, 816d f. (As the reference from the *Gorgias* (Callicles speaking) shows, this is Hellenic, not exclusively Platonic.) [60]*Rep.* 514 f., esp. 515a, *Laws* 644d f., 803b f., 903b f., cf. 658b f. Commentators sometimes suppose the treatment of men as " puppets of the gods " in the *Laws* to have been inperfectly worked out, and to represent the cynicism of a disillusioned old age. But the touch of comedy is never absent from Plato's pictures of Protagoras, Gorgias, and other great men. It is a part of Socrates' character (cf. *Phaedo* 62b), and no Dialogue is without a suggestion of it. Even the pursuit of natural science, as by the so-called Pythagoreans (*Rep.* VI–VII), is regarded by the philosopher as merely an occupation for his less serious hours, an " amusement for his leisure " (*Tim.* 59c, cf. 29cd). The reason for this is because such science rests upon ungrounded hypotheses (*Rep.* 510c f.) and is thus part of the audacious and slightly naive trial-and-error activity so characteristic of biosocial humanity. Like all " pragmatic " activity, it falls short of the transcendental insight sought by the philosopher (*Rep.* 533b f., 534c). [61]Condensed from *Laws* 829b–830d. [62]Condensed from *Laws* 833c–834d. The married women and the *older* men look on and so participate vicariously. [63]*Laws* 947. The biosocial value of dances for later adolescents and those interested in marriage, is fully understood. Cf. *Rep.* 458c f., 459e f., *Laws* 835d ff., cf. 771d f. [64]*Laws* 813d f., 830c f., 832d ff., 942 f. The camping in which boys and girls receive training is presumably like the Boy Scout and Girl Guide work of our own times. This is indicated by the description of the life and self-reliant behaviour of the young men who have received this training, when they enter upon their two years' military service in the country. Cf. *Laws* 760b ff., 813d. Cf. also *Rep.* 416c f. [65]*Prtg.* 326c, *Rep.* 410b f., 441e, *Laws* 743d, 839e. [66]*Rep.* 376e f., condensed. [67]*Soph.* 229e f. ; Cf. *Laws* 810e f. Plato himself, in the *Laws*, has a good deal of " hortatory admonition " too. [68]*Rep.* 378d f., 382a f., cf. 389a f., 414c f., 459d f., *Laws* 663d f. [69]*Rep.* 401c f., condensed. Cf. *Laws* 664. [70]*Rep.* 377e ff., *Laws* 801 f. Plutarch's *Lives* is a fair example of this sort of edifying literature—for adolescents rather than for children. [71]*Rep.* 395b ff., *Laws* 816d f. [72]*Rep.* 381c f., 397d f. Cf. *Laws* 846d. This is in accordance with the ideal principle of " justice " which expresses itself by each member of the community doing " his own work," and not meddling with many matters (*Rep.* 441d f., 443c f.). [73]*Rep.* 398b ff. Cf. *Laws* 816a " out of the imitation of words in gestures the whole art of dancing has arisen." [74]*Rep.* 399a, 400bc. The *Hymn to Apollo*, and the *Hymn to Artemis*, which have come down to us and can be obtained on gramophone records, as well as in the musical notation employed by the historians of Greek music, are usually said to be in the Dorian and Phrygian " mode " (= scale) respectively. But this statement does not accord with either Westphal's or Monroe's reconstruction of the ancient scales ; and the intervals used suggest (to the present writer) the mode called by Plato " relaxed Aeolic." In any case they resemble closly certain of the older Church chants, which may indeed have been descended directly from Greek music. [75]*Rep.* 399, cf. *Laws* 802d f., 816b. The fact that he thus retains only marches and hymn-tunes indicates deliberate insensitivity to the charms of music as such—at least in connection with the education of the immature. Adult experts are (of course) permitted to develop what is immanent in the art of music without these pedagogic restrictions (*Laws* 816d f., cf. 669b f.) which apply only to the three-year course for amateurs. [76]*Laws* 799a f. [77]*Rep.* 377, 386 ff., 401, 595 ff., *Laws* 801, 817d, 829d. [78]*Laws* 809e–812a, condensed. The approved texts apparently include selections from the *Dialogues*. [79]*Polit.* 277e f., cf. *Rep.* 402ab, *Theaet.* 206a. [80]Cf. *Theaet.* 202 ff. [81]*Prtg.* 326cd. [82]*Laws* 811d f. [83]*Prtg.* 325e f., *Laws* 810e f. (The *Laws* passage at least adds Plato's *Dialogues* to the approved school reader). [84]*Cratyl.* 424c, *Phil.* 17–18b. [85]*Theaet.* 202 ff., *Soph.* 253a, *Cratyl.* 424d. [86]Cf. *Cratyl.* 424b–427d, cf. 428bc. See further Ch. IX *infra*.

He does not teach that there is only *one* ideal language.   [87]Condensed from *Laws* 810a, 812c f. Cf. also *Charm.* 160a, *Rep.* 397. *Rep.* 399c f. permits the use of the harp as well as of the lyre in the city. The pipe used by country shepherds is not (of course) handled by citizens themselves.   The flute is essentially chaotic, an impossible instrument for potential idealists (cf. also *Phil.* 56a).   [88]*Cratyl.* 423 f., *Rep.* 397cd, 398c ff., 401d ff.,*Theaet.* 206b, *Soph.* 253ab, *Phil.* 17, *Laws* 657c ff., 664 f., 802bc, 828 f. Vocal music is taught similarly, i.e., in note-for-note unison with the teacher, in the case of solo singing, and in pure unison for choric singing.   In Aristotle's time "magadizing," i.e., singing notes differing by a set interval, as when boys and men sing melodic sequences which are parallel, but the boys' part is set one octave above the men's part, was common and indeed accepted practice.   But Plato disapproves of such mixtures.   His choruses are more like his own abstract " ideas."   Each is kept rigidly apart from the rest. Boys sing with boys, not with maidens, women, or men. Men sing only with men of their own age and character.   From the definite list of disapprovals in Plato's *Laws* it would appear that a good deal of experimental part-singing and of varying the accompaniment, etc., was actually practised in musical circles. But such experts were always foreigners, like the teachers. It is *citizens* who are forbidden to attempt such frills and extras.   [89]*Tim.* 39d f. The intervals of the " cosmic scale " are approximately the same as the classical " enharmonic " scale of the severer type of Greek music. Cf. also *Laws* 659b, 668, etc., and Erich Frank : *Plato u.d. s–g.* *Pythagoreer,* pp. 161–167.   [90]*Laws* 653 ff., 664e f., 672b f., 795e. [91]There is even a suggestion of triennial or quinquennial musical festivals, in *Laws* 834e ; but the details are left to a committee of the law-lords meeting with the director of education and the adjudicators to decide.   [92]Condensed from *Laws* 803d f., 835d. [93]*Rep.* 395bc. [94]*Rep.* 592, cf. 590e f. [95]*Rep.* 402c f. [96]*Laws* 656d f., 659c ff., 665c, 799 ff, 816e, 893 f., 929c. [97]Condensed from *Rep.* 424bc, *Laws* 797b f. [98]So too with the intellectual side of education. For the group of average citizens, who are being prepared for followership only, a little mathematics is acquired in connection with the games of childhood (dividing apples among comrades, when the numbers don't come out even ; arranging" sides " in groups involving a little division, etc.), and in connection with the guessing games of youth, perhaps continued into manhood ; carried further in the business of managing a household, and also in connection with the figures of dancing, and the rhythms of music, etc. Real *work* at mathematics is reserved for the *leadership* class. *Laws* 817e f.

CHAPTER V

EDUCATION FOR LEADERSHIP

Training in music and gymnastic is only one side of Plato's picture of education. It prepares pupils for followership, for a life of docile obedience, of unquestioning loyalty, of ungrounded opinion, of disciplined habits of dependence. His graduates are the great masses who worship in the temples, carry on social and racial traditions in the homes, rally around the government in times of peace, and trail the pikes if it comes to war. They constitute the social background of every festival, every approved entertainment, every worthy cause ; and their cheerful support is always in evidence. They are the cheerful givers whom the Lord loveth—as indeed who does not ?

But followership implies leadership. Obedience implies command. Loyalty implies a cause. Opinion implies knowledge. Dependence implies a leader. The great masses look to leaders, in the temples, in home traditions, in governmental measures, and in warfare. To give their support, they must have someone to whom they can give it : a competent leader. Leaders do not need to be numerous. One at a time will do. But, whether few or many, they must be good : better than the average citizen, better in knowledge, better in experience, and better in character (so far as leadership is concerned). They must be the personification of principle, of the idea of good : in background and in outlook, in techniques and in insight. They must be heroes, supermen, demigods.[1]

Greek tradition knows many such men. Athens has had its Solon, Sparta its Lycurgus. Thales and the rest of the Seven Wise Men are fair as stars, when but a few are shining. Or coming nearer home, have there not been great men like Themistocles, Pericles, Thucydides, and the one original Spartan, Brasidas ? And have there not been the great poets, Homer, and the dramatists, and the great teachers, Protagoras, Gorgias, and their followers ?[2]

True. But such men, pearls beyond price to their own communities, seem to have sprung up spontaneously or by chance.

No community can count on securing the services of a superman or demigod. If it is so vital for a community to secure adequate leadership, is there any way in which it can educate its best citizens for the position ?[3] That is the question which Plato faces, and we now proceed to consider his answer.

In the first place, it is obviously necessary to select the natures most suitable to receive higher education. As the whole body of citizens is being given the standard education for citzenship, and the subject-matter of this education is gymnastic and music : it is necessary to devise some method of selection in gymnastic and music which will pick out the most promising individuals, who may then be separated off as a special leadership class. The selection is accomplished by testing and examining the young people in a variety of ways :

The best guardians will be those who have most the character of guardians : wise and efficient, and with a special care of the state. A man cares most for that which he loves most ; and he loves most that which he regards as having the same interest with himself. We must therefore note in the citizenship class those who in their whole life show the greatest eagerness to do what is for the good of their country : watching them at every age, to see whether they preserve their resolution. We must make them perform actions in which they are most likely to forget or be deceived, and he who fails in the trial will be rejected, and the other selected. And there should be toils, pains, and conflicts prescribed, in which they will give further prof of their quality amid terrors. Again, we will pass them into pleasures, and prove them thoroughly. He who as boy, youth and mature man emerges from the trial victorious and pure will be appointed to the ruling group.[4]

This does not mean that the picked men are the champion runners or fighters in armour, or those who can rattle off the greatest number of memorized poems or accompany themselves most artistically on the lyre. It means, rather, those who have the most steadfast characters, and allow nothing to seduce them from their loyalty. Incidentally, it should be noticed that, unlike the average citizen, to whom education is primarily play and amusement, these picked men are hard workers, industrious, not afraid of toil and pain, and definitely superior to the allurements of pleasure. That is to say, they exhibit pre-eminently the virtues of courage and self-control. It is the second of these on which Plato lays the greatest stress for his purpose. As he sees it, selfrule or selfcontrol is the prime requisite in men who are to be given rule over others. The general mass of the citizens are ruled by others : although it is true that they are trained to be moderate and temperate in their behaviour. But selfmotion, selfrule, and selfcontrol are absolutely essential for membership in the special leadership class.[5]

But are steadfastness and selfcontrolled quietness of disposition, what we nowadays might call the spirit of conservatism, enough ? Enough for the average citizen ? Yes. But enough as a basis for real leadership ? Obviously not. A leader is not someone who sticks to the stereotyped patterns of his party and refuses to budge. On the contrary, he is someone who sets the patterns and prescribes the original lines of development which his followers, it may be, fix in stereotyped legal form :

The best of all is that a man should rule, having wisdom and power both. Law does not adequately comprehend what is noblest and most just for every individual, and therefore cannot enforce what is absolutely best. The differences of men and actions, and the endless irregular movements of human things, do not admit of any simple, universal rule. And no art can lay down a rule which will last for all time. Unchanging rules are the death of art. Its strength has to be superior to law.[6]

For leadership, that is to say, not only steadiness, but qualities of an opposite kind, will be essential. Quickness, acuteness, energy and vigour of mind, which are sometimes comprised under the head of " courage " or " spirit," will be indispensable. But even they will not be enough. The further quality which is a *sine qua non* of leadership is intelligence, knowledge, insight, what Plato calls " philosophy."[7] Natures which have this quality, in addition to the others, are those which are to be selected for membership in the special leadership class.

Let us look at this quality of " philosophy " a little more closely. The philosophic nature has a taste for every sort of knowledge and delights in learning, and yet is to be kept distinct from those whose education qualifies them to be always attending concerts and art exhibitions. For these

are fond of fine tones and colours and forms and all the artificial products made out of them, but their mind is incapable of seeing or loving absolute beauty : and if another leads them toward the knoweldge of that beauty, they are unable to follow. They put the copy in the place of the real object, and are thus dreamers all their lives— dreamers who never wake up. They have opinion, but not knowledge. The philosopher, on the other hand, loves the vision of truth. He recognizes the existence of absolute beauty and is able to distinguish the idea from the copies which participate in it, neither putting the copies in the place of the idea, nor the idea in the place of the copies.

He is no dreamer, but wide awake. He transcends the level of opinion and possesses knowledge. [8]

The philosophic nature, that is to say, has, in addition to courage, temperance, justice, nobility, and grace, the especial qualities of love of truth, a sound memory, and quickness in learning :

> The philosopher is always striving after being   He will not rest in the multiplicity of copies which are appearance only, but will go further. The keen edge will not be blunted, nor the force of his desire abated until he attains knowledge of the true nature of every essence by a sympathetic and kindred power of the soul. By that power drawing near and mingling and becoming incorporate with very being, having begotten mind and truth, he will have knowledge and will live and grow truly. And not till then will he cease from his travail. [9]

Given a few such natures, selected and placed in a special leadership class, [10] what kind of education will fit them for the task of leadership ? Traditional education knows only gymnastic and music. Gymnastic will obviously not do ; for it is concerned, not with the realm of ideal essences, but with their physical copies in the world of generation and corruption. Music also will not do. Like gymnastic, it trains by the influence of habit, making its disciples rhythmical and harmonious, but not giving them scientific insight into truth and value. The various arts included under the term " music " are similarly excluded ; and, as Plato asks, if all these are excluded, what remains ? [11]

Let us look a little more closely at this criticism of " music." Plato elaborates it into what is usually considered a downright attack upon literature and art, and a complete exclusion of all such subjects from the ideal city of the *Republic*. This is, however, exaggerated. It is as pretenders to the place of honour in the curriculum for *leadership*, that poetry, painting, and the rest of the arts are put in their place. In the curriculum for citizenship, where they are used under the direction of philosopher-censors, they are considered perfectly adequate. Poets and artists, as such, are not necessarily persons of philosophic insight. They are childlike figures, with a gift for vigorous and persuasive expression in ways that fasten upon the nonlogical part of the soul, through rhythmic movement, suggestion, and the like. Poets themselves are at times inspired, and much of their work is of the greatest value to the community. Some of it, however, while equally striking as expressive literature, is simply out of touch with reality ;

and to take whatever a poet may say with grace and power, as if it were also gospel truth, would be quite irrational.[12]

The philosopher, in spite of his own perfectly genuine love of art and appreciation of its grace and power over the nonlogical side of life,[13] understands that it is futile to pretend that it can be used as what it is not, namely, a rational instrumentality of rational education. Art appeals, not to reason, but to feeling. It stimulates, feeds, and waters the passions.[14] In so doing, it exercises a very important function. But its function is *not* the function of reason, and nothing can make it so. This has to be recognized as a fact which no wishful thinking can possibly change. Then again art belongs to the realm, not of rational knowledge, but of opinion: that twilight realm hovering midway between being and nonbeing. The realm of " ideas," the patterns of " being " apprehended by reason, are one thing. The fanciful creations of art, floating adjectives flitting in and out of the spacetime world at the bidding of the artist, but with no sure abiding place among the ideal patterns which they sometimes try to copy,[15] are something else again. Titillations of the endorgans of sensation, mirror-images of the brain which gives them momentary birth and a suggested significance not their own, they should never be mistaken for the clearcut concepts of rational thought. They belong to the realm, not of reason, but of opinion.[16]

And further : there is a higher, and there is a lower, level in the realm of opinion. Practical experience, resting upon repeated sensation and use of physical objects for the convenience and comfort of biosocial needs, attains to a certain order and system in its way of living. We need shelter, and the art of the builder evolves a house : a combination of floor, walls, and roof, which actually provides shelter, and can be counted upon to do so. We need rest, and the art of the carpenter evolves beds and chairs : house furniture upon which we can seek and find repose. We need clothing, and the art of the weaver, with the instrumentality of loom and shuttle, evolves a combination of warp and woof-threads which actually clothes us in ways upon which we can rely. These arts have unity, order, and system. They use a good deal of exact science, of measurement, of mathematical calculation ; and it is from this use of principles borrowed from the realm of ideas and applied to the fugitive content of the spacetime world that they are able to provide what will satisfy our biosocial needs.[17] These arts move in the higher realm of opinion, the realm of conviction resting upon practical experience.[18]

So much for the practical arts. They belong in this higher realm. But where are we to place poetry, painting, music, and the rest of the fine arts, usually regarded as higher than the artisan activities of the builder, the carpenter, and the weaver ? They construct images, and nothing but images. You need shelter, and the painter gives you a two-dimensional image which suggests a home. It may be a palace. It may be a hovel. But within its four walls you can never penetrate ; and its suggestion of a roof will never keep the rain or the snow from your head. You are weary, and the painter's wizardry conjures up the semblance of a chair and the illusion of a wonderful bed ; but neither will ever support your fainting limbs. The poet sings of his little grey home in the West and assures you that there is no place like home. He arouses dream-imagery of marble halls, gilded thrones, and tapestry-strewn couches. You ask for bread, and he offers you a sonnet. You ask for a cloak, and he gives you a triolet.[19]

What are these images over which the poet rules ? Are they copies of the ideal patterns, revelations of hidden meaning behind the space-time appearances of ultimate reality ? Or are they reproductions in pigments, tones, or parts of speech, of the physical, space-time objects themselves ? Go into the art galleries of the world. Look at the landscapes, the seascapes, the still-life studies, the portraits of celebrities and their families, the portraits of the artists themselves. Are these intimate revelations of ultimate realities, suggestions of depths to which the eye of sense is forever a stranger ? Or are they expensive and imperfect substitutes for a good photograph of their objects ?

Plato's answer is as follows : Sometimes they are revelations, inspired, pregnant with suggestions of the deepest meaning.[20] Sometimes—far more often in his experience as in ours—they are feeble copies of the spacetime objects : pictures of sail-boats that would never sail, of birds that could never fly, of houses that could never stand up, if they were constructed as the artist seems to imagine. They will not stand the test of mathematics, of the stresses of the space-time world. Such artists have not even the knowledge of the artisan whom they despise. Their work belongs to a lower level of the realm of opinion : a level below practical experience. Plato calls it the level of guesswork.[21]

Sometimes inspired and instinct with significance, sometimes feeble and useless. But the worst thing is this. The artist himself never knows which of his creations are true, and which false.[22] And there is something further. The artist's creations are, in themselves, lifeless. He has lent them what animation he can. But they are dependent, for their life, not merely upon him, but upon his audience. The virtuoso co-operates with the composer, the critic co-operates with the artist, the reader puts his own life into the dry bones left by the writer. And how dry those bones can sometimes be !

Writing is unfortunately like painting. The creations of the painter have the attitude of life, and yet if you ask them a question they preserve a solemn silence. You would imagine that they had intelligence ; but if you want to know anything and put a question to one of them, the speaker always gives one unvarying answer. And once written down, they are tumbled about anywhere among men who may or may not understand them, and know not to whom they should reply, to whom not. If maltreated or abused, they have no parent to protect them, and they cannot defend themselves.[23]

Art is thus a form of communication which the philosopher cannot take altogether seriously. The artist cannot give more than he himself knows ; and he cannot give more than his hearer can take. He can thus stimulate the imagination, but cannot teach a serious lesson, confident that the rational idea in his own mind is passed over to his hearer.[24] As far as an audience of average citizens are concerned, who are through their whole lives cultured playboys, puppets held and guided by the leading strings of art, never rising above the level of opinion, art, under the guidance and direction of community philosophy, has a function to perform. But as far as training for the higher life of leadership is concerned, art is of no use whatever, and its place must be taken by something more scientific, more rational, and more philosophic, something capable cf weaning the soul from the realm of sense and passion, and turning it toward the realm entered only by the mind, the realm of the ideal patterns, the " colourless, shapeless, intangible essences apprehensible by mind, the pilot of the soul."[25]

And there is one further point. Art derives its appeal for the masses, not from its rational side, not from its power to unify, to order in rhythms, to reduce to a central focus. These powers are indeed borrowed from the ideal realm, and it is their application to sense-data and biosocial passion which gives us, in place of crude animal reaction to crude animal stimulation, art.[26] But the application can never be more than fragmentary and temporary. Beneath the refinements of art the crudities of animal feeling continue to lurk : disguised but ever-present. Even the best of us has within him an animal crudity which comes out when the rational control is relaxed, as in the forbidden wish-dreams which trouble our sleep.[27] It is always there. In men of character, given the co-operation of all the resources of the community, art can tame or even sublimate it. But with most men art can do little more than disguise or conceal its presence.[28] In the masses, it is to this original crude vitality which responds to stimulation with a jerk, a cry, or other instinctive movement, that art, however, refined, appeals. Under the forms authorized by society, art provides temporary release, and thus functions as a kind of moral safety-valve which reduces the pressure of our tendencies toward chaos, and so makes possible the continuance of what we call civilization. In our social masquerade, art furnishes the mask which admits the biological urge to the drawing-room.[29]

In fact, just as the mathematical law and order of the physical cosmos studied by science are superimposed upon an original chaos, a seething cauldron of motions lawless, structureless, altogether irregular, by the power of the Divine Artist who called our world into being,[30] so the rhythmic regularities and pattern-suggestions of human art are superimposed (not without Divine inspiration and leadership) upon a seething welter of sensations, passions, and chaotic pleasure-seeking tendencies endlessly irregular in themselves, and thus call into being Hellenic " civilization." This makes its appearance in the form of small city-states which appear unified but are really, beneath the smooth appearing surface, torn by faction, and never very far from the social chaos which the conventions of Greek society claim to have banished forever.[31] Moreover, since the weapons by which the artist conceals, disguises, or partly tames and civilizes the wild streak in man are derived from the ideal realm, and since, further, it is only when controlled and directed by men of trained insight into this ideal realm, that the artist succeeds even in this aim, the question as to how the human soul is to be weaned from the crudities of instinct, even as refined by art, and turned more definitely toward the realm of ideal patterns, so as to be like God, a spectator of all time and existence, becomes more pressing.

Very few men are capable of profiting fully by this higher education. " Wisdom is an attribute of the gods—and of very few men." Assuming, then, that we have a select few whose character and intellectual capacity evidence a tendency to press forward, away from the multiplicity of sense-phenomena, toward the unity of the law which formulates their essence, how are we to educate them ? " Gymnastic " is ruled out. " Music " is deliberately and finally excluded. What remains ?

The answer is, Science. But not science as pursued by scientists. As pursued by scientists, i.e., by the so-called Pythagoreans, science consists in the observation and cataloguing of phenomena, of experimental investigation of their uniformities and sequences, and in the formulation of the uniformities and sequences thus established, in mathematical terms. Mathematical physics professes to discover, by the use of its mathematical techniques and experimental procedure, the laws in accordance with which the mechanism of the universe can be regarded as functioning. Such physicists profess to be able to construct models which will demonstrate, on a small scale, how the thing is done ; and when they have thus " explained " the phenomena of the actual universe, their task is accomplished, and their labours come to an end.[32]

Plato's objection to science, not as science, but as a means of attaining to ultimate, metaphysical insight, is precisely what the scientists regard as its virtue : namely, it sticks to the facts. It refuses to speculate, and confines its efforts to accounting for actual phenomena.[33] As Plato sees the matter, Pythagorean science is a kind of sister of the arts. It uses the weapons of the ideal realm, but only as applied to a field which is essentially non-logical and chaotic. Science, it is true, abstracts from the biosocial feelings and passions which are essential to art. But it accepts sense-data as final—and thus prevents itself forever from constructing a perfectly rational system. For the data of sense are themselves fragmentary and nonlogical : in the end, chaotic. Any system imposed upon them is merely superimposed. It is external. It may work for practical purposes ; but its hypotheses and primary working assumptions are accepted without critical examination ; and it is highly doubtful whether serious criticism would justify such a practice :

As to the mathematical sciences which have some apprehension of true being, they only dream about being, but can never behold the waking reality as long as they leave the hypotheses which they use unexamined, and are unable to give an acount of them. When a man knows not his own first principle, and when the intermediate steps and the conclusion are also constructed out of—he knows not what, how can he imagine that such a fabric of convention can ever become genuine knowledge ?[35]

Pythagorean science, that is to say, turns men into spectators of the temporal and spatial world revealed to our senses. What Plato wants is some study which will turn men into spectators of eternity and absolute existence : i.e., of the ideal realm of which the physical cosmos is a sensory phenomenon. What he needs to do, therefore, is to take the methods and techniques of science, detach them from the actual, detailed, empirical applications which constitute Pythagorean science, and study them in abstraction, as *pure* mathematics, *pure* physics, *pure* theory of method. His study will be, not thinking applied to this or that field, but *pure* thinking, proceeding independently of sensuous perception, in a realm all its own. Plato calls this *dialectic*.

In sensuous experience, for example, we can distinguish two sides or aspects. We apprehend (1) the *qualitative data* of sense, the red, green, and blue, the hard and soft, the light and heavy, as characteristics of concrete objects. In themselves, as ordinarily experienced, such data are accepted and enjoyed. They raise no awkward questionings which might lead us away from the sensuous mode of experiencing.[36] We apprehend also (2) certain *relations* which are given along with the qualitative data, but can be distinguished from them. We apprehend this-patch-of red as *larger*, and that as *smaller*. We apprehend this finger as being *to the right of*, that finger as being *to the left of*, a third finger ; and we apprehend the third finger as being *in the middle of* the other two. So too we apprehend this patch as *round*, that as *triangular*, this third as *square*, etc., Finally, each is thought of as *one*, and they can be added, as *two*, *three*, *four* patches. Relations are not particular like the sense-data. They are *universal*.[37] Relations, too, in ordinary experience awaken no awkward questionings. They are accepted and taken for granted, and some of them are enjoyed.[38] They do not, of themselves, lead us to desert sensuous experience.

But the dialectician is not as ordinary men. He does not accept, but questions ; and in reference to sensuous experience, he finds he can make a distinction which he believes will be helpful for his purpose of turning " the eye of the soul, the instrument of real knowledge, from the world of becoming to the world of being and its ultimate principle."[39]

Objects of sense are of two kinds. Some of them do not invite intellectual thinking, because the sense itself is an adequate judge of them— as e.g., *This is a finger*. In the case of certain other objects the sense is so untrustworthy that further inquiry is imperatively demanded— as e.g. *This finger is large* (relatively to the little finger) *and at the same time small* (relatively to the middle finger) ; or *This object is thin* (relatively to *A*) *and at the same time thick* (relatively to *B*). So too with (relative) softness and hardness, heaviness and lightness. In such perplexities the soul (leaves sensation and) summons to her aid calculation and intelligence. The eye sees both small and large, but confusedly and without distinction ; whereas the thinking mind, intending to light up the chaos, looks at small and large as separate ideas, never to be confused.[40]

That is to say, from the dialectician's standpoint, sense-data, considered qualitatively, are rarely observed to be contradictory and chaotic, and are consequently accepted without intellectual questioning : but relations, "impressions which are simultaneous with opposite impressions " (as in the case of a large which is also small, a thin which is also thick) challenge thought to rise into an intelligible realm in which such contradictions are adequately explained.[41]

The case of number belongs pre-eminently to this second, thought-inviting class of experiences.

If simple unity could be perceived adquately by the senses, there would be nothing to attract toward being. But where there is always some contradiction present (as with the table which is both one and many), so that one is the reverse of one and involves the conception of plurality : thought is aroused and we ask " What is absolute unity ? " In this way the study of arithmetic has a power of drawing and converting the mind (away from sensuous experience) to the contemplation of true being.[42]

That is to say, from the dialectician's standpoint, arithmetic studied, not in its practical applications to buying and selling, but so as to enable members of the leadership class to " see the nature of numbers with the mind only," as " numbers which can only be realized in thought, necessitates the use of the pure intelligence in the attainment of pure truth," and thus " must be made one of the subjects of higher education." It is added that arithmetic has also a secondary usefulness, in that

Those who have a natural talent for calculation are generally quick at every other kind of knowledge ; and even the dull, if they have had arithmetical training, even if they derive no philosophical advantage from the study, always become much quicker than they would otherwise have been.[43]

A second study similarly capable of being used as an instrument of higher education, is geometry. Geometry studied, that is to say, not from the standpoint of the practising Greek geometricians who consider only applications :

They have in view practice only, and are always speaking in a narrow and ridiculous manner of squaring this, extending that, and applying and the like—confusing the biosocial necessities of everyday life with geometric necessity.

From the standpoint of the dialectician, pure geometry abstracts from everyday life and its alleged necessities, as from "everything perishing and transient," and, at least in its " greater and more advanced reaches," aims at knowledge of the eternal, and so draws the mind away from sensuous experience " towards truth," and so " makes more easy the vision of the idea of good.[44] That is why members of the leadership class will study geometry, both plane and solid.[45]

A third study, capable of being used by the dialectician for the same purpose, is astronomy. Not, of course, astronomy considered as mere star-gazing, " gaping at the heavens with the eyes of sense," or astronomy in its practical applications in the construction of charts and reference-books for seamen and farmers, cataloguing the actual motions of the actual celestial bodies.[46] In the hands of the dialectician, astronomy will be used as a means of getting away from the " spangled heavens " with their actuality, and attaining to the absolute ideal : studying

the true motions of absolute swiftness and absolute slowness which are relative to each other and carry with them that which is contained in their orbits, in the true number and in every true figure. These are apprehended, not by sight, but by reason and intelligence. The dialectician will never imagine that the proportions to one another of things that are material and visible can possibly be eternal and not subject to deviation ; and (from his standpoint) it would be absurd to spend much pains in investigating their exact truth. We must let the heavens alone if we are to make the natural gift of reason really useful.[47]

A last special science which similarly contains something which the dialectician can use for the purposes of higher education, is known as " harmonics." This, like astronomy, is a science which studies physical motions ; but whereas astronomy studies the motions which are visible to the eye, harmonics studies motions which are apprehensible to the ear : in a word, physical acoustics. This also is not to be studied as the practising musicians study it, tightening and relaxing the vibrating strings, as they try to catch first, second, and possibly third difference-notes, " setting their ears before their understanding." Nor is it to be studied as the practising (Pythagorean) scientists study it : confining their attention to the tones and consonances which are recognized as such by the human ear, and trying to reduce the physical basis of these to numerical formulation.[48]   On the contrary : they should use the tones and consonances of audible human music as a starting-point only, which is to be left behind as they advance to genuinely intellectual problems : investigating the natural harmonies of number as such and reflecting why some numbers are harmonious and others not.[49] This latter kind of inquiry will assist in weaning the students from the sense-perceivable world, and directing their attention more fully to the intelligible realm of reason : and it is with this object that " harmonics " is added to the studies of which the dialectician approves for their usefulness in higher education.[50]

A further step is now taken. These studies have been pursued without any correlation. Arithmetic is begun first, and is con-tinued indefinitely. Then geometry is started, and is continued indefinitely. Then solid geometry, following upon plane geometry Then astronomy. and finally harmonics. These are all studied as indicated above.[51] That is to say, just as the arts are studied by the citizenship group, not to make them expert artists, but for the purposes of character-education, so these sciences are studied by the leadership class, not to turn them into specialized scientists, but for the purposes of intellectual education : turning their attention away from the world of sense, and making them at home in the transcendental realm of mind, the realm of pure concepts or absolute ideas.

These studies commence in childhood, and thus are, to some extent, pursued by all members of the citizenship group. But these are not expected to go very far. They are the " dullards, who are improved in general " by arithmetical and mathematical training, but are not " able to follow their teachers into the realm of absolute ideas." It is the secondary advantages of such studies which benefit *them*.[52] Let us concentrate upon those who are being selected for membership in the leadership class, and inquire what difference these studies make in their case.

In the first place, they are perplexed and tremendously sti-mulated to intellectual effort. Like Socrates in his own youth, each will be able to say :

Time was, when I seemed to understand the meaning of greater and less. When I saw a tall man standing by a short, man, I fancied the one was taller " by a head." Still more clearly did I seem to perceive that 10 is larger than 8 *by* 2, and that two cubits are more than one, because *two is the double of one*.

But now : I cannot satisfy myself that when 1 is added to 1, the 1 to which the addition is made becomes 2, or that two units added together make 2 by reason of the addition. I cannot see how, when separated, each was 1, and now that mere juxtaposition should cause them to become 2. Neither can I see how the division of 1 is the way to make 2. Nor am I satisfied that I understand the reason why 1 or anything else is either generated or destroyed or is at all ; but I have in my view some confused notion of a new method, and can never admit the other.[53]

In the second place—again like Socrates—this feeling after a " new method " prepares their minds, although dimly, for an ultimate insight into the ideal principle of value, "the good" or " principle of the best," of which Socrates received an unsatisfying but stimulating glimpse from his studies of science. That is to say, the perplexity about the " why " of everything will remain unresolved until it can somehow be shown that the ultimate ground for things being as they are, the x in the equation, is through and through rational, and that the principle of rationality and the principle of value are identified in the conception of ideality. This is a feeling after metaphysical explanation ; but it is felt that the metaphysical explanation must itself be able to throw light upon the physicist's kind of explanation too, before it will be accepted as ideally satisfactory.[54]

The further step, taken in the twentieth year by the select members of the leadership class only, considers these mathematical sciences in their " intercommunion and interconnection " and examines " their mutual affinities." The select students will then be able " to see the natural relationship of these studies to one another and to true being." That is to say, they will realize that arithmetic deals with points, or with one dimension ; that plane geometry deals with points moving lengthwise into lines, and with lines moving crosswise into surfaces, i.e., with points in their first and second " fluxions," or with two dimensions ; that solid geometry deals with surfaces moving depthwise into solids, i.e., with points in their third "fluxion," or with three dimensions ; and from this standpoint they will be able to proceed to solve problems in an·ideal astronomy in which motion is studied in a universe constructed entirely out of regular mathematical solids (tetrahedra, octohedra, eikosihedra, and cubes) compressed in a single revolving sphere : said solids being conceived as consisting entirely and without remainder of ideal points in their third " fluxion."[55]

What we should say nowadays is that these highly select students devote themselves to epistemology or theory of knowledge, gradually tending more and more to metaphysics : using the sciences as starting-points, and, after comparison, learning to transcend the hypotheses or assumptions which make each specific science what it is. That is to say, they will realize that in arithmetic the mind posits, as its subject of study, points as such ; in geometry, it posits the further dimensions of such points, considered as moving length-wise, crosswise, and depthwise. By questioning these hypotheses or assumptions they will find, at the basis of all science, a mind engaged in creating a mind-made world of conceptual entities which constitute so many ideal self-projections of its own nature : an abstract cosmos to be used as a standard in judging the move-ments of the actual celestial bodies.[56]

Out of this process of comparison and co-ordination of the various subjects of study, these students will find themselves in-duced to draw a number of similar conclusions in other fields of study too. They will find in Plato's *Dialogues* (on which they have all been educated) a world created by Plato's mind : in which a Platonic Socrates discourses with a Platonic Protagoras and a Platonic Thrasymachus, not merely about abstract mathematical problems, but about social problems, equally abstract and ideal.[57] Thus, constructed for them in outline they will find an ideal social community,[58] and they will realize that this idealizing method can be applied universally, to every aspect of experience. Thus realizing, they complete what Plato calls " the prelude to the final hymn of dialectic." Here let us leave their intellectual studies for the moment, to consider along what other lines their char-acters are being strengthened for leadership.

For learning alone does not make leaders. Too much theory with too little practice is as harmful as too much practice with too little theory. It fits men for the theoretical life, which they are reluctant to abandon when it is necessary to descend into the cave and take their turn at the tasks of administration :

Neither the uneducated and uninformed of the truth, nor yet those who never make an end of their education, will be able ministers of state. Not the former, because they have no single aim of duty which is the rule of all their actions. Not the latter, because they will not act at all except upon compulsion, fancying themselves already dwelling apart in the Isles of the Blest.[59]

From the age of twenty to the age of thirty, the select aspirants for leadership will not only continue to correlate the sciences and so prepare their minds for the final study of dialectic itself. They will engage in practical life, in military and civil service : not at first as leaders, but as followers, undertaking such tasks in the service of the community as are suited to their abilities, and as will educate them for holding positions of command. Just as music is not studied apart from gymnastic, and gymnastic is not studied apart from music : so the theoretical studies which constitute the approach to philosophy, and metaphysical philosophy itself, are not studied apart from the performance of practical duties in the social economy ; and the practical duties in question are not undertaken without a balancing study of philosophical theory, in the case of citizens who are being trained for leadership.[60]

Just what are these practical duties ? For details, we must consult the *Laws*. It there appears that young men are selected for a two-year term of military service at the age of twenty-five or so, up to twenty-eight. In a city of 5,040 families, 144 of these young men, working in groups of twelve, each group with five officers, are considered sufficient to look after the non-urban area of the country. Their duties are partly military : and the biennial circuit which they make of the various divisions of the country will acquaint them thoroughly with the territory which they may have to defend. Requisitioning the assistance of local labour at suitable periods, they trench and dig fortifications, build roads, take care of streams, fountains, and matters of irrigation, etc. They also construct gymnasia for their own use, and bath-houses for the local inhabitants who require warm baths for some of the ailments of senescence.[61] But they also, acting as a committee of seventeen (i.e., the twelve of each group acting in concert with their officers), exercise a number of definitely magisterial functions in the case of certain rural misdeeds—such as

Interfering with boundaries, pasturing cattle on a neighbour's land, decoying a neighbour's bees, injuring a neighbours' property by carelessness about fires, encroaching on a neighbour's cultivating rights by planting right up to farm limits, or offending against the ancient understandings about the common use of water.[62]

During their term of service, the young men selected pride themselves on being good servants. Each group of seventeen makes its own arrangements. They live simply, serving themselves instead of requisitioning slave or peasant labour. They partly support themselves by hunting and fishing, and in general take as their model the hardy mode of life which characterized their Spartan contemporaries. There is no doubt that the camping experience thus gained would be a great help toward developing self-reliance, sociability, and practical alertness.[63]

Other duties, chiefly of a supervisory nature in connection with gymnasia, school buildings, and other public institutions, under the general and sometimes special direction of important officials such as the minister of education, would fall to the lot of a few assistants who might be in the 20–30 age-group. And it is reasonable to suppose that participation in the choral dancing of the festivals would call for the services of a number of youthful co-opts. Many details are left unsettled, with the general understanding that the older officials (for whom full provision is made) will fill in all such gaps for themselves.[64]

At the age of thirty, young men who have received this sort of training (and are incidentally for the most part now married and beginning to bring up families) are selected as competent to hold certain positions of minor command, and to give orders to men of the 20–30 age-group : acting, of course, always under the direction of superior officers. In the *Laws* such men are selected by the higher-ups (who have kept an eye on their behaviour and development) to act as subalterns in matters military, and as junior officials in the civil service.[65] The most promising of all the young men of this age are picked for the most important administrative service of all : being given junior membership in the immensely important council which revises the laws :

a mixed body of old and young men, consisting of the (15) priests of Apollo and the Sun, the (10) oldest law-lords, the superintendent of education and his predecessors (*emeriti*). Each of these shall take with him a young man of the 30-40 age-group. The whole city will keep an eye upon these young men, especially honouring those who distinguish themselves successfully, and especially dishonouring any who turn out to be inferior.[66]

In the *Republic* this further training in actual leadership on a junior scale appears to be postponed for a five-year period of intensified dialectical study :

Those who have most of this comprehension (power of co-ordinating the sciences) and are most steadfast in their learning, and in their military and other appointed duties, when they have arrived at the age of thirty are chosen out of the select class and elevated to yet higher honour. You will have to prove them by the help of dialectic, learning which are able to give up the use of the senses and, in company with truth, to attain absolute being. The study of philosophy is to be continued diligently and earnestly for five years (30–35).[67]

The reason for postponing the study of dialectic, so that it is only prepared for but not directly undertaken by men of twenty or so, is comparatively simple. The whole method of education hitherto has been playful, nursery and seminary stuff, separated off from actual life. Consequently, the tendency to treat education as a kind of game, not to be taken too seriously, is well developed. If young men of twenty are introduced to the weapons of dialectic while still in this playful mood, their lack of actual experience will interfere with their realization of its supremely serious importance : and they will treat logic-chopping as a new sort of game :

arguing for amusement, always contradicting and refuting others in imitation of those who refute them ; like puppy-dogs, rejoicing in pulling and tearing at all who come near them ; and soon getting into a way of not believing any of the traditional principles about justice and honour.[68]

This juvenile scepticism, which prevents a man from appreciating the serious values of life, is obviated by making the 20-30 period a time of practical social and military experience, and not admitting students (however select) to the class in dialectic until they have reached the age of thirty and are settling down. At that age " the greater moderation of their character will increase instead of diminishing the honour of the pursuit." In fact Plato is trying to solve a very real difficulty. He is attempting to reconcile two tendencies in human nature which are both important for leadership, but happen to be opposed. Steadiness, which is vital for leadership-purposes, does not come except with age and experience. But mental flexibility and ability to profit by intellectual study clearly belong to the period of youth. At the same time, Plato is convinced that we cannot profit by philosophic study until our minds have matured.[69]

The age of thirty thus represents a compromise between the quality of intelligence which gives us " honours students " in the early twenties, and the steadying experience which gives us a basis for sound appreciation of the value of philosophic pursuits in the later forties. Modern teaching experience confirms Plato's belief in the reality of this difficulty. Examiners in scholastic philosophy as taught to (1) college girls and (2) mature nuns selected for teaching are unanimous in recognizing that the subject has far more value for the second group, although there is no doubt as to the intellectual quality of the first group ; and they are convinced that the answers to one and the same examination paper would fall into two distinct groups corresponding to the age-groups. So too in our large graduate schools of education we have no difficulty in realising that experienced teachers of 40-50 who come in to complete their work for the doctorate are able to

appreciate the value of their philosophy classes far better than the
highly intelligent but inexperienced students still in their early
twenties, who are also members of the same classes.

What is this " dialectic " which has to be approached so carefully lest it develop juvenile scepticism and so prove most harmful,
primarily to those who study it, and secondarily to the community over which such students later rule ?[70]   In the first place,
it is a highly abstract study, not altogether unlike the " logic "
developed by Plato's pupil, Aristotle and still taught in Universities to very youthful students.   As such, it devotes itself to
the analysis and clarification of concepts, leading to their arrangement in interrelated systems which follow the laws of classification
and division, and make technical definition possible.   There are
a number of examples of this rather arid application of pure
method in what are called " the *dialectical Dialogues*," especially
in the *Parmenides, Sophistes, Politicus*, and *Philebus*.   But there are
plenty of (minor) examples of the same sort of thing in the
earlier *Dialogues* too ; and no doubt its development originated
in the discussions which centered around the historic Socrates. [71]

In the second place, this study of concepts leads to a number of
broad distinctions between concepts as such, and the multiplicity
of sense-perceivable phenomena which only partly participate
in the determinate and fixed character of the concept.   Sense-
phenomena seem fluid, indeterminate, transient, and inconsistent.
They come and go like moonbeams, and cannot be held fast in
the steel network of conceptual system. They belong to a distinct
universe of discourse, the realm of sensuous opinion, fluctuating,
evanescent, and obscure.   In contrast with these, concepts are
permanent, definite, something that the mind can apprehend
and hold fast. They are consistent and clear.   You can count on
their " staying put," and can use them as bricks in a system, not
of " opinion," but of genuine knowledge.[72]

In the third place, a study of concepts, not in relation to sensuous experience, but in relation to one another, raises a number
of extremely interesting questions.   Can they be arranged in a
single hierarchical system : so that the ideas of *man, ox, horse* etc.,
are co-ordinate species, coming under the higher genus-concept
animal, while *animal*, or *animate being*, is co-ordinate with *inanimate
being*, and both come under the more general concept *being ?*
Where would one place, in such a system, the ideas of *bed, table,
weaver's-shuttle*, etc ?   And where would one locate the ethical
concepts, *courage, temperance, justice*, co-ordinated under the higher

concept of *human virtue ?* Are the virtues all separate, or do even their concepts tend to run into one another : so that ideal *justice* implies *courage* and *selfcontrol*, and *selfcontrol* implies both *courage* and *justice ?* And are there some peculiar concepts (later known as " categories "), " simple notions " which seem to run through all other concepts—notions such as *like, unlike, one, many, rest, motion*, etc ? Does the element of difference and distinction of individual concepts from one another, and of whole classes of concepts from one another, reintroduce into the ideal realm a suggestion of that baffling sense of chaos which accompanies the multiple differences in the field of sense-phenomena ?[73]

> Division according to classes is the business of the science of dialectic. He who can divide rightly is able to see clearly one form pervading a scattered multitude, and many different forms contained under one higher form ; and again, one form knit together into a single whole and prevading many such wholes, and many forms existing only in separation and isolation. This is the knowledge of classes which determines where they can have communion with one another and where not.[74]

In the fourth place, the dialectician exploits to the full what is called " implication." He can deduce the implied consequences of a given hypothesis ; and this technique is helpful to the philosopher in a number of ways. In a case where he is without knowledge, he can assume the *two* hypotheses (*1*) *x is a*, and (*2*) *x is not a*, and can proceed to deduce the consequences of each. If the deduced consequences of (*1*) lead him into a field in which he does possess knowledge, and prove consistent with that knowledge, while the deduced consequences of (*2*) prove inconsistent with that knowledge, he can conclude (provisionally) to the probable truth of (*1*) and the probable falsity of (*2*).[75] Or again, if the deduced consequences of a given hypothesis lead to *two* contradictory conclusions, this is sure evidence that the hypothesis originally assumed as sound contains a lurking dualism which is the source of the contradictions. This was shown to be the case with the Pythagorean hypothesis of the identity of mathematical and physical reality—shown by Zeno, the inventor of this way of reasoning ; and the principle is applied by Socrates in reasoning with Protagoras, Gorgias, Polus, Callicles, Thrasymachus, *et al.*[76]

Finally, by the use of this implicational technique, the dialectician challenges the hypotheses of the sciences, the working fictions or assumptions upon which they proceed, and so eventually seeks to attain to the unhypothetical first principle of all, the principle of ideality itself, the idea of good which is the *ratio cognoscentis*, the *ratio cognoscendi*, and the *ratio essendi*, and as a first principle, transcends both existence and essence :

The good is the author of knowledge to all things known, and also of their being and essence. Yet the good is not itself essence, but far transcends essence in dignity and power. In studying this, the soul passes out of hypotheses and ascends to the principle which is above hypotheses, proceeding only in and through the ideas themselves. This principle once apprehended, the soul descends again : starting from this principle and holding fast to it, and then proceeding to the subordinate principles which depend upon it, by successive steps the soul descends (though the sciences) without the aid of any sense-per-ceivable object : from ideas, through ideas, and in ideas the soul ends.[77]

After five years spent in intensive study of these abstract tech-niques, the members of the leadership class, now thirty-five years of age, are sent out into the world again for fifteen years' experi-ence of actual leadership :

After five years, they must be sent down again into the " cave " and compelled to hold any military or other office which men of their age are qualified to hold. In this way they will get their experience of life, and there will be further opportunity of trying whether, when drawn all manner of ways by temptation, they stand firm or flinch.[78]

Quite a number of leadership positions of an intermediate rank in the military, civil, and judicial services are open to men of merit in the 40–50 age-group in the model city of the *Laws* ; and it is to be presumed that positions of this type are in the mind of the author of the *Republic*. Adjudicators in the music festivals, while usually in this age-group, are in the case of solo-performers sometimes as young as thirty-five. And the adjudicators in the gymnastic sports meets are presumably in the same age-class.[79] Such persons, sitting in committee with the law-lords and the minister of education, exercise a number of important legislative and administrative functions.[80]

Eventually, the select members of the leadership class reach the mature age of fifty, which, both in the *Republic* and in the *Laws*, marks a definite turning-point in a man's life. The period of probation is now over, and the community is prepared to entrust its most important offices to their hands : in some cases for a five-year period, in others, for life.

When they have reached fifty years of age, let those who have dis-tinguished themselves in every action and in every branch of knowledge come at last to their consummation. The time has arrived at which they must raise the eye of the soul to the universal light which lightens all things, i.e., behold the absolute good. This is the pattern according to which they are to order the life of the state, of individuals, and of themselves : making philosophy their chief pursuit, but, when their turn comes, toiling also at politics and ruling for the public good. This is their duty. And when they have brought up in each generation others like themselves and left them in their place to be governors of the state, they will depart to the Isles of the Blest and dwell there : being especially honoured by the city. [81]

The duties undertaken by such trained leaders are duties of deliberation, supervision, and direction. They meet together in councils and deliberate upon policies. They decide upon the church calendar, settling the dates of the various festivals of the church year. They decide upon the civil calendar, settling the dates of the court-of-justice sessions, and the dates of the various peace-time military sports meets. They initiate and revise laws as occasion arises. They scrutinize the qualifications of magistrates, and supervise their conduct in office. They supervise the behaviour of citizens in the home, in the streets, in the temples, in peace and in war. They appoint visitors to travel and observe foreign institutions and report back with suggestions (if any) for improvement of the home institutions. Finally it is members of this group who are elected to all the important administrative positions, such as that of minister of education, to all important judicial positions, and (in their later years, after they reach the age of sixty) to all important representative positions, positions in which they represent the community as ambassadors, or as priests. In each and every election, care is taken to see that the principle of merit (the " idea of good ") is strictly observed. The very best of the civic material available is always appointed to the offices, whether civil or military. [82] The importance of these offices requires the education for leadership, and the thoroughness of the education for leadership justifies appointment to such offices. As long as the supply of trained leaders does not fail, the community can expect to continue to improve. If the supply falls short, for whatever reason, the community will degenerate. [83]

Let us summarize Plato's account of education for leadership by applying it to an individual case. We imagine a boy (or it might be a girl) of good parentage and excellent physique. In the home nursery (or, in the *Republic*, the state nursery) and the community playground he acquires the rudiments of courage, selfcontrol, friendliness, respect for elders. From the age of six to somewhere in his later teens, he acquires, in community sports schools and arts schools, supplemented by participation in monthly festivals of a variety of sorts, a gentleman's degree of proficiency in " music " and gymnastic, and possibly some apprentice-like acquaintance with actual warfare. The education received, however, is less a matter of proficiency in specific subjects, and more a matter of development of character. He had become a walking pattern of the community virtues, with a loyalty which rests upon " opinion " rather than " knowledge," but is thoroughly inculcated. He is now qualified to enter the army and gradually, i.e., when there is a suitable vacancy among the 5,040 citizenship positions (for which he is on the waiting list) he becomes a citizen, marries and settles down.

We are supposing, however, that our imaginary boy is unusually intelligent and shows remarkable promise in his education. If so, he is especially stimulated to take part in mathematical games and all sorts of problem-solving activities : especially such as will draw his attention to the beauty and intellectual satisfactoriness of conceptual abstractions. If in addition he shows a disposition to work hard at his problems, and not merely to take them play-fully : then, somewhere at about the age of twenty he is placed in a select leadership class and encouraged to reduce his scientific studies to a common focus, looking into their interrelations and the principles which they share in common, and probing into a number of highly advanced problems. At the same time, he is tried out in a number of positions, military and judicial, which give him a certain amount of responsibility and call for the exercise of independent judgment as well as loyal obedience to superiors. This kind of training continues until he reaches the age of thirty.

If his qualities of character and intelligence still make him out-standing among his contemporaries, so that he still (though married) presses on to higher aims, he is admitted to a five-year course in abstract dialectics, a severe training in logic, theory of knowledge, and the beginning of metaphysics. At the end of this period he is returned to military, civil, and educational duties as a minor official : being given training in actual leadership in all suitable fields for fifteen years. If at the end of this period, i.e., at the age of fifty, he has shown himself in every activity, practical and theoretical, among the very best of his generation, the period of probation is over, and he is elected to the most important state offices : with adequate provision for sabbatical leave (to refresh his vision of the ideal realm) and eventual retirement.

It remains to bring out clearly one further feature which is characteristic of Plato's thinking, namely, its transcendentalism. The words used above in summarizing the account given of higher education might almost have been taken from the speeches attributed to Protagoras. For Protagoras, the great " humanist " and early founder of " pragmatism," also endeavours to turn out pupils who are patterns of the community virtues and have been trained in techniques which are at least successful in getting their practitioners elected to important offices.

In Protagoras' thinking, however, the empiricism is radical. There is no transcendental basis whatever. What the community thinks right, *is* right, and the pupil is taught to treat social objectivity as the only kind of objectivity to which man has access. The pupil learns to excite and soothe the many-headed beast by appropriate oratorical utterances, to study its ways of behaviour and accept its judgment as final. In the chaotic welter of motions which constitutes the only " reality " there is, the community will-to-believe is the sole authoritative court of appeal. Respectful study and artistic catering to that will-to-believe constitute the only safe pathway to success in life ; and the pupil is taught to govern himself accordingly, and believes this information and this training to be worth a large fee.[84]

To Plato, this seems entirely false. He endeavours to demonstrate its falsity on occasion, but doubtless realizes that he can only prove it false if he presupposes his own transcendentalism as true.[85] Be that as it may, his own view is that behind the flux of sensations and opinions there is a realm of intellectually consistent ideal patterns, in accordance with which God has constructed (out of chaotic materials) the physical world. He believes that, by following through the higher education which he provides, it is possible for men of great natural gifts to acquire insight into this ideal realm, and to construct, in co-operation with God (out of relatively chaotic human materials) some approximation to the pattern of an ideal social world. Insight into these ideals transcends sensation and opinion, but Plato hopes by having his community leaders trained to appreciate, understand, and incorporate these ideals in their own lives and in the life of the community, to make the dream (God's plan for humanity) come as nearly true as such a dream can. Behind biosocial impulses he glimpses an ideal reality, and his view is thus opposed to the view of Protagoras as " idealism " (in the transcendental sense) is opposed to " pragmatism " or " radical empiricism."

[1]*Rep.* 505e f., cf. 474b, *Laws* 640a f. [2]*Prtg.* 316c, 343a, *Ion* 530b, 531a, 536a f., *Rep.* 595b, 598d f., *Theaet.* 152 e, *Laws* 631d. [3]*Lach.* 179 f., *Prtg.* 320, 324d ff., *Meno* 93 ff., *Rep.* 521b f., *Laws* 694d. [4]Condensed from *Rep.* 412–414a. The character tests, as appears from the *Laws*, take place largely at the monthly festivals in military sports, and doubtless at the other festivals, in which competent adjudicators select the prize-winners, paying more attention to character than to technical proficiency (Cf. *Laws* 658 f., 764d f., 828cd, 829b f., 840b ; *Laws* 833d f. however seems to imply that technical proficiency (and not character) is the important thing).   The " young " men of thirty or so co-opted in the highest council of all (in the *Laws*), of which they constitute 50 per cent of the membership (Laws 951d f), are presumably picked from the ranks of the prize winners. [5]*Laws* 643e f., cf. *Gorg.* 491d, *Rep.* 590d f. Cf. also *Laws* 734e f., 817d f. [6]*Polit.* 294a ff., condensed. [7]Cf. *Charm.* 159b f., *Rep.* 375 f., 537d ff., *Polit.* 306 ff., *Laws* 964 ff. [8]Condensed from *Rep.* 475c–476d. The same argument is continued to p. 480. [9]*Rep.* 490ab, condensed. The passage expresses the essence of *Rep.* 484–490d. [10]*Rep.* 503b f., cf. 412d ff., *Laws* 734e f., 964 f. [11]*Rep.* 521e f. [12]*Phaedr.* 275c f., *Laws* 682a, 719b f., 817. [13]*Rep.* 595c, cf. 391a, *Phaedr.* 245a, 265b. [14]*Rep.* 604 ff. [14]*Phaedr.* 248cd, 250bc, 276a f. [15]*Rep.* 596c f., cf. 476 ff., 509e f. [17]*Rep.* 596 ff., 602c f. *Soph.* 266d f., *Phil.* 55c f. [18]*Rep.* 510ab. [19]*Rep.* 597b f., *Soph.* 266de.   Critics belive that Plato neglects the fact that that artists provide for higher, more spiritual needs. [20]*Ion* 534, *Meno* 99c f., *Apol.* 22b f., *Rep.* 484c, *Laws* 682a, 719b. [21]*Rep.* 509e f., 597e ff., 602c f. [22]*Ion* 534b f., *Apol.* 22bc, *Meno* 99c f., *Rep.* 602a, *Phaedr.* 245a, Laws 682a, 719b. [23]*Phaedr.* 275d, slightly condensed. Cf. *Prtg.* 329a. [24]*Phaedr.* 276. [25]*Phaedo* 247c. [26]*Laws* 653d f. [27]*Rep.* 571 f. [28]*Rep.* 461bc, *Laws* 790d, 836–841, cf. *Phaedr.* 244de. [29]*Tim.* 47d f., *Laws* 653d f., 672c., cf. 673e f. [30]*Tim.* 53a f., 69b, *Polit.* 273b f. [31]*Rep.* 422e f., 546 ff. [32]*Rep.* 527–531c, *Tim. passim.* As to models, cf. *Tim.* 40d. [33]*Rep.* 530b, " In astronomy, as in geometry, we should employ problems, and let the heavens alone if we would make the natural gift of reason to be of any real use." Cf. 531c, " The Pythagoreans are in error. They investigate the harmonies which are heard, but never attain to problems." Cf. 529c " Nothing sense-perceivable is matter of real knowledge." [34]*Rep.* 510b f. [35]*Rep.* 533, slightly condensed. [36]*Rep.* 523b f, *Phil.* 51. [37]*Rep.* 523c f. [38]*Phil.* 51c. Cf. also *Phaedo* 96d. [39]*Rep.* 518cd, 534cd. [40]Condensed from *Rep.* 523–524. [41]*Rep.* 524. Cf. also *Phaedo* 96d f., *Parm.* 129. [42]*Rep.* 524d–525a, condensed. Cf. *Theaet.* 185 f. [43]*Rep.* 525–526c, condensed. Cf. also *Laws* 747a–c, which brings out even more sharply the uses of number in assisting the trained leader to organize his community for greater efficiency in matters domestic, civil, and military. [44]*Rep.* 526c–527c, *Theaet,* 185de, *Laws* 817e. It is traditionally supposed to be on the authority of these passages that colleges still demand " first year mathematics " of all students—although it is not so much geometry as Plato knew it, as the analytic geometry invented by Descartes, which is used nowadays. [45]*Meno* 82, *Rep.* 528, cf. *Theaet.* 147d ff. [46]*Rep.* 527d, 529a–c. [47]*Rep.* 629d f., condensed. [48]*Rep.* 530d–531c. [49]*Rep.* 531c. Cf. *Supra*, 317 [50]*Rep.* 530e, 531c, 533d. [51]*Rep.* 536d, 537bc. That is to say, they are studied playfully (cf. *Laws* 819b f.), and by means of problems. [52]*Rep.* 476, 526b, *Laws* 747b. [53]*Phaedo* 96d–97b, condensed. [54]*Phaedo* 97b ff. The *Timaeus* provides, in general, the kind of answer which would have satisfied Socrates (or these youthful searchers for metaphysical explanation in the field of science). [55]*Rep.* 531d, 537c. For an example of this ideal astronomy, cf. the *Timaeus, passim.* For a brief statement of the different " fluxions " of a moving point, see *Laws* 894a, and for its explanation see E. B. England's note *ad loc*, and also Erich Frank : *Plato u.d.s–g. Pythagoreer*, pp. 369–371. Doubtless, the students will also be able to appreciate " cosmic music " or the " unheard music of the spheres " in such a purely ideal world. [56]*Rep.* 510c f., 533cd. This construction, which is the highest stage reached by such students, is regarded by the philosopher who has completed his work and seen the final vision, as " recreation for his leisure hours " (*Tim.* 59c). [57]*Laws* 811d f., cf. *Rep.* 340d ff. [58]*Laws* 739b f. [59]*Rep.* 519c. [60]*Rep.* 537d, cf. 539d ; *Tim.* 87b ff. [61]*Laws* 760 f. [62]*Laws* 843 f., highly condensed. Cf. 761d f. The cases of lesser importance are settled by the officers alone. More important cases require the consideration of the whole body of seventeen. [63]*Laws* 762s f., cf. 633 (for the Spartan parallel, which is both striking and deliberate). Cf. also

Rep. 416d f. [64]*Laws* 770, 813cd. [65]*Laws* 756a. [66]*Laws* 951d f., condensed. This is the "Nocturnal Council" described as "the anchor of the state." In 961a the visitors to foreign states who have proved themselves worthy, are also included. [67]*Rep.* 537d and 539de, condensed. Cf. *Laws* 967d f. [68]*Rep.* 538c, 539bc, condensed. Cf. also *Rep.* 498a f. and *Laws* 887c ff. Cf. also *Phil.* 15e. [69]*Rep.* 503c f. ; *Polit.* 306 ff. [70]*Rep.* 497d. [71]*Parm.* 130b f. is usually interpreted as ascribing a certain degree of originality to Socrates. But there can be no doubt that the philosophical exploitation of conceptual techniques as such originated in the Eleatic school, in the work of Parmenides himself and his polemical associate, Zeno. Scholars believe that the "torpifying" effect of the destructive part of Socrates' discussions was simply an application to ethical questions of the method which Zeno had invented as a weapon against the Pythagorean hypothesis of the identity of mathematics and physics. [72]*Rep.* 475c ff., cf. *Tim.* 49 ff., *Theaet.* 156 ff., 182 ff. [73]*Parm.* 129 f., 137b ff. For the "categories" cf. also *Theaet.* 185 f., *Soph.* 250 f. [74]*Soph.* 253d, condensed. Cf. *Phil.* 16c ff. [75]*Meno* 86d f., *Phaedo* 100. Cf. also *Rep.* 510, 533, *Parm.* 136 ff. [76]Cf. *Gorg.* 505e f., 509a. [77]Condensed from *Rep.* 509bc, 510b, 511b. [78]*Rep.* 539de. [79]*Laws* 764e f. [80]*Laws* 801c ff., 812e f. [81]*Rep.* 540ab, condensed. Cf. *Laws* 964b ff., cf. also 947. [82]*Laws* 755 ff. [83]*Rep.* 449a, 546a f. [84]*Prtg.* 328. [85]Cf. e.g., *Theaet.* 165e f., 179c. Cf. also *Rep.* 354b, 357a, 358c.

CHARTER VI

ASSOCIATION AND IMITATION

So far we have discussed Plato's Theory of Education in general outline, following the well-known grooves but stressing the transcendentalism which differentiates it from the rival " humanist " theory of Protagoras, as well as from the traditional Hellenic practice, and its highly extracurricular nature which differentiates it from almost all modern theory and practice except in the " progressive " or " new " movement associated with the name of John Dewey. But before we can discover in any final way precisely how much of Plato's theory is to be regarded as characteristically original and as distinguishing his suggestions not only from his own age but from our own present-day theories and practices, we shall have to carry through a number of investigations into particular problems which may seem at first sight unimportant, but will be found to have far reaching implications both for theory and for practice. The first of these is indicated by the title of the present chapter : " Association and Imitation."

To the modern educational psychologist, interested in establishing the main laws of the psychology of learning, *Association* is a word with which to conjure. It is usually believed that the chief types of association, namely (1) association by contiguity in place, (2) association by contiguity in time (3) association by similarity, and (4) association by contrast, whose tradition is established in modern thought by the work of David Hume and his successors,[1] go back to the father of psychology, Aristotle,[2] and even its grandfather, Plato.[3] But whatever the details of the tradition, *Association* is understood at the present day in a very definite sense, as one of the three fundamental " laws of learning."

The modern view is extremely simple. It is believed that learning proceeds by habit-formation, forging links or bonds of connection between A,B,C, . . . by processes strictly mechanical in character, processes of repetition, or the hammer-blows of *intensity*, *recency*, and *frequency*, as the textbooks have it. When a series of terms to be " learnt," A,B,C, . . . has been repeated a number of times, it is said that *A has become associated with B, B* with *C, C* with *D*, and so on. When we see *A*, we think of *B* ; when we see *B* we think of *C*, and so forth. Experimental evidence indicates that many further links or bonds of connection are formed, as between *A* and *C, A* and *D*, and indeed that the association works backwards as well. When we see a picture of Mutt, we think of Jeff ; and when we see a picture of Jeff, we think also of Mutt. The learning process is conceived on the analogy of a physical chain, and the chain of association is said to be no stronger than its weakest link. To " learn " anything whatever, you just keep hammering away at the weak links, strengthening them by *intensity, recency*, and, above all, by *frequency*, until the association becomes " stamped in " in the plastic nervous system, where the mechanism of the process resides.

The evidence for this extremely clear and simple view in modern educational psychology is experimental ; but its interpretation in the textbooks used in teacher-training is dogmatic and far removed from the caution usually exhibited by experimental scientists. Its " laws " and the pedagogic deductions made from them are formulated and driven home with a certitude[4] which would have left an experimentalist like Ebbinghaus gasping, and would have reduced a master of method like Aristotle or a dialectician like Plato to offering ironical congratulations. Before anyone brought up on this modern doctrine can hope to understand what a writer like Plato means by *association*, he will have to face and answer a few questions which will shake his naive conviction of certainty.

In the experimental work there are a good many points which do not fit into this dogmatic interpretation at all easily. The mental activity which selects these or those features of a situation and grasps their intelligible inter-implications in a single system ; the biosocial or other patterns into which we naturally group whatever we take an interest in ; the tendency to unify and systematize along aesthetic, ethical, economic, and logical lines ; the tendency to exclude actively from our attention everything which has no especial appeal to our interests and hopes, whether natural or acquired. Consideration of these and similar factors undoubtedly present in the learning situation make it look as though strictly mechanical association (in the modern sense) is an unwanted child, kept alive only by repeated doses of intensity, recency, and frequency, but lapsing, if left to itself, into a state of coma. Better dead—and buried !

When we have reached a point at which we can agree wholeheartedly with this conclusion, we can effect a transition to the Platonic point of view. In Greek medical practice it was usual to treat patients in the non-fee-paying class a little roughly : giving a pill or potion intended to affect, not the body as a whole, but a single part of it. Such violent local irritation might, or might not, prove effective ; but as contrasted with the kind of treatment which does not forget that the patient is not this or that local organ, but a man, a " whole " whose " unity " is to be respected, Plato entirely disapproves of it.[5] In precisely the same way, a " law of learning " which professes to deal, not with the pupil as a whole, but with this or that mechanical link or bond of connection, by drill-methods which may or may not be effective, would be regarded by Plato with extreme disfavour.

This means that, for Plato, *association* has never a mechanical, but always a personal significance. It affects the persons concerned as wholes, as unities whose unity is all-important. You do not educate a man by filling up his plastic nervous system with all kinds of artificial complexes, fixed ideas driven in by intensity, recency, and frequency. A man so trained would have bitten off more than he could chew and would suffer to the end of his days from chronic mental indigestion. A man is educated when he is master of himself ; when the self-initiated motion residing in his brain is in full control of everything taken into the system, whether of body or of mind.[6] Such a man is always master of his fate because he is the captain of his soul and body ; and Plato's education is always an education of free men for even greater freedom.[7]

Consider the different stages of education. The games of children in the community playground are spontaneous. " Tag," " Hide-and-seek," " Racing," " Ball-playing," and the rest are games which do not vary much from generation to generation, or even from century to century. But the point is, that children associate with one another naturally and spontaneously in such games. " From three to six years, the childish nature will require sports. Such children have certain natural modes of amusement which they find out for themselves when they meet."[8] It is also natural for them in such games to develop the childish beginnings of such virtues as courage, selfcontrol, friendly co-operation, respect for elders, and to accept a certain measure of direction from above, both positive and negative. In this way they learn to control tendencies toward " tantrums " and " self-will " and learn to behave as freeborn citizens should.[9]

So too in the sports schools from the ages of six to ten. Rhythmic dancing is both natural and spontaneous,[10] and so is the tendency of " boys to live with boys, and girls with girls."[11] Both sexes take naturally to throwing, hurling, and shooting missiles in sport, and to learning to ride the horse, and to take sides in mimic warfare. They thoroughly enjoy going to school and associating together, and receiving direction in acquiring skilled control over their own bodies.[12]

So too in the " music " schools from ten on. The youngsters take kindly to reading, writing (for the most part), and arithmetic, when taught without tears, by way of games. They take naturally to " speaking pieces " and to playing on the lyre as they accompany their own singing. Their association with one another and with their instructors is the natural relationship of freeborn citizens during the instructional period, and seems to them perfectly natural.[13]

So too with the community festivals, the community marches, processions, and chants. Association in such exercises, where the community is just one great family, is perfectly natural, and freeborn citizens feel no sense of compulsion or artificiality. It is sometimes supposed that the young are being drilled mechanically into acquiring community habits : especially when we read such passages as the following :

The legislator has to find out what belief will be of the greatest public advantage, and will then try to make the whole community utter the same word in their songs and tales and discourses all their life long. All our three choruses shall sing to the tender souls of children, reciting these noble thoughts whose sum is that the life which is by the gods deemed happiest is also the best. First the sacred choir of children will sing lustily the heaven-taught lay. Next the choir of young men will call upon Paean to testify to the truth of their words, and will pray him to be gracious to the youth and to turn their hearts. Thirdly the choir of men will sing. Finally, those too old to sing will tell stories, illustrating the same virtues, as with the voice of an oracle.[14]

But, as Plato understands the matter, there is no mechanical " conditioning " involved. A " habit " for Plato is not an artificial action-pattern drilled into an isolated section of the nervous system, whether the human individual wants it or not. It represents rather a freely chosen activity in which the whole person is interested : as children love to march, to dance, and to sing together. And as to the sentiments, they are not pious texts inculcated *de haut en bas*. They are perfectly natural and spontaneous. " The minds of our young disciples will be more likely to receive these words of ours than any others which we might address to them." Community religion is not something external, but is entirely natural.[15]

So too with membership in the army, with marriage, and with the other community institutions. The association of free citizens with one another in such institutions is not something forced and unnatural, splitting up the life of individuals into artificial fragments. The community sense integrates such activities into a unity, and the man feels most himself when he feels himself a citizen who "belongs," a full member of the civic group, in each and all of his activities :

> Our men and women are to have a common way of life : common education, common children ; and they are to watch over the citizens in common whether abiding in the city or going out to war ; they are to keep watch together and to hunt together—always and in all things, as far as they are able, to share in the same experiences. And in so doing they will do what is best, and will not violate, but preserve, the relations which are natural.[16]

Finally, in the special class which is trained for leadership, the youths selected are those whose natures take kindly to intellectual and philosophic problems. They too are educated without the slightest suggestion of compulsion,[17] and their association with one another is as natural as the association of the members of Plato's "Academy," known as "The Friends," or as the association at the present day of the members of fraternities and sororities, or (in later life) of the members of learned societies.

In all such cases, "association" affects individuals as individuals, as wholes, as irreducible units, members one of another ; and education by means of association takes place by a kind of merger of personalities, such as we see nowadays in the case of hero-worship and friendship. The interest and capacity for education must be there ; but it is stimulated into activity not by introducing some foreign body which sets up local irritation, but by partnership, co-operative activity which appeals to the pupil to engage his whole self in the pursuit of common aims. " It is only by the movement of the whole soul that the instrument of knowledge can be turned from the world of becoming to the world of being."[18]

Association for Plato thus means friendly companionship in a common activity. The companionship of fellow-workers in the arts, of fellow-pupils in the sport-schools and "music" schools, in the army, and in the dialectic class, illustrate what is meant.

Or we could illustrate associative companionship by referring to the relation between teacher and pupils, whether in the arts, the sport-schools and music-schools, or in the army and in the dialectic class. This academic pupil-teacher relation is what Plato has most commonly in mind when he discusses education ; and it coincides, in detail and in principle, with what is known as " Platonic love." For the companionship of educational association is more than spacetime juxtaposition at adjacent workbenches. An *esprit de corps* is developed as each pupil tries to improve his nature by participating in the broader and deeper experiences to which his teacher leads the way. The passionate idealism of hero-worship lends emotional drive to his efforts, and the enthusiastic inner glow which suffuses his whole nature makes him assimilate himself, as much as he can, to the leader whom he admires, becoming more and more like him in spirit.

And further : this enthusiastic association is more than a merely social, human togetherness. Just as two lovers feel that life is opening out before them with new and almost unimaginable sublimities, which transcend the merely empirical actualities of everyday spacetime association : so there is about the vast sea of learning, in which fellow-pupils are endeavouring to follow their leader, a magical quality suggesting transcendentally unfathomable depths of more than earthly resplendence and vitality :

They perceive beauty absolute, separate, simple, and everlasting, which without diminution or increase or any change is imparted to the ever-growing and ever-perishing beauties of all other things. The true order of going (or being led by another) is to begin from the beauties of earth and to mount upwards for the sake of that other beauty, using these as steps only : proceeding from one to two and to all fair forms, from fair forms to fair practices, from fair practices to fair notions, and to the notion of absolute essential beauty. If man had eyes to see that true beauty, beholding beauty in that communion with the eye of the mind, he would be enabled to bring forth the reality of true virtue and would become the friend of God and enter upon life immortal, so far as is granted to mortal man.[19]

That is to say, behind the arts teacher the pupil glimpses the Muses and their leader Apollo, and behind the pedagogic association there is always a fluttering of wings which indicates the presence of the spirit of Eros, guiding the pupils to the plain of Truth in that heaven beyond the heavens where live the transcendental forms of beauty, goodness, justice, and ideality itself.[20]

So much for the term *association* as used by Plato in his theory of education. Let us now turn to a term which at first sight looks

somewhat different : the term *imitation*. This is used about as
frequently by Plato as by modern writers upon educational
topics ; but with certain differences which are characteristic.

The modern educational writer is influenced by the recent
sociologist Tarde : whose work *Les Lois de l'imitation* has been
echoed respectfully even by those whose agreement with him seems
to be purely external. It has been observed that man has an
instinctive tendency to mimic or copy. If you go into a school,
you will find that many of the scholars mimic the mannerisms
of their teachers, and indeed copy the clothing, bearing, and
general behaviour of their elder companions, especially those who
are regarded as school leaders. In the same way, fashions are set
by a few leaders, whether in " Society " or in the " Movies,"
whose clothing, language, and behaviour awaken a tendency to
imitate and reproduce in one's own life. You can always tell a
teacher. You can always recognize the Oxford " accent," military
or nautical " bearing," and the evidence of other group influences.
And modern educational authorities insist upon the importance
of a school-teacher's clothing, language, and behaviour, both in
school and out of school, because of the educational significance
of the tendency of pupils to imitate. This means that, in the
association of teacher and pupil, the imitation, direct or indirect,
of the teacher by the pupil, is an educational factor whose value
can hardly be overemphasized.

That children are " copycats " can hardly be denied. They
mimic things or persons. Candidates for Major Bowes'
" Amateur Hour " sometimes mimicked, with surprising fidelity,
police sirens, assorted birds, and the various characteristic noises
heard on our city streets. In exactly the same spirit the ancient
Hellenic mimic would imitate

smiths and other artificers, oarsmen, boatswains and the like ; the
neighing of horses, the bellowing of bulls, the murmur of rivers and
roll of the ocean, thunder and the noise of wind and hail, the creaking
of wheels, and the sounds of flute, pipe, trumpet, etc. He barks like a
dog, bleats like a sheep, crows like a cock, etc., etc.[21]

In modern educational literature[22] it is taught that this
tendency to mimic is reinforced by the advantages which go
along with conformity to group usages and group standards.
Children seek the approval of their group, and so do what the
group regards with approval. The tendency to reproduce
manners and mannerisms characteristic of the family group,
while partly, perhaps, due to the instinctive tendency to mimic,

owes far more to the desire to be a regular member of the group, enjoying all the advantages which accompany group approval. In fact, in most groups, conformity is enforced by tangible rewards and punishments. It is hardly mimicry which makes recruits salute smartly and develop " soldierly bearing." It is rather the tangible rewards and punishments within the control of the drill sergeant and his fellows. It is hardly mimicry which is responsible for the bowed legs of the cavalry man, the rolling gait of the sailor, the top hats and short jackets worn by schoolboys at Eton, and the long hair and yellow stockings worn at Christ's Hospital. It is highly realistic environmental influences, partly social, but all definitely physical, which similarly account for polite behaviour at the race-course, the business banquet, and the court ball. And as to school children acquiring polite manners by directly mimicking their schoolteachers, it is as true today as in Plato's time that the co-operation of parents and attendants, using direct physical pressure, is of very great help :

> Teachers are enjoined to look to the child's manners even more than to his reading and music ; and the teachers do as they are desired. (Like the parents) they tell him that " this is right, that is wrong ; do this, and abstain from that." And if he obeys, well and good ; if not, he is straightened by threats and blows, like a piece of bent or warped wood. And when they have done with masters, the state again compels them—to live after the pattern of the community laws, and not after their own fancies ; and the transgressor is corrected.[23]

A pragmatist educational authority like John Dewey teaches that there is a direct place for imitation in the sense of reproducing the teacher's movements, when the teacher is showing how to handle tools in the most efficient way. The child learns by doing, but by doing as the teacher does, and finding that such " imitation of techniques " assists the child also to success in his efforts. It is highly probable that part of the work of " association " in Greek education is accounted for by a similar " imitation of techniques," the potter's child or apprentice directly imitating the skilled movements of the potter, in throwing the clay, hollowing out the vessel with his thumbs as the clay revolves before him on the wheel, etc.[24] So too the pupil of the lyrist, who learns to play note for note in unison with his master, presumably holds his lyre in the same way as his master, and imitates directly the way in which his master strikes the strings with the plectrum[25] ; and it is incredible that the patterns and rhythms of dancing are not acquired in the same sort of way, by direct imitation of the spacetime movements of the dancing instructor, coupled with an inner feeling of satisfaction in the gradual mastery over artistic results which tends to follow upon such imitation.

But imitation in this sense, while it doubtless has a wide scope in all the arts which involve skilled movements, is not the whole matter by any means. The modern educationist refers to the inner feeling of personal satisfaction in success. This is not an imitation, but a direct experience. However, idealistic authorities like H. H. Horne refer to a further form of imitation which is not external, a spacetime affair, but represents an attempt to project the self into an attitude like that of the instructor. The pupil does not merely attempt to reproduce the external, spacetime movements of his instructor, but tries to project himself into the same attitude of mind : to feel as his instructor feels, and to value as his instructor values. He tries, that is to say, to assimilate himself to his instructor as a person with a selfconsciousness : to merge his personality with the personality of the instructor and to be like him in thought, as well as in word and deed.[26] This is how the pupil becomes a musician, a dancer, a poet, or master in some other creative field : not merely a reproducer of external techniques, but a living, selfcontrolling artist in his own right.[27]

It is in this idealistic sense that Plato especially uses the term *imitation*. It shades rather easily into the term *assimilation*, a form of dramatic impersonation of which he also makes use. A human being who associates reverently with persons whose lives exhibit orderliness, system, and law, feels drawn by the nisus towards unity within him to assimilate himself to his associates.[28] Imitation of this sort is not external, the reproduction of a number of " techniques " or spacetime behaviour-patterns. It is internal, the forming of one's own self-determining character upon the self-determining character of another person, as in the case of religious worship, or of two lovers, or of a pupil imitating a teacher whom he admires. It is a merger of personality, taking place by a dramatic impersonation which becomes second nature. As we imitate ideals, we assimilate ourselves to them and participate in their ideal reality, becoming their living impersonation :

Evils can never pass away. Having no place among the gods in heaven, they hover around this earthly place and our mortal nature. Wherefore we ought to fly from earth to heaven, from mortality to immortality. And the manner of the flight is on this wise : we must assimilate ourselves to God, becoming, like Him, holy, just, and wise ;

growing like the divine pattern by reason of good deeds and leading a life answering to the pattern we are growing to resemble ; departing from the cunning of evil, so that the place of innocency will receive us after we have put on immortality.[29]

In the same way, as we pass through life, we project ourselves into our " other," viz. personalities which resemble our own and confirm us in developing into our full selves. We love and worship our own image, thus growing to resemble it more adequately : especially when it seems to have a basis which transcends everyday life and is " divine " :

> Every one chooses his love according to his character. This he makes his god and fashions and adorns as a sort of image which he is to fall down and worship. The followers of Zeus (wisdom) desire that their beloved should have a soul like Zeus ; they therefore seek out some one of a philosophical and imperial nature and do all they can to confirm the Zeus-nature in him, and themselves follow in the same way. As they gaze intensely upon their beloved, they become possessed of the Zeus-nature, and they receive their own character and disposition, so far as man can participate in God. The qualities of their god they attribute to the beloved and therefore love him all the more : wanting to make him as like as possible to their god, as together they walk in the god's ways.[30]

That is to say, in imitation, the person who imitates projects his personality into a new merger of selves, and takes on the character of that which he imitates : acquiring from the enhanced principle of selfmotion which thus comes to him all the capacities which the new principle is competent to initiate. The pupil, as Plato sees him, imitates, not the external techniques of the artist, but his spirit ; and having acquired the artistic spirit, he has acquired, along with it, all the artistic techniques in which it expresses its creative self. This is, however, not a matter of external observation, but an inner merger of the spirit, such as we realise only in personal experience. The enthusiastic reader of Homer acquires something of the Homeric spirit ; and presently we find him, not repeating the words of his master, but inspired from within to write new quasi-Homeric poetry.[31] So too Socrates inspires his followers to be, not little replicas of Socrates, but themselves : an Aristippus, a Euclid, a Plato : creating new schools of thought arising out of their spiritual merger with the great teacher.[32]

> On the essence of my philosophy a good deal has been written : by pupils of mine, by pupils of other teachers, and by some who think they have found out my secret for themselves. Of all such I say

this : It does not matter who they are or what they write—and this applies to the future quite as much as to the past—the very attempt to reduce my teaching to written words demonstrates complete and utter misunderstanding. For the thing simply cannot be done. I have never attempted it myself, and never shall ; for it is not like other things that men study. In these other fields there is a content which can be set down in words, and so passed on from teacher to pupil. But the spirit of philosophy is not like this. It cannot be reduced to any verbal formula. When teacher and pupils of philosophy associate intimately in their researches, so that their life is one life : in this continuous merger of personality, something happens. As a leaping flame shoots sparks which kindle to an inner glow, the philosophic spirit by spontaneous combustion comes to birth within the soul and develops and grows by self-nurture.[33]

That is to say, for Plato such terms as *imitation, assimilation, impersonation,* and *inspiration* converge in their wider fringe of meaning, and tend to coincide. The focal point from which they all emerge like radii of the same circle is the central unity of the person, with its principle of selfmotion controlling both body and mind. Just as the mathematical unit cannot possibly be fractioned in such a way as to destroy the fundamental concept of unity,[34] so the unifying power of mind and the self is of the essence of mental life : its most fundamental law, which can never be set aside or fractioned into something devoid of unity.

The soul which has never seen the truth will not pass into the human form. The condition of the soul's passing into the form of man is that it shall have beheld true being. For a man must have intelligence of universals and be able to proceed from the many particulars of sense to a unified conception of reason : beholding in the earthly copies an image of the ideal realities, justice, temperance, and the higher ideas.[35]

Imitation is thus always a form of self-projection, in which the person merges his self with the self of another person, or at least takes on the colouring of some action or passion. Hence the immense importance of the environment, especially the social environment, for educational purposes. Surround a growing youth with images of good, with persons, actions, and passions which encourage and strengthen the native idealism of the soul. By merging his self with these, he will tend to grow like them, becoming stronger and stronger in courage, self-control, justice, and the other virtues which make a man a good and useful member of the human community. Surround him with images of evil, with forms of vice in dance, song, and action, and you will find that, if he projects his self into these, " they will have the same effect as when a man associates with bad characters. He who takes pleasure in them will surely become like those in whom he takes pleasure."[36] He will become more and more blind to the ideal realm which is the source of all human power and value :

Those who know not wisdom and virtue go down and up only as far as the mean, never passing into the true upper world. Thither they neither look, nor do they ever find their way ; neither are they truly filled with true being. Like cattle, with their eyes always looking down and their heads stooping to the earth, they fatten and feed and breed, and in their excessive passion for these delights they kick and butt at one another with horns and hoofs of iron. They fill themselves with that which is not substantial, and the part of themselves which they fill is also devoid of substance.[37]

This imitative self-projection is distinguished by Plato from the copying of techniques by external observation in the handicraft arts, and is alone dignified by the name of " education."[38] The teacher stimulates its development in the pupil, not only by himself illustrating the character or action which is to be imitated, but by direct appeals in the form of admonition and advice, and also by the Socratic method of " refutation " which convinces the pupil that he is in a state of ignorance, and must make every effort of himself to escape from his prejudices.[39]

Gymnastic, for instance, is not to be regarded as an external affair, a matter of going through a course of specialized physical jerks in order to develop this or that muscle. The pupil projects himself into the gymnastic spirit, and so develops his nature as a whole on its spirited side, thus becoming courageous on every detailed occasion which calls for this virtue :

Gymnastic is not really designed for the training of the body. The exercises and toils which the youth undergoes are intended to stimulate the spirited element of his nature. It is not a question of merely increasing physical strength. Common athletes use exercise and regimen to develop their muscles. Our youth uses them to develop courage.[40]

In fact, such forms of gymnastic exercise as are approved for citizens of the *Republic* and *Laws* are designed specifically to develop military spirit : that is to say, courage tempered by disciplined selfcontrol. The war-dances, military sports and field-days prescribed for all citizens have this as their chief objective ; the idea being that, where the spirit is present, the appropriate detailed activities will readily be forthcoming—whereas, if the spirit is absent, the utmost attention to technical details will be utterly futile.[41]

Where gymnastic exercises and diet coincide with the regimen which confers and preserves health and good looks, the arts of the kitchen and beauty parlour, which attend only to details and imitate only external appearances, are discarded in favour of a way of living which produces health and good looks from the inside, as its consequences. The student who projects himself into a sound way of living acquires, not merely the appearance, but the reality of these consequences, growing from the inside outwards and so participating in the vitality of the controlling selfmotion :

Cookery is a deceiving art which assumes the appearance of medicine. Tiring similarly assumes the appearance of gymnastic. It is a knavish, false, ignoble, illiberal art, working deceitfully by the help of lines and colours and enamels and draperies, and so makes men affect a spurious beauty, to the neglect of the true beauty which is given by gymnastic.[42]

Choric dancing, which is partly treated under the head of gymnastic and partly under the head of music, is almost identified with education for citizenship.[43] It is treated in the *Laws* as a form of community association in rhythmic control of animal motility which " imitates character," and thus educates those who project themselves into the dispositions and activities which are dramatically reproduced. In fact, almost all the activities which come under the head of gymnastic—representative dancing, ceremonial marching, sports of all sorts, and the war-game practised at manœuvres—are a sort of make-believe, in which the pupils assume in play

those characters which are suitable to their future profession as citizens and guardians—courage, temperance, holiness, freedom, and the like. From such imaginative self-projection they come to be what they imitate. For make-believe characterizations, beginning in early youth and continuing far into life, at length grow into habits and become a second nature, affecting body, voice, and mind.[44]

That is to say, what makes gymnastic *educative*, is not the spacetime motions of the limbs and muscles and the acquisition of physical strength, but rather the spirit in which the pupil imagines himself as a good citizen, a loyal comrade, a gallant soldier who throws all he has within him into the defence of his community, and so grows from within into what he accepts as his ideal :

We are not speaking of vocational training, but of that education in virtue from youth upwards, which makes a man eagerly pursue the ideal perfection of citzenship, and so *teach himself* how rightly to rule and how to obey. This is the only education which, upon our view, deserves the name. That other sort of training which aims at the acquisition of wealth or bodily strength or mere cleverness is illiberal, unworthy to be called *education* at all.[45]

If we pass to consider " music " as a medium of education, Plato's position becomes even clearer. The world of literature and art is emphatically *not* the actual spacetime world, but an imaginary realm in which child, adolescent, and adult alike " charm themselves " by artistic make-believe into dreaming the selfsame dream, the dream of a perfect civic life under the guidance of divinely inspired wisdom, and so make their dream-citizenship come true. They are *dramatis personae* in a community play which seeks to reproduce upon the human stage God's plan for humanity, and the whole of the literature and art authorized to educate them for this performance is settled upon the best and surest foundations, namely upon the ideal realm revealed in the Platonic *Dialogues:*[46]

We too, according to our ability, are authors, and our tragedy is the best and noblest ; for our whole state is an imitation of the best and noblest life, which we affirm to be indeed the very truth of tragedy. We are authors in the noblest of dramas which true law alone can perfect, as our hope is.[47]

Every man and boy, both sexes, and the whole city, must never cease charming themselves with these strains : so that the whole community utters one and the same word in song, dance, and story, all their life long, varying the details so as to take away the effect of sameness, in order that the singers may never weary of their hymns.[48]

So far we have considered gymnastic and music, which educate for citizenship by training the imagination in a regulated make-believe which develops the average citizen into a cultured " puppet," a refined and reliable follower of the divinely-inspired government. That such education for citizenship takes place almost wholly by appealing to and developing a *dramatis persona*, at first transient and imaginary, but eventually permanent and a genuine second nature : a centre of selfmotion competent to govern and direct the man in all his thoughts, words, and works, is clear to the Plato student :

Everyone had best be ruled by divine wisdom dwelling within him ; or (if this is impossible) by an external authority, in order that all may be, under the same government, friends and equals. This is the intention of law, the ally of the whole city ; and is seen also in the authority we exercise over children : refusing to let them go free until we have established in them a principle analogous to the constitution of a state and have set up in their hearts a ruler and guardian like the ruler and guardian of our ideal state.   When this is done, they may go their ways.[49]

We now pass from gymnastic and music, which train, by imaginative self-projection into desirable characters, for a life of followership, and consider the higher or intellectual education which trains for a life of leadership. What place, if any, is there for " imitation " or imaginative self-projection, in this kind of education ?

At first sight, it might seem that there is no place for " imitation " in this kind of life. Is not imagination, it will be asked, distinct from reason ?   Is it not sub-rational, vital, if you like, but to be trained by rhythmic suggestions and other definitely non-rational appeals to the feelings ? And is not imitation essentially imaginative, essentially, that is to say, non-rational ?   All-important, perhaps, in developing self-chosen character -but is not higher education an affair of something distinct from and superior to character, namely, reason ?   Are not the virtues of citizenship *habits*—habits of will and personality acquired, like bodily qualities, by exercise until they become second nature— whereas intelligence is essentially a permanent and original capacity, the eye of the soul which can be obscured or set free to see, but cannot be put into the mind by any pedagogic devices whatsoever ?   Reason feeds, not upon spacetime images devoid of substance, but upon the reality of the transcendental ideas.[50] How can there, then, in the life of reason, be any place for " imitation " as a method of self-education ?

This question raises a difficult problem, a problem which derives its significance from the technique of dichotomizing experience into two factors (1) sensuous imagination which is human, all-too-human, and (2) purely rational conception which is perhaps more-than-human, and contrasting these so sharply that they seem to have nothing in common. If this technique is accepted uncritically, and we asume that there *are* (or can be) beings purely rational, raised above sensation, imagination, and feeling, and devoting themselves to unalloyed contemplation of the ideal realm and its principle of absolute ideality, there is only one possible consequence for the theory of education : Such beings are already in possession of absolute knowledge, and stand in no need of any sort of " education."   They are already at the end of the pedagogic rainbow, in full enjoyment of the pot of fairy gold. They stand altogether outside of and above humanity as we know it, and are as gods, knowing both good and evil, and having no need whatever to *educate* themselves, to prepare themselves to advance one rung higher on the ladder of wisdom by projecting themselves there in imagination. Already on the topmost rung, they transcend imitation, assimilation, imaginative impersonation of the ideal ; and such activities have no place whatever in their lives.

But this technique is not accepted uncritically. Plato is well aware of the traps it contains for the unwary reasoner,[51] and indeed subjects them to severe criticism himself :

> The knowledge we human beings have answers to the truth which we possess. It is human and relative to humanity. But the absolute ideas (of the beautiful in itself, of the good in itself, etc.) are beyond the truth which we possess, and thus are unknown to us. Absolute knowledge (if there is such a thing) must be far more exact than human knowledge ; and, if any one possesses it, that possessor will most likely be God. These absolute ideas are not valid in relation to human things ; nor are human things valid in relation to them ; the relations of each are limited to their respective spheres ; and the spheres of (1) human knowledge and (2) transcendental or absolute knowledge are distinct. These are only a few of the difficulties in which we become involved if we try to define the ideas generally without adequate dialectical training.[52]

In a word, Plato's leadership class consists of beings who are, and remain, human. They do not begin to rule as governors of the ideal community until they reach the age of fifty ; and from the age of twenty, when they are first separated from the citizenship class in whose " imitative " education they have fully participated, to the age of fifty, they receive a kind of education which, while preparing them for leadership, does not raise them beyond the highest rungs attainable by humanity. The starting-point of this higher education is reached by processes of imitative self-projection; and while it is true that the higher education proceeds with the help of the sciences rather than of the arts, it is still true that it is the imaginative selfconsciousness which is educated and is rendered at each stage more capable of taking up the final task of governing the community.

Selected in the first place from a group which has acquired some twilight awareness of the beauty of reason, but is incapable of attaining to any clear intellectual vision of what this involves,[53] the members of the leadership class proceed to imagine themselves as dedicated to the discovery of truth. This use of imagination

enables them to assimilate themselves to the ideal of the philosopher :

> They love knowledge of a sort which shows them the eternal nature
> not varying from generation and corruption and love all true being ;
> and they will never intentionally receive into their minds falsehood, and
> they will love the truth, desiring all truth.   Their desires setting strongly
> in this one direction will be weaker in others : so that, being absorbed
> in the pursuit of truth, they will hardly feel bodily pleasures.   They
> will be temperate, uncovetous, generous, and altogether manly.   As
> spectators of all time and all existence, they will be above all little-
> nesses of spirit and will be just and gentle, devoted to study and
> participation in being.[54]

The studies which assist them in confirming their growing
idealism are the mathematical disciplines of arithmetic, geometry,
physics, etc., and finally dialectic or ultimate philosophy.
But a certain training of the imagination is necessary
throughout.   They have to become conscious that they are
studying mathematics, *not* in order to make themselves mathematicians, but in order to familiarize themselves with abstract
ideas and techniques, and so to withdraw from unthinking
confidence in the world of the senses and emotions and to acquire
critical trust in the concepts with which the dialectician operates
in the realm of reason.   Studied in this spirit, the mathematical
sciences carry the pupils a step further than students of the arts
have gone ; but these sciences themselves

> only dream about being and never behold its waking reality.
> Conventionally termed " sciences," they ought to be given some other
> name—implying greater clearness than " opinion " but less clearness
> than " science."   They are employed by the dialectician as handmaids
> and helpers in the work of turning the soul from the outlandish slough
> of the senses and opinion towards contemplation of the realm of ideas.[55]

The second step is taken when the student sets himself in
imagination the ideal of studying these sciences not separately
but together, in order to " discover the natural relationship of
them to one another and to true being."   This step he can take
only after he has devoted some time in his twenties to studying them
separately.   To mount this rung of the ladder of wisdom takes him
till about thirty, when he begins to give evidence that he is
" able to surrender the sight and the other senses, and in company with truth to attain, as far as a human being can, absolute
wisdom."[56]

In the following five years of dialectical study, the value of the imaginative development of character is seen in the steadiness and orderliness with which the student devotes himself to a pursuit which in less well-prepared characters might well become barren logic-chopping, contradicting only for the sake of amusement. Plato's thirty-year old dialecticians, however, have learnt to regard themselves as " serious students," and this imaginative way of regarding themselves helps them to become something more than " eristics " who argue for victory or merely for amusement : namely, genuine philosophers.[57]

When these very human and far from perfect students are then sent out into practical life, setting themselves for fifteen years to distinguish themselves in every office which men of their age can hold, they imagine themselves in the character of men of action. During this period there are ample opportunities of trying " whether, when drawn this way and that by temptation, they will stand firm or flinch." · That is to say, there will be opportunities of testing whether education by means of imaginative projection which prepares their selfconsciousness for positions of rule has merely furnished them with daydream imagery of greatness, or has succeeded in developing an entirely firm and trustworthy character.[58]

Finally, those whose powers of imagining themselves as always capable of self-advancement have kept them till the age of fifty always looking one step higher and working steadily upwards, are selected to be philosopher-kings, governors of the state and chief leaders of the citizens. Their position is surrounded with " public memorials and sacrifices and honours " which appeal to the imagination of the other citizens and doubtless also to their own. But what especially attracts their trained imagination, is the ideal of public service. All their lives they have been educated to fill just this position, and it has been held by themselves as well as by their fellow-citizens before their eyes ; so that they govern " not as though they were performing some heroic action, but simply as a matter of duty."[59]

Thus we realize that education in Plato's *Dialogues*, from beginning to end—from its beginning in music and gymnastic to its end in philosophy and administration—involves *imitation* in the sense of imaginative self-projection into the next highest rung of the ladder of advancement, and selfconscious assimilation to the duties and powers of the position thus imaginatively envisaged. It is not an external matter, the copying of spacetime techniques, but rather the inner development of the whole soul by merging it with the higher personality set before the eye of the soul as the next goal of achievement.

[1]See e.g. Hume : *Enquiry*, Sect. III *ad fin.* (Rand : *Modern Classical Philosophers* pp. 312–313) Actually, the process is fairly well described before Hume. See Hobbes' *Leviathan.* [2]Cf. the article on " Association of Ideas " in *Ency. Brit.* (14th Ed.), Vol. 2, p. 563. [3]*Phaedr.* 73c f. ; cf. *Theaet.* 198d ; *Phil.* 38e f. [4]The especial reference is to the well-known and highly authoritative textbooks of Professor E. L. Thorndike. See especially the second volume of his *Educational Psychology*, namely, the volume entitled *Psychology of Learning*, and read chapters I and IX. [5]*Charm.* 156 f., *Tim.* 88 f., *Laws* 720, 857d f.   The Greek language does not say " my finger hurts, or my head aches, " but " *I* am pained—in respect of my finger, or my head " (*Rep.* 462cd). [6]*Phaedr.* 245d, *Laws* 895 ff., cf. *Tim.* 88e. [7]Cf. *Rep.* 395b. [8]*Laws* 793e f., cf. 797b f. [9]*Laws* 793e–794a. [10]*Laws* 654a, 672b f. This tendency toward self-directed and controlled orderly motion is the origin, not only of dancing, but also of gymnastic and music. [11]*Laws* 794cd. [12]*Laws* 643a f., 794d., cf. *Rep.* 466e f. [13]Cf. *Lysis* 207d ff. [14]*Laws* 664, condensed. [15]*Laws* 664bc. Cf. also *Laws* 885b, 886a ff. [16]*Rep.* 466c, slightly condensed. Cf. *Laws* 739c f., 942b f. [17]*Rep.* 536d f. [18]*Rep.* 518c. Cf. also *Theaet.* 150b ff., and the many passages throughout the *Dialogues* which indicate that it is by the association of two or more interlocutors that truth is found.   There is an effect as of dialogue in the thought of a single individual, suggested by describing it as " the conversation of the soul with itself," and Socrates, in giving his own conclusions, takes both sides in such a " conversation." (Cf. *Gorg.* 505d f., 507a, *Theaet.* 187a, 190, *Soph.* 263e f.). [19]Condensed from *Symp.* 211 f. I understand by " life immortal " in this passage the life of the immortals, i.e., the life of holiness, justice, temperance, and wisdom : in a word, the life of idealism. Cf. R. C. Lodge : *Plato's Theory of Ethics*, 1928, Ch. XVI. [20]Cf. *Symp.* 202d f., *Phaedr.* 252b f., cf. 247c f., *Laws* 653d, 654a, 665a, 672c. [21]*Rep.* 396a, 397a, slightly condensed. [22]See, e.g., John Dewey : *Democracy and Education*, 1918, Ch. XII ; R. C. Lodge : *Philosophy of Education*, 1937, Ch. XV. [23]Condensed from *Prtg.* 325d f. The " blows " in the original are administered by parents. Cf. *Laws* 808e. [24]*Rep.* 466e f., cf. 421de. [25]*Lysis* 209b, *Laws* 794e. [26]Cf. H. H. Horne : *Philosophy of Education*, 1930, pp. 175–188, and R. C. Lodge : *Op. Cit.*, pp. 237–242. [27]Cf. *Rep.* 590e f. Cf. T. Percy Nunn : " Our proper aim is to make our pupils feel what it is like to be inside the skin of the man of science, looking out through his eyes, using his tools, experiencing his sense of joyous adventure." (*The New Teaching.* p. 160, condensed.) [28]Cf. *Rep.* 500bc. [29]Freely paraphrased and condensed from *Theaet.* 176 f. Cf. also *Phaedr.* 246c f. [30]Condensed from *Phaedr.* 252d f. Cf. also *Symp.* 209, which relates this sort of experience definitely to education. [31]*Ion* 533d f. [32]Cf. *Theaet.* 150c f., *Apol.* 23b, 33a. 245c f. [33]*Epist.* 341b f., freely translated. Cf. *Phaedr.* 276b f., *Laws* 968d f. [34]*Rep.* 525a, e, cf. *Phil.* 14c ff., *Soph.* 251bc. [35]Condensed from *Phaedr.* 249c f. Cf. also *Rep.* 475d ff. " Self-motion is the very idea and essence of the soul " (*Phaedr.* 245e.). [36]*Laws* 655d f., condensed. Cf. *Theaet.* 176 f., *Gorg.* 511a, *Rep.* 409, etc. [37]*Rep.* 586ab. [38]*Soph.* 229d f., cf. *Rep.* 590c, *Laws* 643d f. [39]*Theaet.* 150b f., *Soph.* 230. Cf. *Phaedr.* 276e f., *Laws* 648b. [40]Condensed from *Rep.* 410. [41]*Laws* 813, 830e, 832, 942 f., cf. *Rep.* 423d f. [42]Condensed from *Gorg.* 465ab. Cf. also *Tim.* 88b f., *Laws* 720, 857d f. [43]*Laws* 653 f. [44]Paraphrased from *Rep.* 395c. Cf. *Laws* 643, 653e f., 655d f., 657d f., 664e f., 672b f., 830 f. [45]Condensed from *Laws* 643d f. Cf. *Rep.* 590c f., *Soph.* 229 f. [46]*Laws* 811b f. Cf. P. E. More : *Platonism.* [47]*Laws* 817, condensed ; cf. *Rep.* 394c ff. [48]*Laws* 664a, 665c, condensed. [49]*Rep.* 590d f., condensed. [50]*Rep.* 518b f., cf. 475c ff., *Phaedr.* 246c ff. [51]*Gorg.* 482c f., 487ab, cf. *Rep.* 345c f., 360d f. [52]*Parm.* 134 f., condensed and slightly paraphrased. [53]*Rep.* 475 ff. Cf. *Laws* 964 ff. [54]Condensed from *Rep.* 485 ff. [55]Condensed (and slightly paraphrased) from *Rep.* 533. [56]*Rep.* 537b f., cf. 533a. [57]*Rep.* 537d ff. [58]*Rep.* 539d f. [59]*Rep.* 540a f., cf. 520d f., *Laws* 947.

IMAGINATIVE SELF-PROJECTION AND EDUCATION

In Plato's theory of education, we note an ever-present appeal, not merely to " play," but to the " imagination." The carpenter's son, playing with his little hammer and saw in imitation of his associates, *imagines* himself at each stage of the game a more skilful carpenter. And eventually he grows into what he has *imagined* himself as being. The soldier's son, playing with his light shield and javelin in association with his schoolfellows under the guidance of a professional, *imagines* himself a master of his weapons. Eventually he becomes what he has imagined himself as being. The selected understudy, co-opted into the nocturnal council by a real magistrate, *imagines* himself a bigger and better executive ; and what his 'prentice judgment has within it to be, he eventually becomes.

Imaginative self-projection into this or that status is, in fact, an almost universal method of education in the *Dialogues*. Yet if we stop and look at it we find that it looks like—magic. It resembles the empty magic with which the artist pictures all things in heaven and earth : by his trick of holding the mirror up to nature. A word-wizard with little Latin and less Greek can fill the stage for us with imaginary intellectuals and men of action, lords and ladies, priests and peasants, life and death, and the beyond. The simple-minded revere him as a great educator ; yet what he sets before us is—pure illusion : the airy nothing of a dream.[1]

That each of us has his dream : picturing himself as this or that—is certain. That Platonic *personae*, from Protagoras to Socrates and the Athenian Stranger, naturally appeal to this imaginative tendency : setting before the interlocutor this or that protreptic and persuasive picture, so as to induce the interlocutor to accept the picture and dream the dream set before him—is also certain. That Plato's education for citizenship systematically and deliberately surrounds the growing neophytes with sights and sounds, with art and literature, with actions and persons, all calculated to induce in the educands one and the same dream : the dream of good citizenship—is equally beyond dispute.

Yet there is a problem involved. When Homer waves his magic wand, the pictures are attractive, dreadfully attractive. Socrates himself feels their power.[2] Yet Homer is mercilessly excluded from the ideal republic and the model city. He is no true educator. When Socrates or the Athenian Stranger uses precisely the same appeal to the imagination, it is quite all right. It is adopted as the official method of educating for citizenship. Why is it right for the one, and wrong for the other ? What is it that distinguishes Plato from Homer ?

From the modern standpoint, the problem becomes, if anything, even more accentuated. Our present-day educationists look askance at all forms of *reverie*. Imagination is easy, simple, and it may accomplish nothing : absolutely nothing. To picture oneself as this or that : as prize-winner, as good citizen, leader of the community, or what not—is not enough. It takes years and years to educate ; and those years must not be spent in mere picturings, however attractive. The modern educationist accordingly says very little about the imagination : except to warn us against encouraging daydreaming. We learn by *doing*, not by playing with images : whether the images are induced by book-reading or by attendance at our picture-palaces. It is not among our movie-habitués that we look for the men and women who do great things in our modern world.[3] Perhaps not even among our Plato students—unless they do something more than enjoy the images. What is this something more ?

What we are told in the *Laws* might almost have been written by a Piaget or a Pareto or some equally modern-minded sociologist. All animals have an original tendency toward action : toward doing something, no matter what. Their animal nature expresses itself by flinging its fore-limbs about, by kicking spasmodically with its feet, by uttering cries with its voice, and so on. We see this especially with babies. With human, however, as distinct from other animals, these motion-tendencies become humanly patterned. We observe a blind but persistent groping toward rhythms, ordered recurrences of motion which have a certain method in them. As in the play-tendencies of young children, they are not satisfied until they have worked their way toward the acceptance of certain rules and principles. Thus arise the games of children, the dances, the songs-and-dances : at first spontaneous, and later, as the children become more socialized, woven more fully into a single group-life pattern.

So arise what are called " unwritten customs " : folk-ways,

including folk-dancing, folk-singing, folk-language, folk-mentality. Eventually, under the influence of an artist like Homer or a sophist like Protagoras, we have a national literature, a national poetry, and a variety of theories which profess to account for this national culture. One and all, however, from the simplest folk-usages of peasants to the most pretentious of the poems and theories discussed in the home of the millionaire Callias, are projections and outgrowths of the original action-tendencies which characterize the human animal. Their basis is nonlogical.

That is to say : the airy flights of a Homer's fancy, no less than the temple-rituals based thereon, and the sociological theories propounded by a Protagoras—are merely clever games. They are ways in which the human puppet satisfies his original motility. Human poetry is a game played with images. Human religion is a game played with dancings, posturings. Human sociology is a game played with words, words, words. Throughout, the action-tendency and its satisfaction are primary. All the rest : the poetry, the religion, the culture, the theoretical elaborations : are secondary—make-believe from end to end. Each new poet, prophet, and sophist, merely feels his way downstream : dreaming the age-old racial dream ; broadening and deepening the folk-ways of his folk-world.[4]

That is why Plato rejects them ; for he has, as he believes, something more to offer : something which is not merely imaginary, make-believe, non-logical. What is this something more ? It is his vision of the " Ideas " : the transcendental patterns followed by the Divine Artist in creating, out of relatively chaotic material, the space-time world in which we live and move and have our physical being.

The Ideas are in no sense arbitrary, imaginary, or merely human. They are strictly objective. Objective, not in a merely biosocial sense : like the simple patterns followed by a Homer in depicting the mythical schemings, quarrellings, and relaxations of those all-too-human *personae*, his Olympian gods and goddesses. Not in a merely physical sense : like the hypotheses accepted by Pythagorean scientists without question ; make-believe assumptions found useful in playing their little game of consequences and verifications—whose mind-made constructions sometimes seem to apply to the phenomena of our world, but are entirely devoid of ultimate foundation.

The Ideas are not make-believe at all. They are ideally actual, really, metaphysically, there.[5] It is unconscious parti-

cipation in their reality which lends to the speculations of a
Homer, a Protagoras, or a Pythagoras, what elements of value
those speculations at times (not without divine influence) chance
to have. But even at that, those speculations are just dream-
stuff. The vision of the Ideas is the waking reality.

What Plato has to offer is education : education in a new sense,
a sense not even glimpsed by the folk-leaders. For human beings
it is vital that they should awaken from their dreamings. They
should learn to see clearly and distinctly the structural patternings of a world which utterly transcends their biosocial imaginings. Once enlightened by this vision, they will be able to make
over their social living, their science, their art, their religion. It
is high time that these should be something more than the
reachings out after superficial satisfactions : blind stretchings of
our human pseudopodia into the void. It is time to work together
in bringing to fruition God's plan for humanity : the maximal
realization of our value-potentialities.

The outlines of this plan Plato sets before us in his *Republic*.
The educational steps by which we may climb to a point at which
the ideal vision may itself come to a point within us, are set forth
in the same *Dialogue*. In writing what he has written, Plato is
himself appealing to our imaginations. He is using words, manipulating images, suggesting symbolically the possibility of a
vision. But the vision itself is something that words, even Plato's
words, cannot give. It is something more than the imagination,
even when stimulated to the utmost, can quite realize. Platonic
education carries us only as far as the threshold.

What Plato does, that Homer and Protagoras (and their modern
equivalents) do not, is to tell us of the vision that awaits the
seeker : to show us the pathway that may be followed by the
pilgrim ; to stimulate us in all manner of ways to take the first
step, the second step, and to proceed on our forward way. Beyond
that, no system of education which starts from scratch, appealing
to us in ways that ordinary, biosocial humanity can conceive in its
imagination, can go. It is only those who respond to the appeal,
who take the steps and follow the path, who can hope to arrive.
It is they who become friends of Ideas ; who, having received
enlightenment, co-operate forever after in living after the fashion
of the ideal pattern : descending into the cave, manipulating the
images in quasi-Platonic ways, and assisting their fellows, in their
turn, to achieve transcendental freedom.[6]

¹*Rep*. 596c f.   ²*Rep*. 595c, 607c ; cf. 391a.   ³Cf. *Rep*. 475c ff.   ⁴*Laws* 653 ff.   For

Piaget's views, especially in connection with children's games, cf. his *The Moral Judgment of The Child*, 1932. For Pareto's views, see his *Trattato di Sociologia generale* (E.T. *Mind and Society*).   ⁵This is the traditional interpretation.   Natorp (*Platos Ideenlehre*) and J. A. Stewart (*Plato's Doctrine of Ideas*) interpret them, not metaphysically but methodologically.   Both interpretations rest their case upon a meticulously complete study of the evidence of the *Dialogues*.   ⁶Cf. *Rep.* 533 f ; *Epist.* 341c f.   Cf. also J. Stenzel : *Platon der Erzieher*, 1928, pp. 310 ff.

CHAPTER VII

TEACHERS AND TEACHING

If we inquire " Who does the teaching in the ideal republic and the model city ? " we discover, somewhat to our surprise, that we have raised a problem to which the answer is far from easy. If we go to the literature, we find without difficulty authoritative information. German scholarship assures us, almost with one voice, that in the ideal republic there are three *Stände* : *Nährstand, Wehrstand, und Lehrstand.* So at least the highly authoritative Windelband[1] and so also the recognized dean of classical scholars, the great Wilamowitz himself.[2] But when we try to make clear to ourselves just what this means, we come upon unsuspected difficulties.

The *Nährstand* is easily enough identified. It is constituted by the farmer class—and presumably also the artisans who build the farm-houses and other homes with their ploughs, utensils, and other furnishings, and the business men who market the farm-products and make possible the exchange of goods and services so necessary in any but the most primitive of communities. Taken all together these constitute by far the largest group in the community. They are not exactly citizens. That is to say, they do not attend meetings and vote upon policies and elect executive magistrates ; and most of the business men are definitely *metics*, that is to say, aliens operating upon a limited residence-permit. All hand-workers similarly are excluded from the class of free self-determining citizens. No artisan is permitted to hold a city lot, and no lot-holder is permitted to practice any handicraft. Everyone connected with the detailed work of providing the community with food and the material side of life generally thus belongs to this immensely large, non-civic class.[3]

The *Wehrstand* is also easily identified. It corresponds in principle to the " silver " class of auxiliary guardians in the *Republic*, whose duties are primarily of a military nature. These " auxiliaries " are undoubtedly of the freeborn citizen class who elect their executive officers in a number of cases and grow gradually into exercising all the functions of citizenship. They exercise, however, a number of functions quite distinct from defence, so that the name *Wehrstand* is only partially correct as an indication of what they do. In the ideal republic they are said to be " not less than a thousand " in number. In the model city of 5,040 families, there would be, presumably about 4,000 persons between the ages of twenty and sixty who would be theoretically available for military service.[4]

It is when we come to the *Lehrstand* that difficulties begin to multiply upon us. Presumably the *Lehrstand* is identified by German scholars with the " full " guardians, i.e., the extremely small group of highest magistrates who from the age of fifty till the period of retirement direct the community in all its ways, " making philosophy their chief pursuit, but when their turn comes ruling for the public good ; and when they have brought up others like themselves to be governors of the state they will depart to the Islands of the Blest."[5]

He who at every age, as boy, as youth, and as mature man, has come out of the trial victorious and pure, shall be appointed a ruler and guardian of the state. The word " guardian " in the fullest sense ought to be applied to this higher class only which preserves us against foreign enemies and maintains peace among our citizens at home. The younger men before called guardians may more properly be named " auxiliaries " and supporters of the rulers' principles.[6]

The members of this class of philosopher-kings devote themselves, it is true, to philosophy. But is it correct to regard them as a specifically *teacher*-class ? Are we to suppose that members of this highest of all classes " which preserves us against foreign enemies and maintains peace at home "—i.e., occupies the highest military and civic positions of command—actually does the detailed work of teaching ? In the first place, it should be obvious that their numbers are insufficient for such work, if they do nothing else ; and in the second place, it should be obvious that they have laborious duties in other fields, as they " *toil* at politics." Their duties, on the practical side, are mainly deliberative, and partly directive. On the directive side they are doubtless assisted by junior executives ; but comparison with the functions of the higher magistrates in the model city makes it plain that, if they are concerned with education—as they doubtless *are*—this can only be in a supervisory and directive capacity, *via* the office of " director of education." It looks as though identifying the leadership class with a *Lehrstand* is misleading.

Suppose we go further, and inquire, insisting upon adequate

documentation, who does the actual teaching. Who teaches, for instance, the young children born to the citizens in the ideal republic ?   The mothers and nurses, of course, and similar attendants, for whose use an authorized anthology of suitable stories is prescribed :

We must establish a censorship of story-writers, and let the censors accept any tale of fiction which is good and reject the bad ; and we will desire mothers and nurses to tell their children the authorized ones only. Let them fashion the mind with such tales.[7]

This statement occurs in the earlier part of the *Republic*, before the point is made that children are wards of the state, rather than members of their individual parents' families.   But the only difference involved in this change is that " parents " are under- stood in a wider sense, as members of the parental group, who regard all members of the children group born within certain dates as " their " children.   A group relationship is substituted for the family relationship,[8] and the nurses and other attendants are state officials rather than family servants.[9]   But it will still be the group mothers and the nursery officials who educate and look after the child-group, and they will presumably use the pre- scribed children's reader for this purpose.   So too in the *Laws*, it is a " playground matron," a definite representative of the older generation, who, with the co-operation of nurses and attendants, takes charge of the early education of the group children from the ages of three to six.[10]

So too in the war-expeditions, at a slightly older age.   It is the parents (group parents, of course) who take the children along with them " to look on at the work they will have to do when they are grown up," " to help and be of use in war, waiting upon their fathers and mothers."   This constitutes part of the early education for military duties ;[11] the other part is played, not by the parents directly, but by their appointees, military officers of age and experience :

The parents will place the children under the command of experi- enced veterans who will be their leaders and teachers. Thus they will get an excellent view of what is hereafter to be their own business ; and if there is danger they have only to follow their elder leaders and escape.[12]

Who are the teachers of gymnastic, i.e., military sports such as " horsemanship, archery, hurling the javelin, slinging the shot, and managing heavy arms ? "[13] Can we suppose that these are taught by the highest magistrates of the city, the philosopher-kings who are fifty or more years of age ? The very idea is absurd. Just as there are state officials appointed to have care over infants, so it is to be presumed that there are state officials appointed to have care over the sports schools which children attend from about the age of six to about the age of ten. The matter is settled by an explicit passage in the *Laws* :

> We include under gymnastics all military exercises, such as archery and all hurling of weapons, the use of the light shield and heavy armour, military evolutions, movements of armies, and encampments, and all that relates to horsemanship. Of all these things there ought to be public teachers, receiving pay from the state, and their pupils should be the men and boys, the women and girls, who are to know all these things.[14]

If we inquire further into the personnel of gymnastic teachers, we find that they are under the control of the director of education, and may conceivably be " citizens, male or female," the best he can choose for the purpose.[15] But the reference to pay, and the general rule that no citizen may practice any art except agriculture, and this must be the sole source of money-making,[16] indicates that the public teachers, while possibly supervised by citizen-officials, cannot themselves be lot-holders ; and we find that the gymnastic teachers are, in point of fact, non-citizens :

> In the schools of horsemanship, archery, etc., let there be dwellings for teachers, who shall be brought from foreign parts for pay, and let them teach those, who attend the schools the art of war ; and the education shall be compulsory.[17]

It is sometimes supposed that because, under the director of education's authority, any father, i.e., full citizen, acting on behalf of the whole group of parents, may and indeed must correct, not only any child whom he finds misbehaving, but also " his instructor," that these " foreigners, attracted by pay " cannot be persons of any great importance.[18] But the reference to the director of education assures us that they are experts in their line, the best that can be obtained for love or money. Furthermore, the teacher-training which enforces successful study of Plato's *Laws* " and similar writings " as a necessary preliminary to state appointment as teachers, assures that such teachers will be adequately acquainted with the usages of the model city, as well as being masters in their own lines of *expertise*.[19]

Who are the teachers of " music," i.e., of reading, writing, lyre-playing, and the elements of song-and-dance which are essential

for choral performances ?   Are we to suppose that the senior
guardians, whose time is explicitly devoted to philosophy and
administration, are intended to give instruction in these elementary disciplines to about sixteen hundred children of school age ?
The mere question of numbers makes such a notion impossible,
entirely apart from the further question of citizens devoting themselves to professional work.   In a city of 5,040 families, there
would simply not be enough senior magistrates to set aside for
this purpose.   The only possible conclusion is that the teachers
of these elements are, at least for the most part, like the teachers
of military gymnastic, " foreigners attracted by pay " and given
state appointment under the authority of the director of education.
As a preliminary to receiving state appointment they are " con-
strained to learn and approve " Plato's *Laws* and similar works,
which are partly to be used as instructional material with the teen-
age pupils.[20]

The teaching, both of military gymnastic and of " music,"
while attendance in the schools is compulsory upon all children
of school age, is attractive to children, and takes the form of
interesting play.   As pointed out elsewhere, it is of a distinctly
extracurricular character, and accordingly, in Plato's opinion, is
not only suitable for the development of citizens whose lives are
to be an exposition and defence of freedom, but will actually
awaken the willing co-operation of the child as a whole and so
carry him further than insistence upon " discipline " would do.
It is this appealing to the child's imagination as a whole which
induces him to throw himself wholeheartedly into the educational
games and so identify himself with success in them, that really
accomplishes the " education."   This is quite distinct from the
practical training in techniques for professional purposes, which
tends to be " slavish " and is entirely unworthy of the name
" education."[21]

This extracurricular teaching in schools which deal with sports
and accompanied song-and-dance activities is cued to the
monthly sports-meets and music festivals, in which the children,
like their elders, take an " innocent delight " in expressing themselves in public, competitive performances, with the community
and expert adjudicators sitting in judgment and conferring prizes.
These festivals also are of a distinctly educative character and
come under the control of the director of education and his staff.[22]
Here, as in our modern music festivals, the adjudicators furnish
a sort of education, by providing opportunities, standards, leader-

ship, and criticism, and thus may reasonably be regarded as at least quasi-teachers. They receive state appointment, as follows :

Let persons who commonly take an interest in such matters[23] attend, under penalty of being fined for non-attendance ; and let there be proposed as directors (i.e. leaders and adjudicators)—one for the choruses, and one for the solo performers, to hold office for one year— ten experts in choral music, and ten experts in solo performance (in singing, and in playing the harp, flute, etc., and in reciting), whose *expertise* is subject to challenge. Of each group of ten, let one be chosen by lot, to undergo scrutiny and function as adjudicator.[24]

The corresponding adjudicators for military sports are selected from a wider group ; for almost all citizens are competent to exercise a vote upon military matters ; and in this case there seems to be no doubt that the adjudicators finally chosen by lot will be citizens rather than imported teachers. At least there is a definite passage which reads

In our equestrian games, let the competitors have conflict and rivalry in accordance with the law, and let the colonels and generals of horse decide together about all courses and about the armed competitors in them.[25]

At the same time, in relation to the contests in armour " of one against one, two against two, and so on up to ten against ten," it is stated that :

We ought to call in skilful persons who shall judge for us and be our assessors in the work of legislation. They shall say who deserves to be victor in combats of this sort, and what he is not to do or have done to him, and what rule determines who is defeated.[26]

This is more nearly parallel to the case of music, and possibly indicates the appointment of foreign experts who are associated with the work of a legislative committee.

Teen-age children study also the elements of mathematics, including arithmetic, geometry, and astronomy : the barest elements which it would be " disgraceful not to know." The study is not serious, but playful, as in the Egyptian number-games, and apparently is continued into adult life, with the aim of developing a certain mental alertness. The serious investigation of such subjects is restricted to " a very few " who apparently coincide with the students in the pre-dialectic course in the *Republic* :

There remain three studies suitable for freemen : arithmetic, the measurement of length, surface, and depth, and the revolution of the stars in relation to one another. All freemen should learn as much of these branches of knowledge as every child in Egypt is taught when he learns the alphabet. It is disgraceful not to know what is necessary for mankind in general. But not everyone has need to toil through these matters in a scientific manner. This is reserved for a few, to be indicated hereafter.[27]

Who are the teachers of elementary mathematics? Mathematicians, of course ; but it would be absurd to suppose that the mathematics teachers are taken from the higher guardians who have been graduated in dialectic. For while it is true that these fifty-year old magistrates have studied mathematics seriously— they are indeed the " few " to whom reference is made above[28]— (1) there will not be enough of them available to teach the whole teen-age group, and (2) there is a rather sharp distinction made by Plato between competent mathematicians and graduates of the class in dialectic.[29] We conclude, rather, that the mathematics teachers will be, like the other teachers, imported professionals, probably of the Pythagorean Order, who are good mathematicians and nothing further.

So far we have been considering the public teachers appointed to teach to every potential citizen of school age the gymnastic, music, and mathematics which are regarded as essential for every citizen to know. The special reason for teaching the elements of these subjects, is that such subject-matter can be made helpful in appealing (in play) to the imagination of the pupil, to project himself as a whole into these activities, merging the stage of development which he has reached with the stage he is planning to reach, and which is exemplified before him in the person of his teacher. By this appeal to his imagination he is encouraged to educate himself for citizenship, and to form his character upon the normative ideals approved by the community authorities.

Such public teachers, we have discovered, are not themselves citizens, but are experts imported for the purpose, the best than can be attracted by state positions and state pay, and they receive special training in the laws and customs of the community before they are given final appointment. There cannot be the slightest question of their ever being regarded as members of the *Lehrstand*, the " golden " class from whom the chief magistrates come ; and if this were the whole truth, it would be simply incomprehensible how German scholarship ever came to suppose for a moment that the highest magistrates occupied themselves—except in a purely administrative capacity (as in the case of the director of education)—with the work of teaching. In fact, as these public teachers constitute the immense majority of all the teachers in the state, it is clearly misleading to speak of the highest class of magistrates as a *Lehrstand* at all. As educated men they are doubtless competent to teach part of what they have learnt,[30] but as full-time magistrates they are obviously occupied with other duties. Plato never calls them anything which could be translated *Lehrstand*, but always " magistrates," " rulers," or (more frequently) " guardians," a name which does not mislead as to their functions.

It is when we pass beyond the general mass of the citizens and their education for citizenship, and approach the special leadership class in their twenties with the question, who are their teachers, that we begin to see the point of the German terminology. For this leadership class cannot possibly be educated by imported professionals. No professionals anywhere in the world outside Plato's imaginary state are really competent. A man of native genius, possibly, here or there, a divinely inspired poet or an entirely exceptional lecturer of the stamp of the great Protagoras, might have penetrated into these advanced studies with some success. But it would clearly be improper to rely, in such important matters, upon casual rarities. " Shall some poet who has found his way into the city, or some chance person who pretends to be an instructor of youth, show himself better than—our guardians, and to possess a more precise knowledge of virtue ? No ! "[31]

Plato himself is well aware of the difficulty of finding competent teachers for the members of such a leadership class :

First, a list would have to be made out of those who by their ages and studies and dispositions and habits are well fitted for the duty of a guardian. In the next place, it will not be easy for them to discover themselves what they ought to learn, or become the disciple of one who has already made the discovery. The learners do not know what is learned to advantage until the knowledge which is the result of learning has found a place within their souls. And so the details as to what they should study and at what times, while not exactly a " secret," can hardly be stated beforehand.[32]

The conclusion is, that this higher education is vital to the realization of Plato's dream-city and that it can only be further described and implemented by co-opting " the Athenian Stranger," who is a thinly veiled disguise for Plato himself, the founder of the original Academy in which higher education was taught by a citizen to potential leaders :

We must detain the Stranger and by supplications and in all manner of ways make him share in the foundation of the city, or else we must give up the undertaking.[33]

That is to say, the teachers of the small class in dialectic will certainly be citizens, presumably graduates of Plato's own Academy or of some similar institution of higher learning. It is with reference to citizen-graduates of this kind that we read that

The teachers ought to excel the rest of mankind, and perfectly to show him who desires to learn and know (or, on the other hand, whose evil actions require to be punished and reproved), what is the nature of virtue and vice.[34]

and it is presumably with reference to its proven competence in dialectic that this small group of higher magistrates is called, by German scholarship, the *Lehrstand*. It is doubtful, however, whether more than three or four at most would be giving much of their time to teaching. They are magistrates with a highly developed interest in philosophy, or philosophers with the duty of acting as administrators, rather than anything which could be regarded as a Teaching Order.

It remains to discuss the Ministry of Education in the model city of the *Laws*, the central authority from which all education for citizenship (if not for leadership) radiates. The minister himself is of course a member of the " nocturnal council " and one of the very highest magistrates.[35] He is thought of as an old man, with a specialized interest in education, charged with the most important of all the state offices :

The minister of the education of youth, male and female, must be fifty years of age and must have children lawfully begotten and preferably of both sexes. Of all the great offices of state this is the greatest, and care must be taken that the very best of all the citizens is elected. The magistrates (with certain exceptions) are the electors, and they are to select the best of the law-guardians. The official they select holds office for a term of five years.[36]

The minister's staff consists of (1) a rather special assistant, the junior member co-opted by him into the nocturnal council (2) an indeterminate number of administrative assistants, selected from the citizens " both male and female " for their efficiency, and (3) the general body of full citizens (lot-holders) who have the duty (enforced by penalties) of maintaining order and good behaviour in public on the part of all children of school age and their attendants and instructors.[37]

Assisted by this staff, the minister sits on a number of important legislative committees. He acts (1) as a member of the highly important nocturnal council, a deliberative body which considers all matters involving fundamental change in the community institutions, including the recommendations of the " travelling inspector of institutions,"[38] (2) as chairman of the extremely important committee on education. This is a legislative committee of the law-guardians, assisted by the advice of educational experts, namely, on questions of gymnastic, by the adjudicators in gymnastic, and, on questions of music, by the adjudicators in music. The committee has a number of duties. (1) It arranges the times, programmes, and rules of the sports-meets and music festivals.[39] (2) It acts as a board of censors, administering the law which permits certain types of publication and excludes certain others, in the case of both native and foreign poets and artists, especially such as are intended for performance on festival occasions.[40] The minister also acts (3) as a regular member of the law-guardians in all their more general activities. Finally (4) he is *ex officio* host to " travelling inspectors of institutions " who come from other countries to see how things are done in the model city.[41]

These duties are partly deliberative, partly administrative. In addition, the minister has a tremendous amount of work to do of an administrative and executive sort. His office selects, trains, appoints, and supervises all public school teachers, both in the sports schools and in the literary and music schools. He sees to it that the curriculum follows the straightforward simplicity of the lines laid down by the law, with a minimum of frills and innovations. He exercises general oversight over all children of school age, not only when on school premises, but also on the street ; and in general, wherever educational matters come up or the proper behaviour and treatment of the rising generation are concerned, he sees to it that his fellow-citizens are adequately instructed as to the principles and applications of the far-reaching school law.[42]

If we now ask again the question with which we started, namely, *Who are the teachers?* we find ourselves in a position to give a definite answer. (1) As far as children up to six years of age are concerned, the teachers are the parents, nurses, and other attendants, with the place of the parents partly occupied by a state-appointed official, the playground matron who holds office for one year. These teachers belong partly to the citizen class. Some will be members of the " auxiliaries " or *Wehrstand*, while others doubtless will consist of the very small group of higher magistrates referred to as the *Lehrstand*. The nurses and attendants are non-citizens, and, as slaves, possibly fall even outside the official *Nährstand*. (2) As far as children from six or seven to ten years of age are concerned, their teachers are state-appointed officials, normally and usually (if not exclusively) non-citizens : professionals earning their living in a way not permitted to lot-holders. These obviously belong, neither to the *Wehrstand* nor to the *Lehrstand*, but to the *Nährstand*. One exception should be noted. The veterans who have charge of the children when taken on military expeditions as spectators and act as " teachers " of these children, may well be citizens. So too the adjudicators in certain military games, who are " colonels and generals of horse " are presumably citizens ; and such persons belong to the official *Wehrstand*, unless the " veterans " are of more than sixty years of age, in which case, as *emeriti*, they hardly belong to the *Wehrstand*, except by courtesy.

(3) As far as teen-age children are concerned, their teachers in the literary, music, and mathematics classes are state appointees under the control of the director of education, and so are presumably non-citizens. They would be ranked in the *Nährstand*. Finally (4) members of the very small class in dialectic for candidates for the higher magistracies would be taught by dialecticians, i.e., graduates of some institution like Plato's Academy, who would presumably be ranked with the official *Lehrstand*.

That is to say, in general, children of school age are taught by state appointees of a definitely non-civic group, " foreigners attracted by pay," with possibly a few military officials acting as adjudicators and advisory experts. The only individuals taught by the higher magistrates (the *Lehrstand*) are (1) their own very young children, and (2) candidates for magistrate positions of the highest class who are admitted to a course in dialectic— and possibly (3) misguided adults who are committed to the House of Correction. The teaching for citizenship is a state function of great importance for which the state is prepared to offer state positions and salaries to competent instructors, under the authority of the director of education.

[1]See Fr. Windelband : *Platon*,[6] 1920, p. 151 (in Fromann's *Klassiker*—a very widely used text). [2]See U. v. Wilamowitz-Moellendorff : *Platon*[2], 1920, Vol. I, p. 397. [3]In the model city, the supply of food depends upon the operation of the 5,040 farm lots. These are " owned " by the 5,040 citizens, although the practical work connected with operating them is of course performed by members of the non-civic class (Cf. *Laws* 743d, 745b f., 760e f., 806d, 949e). If these gentlemen farmers are regarded as " *Nährstand*," then the *Nährstand* is not *one* group connected with the model city, but consists of *the whole body* of full citizens, whose full citizenship is defined by reference to lot-holding. [4]Cf. *Laws* 785. If women are needed for military service, their service period is from about forty (cf. *Rep.* 460e) to fifty. For the basis upon which numbers are calculated for the various groups in a community of 5,040 heads-of-families, see *infra*, Appendix I. [5]*Rep.* 540ab. Cf. also *Laws* 946, 964d f. [6]*Rep.* 413e f. These full guardians are identified with the " golden " class, *Rep.* 415a. [7]*Rep.* 377c. Cf. *Laws* 791e–794a. Cf. also *Prtg.* 325cd, where *fathers and tutors* are also mentioned. [8]*Rep.* 461c. [9]*Rep.* 460bc. [10]*Laws* 794ab. The matrons are appointed, for the term of one year's service, by the committee of women magistrates who have authority over marriage and childbirth, and thus will be appointed from the group of young mothers (married not longer than ten years) under the control of the magistrates' committee. Children, here too, are state wards (*Laws* 804d). [11]*Rep.* 466e f. In the *Laws*, children are taken to manoeuvres, along with their parents, but not (apparently) to actual warfare. Military science is taught by officers who are state officials (*Laws* 813d f) acting under the control of the director of education. [12]*Rep.* 467d f., condensed. [13]Cf. *Laws* 794c f. In the *Laws*, the boys go to men, and the girls to women teachers ; although all learn the same techniques. [14]*Laws* 813de. [15]*Laws* 813bc. [16]*Laws* 743d, 745b f., 760e f., 806d, 949e. [17]*Laws* 804c f., slightly condensed. [18]*Laws* 808e f. [19]*Laws* 811, referring primarily to teachers of letters, rather than of gymastic, and 813b f., referring primarily to teachers of gymnastic, may be compared with 804d, which brings the two groups of teachers together. The general context shows that all are equally foreigners and all paid officials, and all under the authority of the director of education. *Laws* 964b ff., which groups " teachers " along with interpreters, legislators, and guardians—i.e., with the higher magistrates who have received the higher sort of education—I take to refer primarily to the higher teachers, rather than to the teachers of military sports and the elements of reading, writing, and music. The higher teachers are discussed *infra*, pp. 159–ff. [20]*Laws* 810–813. [21]*Rep.* 590c, *Soph.* 229d f., *Laws* 643d f. [22]*Laws* 764c ff. The control of the director over adjudicators is indirect, and takes place *via* a committee of law-guardians (of whom the director is one) sitting with the experts to settle programmes and rules (*Laws* 835a). [23]As regular citizens with no especial interest in music are held excused, I assume this means members of the music-teachers association, i.e., chiefly " foreigners attracted by pay," but possibly including a few citizens. But where the short course in music is all that is permitted to citizens (*Laws* 810a, 812c f.), it is not likely that many citizens would be qualified to judge such matters. State authority is given by the adjudicators sitting with a committee of the law-guardians to decide upon the content of programmes, etc. (*Laws* 835a). [24]Condensed from *Laws* 764d f. [25]*Laws* 834c. [26]*Laws* 833d f. The same regulations apply, apparently, to military wrestling. The passage as to election of adjudicators (*Laws* 765c f.) in gymnastic does not make it clear whether the experts so chosen would be citizens or imported teachers. [27]Condensed from *Laws* 817e ff., cf. 747, and *Rep.* 537c f. [28]*Laws* 965–968a. [29]*Rep.* 531e, cf. *Theaet.* 165a. [30]*Laws* 964b, 966ab. [31]*Laws* 964c, slightly condensed. [32]*Laws* 968d. Cf. *Rep.* 533a. [33]*Laws* 969b. [34]*Laws* 964b. Cf. 909a, which seems to imply that those graduates who are members of the " nocturnal council "—presumably the older members—are competent to undertake the reformation of such offenders as require instruction. [35]Education is represented on the nocturnal council (1) by the director and (2) by his co-opted assistant, a man of between thirty and forty co-opted as " junior member " of the council, (3) by the director emeritus, whose service on the council is thus continued for a second term of five years, and (4) by the director emeritus' " junior member." (*Laws* 951e.) [36]Condensed from *Laws* 765d f. [37]*Laws* 808e f., 813c f., 951e. [38]*Laws* 951 f. The inspector holds office for ten years. [39]*Laws* 813, 828b, 830d, 835a. [40]*Laws* 764c, 801d, 816bc, 817, 829d, 936a. [41]*Laws* 953d. [42]*Laws* 811 ff. His authority over school buildings seems to be exercised indirectly, through the instructors who are his appointees (764d), who also are more directly concerned with the regular attendance of pupils.

CHAPTER VIII

SUBJECT-MATTER. COMPOSITION

As an example of subject-matter and its treatment in the Platonic theory of education, let us investigate Plato's account of composition. Let us consider how its creation and use are directed and controlled for educational purposes in the ideal Republic and in the model city of the *Laws*.

The use of verse and prose composition for educational purposes commences early in the child's life. Mothers and nurses sing the children to sleep and tell them stories, even before the children are sufficiently developed mentally to appreciate the significance of what they hear. The appeal of the traditional subject-matter is largely nonlogical. It is as forms of play, and as associated with rhythmic motions which have a definite nonlogical function, that the songs and stories influence the children and indeed begin to educate them.[1]

Very young children, like most young animals, have a tendency to move their limbs spasmodically, and to utter a variety of cries. These cries and these movements are expressive of uneasiness of one sort or another, and are at first without any regular principle or control.[2] Mothers and nurses, on such occasions, take up their children in their arms and impart to them a rocking motion—usually associated with some sort of rhythmic song—which apparently soothes the temporary uneasiness and induces well-being. The steady rhythm of this motion is believed to assist the body in mastering the alien elements which have been introduced in the form of food and drink—on much the same principle as an ocean voyage is considered helpful for adult dyspepsia.[3] That is to say, the rocking or surging motion facilitates the distribution throughout the body of the nutritive material, and assists its absorption and transformation, at appropriate points, into bodily tissue. In so doing, this motion, imparted from without, reinforces the efforts of the central selfmotion within, located in the cerebrum, to dominate, direct, and control the functioning of the various bodily organs.[4] All this is physical and biological : that is to say, definitely nonlogical ; although in the mastery of quasi-chaotic motion-tendencies by means of regular, orderly rhythm we can doubtless suspect the rudimentary beginnings of something analogous to the Divine Artist's superimposition, upon primordial chaos, of regular geometric patterns : thus creating a universe in which values of an aesthetic, an ethical, a religious, and a logical order, as well as values of a biological type, become realizable, if only we can learn to co-operate with our Divine Leader.[5]

And further : the rhythmic motion of the mother's arms, re-inforced by the rhythm of the lullaby or other chant which accompanies it, has upon the young child an effect which is not merely hypnotic in a physical sense. The structural patterns developed within the cerebral selfmotion of the child have a function which is social. They do more than facilitate and render possible education at a later stage. They are themselves directly educative. By participating in one and the same motion, in a rhythm which regularizes the vocal gestures as well as the movements of the cradling arms, parent and child are brought very close together. There is effected a kind of social merging which helps to make the growing child a member of his family : as he shares in its activities at playtimes, at mealtimes, and at sleeping-times, gradually taking up into his system the rhythms of family and community life. In fact, here at the infantile level we have something analogous to the social merging which takes place in the ritual temple-dances of the community festivals, when the citizens, young and old, unite in fellowship and worship and mingle their personalities with the personality of their Leader, the god whose praise they chant, and who participates in, as well as guides and inspires, their choral dancing.[6]

As the children grow older, they are taken out, from the age of three to the age of six, to play with the neighbourhood children. Their customary nurses are still in attendance, and the mothers are represented in the model city of the *Laws* by a matron who is a state official appointed for that purpose. Playgrounds are provided by the state. The matron functions as a playground supervisor, armed with all necessary authority ;[7] and the children's games are treated as a part of the state educational system, receiving a certain amount of state impulse and state control.

These games have, in fact, two sources. On the one hand, they are said to be spontaneous. Young children take to play naturally. " The childish nature requires sports " and expresses itself freely and readily in activities which are playful. Children run,

skip, and jump, and they handle things : everything in their
immediate neighbourhood, and especially what they see other
children or their parents handling.[8] In the group playing, the
running, skipping, and jumping easily take on certain rhythmic
forms, usually associated with the patterns of some rhythmic
chant. They become marching games, dancing or action games,
and acquire definite structure.[9] The words chanted in these
childish games may have for the children little more significance
than the words sung by mothers have for the babies who are
being played with or lulled to sleep. Their influence is thus
predominantly nonlogical.

And further : the tendency to do what others are doing and
thus to participate in group activities lends to the structure of
these group games a certain stability. Such group ways of
playing easily take on the form of community traditions.[10]
In effect, children's games thus become a sort of play-level reflex
of the activities of family and neighbourhood life and interests.
Rooted in the nature of the child, his family, and his neighbourhood, they acquire a certain biosocial significance ; and the
child, as he throws himself into such games, becomes both in
action and in feeling a full member of his group. That is to say,
by participating in such games, the family baby becomes a
neighbourhood child.[11]

On the other hand, these games both require and receive a
certain measure of direction and control. The spontaneity of
childhood, if left entirely to itself, may easily run wild. It may
follow directions of which nurse and matron (representing the
family and the community) cannot but disapprove. In such cases,
nurse and matron interfere at once and check such tendencies in
their origin. Children are sometimes mischievous, boys especially
so. If left to themselves, they may do serious damage to whatever
they handle : inanimate objects, living things, other children, or
even themselves. They thus require and receive discipline and
wise direction.[12] The matron appointed by the state sees to it
that their games, while following the patterns inherent in the
spontaneity of child-growth and in the group-life of young
children, are so developed on the biological side as to fit the
neighbourhood child to participate before long in the more
definitely organized sports of the school and community, and
eventually to take his place as a member of the wider group
as a citizen in the model city. That is to say, while these neighbourhood games are nonlogical in their operation, the child who

takes part in them is learning, without knowing it, to take on something of the ideal forms of manliness, fair-play, loyalty to his fellows, and a host of similar virtues, all making for good citizenship.[13]

In calling these impulses and group-rhythms "nonlogical," what is meant? It is meant that the children who participate in them do not clearly understand what they are doing, and what the ultimate purpose of these games is. There is on their part no clearcut conception of objectives, and no deliberate selection of means best calculated to realize such objectives. The impulses which move them to play and to play in such groups are not "reasons" of which they could give and receive an account in well chosen words. They are instinctive, racial, vital, a part of the obscure background of impulse which furnishes so much of the motive power in the human life-cycle. To the participant in the different phases of this life-cycle, much in this background is and remains obscure. He feels it, he lives it, he acts in accordance with its promptings. But an effort on his part to bring it into the foreground, and focus intelligent apprehension upon it, tends to be unsuccessful. The effort either makes nonsense of his logic, or makes nonsense of his life. The background contains an element which can only be called nonlogical, irreducible to conceptual order, system, and law : an element which is vital, but is also chaotic, essentially unidealizable.[14]

And yet, something can be done with it. In so far as it can be induced to take on structures which are mathematical in pattern and follow regular geometric forms, the Platonic student of education believes that he has something which his mind can grasp and can use in building up more complex structures whose every phase is logical.[15] For example, when the rhythms of group play take on the forms of marching, dancing, and action-songs, these rhythms have a definite pattern which can be expressed in mathematical formulas. The *anapaest* of the Hellenic march is very definite. You can build upon it the "marching into war" patriotic song-and-dance associated with the name of Tyrtaeus : a traditional composition of which the community usefulness is conspicuous. It sends the citizens into battle shoulder to shoulder, ready to do or die. So too with the simple dance-rhythms of the *trochee, iambus, spondee, dactyl*, and the rest. The mathematical basis is clear and unmistakable. Once thoroughly grasped, you have something which you can use in your most complicated war-

dances and ceremonial peace-dances : dances whose civic usefulness is plain beyond question.[16]

Here indeed we are speaking of human art. But there is in
nature itself something analogous to this, some trace of patterning
which seems to take geometric form. God, the Divine Artist, has
created the world, Plato teaches, on geometric principles, by super-
inducing upon a primordial welter of motion-tendencies conceived
as utterly chaotic, mathematical patterns of extreme simplicity
and regularity.[17] The leaders in this field are the so-called Pythagorean scientists, who seek everywhere in nature the secret formulas, the numerical proportions in terms of which the trained
intelligence can rediscover the outlines of God's plan in the
creation, and can account for the behaviour of phenomena. Thus
what commonsense calls " earth," "water," " air," and "fire,"
and regards (since Empedocles) as the elements of which physical
matter is made up, are conceived by Pythagorean science to be
the sensuous appearance of what the intellect thinks under the
form of regular solids : the cube, the icosahedron, the octohedron,
the tetrahedron. These solids are treated by Pythagorean science
as composites, whose regular surfaces are built up out of certain
elementary triangles ; and the ultimate secret of these triangles
(doubtless the well-known " tetrachtys of the dekad ") is a
Divine mystery revealed only to the Pythagorean Brotherhood.[18]

The birds, the fishes, the land-beasts, and man are all alike
made up, on their material side, of these same four elements,
earth, water, air, and fire, mingled in a certain balanced proportion. But the formula which holds the elementary triangles
in stable balance differs from one species to another. Some have
more air in their composition, some more water, some more
earth, and some more fire, and the preservation of each species
depends upon the maintenance of the balanced pattern characteristic of that species.[19] Each species thus has its own vital
rhythms, which are characteristically related to the secret formula
of the species. Interfere with this formula, and you have disease.
Dissolve the intimate relation of the elementary triangles, and you
have death.[20]

The vital rhythms characteristic of human beings are expressions, in the nonlogical form of play, of the secret formula of the
species ; and the balanced patterns of the marches, dances, and
action-songs developed " naturally " by children as a group and
providing human artists with a basis on which to work creatively in
the service of the community festivals, are not to be regarded as

arbitrary and unnatural. On the contrary, they are definitely in the order of nature ; and such regulated play-activities assist in developing and strengthening what is characteristically human in humanity.[21]

Hence their importance for the purpose of education, an education which seeks to co-operate with the Divine plan in developing to a balanced maximum the biosocial potentialities actually inherent in human nature. The further action-patterns to which neighbourhood play-life leads : the patterns of school life, of army life, of farmer-legislator life, of magistrate and priest-life : in a word, the patterns of citizenship in Plato's " model " city, are not idle dreams, arbitrary thought-webs spun out of itself by an abstract, etiolated intelligence which has become lost in its own over-developed techniques. They are the very stuff and substance of life as it grows into more life and eventually flowers into the self-maintaining community whose balanced interactivities constitute the good life, the life of maximum human value.[22]

Against this background, we can now proceed to draw in outline the essential characteristics of literary composition, the characteristics which make it possible to use it as an instrument of education, a highly important part of the subject-matter studied in the school curriculum. Structurally regarded, literary compositions can be analysed into sentences, sentences into words, words into syllables, syllables into letters, and letters into vowels, consonants, and mutes.[23] Vowels, consonants, and mutes, together with all that can be built up out of them, are actions, forms of motion, of moving air as it passes through the vocal organs and is guided and shaped by lips and tongue. That is to say, they are a sort of gesture, precisely analogous to certain other types of gesture.[24] The first and closest analogy is with the vocal gestures which furnish the tones of which music is composed. The second analogy is with gestures of other parts of the body which issue in dancing and other forms of gymnastic exercise. All three forms of gesture, linguistic, musical, and terpsichorean, may exhibit identical rhythmic patterns ; and it is both natural and proper for all three to be associated together in this way in choric dancing, which is indeed stated to be the chief subject-matter of education in the model city of the *Laws*.[25]

" Both natural and proper." What does this mean ? It means that in a song-and-dance composition the words, the music, and the dance-movements may all follow the same identical rhythm. They may be all anapaestic, or all spondaic, or may all follow some other rhythmic pattern. The number of notes sung, one for each syllable of each word, may be identical with the number of notes played on the accompanying instrument, and with the number of dance-movements of the foot or hand or swaying body. The accents all come at the same time ; and indeed the pitch of the singing voice may be identical with the pitch of the instrumental accompaniment. As far as the song-and-dance compositions performed by citizens are concerned, this thorough-going and almost archaic simplicity is precisely as Plato would have it.[26] As far as professional performers are concerned, Plato is of course well aware that technicians can hardly be kept from experimenting, varying the pitch of melody and accompaniment to an octave or a fourth or fifth, and perhaps combining voices of different registers, so that, e.g., men and boys would sing an octave (or so) apart, or men and women would sing a fourth or fifth apart. He also fully understands that technicians might play two or more notes of the accompaniment to one note of the melody and might even vary the rhythmic, as well as the tonal pattern of the accompaniment. For professionals and for advanced performers he does not regard such experimentation as inappropriate, especially before a popular audience, which enjoys trills and the virtuosity of cadenzas.[27] But for citizen-performers, who are trained along strictly traditional lines, he regards archaic simplicity and the observance of the conventional patterns in vocal, instrumental, and terpsichorean motion, as essential for the purposes of an education which is to fit them for citizenship.[28]

Assuming this analogy between the three arts, and the fundamental identity of their underlying human rhythms, let us focus our attention upon the functions of the vocal movements which issue in language and finally in literary composition. We have considered their structure. Let us pass to consider their function. Their function is expressive, and expressive in a twofold reference. In the first place, in reference to the body. Some form of vocal movement issuing in human cries with definite syllabic and letter-structure is naturally expressive of bodily emotion. In joy or in sorrow, in courage or in fear, human beings, like other animals, express their feelings in characteristic cries, as well as other forms of motion.[29] It is these expressive utterances which form the raw material from which words and ultimately sentences are composed ; and it is with reference to such underlying emotions that language and literature develop as they do. Any form of literary composition which becomes popular will thus be sure to exhibit a definite appeal to the standard human emotions.[30] Hence the popularity of patriotic literature, of the weepy lamentations characteristic of Greek tragedy, of the creepy thrills of ghost-story stuff, and of the erotic stimulation associated with Greek love-stories.[31] The rhythms, the words, the syllables, and even the letters used in such compositions, are expressive of the corresponding emotions, and the patterns of such literature are simply a stylized expansion of rhythmic patterns which are fundamental in the human organism.[32] Greek literature is always read not silently, but aloud. It is performed, acted out ; and the performer throws himself into the movements which express whatever emotion is being portrayed, and himself feels directly, in the rhythms of his own body, the passionate tears, the patriotic fervour, the misery of desolation, the horror of doom ; and the emotions thus portrayed are experienced directly by the sympathetic audience.

Tell me, Ion (asks Socrates), when you produce the greatest effect upon the audience, when reciting the apparition of Odysseus leaping forth upon the floor, recognized by the suitors, and casting his arrows at his feet, or when describing Achilles rushing upon Hector, or the sorrows of Andromache, Hecuba, or Priam : are you not carried out of yourself, does not your soul in an ecstacy seem to be among the persons of whom you are speaking in Ithaca or Troy ?

Yes (replies Ion), I confess that at the tale of pity my eyes are filled with tears, and when I speak of horrors, my hair stands on end and my heart throbs. And I look down upon the audience and behold the various emotions of pity, wonder, sternness stamped upon their countenances. I make them weep.[33]

Thus we see that one function of literary composition is expressive in reference to the organic emotions of the human body. The rhythmic motions of the two correspond to such an extent that whoever throws himself into the rhythmic patterns of the words and phrases of the literature expresses directly the pulsations of the corresponding vital rhythms in his own body. This effect of literature is largely nonlogical ;[34] much as the effect of a modern symphony orchestra is largely non-logical : as the expansions and contractions of its dynamics expand and contract the audience to such an extent that, even when not musically educated, they experience directly the sweep and pulsation of the rhythmic patterns, and emerge from the concert, not merely stimulated, but emotionally exhausted.

What is the second expressive function of literature ? The organism is thought of as interactive with its environment ; and where the one function is expressive of the state of the organism, the other is expressive of the environment. In this sense, the letters, syllables, words, and sentences of literature (conceived always as spoken, acted out) are expressive of the objects, things and persons, which constitute the environment with which the organism is interactive. The motions of literary structure are said to convey " information," not (in this reference) of the state of the body, but of the nature of the objective world. They are " imitative " of the motions of the objective world.[35] There are certain root-words and root-letters which directly express certain forms of motion. The letter R is uttered with a violent motion of the tongue, and will be found to be prominent in all words expressive of violent motion, such as " rush," " rapid," " run," etc. The letter O is formed with a round motion of the mouth, and will be found prominent in all words which express " roundness," " rotundity," " orotundity," and " mouth " itself. On the other hand, such letters as ST indicate the termination of motion, as in " rest," " stop," " stay," " stabilize." Names built up out of such letters on " onomatopoeia " principles : words like " crash," " bang," " smash," " whistle," " whisper," etc., which are common in most languages, are a kind of picture-image of the thing to which they refer, and root-words, " primitive or first names," are thought by Plato to have been formed, for the most part, in this way[3.6] Thus we read :

That objects should be imitated in letters and syllables, and so find expression, may appear ridiculous ; but cannot be avoided. There is no better principle to which we can look for the truth of first names. The name is an imitation of the thing, as a picture is an imitation of the thing. Primitive sounds may be compared to pictures, by syllables and letters imitating the nature of things.[37]

And, as we all know, literature abounds in passages in which the sense and the sound keep pace. This is particularly well established in the case of poetic picture-images. But there are plenty of prose passages where the same end is achieved by the same means. The most famous example in Plato's own writing is the *Republic* which describes the effect upon the soul of too much music, poured unceasingly through the funnel of a man's ears ; he warbles and wails and weakens his spirit until he becomes but a feeble wielder of the lance.[38] A still more famous passage in Greek literature is the professional rhetorician Lucian's depiction of the Elysian fields, what time the breezes whistle and whisper through the tree-tops as they sway gently to and fro, shading the tables at which the heroes sit banqueting ; and hosts of onomatopoeic words in which the Hellenic language is so rich are assembled and pressed into service : advancing in formation, performing their ordered evolutions, and finally retiring at the wave of their master's hand.[39]

Picture-images, as such, exhibit a certain " rightness " or " wrongness," according as they resemble, or fail to resemble, the objects which they profess to portray. Word-imagery, Plato is inclined to think, possesses also a sort of " truth " : namely, in so far as the " information " conveyed by the word-picture is correct.[40] Its correctness, however, is not strictly objective. For linguistic images depict things, not as they are in themselves, but rather as they appear in relation to human desires and human needs. That is to say, we must put together the two sides of the two-fold function of language and literature. For the truth is that the medium in which objects are pictured by language is the medium whose rhythms are the rhythms of the natural human emotions. Literature presents us with an emotional picture of the world, a picture transcribed, as it were, into the human clef, a biosocial picture.[41] Thus in both of the functions in which language and literature are expressive, the expression is biosocial and emotional, rather than anything which could be recognized as scientific and objective. Literature is instinct with feeling, with vital rhythms and patterns which are human. But, however cunningly contrived, whether interwoven by the forces of group life or unified by the skill of an individual word-artist, its feelings, rhythms, and patterns are, from end to end, nonlogical.[42]

That is to say, just as most dances are folk-dances, most melodies folk-melodies, and most songs folk-songs : so most of the literature which is built upon folk-language, is folk-literature, instinct with the feeling, the passions, and the rhythmic patterns which make human life the thing that it is : a game, a sport, a gamble with destiny, a noble art, if you will—but not science, not logic.[43] Consider the content of traditional Hellenic poetry of the Homeric stamp : adventure, ambition, feasting, high life, romance, wedded love. Each phase of the human life-cycle is pictured with human sympathy as well as consummate artistry ; and pictured with a certain " universality " too, if you insist. But the universality is not the universality of the logician. It is racial and vital, rich in subjective valuings. For in the world as depicted by Homeric literature we have, not an impartial sociologist's description of scientifically surveyed phenomena, but an aristocratic world-picture, the living expression of a living culture.

One further point. As contrasted with " primitive " vocal expressions, " primitive " syllables and letters, whose racial origin and significance are unmistakable, we have in more richly developed language and literature a number of sophistications which partly embellish and partly conceal the original stark forms and patterns which are the creative source from which all emotionally significant development of literary composition takes rise. Nouns and verbs, adjectives and adverbs, develop patterns of their own, technical patterns of accidence and syntax whose systematic implications are studied by the art of the grammarian. So too sentences and paragraphs, both in verse and in prose, develop patterns of their own, technical patterns of form whose systematic implications are studied by the art of the rhetorician. Under this influence, words become prettified, with letters omitted, altered, or inserted " for the sake of the euphony." They lose something of their pictorial significance and take on something of the tonal quality of music, but without relation to the original sources of musical significance. They sound fine, but no one knows quite what they mean.[44]

So too with the old simple patterns of speeches and stories. " To suit the modern sophisticated taste," all kinds of innovations and mixtures make their appearance. But in spite of the fearsome modern nomenclature and technology,[45] something of the old vigour is lost, and with the newer-style compositions—well, you could put the topics in almost *any* order, and no one would see the difference.[46] All this over-sophistication, with its own conventions and techniques, casts over the surface of the newer literature an appearance of system, order, and logicality which is really illusory. The trained grammarian or rhetorician who is at home in this field of study is not himself a poet or an orator. He is a secondary student, a professor whose whole stock-in-trade is the definition and classification of such techniques and conventions. But these are the merest elements of the art which genuine authors practise.[47] The *creative* artist is no museum-curator, arranging dessicated specimens under glass covers. He cultivates the blooms of literature outside in a living garden, in vital contact with the soil and the sun, the water and the air of nature. He seeks inspiration, not in processes which are rational and logical, but in something deeper : projecting himself into the primitive, racial sources of literary value whose rhythms and patterns, derived from the original formula of human existence, have been hammered into definite forms and structures which are expressive of the biosocial background and outlook of the specific group in which his own life is cast.[48]

Regarded as an instrument of education, folk-language and its development into folk-literature, whether in the pre-school, school, or post-school period, permeate the environment of the young human animal who is gradually being initiated into the brotherhood of community life. Such literature surrounds the neophyte with a kind of *aura*, a persistent atmosphere redolent of everything which the group holds dear. The hymns and other word-picturings of the spirit-world in which the community expresses its religious aspirations, the poems and funeral orations glorifying heroic leadership, in which the community renews itself by giving expression to the patriotic norms and action patterns which constitute its traditions and indicate its historic mission, the lyric and comic word-sketches of everything in group life which has beauty and charm : all these exercise persistent pressure upon the growing mind.[49]

In so far as they are artistically balanced and graceful, they make those upon whom their influence is extended, balanced, graceful, and charming.[50] And further : when we recollect that not only are these storied themes a large part of the young citizen's constant environment, but also that he himself from an early age participates in them actively, learning them by heart and singing, speaking, and acting them out all his life long : we realise how potent an instrument of education folk-literature is. In spite of its fundamental nonlogical character, it helps to turn the young human animal, not merely into a family baby, a neighbourhood child, a schoolboy or schoolgirl, an adolescent, an army man or woman, but into a citizen : a full member of a specific community, who responds with every fibre of his being to the rhythms of the community life—as a Spartan, a Cnossian, or a native Athenian. When the songs and stories, the games and sports, the religious, dramatic, and civic gatherings are all imbued with the self-same community ethos, their all-pervasive influence is simply overwhelming.

It is the community which educates young and old, men and women : educating them in every detail and fashioning them into what the community wants them to be.

When all are gathered together, in assembly, law-court, theatre, camp or other popular resort, and there is a mighty uproar, as they praise some things which are being said or done, and blame others, both to excess : reinforcing the words they shout with hand-clap, and the sound of their praise or blame is redoubled by the echo of the place of assembly—a young man's heart leaps within him, and he is carried headlong by the overwhelming flood of popular opinion. He will say what the public says. He will do what the public does. And he will become such as the public is—and necessarily so.[51]

Such is the educative effect of folk-language and folk-literature upon the young. Literature, with its word-imagery, influences directly the range and quality of rhythmic picture-thinking. It broadens and deepens the imagination of the young, as they project themselves into this or that community-approved situation. Furthermore, as a constant influence, it lends to their imaginations its supporting structures and so standardizes them. Acting in concert with other community institutions, it gradually adapts and shapes them, in thought word, and deed, for full citizenship, and at all times confirms them in the spirit of that citizenship. And this is inevitably so.[52]

All this is universal-Hellenic. These are simple facts of city-state life in Ancient Greece, easily verified by observation ; and the value of folk-literature in educating for citizenship is universally admitted. It is accepted as a traditional instrument of education, and is everywhere acclaimed as appropriate subject-matter for the school curriculum.[53]

How about Plato ? Does he accept this traditional attitude ? Not entirely. He does not deny that, provided you wish to bring up a boy to be a Spartan, you must bring him up on the action-songs ascribed to Tyrtaeus, which constitute the literary side of the traditional school of Spartan discipline. Or provided you wish to bring up a boy to be an Athenian, you will bring him up on the choruses of Aeschylus and the orations of Pericles, which constitute the school of freedom, Athenian style. All this is obvious, accepted as a matter of course.[54] But for himself, Plato does not accept this proviso. It is not his purpose to educate for membership in an actual community with its historic entanglements, its historic mission, and its distorted emphasis upon whatever one-sided character-development is deemed essential to its safety or its mission.[55] On the contrary, his aim is to educate for citizenship in a community which is more universal : Hellenic, indeed, in general pattern, but idealized as far as is humanly possible, a " model " city, which starts with a clean slate.[56] For this purpose, literature will be needed. Of course. But it is literature which has not yet been written. The literature which has sprung from the soil is local, all-too-local. And it has many other faults which entirely unfit it, at least in its present form, for use in converting young human animals into ideal members of a model city.

Just what is wrong with existent literature ? In the first place, the precise relation of the various rhythms and formal patterns followed by authors to the vital rhythms and patterns inherent in the human life-cycle at its more instinctive level, and of the stylistic conventions of literature to the different type-forms inherent in human nature, has never been worked out adequately. Consequently a good deal of extant literature does not succeed in expressing what it intends to express. A prayer or hymn intended to express praise and thanksgiving may be imperfectly expressive of the natural sentiment, and may even (involuntarily) suggest feelings of ill omen. [57]

In the second place, as picture-images which are intended to resemble, at least in essentials, the objects to which they refer, the creations of the extant literature are, for the most part, pretty poor copies. They are falsifications, not deliberately so, but with an effect, upon all who look to them for ideal truth, which is misleading. Word-pictures which represent the gods as ungodlike, great heroes as unheroic, men as unmanly, and women as unwomanly are bad art, [58] poor pictures. Moreover, their influence is bad in a moral sense. If learnt by heart, spoken and acted out, they can hardly fail of inducing in the younger generation dispositions which would be considered unfortunate. [59] And if the artist's efforts, as is sometimes demonstrably the case, are directed, not so much to portraying ideal truth as to imitating the physical phenomena of this world : so that he reproduces, not the inner significance of such phenomena, but their merely external sound-effects—as when he mimics the whistling of the wind, the creaking of ship's blocks, the barking of dogs, and the like—in such " art " there is nothing calculated to develop the young human animal into an ideal citizen of a model community. Such " literature " is pure nonsense. [60]

In the third place, literature which springs up unguided and undirected is liable to run wild. Instead of fine blooms, we find great overgrown weeds. Dependent as the author is upon satisfying the popular taste, he necessarily aims at pleasing his audience, i.e., at entertaining and amusing before all else. This means that he will aim at display and will exhibit a certain virtuosity. He will concentrate upon whatever is striking, registering fear, rage, and grief to excess : overemphasizing the already sufficiently emotional appeal of his art.[61]   The dignified, self-contained, self-disciplined character of the good citizen will be considered dull, unsuitable for literary depiction ; and the effect of all this will be to place emphasis, in education through literature, upon staginess and other undesirable qualities of character.   In fact, Plato feels about an unvaried diet of Greek literary successes much as we should feel about a curriculum devoted chiefly to the study of thrillers and crime stories.[62]

What can be done about this ?   It would not be practicable to scrap the whole of the extant Hellenic literature, merely because, in the form in which it has come down to us, it is unsuitable for school purposes.   The new-born baby starts from scratch, and if it is to be prepared, in a few short years, to become a full-fledged member of a Hellenic community, it must somehow interact with the traditional background and outlook enshrined in Hellenic literature.   In this nonlogical sphere, tradition has a definite value, which is indispensable.[63]   The traditional content of Hellenic literature must, then, somehow be preserved.   The question is, how ?

As Plato envisages the difficulty, two solutions commend themselves.   The first is to select, edit, revise and rewrite the traditional literature *in usum scholarum.*[64]   The second is to create an entirely new literature, a literature which will incorporate within itself the resources of the storied past, but will reorient and reinterpret them in the new spirit of idealism in education.   Let us consider these two solutions separately.

To rewrite the works of Homer and Hesiod, Aeschylus, Euripides, and the rest of the venerable writers of the past, sounds like a formidable task (one would think), not to be undertaken lightly.   Yet Plato does not hesitate.   He faces the problem precisely in the way in which an ecclesiastical authority would face the problem of bringing the traditional hymnal up to date, or a movie magnate would have a literary classic re-written for presentation upon the modern screen.   A small committee of technical experts—script-writers—is engaged and is put under the direction and control of some trustworthy representative of the powers-that-be.   In Plato's *Dialogues* this representative is referred to as the dialectician, the philosopher-king, or a member of the highly-trained senior legislative council : that is to say, a man not himself likely to be a creative author, but outstanding in respect of trained intelligence as well as of community spirit.[65]   He insists upon the observance of certain standards ;   and under his authoritative guidance the script-writers find their task simplified for them. A good deal has to be thrown out. But a good deal can be retained. A word or a line altered here and there, a new stanza inserted once in a while, and the problem becomes a mere matter of detail. You tackle your material piecemeal and presently you have reached your objective.[66] Writers in our own time do much the same without much difficulty. We have a *Boy's Homer, Tales from Herodotus*, and simplifications (for children) of Shakespeare and the Bible. The thing can be done.

What are the principles which guide the Platonic rewriting? They fall under three heads, corresponding to the three faults in Greek literature which have to be remedied. In the first place, the precise relation between the rhythmic patterns suitable for literature and the vital pulsations inherent in the human life-cycle will have to be established definitely. These rhythms are essentially identical for chant, melodic accompaniment, and associated dance-movement, but, in deciding what precise rhythms a composition should follow, sense is to take precedence over sound.[67] Certain types of sentiment are appropriate for young men in warlike mood. Words expressive of this martial sentiment are arranged in the appropriate martial rhythm (the revised " enoplion " rhythm) and so furnish the chant. A tonal sequence or melody expressive of the same sentiment (set in the revised Dorian mode or scale) is arranged in the same rhythmic pattern, and the appropriate quick-step or other dance-movement follows and reinforces the selfsame rhythmic sentiment.[68]

Modern concert-goers feel that there is something definitely " natural " in the themes of classical music. To Western civilisation these themes seem almost to sing themselves and to dance themselves. This is especially obvious in the case of composers like Mozart and Beethoven ; and in addition, their themes are definitely expressive of human moods, of joy and grief, of manliness, of love .and religious aspiration. We find this essential naturalness not only in the work of our greatest composers, but every now and then in the work of quite minor composers— corresponding to the inspired poem, perhaps, of Plato's " One-poem Tynnichus."[69] But Plato thought this contact with the deeper pulsations inherent in human nature did not need to wait upon inspiration. It would not (he imagined) take his official committee of experts long to discover by deliberate research the mathematical basis of these rhythms existing in human nature. It would then be a simple matter to establish for all time the standardized melodic rhythmic patterns which connect with the vital pulsations of the race and are at the same time expressive of moods and dispositions considered desirable for members of his model city : patterns manly for the men, womanly for the women, civic for the citizens, and so on and so forth.[70]

In the second place, since human nature and world-nature are after all based on the same general principles, the rhythmic patterns discovered by scientific research may be expected to connect with the patterns of the objective world.[71] In this case the picture-images of the rewritten literature will be found to furnish an indirect but reliable imitation or copy of the original to which they refer. If the dance of the stars in their courses is expressive of such cosmic moods as steadiness, orderliness, discipline, and control by a centralized principle of selfmotion, and stellar movements are expressive of a definite geometric pattern which can be reproduced in a man-made model : human art may conceivably succeed in reproducing, on a small scale, the orderly rhythms of the great world.[72]

Plato suggests that, by basing the scales constructed by his experts to express human moods upon a system of intervals corresponding exactly to the intervals which separate the orbits of the chief planets from one another, a " perfect system " of scales can be devised which will correspond to the great cosmic scale.[73] From this he concludes that the revised song-and-dance material used in his model city will be expressive of the great cosmic moods, transcribed, as it were, into the human clef. In this way literary and musical art can serve purposes directly educative. It can strengthen the cerebral selfmotion and assist it in its task of controlling and guiding the human organism as a whole. It can attune the young to the great harmonies of the cosmic system in which their lot is cast ; and it can encourage the mature and the ageing to continue in the straight and narrow path of a destiny which they realize to be of cosmic, as well as human, significance.[74]

In the third place, literature must not be left without some yet higher kind of guidance. Its revision must be directed and led beyond where the popular taste, if left to itself, would go. It must be directed beyond satisfying biosocial group feeling, if it is to unfold its full potentialities. It must be directed even beyond reproducing the orderly rhythms of the physical cosmos. For biosocial and physical patterns are not final. They are imperfect copies of something yet finer and more noble. Inherent in our feeling for art is a demand for something perfect. We reach out toward ideal rhythms glimpsed as transcending and glorifying human, earthly, and even cosmic motion-patterns, For it is these that we desire to have brought into intimate contact with us, through the medium of truly great art.[75]

This ultimate source of value, while expressible, no doubt, in mathematically apprehensible formulas, can be reached by us only through some process higher than the processes known as mathematical, logical, or dialectical. We call them "inspiration" and attribute them to a creative influence which transcends the cold reason of the scientist. Human reason, with its training in the elements of literary craftsmanship, with its scientific insight into the mathematical forms of the standard metrical rhythms, can go just so far. We soon come to the end of this sort of knowledge ; we have not yet begun to develop the feeling for guidance from above which inspires the creative writer. The genuine artist goes further. He submits himself to guidance, reaching out toward a divine source ; and the source which has created both man and the cosmos can take the artist's outstretched hand and can so guide it that it succeeds in expressing the secret values which underlie both men and the cosmos, and are ideal.[76]

In Hellenic literature from Homer down there is plenty of material whose inspiration from this source is beyond doubt. The task before the dialectically trained legislator and his committee of revisers is to see that the material is so arranged and rewritten that the spirit of idealism shines through unmistakably. As it might have been expressed by a later poet,[77]

> Into the melting-pot when *Homer* comes,
> What horrid stench will rise, what noisome fumes !
> How will he shrink, when all his lewd allay
> And wicked mixture shall be purged away !
> But what remains will be so pure, 'twill bear
> Th' examination of the most severe.

That is to say, as finally revised *in usum scholarum*, the traditional literature of Hellas is not merely simplified, so that children can understand its stories. It is so rewritten that its readers will not fail to grasp the underlying message, to experience it directly, to feel it with every fibre of their being. The revision will bring out, in rhythmic patterns which get under the skin of ordinary biosocial humanity, the ideal message of the Divine Leader, God's plan for the guidance of men, women, and children, as they make their way through the phases of the human life-cycle on this earthly planet.   It will guide and lead them toward the life-giving vision of the realm which lies beyond this visible world : the Plain of Truth, the realm of values which is the eternal source of whatever in human ways of living is worth while.[78]

So much for the rewriting of the traditional literature : a re-writing which makes it suitable for the education of human beings who are being prepared for membership in a community inspired by the spirit of idealism.   Such rewriting requires the combination of two gifts rarely found in a single person : the gift for creation (or rewriting), and trained philosophical insight ; and Plato arranges for this combination by having a committee appointed which contains men of both kinds.[79]   But while rarely united in a single person, these gifts are actually—in a case known to Plato—found existing together ; and where they co-exist, we can expect to receive, from the doubly gifted philosopher-author, an altogether new *genre* of literary composition. This new litera-ture will not need to be rewritten for educational purposes, because it is already, in its original form, so conceived and so written.

What is this perfect example of the new idealistic literature ? It is *The Dialogues of Plato* themselves.[80]   Compare these point by point with the literature which has had to be rewritten, and you will find that they have everything you could desiderate.   They exhibit all the genial mastery of language, rhythm, technique, and style which you could ask of any author.   Their content is deeply rooted in the soil, in the nonlogical vitality of the myths and tribal dreams of Hellas and the ancient world.   They possess humour, drama, suggestiveness, depth.   Undoubtedly inspired, they are permeated throughout by philosophic insight into the ideal realm and the principle of its power : The Idea of Good. In their great hero, Socrates, we have concrete proof that good-ness is not necessarily either sissified or dull.   A model of all the virtues, courage, justice, piety, temperance, and love of wisdom, he is no mere logic-chopper.   So vital that his nature eludes definition and cannot be confined within any verbal formula, he remains to the end a living enigma, the personification of the spirit of Eros, the almost-divinity who mediates between God and man, and operates not by logical techniques, but by merger of personality.[81]

And further : in addition to their freshness and the unusual qualities of their great hero, the *Dialogues* possess three definite advantages which the traditional literature lacks. (1) The older literature, once separated from its creators, is helpless. You can take it or leave it—or you can mistake it ; and it cannot defend itself against your misunderstanding. [82] Plato's *Dialogues* are in a different position. They too are plausible. They present vivid pictures. They suggest and they indicate. But that is not all. They argue, they refute objections. They prove their points. Once you enter into the argument, it will go hard but you will be convinced, and convinced by methods which are not merely persuasive in a nonlogical sense, but are susceptible of rigorous proof and disproof. The new literature can defend itself. In the second place (2) the *Dialogues* are not merely depictive (like Greek tragedy) or even merely protreptic. It is true that they draw their readers into the discussion and initiate them into philosophy ; but they also prepare them for active citizenship. They have a definite practical aim. And finally (3), the *Dialogues* are thoroughly reflective. Plato knows what he is doing, and how, and why, and his selfknowledge is not concealed in the *Dialogues*, but is plainly revealed. It has long been known that the *Republic* is essentially a treatise on Education : a specialized treatise which actually performs the service of which it talks. It discusses education for citizenship in an ideal community ; and at the same time it stimulates and actively prepares its readers, even at the present day, for such membership. The *Laws*, as Plato explicitly declares, is similarly an educative treatise on Education. [83] And as to the other Dialogues, of which of them is not the same statement approximately true ?

Dialogues of the Platonic type, then, are to constitute the curricular material, the new literature which is to be especially useful in stimulating and assisting the educational development of the rising generation in Plato's model city. Just how is the new material to be used, and by whom ? Is it just to be put into the hands of promising youth, as we distribute prize books at our Speech-day exercises ? Clearly, not. If *any* literature can be trusted to explain and defend itself, and to attract and educate its readers, Dialogues of the Platonic type can be so trusted. But education, with Plato, is always a process which involves two or more persons, merging their personalities ; and the new books, like the revised literature, will have to be studied, learnt by heart, and acted out, performed. They will need, not only pupils, but teachers, highly qualified teachers, if their use for the purposes of education is to be successful. [84]

The Platonic *Dialogues* are used first, then, in training the teachers. The new teachers are to be imbued with the spirit of idealism and are to pass this on to their pupils. The literary part of the teacher-training curriculum is thus to be derived from the *Dialogues* ; and it is only graduates who have lived their way into these *Dialogues*, have mastered their content, and have accepted their message, who can be given licences to teach. The literature which they will themselves use in teaching will be (1) the Platonic *Dialogues* themselves and (2) whatever other prose or verse literature they can find which is permeated with the same spirit—i.e., the traditional literature of Hellas which has been selected and edited by the committee of revisers. [85]

The teacher-training institution to which reference is here made is presumably intended to indicate something like Plato's own Academy at Athens ; and the suggestion is that it is to graduates trained in precisely such an Academy of higher learning that we are to look for a supply of teachers competent to initiate youth into the new idealism.

Thus trained and imbued with the spirit of Platonic idealism, to whom are the new teachers to introduce the study of the *Dialogues* ? To boys and girls of school age ? Hardly. The earlier schools, attended separately by boys and girls from the ages of six to ten, are primarily sport-schools. Gymnastic rather than the new literature constitutes their chief subject-matter. [86] It is true that the folk-gymnastic which is taught exhibits a rhythmic patterning, and it is doubtless expected that the girls and boys will sing or chant as they go through the motions of their folk-marches and folk-dances. But the words of these action-songs cannot consist of anything taken directly from the *Dialogues* themselves. For the *Dialogues* are not intended for young children. We can see this from the fact that not a single child is ever present—even as a *kophon prosopon*—among the *dramatis personae* of a single Dialogue. The chant-words of the sports-schools will thus be traditional. They will belong to the literature which has been revised and rewritten so as to conform to the Platonic pattern.

Will the *Dialogues* be taught, then, in the teen-age schools, in which instruction in the elements of expressive reading, singing, and dancing is made compulsory ? The reference to the *elements*, the three R's of the model city, indicates that nothing requiring intellectual maturity or depth of philosophic insight into principles underlying civic institutions is to be expected in these schools.

The literary subject-matter utilized will thus, for the most part, be derived from the rewritten literature of the Hellenic tradition; although it is conceivable that some of the vivid pictures of Plato's early and middle *Dialogues* might be introduced in the form of selections to be memorized and acted out, especially in the final school-year.

If it is not, then, to the school-age pupils that we are to look for students who are to be initiated into Platonic idealism *via* the *Dialogues* themselves, to whom are we to look? There remains only a somewhat older group, the group constituted of the young men and women who are being selected, tested, and trained for leadership : for positions as magistrates, adjudicators, and accredited representatives of the directorate of the model city. Somewhere in their career, these persons have to receive a higher education : an education analogous to the training which fits young men and women of the requisite technical gifts for the profession of teaching, but different. The higher education fits its graduates for positions of supervision and administrative direction, rather than for the performance of tasks which require mere technical capacities. It is such persons pre-eminently who will devote thorough study to Plato's *Republic, Politicus,* and *Laws,* and indeed to the more " dialectical " *Dialogues.* Such persons, carefully selected for their competence, will carry on their studies, presumably, in an institution which is analogous to Plato's own Academy ; and while many of their studies will be of a strictly scientific nature, their curriculum on its literary side will be constituted, not by the traditional literature revised for school use, but by Plato's own *Dialogues.* These will be utilized, then, primarily by adults, in what we might characterize as a post-graduate school of idealism. [87]

How is literary composition taught in the schools ? The models used are chiefly vivid pictures, each teaching a lesson, derived (by the revisers) from traditional literature. The pupils learn these by heart and then recite them, acting them out before their fellows under the eye of a competent teacher : a teacher competent to bring out the spirit of idealism as well as to assist in elocution and gesture. [88] But this is only a part of their use. Their chief function is to serve as models for composition : as patterns to guide the beginner in his early attempts to express himself, to create something of his own. Just as in learning to write : the beginner first moves his stylus in the grooves of the pattern, learning to get the feel of the letters. He then reproduces the form of the models in his own way, and eventually learns to express himself freely in the standard way of writing. So too with grammar and the accepted rhythmic and stylistic forms of literature. What is taught to pupils is the approved patterns. They learn to follow these, at first very closely, and gradually, as they acquire facility, with greater freedom : until they cease to repeat mechanically and succeed in expressing themselves, their own thoughts and feelings, in the accepted forms. That is to say, they learn to write letters in the accustomed epistolary style. They learn to prepare forensic and political speeches, recognizable as such. And they learn to compose familiar poems and speeches of approved pattern, so that they can entertain their friends in postprandial discussions like those of the *Symposium*. [89]

For citizens of the ideal community, the approved patterns are standardized and fixed. No one needs to be perpetually changing the shape or function of the letters of the alphabet. Individuals develop, it is true, somewhat different and indeed distinctive ways of writing, especially if they are not professionals, but citizen-amateurs. But no one really makes innovations in the accepted letter-forms. So too with grammar. The approved type-forms —noun, verb, adjective, preposition, and the like—are standardized, and the rules are there to be obeyed. It is not in the public interest that experimentation and innovation should keep grammar in a state of flux. It is true that in the course of time variations and corruptions have crept in : with peculiar effects upon spelling and upon certain grammatical usages. But this sort of thing is due to ignorance, to foreign influences, and to pretentiousness. It is in the public interest that the correct forms should be restored and standarized. [90]

So also with the formal patterns of literary expression. There is a reason in the nature of things for the differences between lyric, epic, and dramatic poetry, between forensic and political oratory, between a treatise, an epistle, and an epigram. Nothing whatever is gained by mixing these things up. When you are talking to an individual you don't express yourself as if you were making a formal motion in a legislative assembly ; and when you are offering a solemn prayer at an ecclesiastical festival, you don't make wisecracks. You have to accept the established distinctions between literary type-forms : precisely as you have to accept the established distinctions between men, women, and children. Only by recognizing these objective distinctions will you know what kind of speech to use in, addressing this audience or that ; and only so will you succeed in communicating what you have it in you to express.[91] The formal patterns of literary expression, once adequately determined, are standardized and remain, for the citizen of the ideal community, fixed.[92]

Fixed, *more egyptiaco*—just what does this mean ? Modern commentators, for the most part, consider that Plato goes too far. They believe that his standardization would sterilize art and would destroy the spirit of creativity in its cradle. He leaves, they assure us, no possibility of progress. Progress, they tell us, comes only from a revolt against the established norms, and from free experimentation, unhampered by the *mortmain* of the past. Is this position, however, in accordance with the evidence of the *Dialogues* ? Does Plato really mean what they think he says ?

Let us consider their position a little further. It takes the following form : if there is only one right way of composing in sonnet or sonata form, does not this mean that in a few short centuries the possibilities inherent in this form will be exhausted, and that creative composers will turn to something else—e.g., to free verse and impressionism,—as providing more scope for selfexpression ? If such new outlets are denied them, the source of their inspiration will surely dry up. Similarly, if there is only one right way of reciting Shakespeare or playing Beethoven's piano sonatas, does not this mean that artists will soon cease to perform Shakespeare or Beethoven, just as no one can endure the same gramophone record, however good, played over and over again ? In fact, if there is only one right way of expressing a given biological emotion or rhythm in vocal sounds, does not this mean that, in the end, there is only one fundamental language which is correct, and that consequently the many extant tongues represent variations which are corruptions of the archaic original, variations pursued because people grew tired of repeating the same sounds on the same occasions ?[94]

So much for the position of the critics. It is not, in itself, unreasonable. Perhaps we should take it in connection with the views of those interpreters who see in Plato's literary and philosophical development an increasing love of formal outlines and conceptual patterns, of triangles and circles, of " ideas " which are ultimately reducible to pure mathematics, and a growing devotion to dichotomic processes of analysis so abstract that they dehydrate and completely desiccate the vital material upon which they are so relentlessly superimposed. [95]

Is it however, *Plato* who is essentially attacked by this line of criticism ? Is he caught in his own web, smothered by his own techniques ? Let us consider. Even in his latest *Dialogue* he appears to be perfectly well aware of the barrenness of abstract conceptualism ; [96] and is not this the essential lesson of the *Parmenides*, that *Dialogue* which most readers find paradoxical precisely because it refutes, first the technical " theory of Ideas " attributed to Socrates, and, second, the yet more abstract theory of the One attributed to the great Parmenides ? Does not this mean that Socrates is greater than his " ideas," that *der Mann ist unendlich viel grösser als sein Werk*, that life is essentially more than its techniques ? [97]

It is true that Plato is a great lover of the processes of analysis and synthesis—but not *per se*. Their value is auxiliary. They help him to speak and to think. [98] The divine creation of our articuculated world of law and order is not less vital than the original chaos upon which its geometric structures are superimposed. On the contrary, it is more valuable in every way. The mathematical structure brings out and reveals values which would otherwise have remained forever a-slumber in the limbo of nonbeing. [99] So also in the case of language. The grammatical and literary forms and rules superimposed upon the inarticulate cries of primitive emotion do not smother, but unsmother. They bring out and develop to advantage, in language and literature, values which humanize our animal nature. The new forms of expression reveal man to himself, and reveal nature, the world of humanized nature, to man. Great literature is no second-hand, devitalized substitute for direct living. On the contrary, its creations enlarge and set at liberty our essential humanity. That is why it is so important as an instrument of education. It is indispensable, not only for tribal conditioning, but also for preparing for Platonic citizenship, for membership in the life of an ideal community. [100]

Do the permanent forms of language and literature eventually stifle the growth which at first they stimulate ? From the very beginning, Plato expects, admits, and insists upon the need of variation in matters of detail. Thus he never believes that once upon a time there existed a single archetypal language, of which all extant tongues are corruptions. On the contrary, while recognizing the functioning of a single language-producing principle (the principle of emotional reaction *via* rhythmic sounds, to biosocial stimulation), he recognizes, from the beginning, variations in the patterns in which such emotions express themselves.[101]

In the same way there has always existed, and there will always exist, considerable variety among the grammatical and literary forms of self-expression. The possibility of novelty, of alternation and variation of expression in matters of detail, is practically unlimited. No two individuals express their own feelings, or picture the world in which they live, in precisely the same words. Biosocial situations, such as come to receive expression in literature, are doubtless limited. But their expression in words, whether in lyric, dramatic, or epic, or forensic form, is susceptible of an infinite variety in detail. Even the subject-matter of Greek tragedy—which, being practically confined to borrowings from a single author, Homer, might be regarded as definitely limited—is still far from indicating that its vital possibilities for literature have all been exhausted. And the same is doubtless true of modern sonata-form or fugal form in music.

In fact, while individual writers may tire of writing plays, the drama form persists. It is grounded in human nature. And the same is true of all the major literary forms discovered by the Greeks. They are still in use in our modern world ; and while here and there a writer claims that they cramp his style, and that he needs a radically new form of self-expression, it is altogether likely that the chief forms of artistically balanced expression have by now demonstrated their *Lebensfähigkeit* and will continue to exist.

As to the question whether the discovery and invention of new literary forms is absolutely prohibited by the Platonic regulations, interpreters who maintain this forget three things : They forget (1) that the prohibition applies primarily to young persons who have taken a " short course for amateurs " in the elements only, and are still *in statu pupillari*. It is altogether reasonable to suggest that beginners learn to grow into the established patterns before they start outgrowing them.[102] As far as older professionals are concerned, Plato nowhere suggests that it is inappropriate for mature artists to experiment with the limits of their art, and to try out new combinations which go beyond the established patterns.[103] In fact, he plainly extends an invitation to one such independent artist to come and join him in the work of his own Academy.[104]

They forget (2) that Plato sets up definite machinery, not merely for establishing the standard art-forms, but for passing upon the desirability of introducing art-forms other than those already accepted as standard for the citizens.   More particularly, in his device of the " Visitor " who makes annual reports to the appropriate committee of the law-lords, he has provided a representative institution for investigating and testing novelties of all sorts, with the explicit intention of finding whether they are more likely to assist in carrying out the community programme than the forms which have already been accepted.[105]

Finally, they forget (3) that Plato himself invented and developed a new literary form : the philosophical *Dialogue*, and that he definitely experiments with this, varying it considerably from one dialogue to another.   The new form reaches a perfect artistic balance in the *Republic*, and a perfect artistic balance of a different type in the *Symposium*.   In some of the later *Dialogues* we can almost see it making way for the (still newer) forms of the treatise and the sermon.

We conclude, therefore, that the position taken by the critics, while not unreasonable in itself, cannot be regarded as directly opposed in spirit to the teaching of Plato.   Plato allows both for individual self-expression and for the guiding value of group norms which rest upon nature.   Both fáctors are, he believes, necessary if we are to have significant literary creativity.

And Plato goes further.   He investigates the philosophy implicit in the reference to nature and nature's group-norms.   In this way he teaches the writers of the future, who are expected to co-operate with the dialectician.[106]   He teaches them to see in nature something more than biosocial impulse, something more, even, than geometric patterning and the texture of the " ideas."   He reveals to them a vision of a life like ours, but vaster and greater, a vitality superior to the norms which it superimposes upon impulse :   a spirit of vitality which, speaking to us *via* the stylized patternings of impulse which we call " literature," sets aglow and fans into flame the spark of vitality which is within us.   In this way the creative spirit of humanity is kindled, developed to maturity and set at liberty.[107]

Liberated by literature selected and interpreted by teachers imbued with the spirit of idealism, humanity is stimulated to realize its highest self, to express the best that it has within it, by creating co-operatively a community life in the form of a model city, an ideal republic which is the City of God.   Firmly based upon human nature, upon mathematics and the techniques of reason, and upon the Divine plan for humanity (namely, the maximal realization of human value-potentialities in the service of the Whole),[108] this ideal furnishes an ultimate standard by which the significance of all human functions, including the function of creating literature, can be evaluated.

Judged by this standard, the best and only truly significant literature is such literature as supports men and women in the characteristic human effort of co-operating with God in creating and continuing the life of the model city : that is to say, such literature as we find exemplified in Plato's *Dialogues*, especially the *Republic*, *Politicus*, and *Laws*.[109] Next best is the literature created by inspired writers who have not indeed attained to this final vision of what human life could be and should be, but have in them something of the spirit of idealism : especially if their compositions can be revised and rewritten so as to reinforce the message conveyed by Platonic literature.[110] Last of all come the compositions of artists who, although technically gifted, have been blind to the vision : writers who stimulate unenlightened emotionality, or who mirror in their word-pictures a nature which is merely external, devoid of living meaning. Literature of the third kind cannot possibly be accepted and adopted. However undeniable its technical wizardry may prove to be, judged from the standpoint of stimulating and supporting the ideal city-life of humanity it is fundamentally worthless.[111]

So far we have been considering literary compositions primarily with reference to the curriculum of the state schools. But their educational use with Plato is far wider than that. They are used by mothers and nurses in forming and guiding the pre-school play of children—and who shall say that in such association the mothers and nurses are not also forming or re-forming themselves ?[112] They are used by old men who form and guide the spirit of youth by telling stories—and who shall say that the old men are not, in that association, reliving their past and re-forming their own spiritual strength ?[113] They are used daily in the temple services which the citizens of all ages attend regularly their whole life long. They are used in the monthly sport and music festivals, the field-days in which the whole community recreates its physical and spiritual vitality. They are used in the great festivals, occurring at wider intervals of time, in which the whole community rededicates itself to its great purpose. They are used in forensic and political business, and on all solemn occasions of public life.[114]

On all of these occasions the spirit and message of the literature used is one and the same.[115]

Thus the citizens who participate in the influence of these literary compositions, whether as hearers, or as performers, composers, teachers, and adjudicators, live in a perpetual atmosphere of community spirit. They emerge from their intimate contacts with literature spiritually cleansed, refreshed, strengthened and re-conditioned for life, with their vision renewed and refurbished. Such is the magic, the wizardry, of the new literature, and so varied its appeal, that, where the theme is life and what makes life worth while, the citizens are never satiated or bored by the essential simplicity of its message.[116] On the contrary, they are revitalized, inspired, thrilled. The new literature helps them to see things in their ideally true colours, to name them by their ideally true names, to realize their transcendental significance and function in ideal living.[117] Each day is a new and rather special sort of Christmas Day. Each citizen is a new embodiment of the spirit of his family group, a rather special Odysseus or Nestor. Each wife is a new and rather special sort of Penelope or Andromache. And each child is a very special sort of little Telemachus or Nausicaa.

The glamour of such names is no merely fanciful embellishment or literary make-believe. It is indeed dream-work, but it is a racial dream-work which reinforces the racial dream-purpose, and assists it to come true. For the literary tradition has an outlook as well as a background. It embodies and expresses the inner significance, as well as the history of the race. It whispers hope, inspires courage, and breathes prayer : that the new spearhead of the race may prove itself worthy of the name it bears.[118] The halo which literature places upon the brow of each citizen is intangible but real. Its help is demonstrable. As the citizens associate more actively with the storied heroes and storied gods of Olympus, they assimilate themselves more sincerely to the living principle of heroism and Divinity. They gradually become, while here on earth, more genuinely fellow-citizens of the ideal community whose home is in Heaven.[119]

It remains to inquire how literary form is related to scientific form. The differences spring to the eye. Literature is stylized expression, in rhythmic patterns which appeal to the race, of the cries and movements with which humanity reacts to its biosocial environment. Its pictures of the world are emotional, biosocial, related to action, concrete : expanding and enriching our experience, but keeping it always human in intimate contact with racial feeling. Science utilizes a very different medium of expression. Its mathematical and other symbols and rules are severely formalized. They are kept as separate as possible from the biosocial point of view. Their pictures of the world are skeletal outlines, diagrams which are standardized, abstract, unemotional, and dry. The scientist tends to think of human beings as triangles, and of their idealism as explicable in terms of the mechanics of their anatomical structures.[120] He thinks of the starry heavens as moving orbits tracing complicated geometric patterns. He thinks of architecture, painting, and music, as so much applied mechanics. In fact, it is the mathematics rather than the poetry of motion that he sees everywhere ; and what is poetry itself— e.g., in a Pindaric or choric ode—but a tangled texture of rhythmic equivalences requiring a slide-rule for its interpretation ?[121]

We have here a certain tendency, on the part of literary and scientific form, to diverge and develop along different lines, with a growing hostility which suggests fundamental incompatibility.[122] Most creative literature would be classed as fiction. It has high standards of its own, but ultimately it rests upon feeling, biosocial feeling ; whereas science aims at truth and rest upon a mixture of sensation and logic.[123] Literary and scientific methods thus differ as feeling differs from technique, as subjective differs from objective, and as opinion differs from knowledge. As thus differing and continuing to differ, each party to the difference becomes a little one-sided. It can and does criticize the party of the other part severely ; but it is not immune to an equally crushing reply.[124]

As Plato envisages this situation, this divergence and one-sidedness need to be overcome. The origin of both literature and science is the same. The ideal goal of both is the same. And while they necessarily diverge in technical methods, they should converge in purpose and so should manage to co-operate. In the new literature which is to be used for educational purposes, there is room for both ; and the revisers will see to it that neither diverges too far from the spirit of the other.

The origin of both, as forms of expression, is the same. Scientific form—roughly called mathematics—is itself a sort of language. It can be spoken and written. It constructs picture-images of a

sort—geometric diagrams and their arithmetical equivalents—
and it can be used to persuade and convince beings who are
sufficiently intelligent and sufficiently educated to apprehend
the conclusiveness of its abstract patterns.   It constitutes an
artificial language, created deliberately for highly specialized
purposes.   Its patterns represent a technical standardization of
the patterning-motif already present in ordinary biosocial language
and literature.   The Hellenic equivalents of the " foot " and the
" ell " are as biosocial in origin as the modern terms.   But in
scientific language the emphasis is upon the technical standard
rather than upon the biosocial background.   Scientific language
thus seems to be logical rather than nonlogical ; although the
logical quality belongs to its technical methods rather than to its
ultimate background and its ultimate outlook.[125]

As a special language, it builds upon and presupposes much of
the structure and function of general biosocial language ; and
thus the training it gives in techniques comes somewhat later in
the child's development than the acquisition of general language.
The early education of the child is necessarily through fiction
rather than through science, and artistic fiction develops the
imagination rather than the reason.[126]

But the Platonic board of censors sees to it that the literature
used for educational purposes develops not only friendliness, self-
control, and other socially commendable attitudes.   It is so
selected, written, and taught, as to develop also a love of truth.
It prepares the growing mind for making an enthusiastic as well
as a prudent use of its reasoning powers when the times comes,
and meanwhile encourages it to take kindly to mathematics in
the concrete.[127]

The prose and verse rhythms of the action-songs are selected,
not merely for their biosocial appeal, but also for their orderly
metrical and logical patternings : so that the child-mind develops
structures which are already, in their essence, geometrical and
logical.   So too the games of childhood are formed upon the
solution of problems which have, not only a biosocial, but a definitely mathematical appeal.   Dividing children into groups
which take sides for the purposes of play, distributing apples and
toys so as to give each child an equal share, involve quite a little
concrete mathematics.   So too the petty commerical interests of

family life involve a good deal of buying, perhaps also of selling, in which concrete reasoning of a mathematical kind will develop naturally.[128]

In such ways the play and biosocial background of the child's life can be made to harmonize with the geometric rhythms of the revised literature : both alike preparing the mind for a systematic and detached study of mathematical techniques and their logical implications when the times comes. They make the transition from concrete to abstract, from imagination to reason, easy and natural.

On the other hand, Plato does not encourage the development of scientific techniques merely for themselves, in complete abstraction from the home environment and its place in the ideal city. It is only children with sound literary training and with imagination developed along the approved lines, who are selected, when the time comes, for the advanced scientific training.[129] And their training in scientific method is never in scientific method for its own sake. The young citizens are not being trained to be scientists, as such. On the contrary, their study of science is a means to an end which has been present all along ; and the technical training is intended to fit them for leadership in the model community. They are to be trained leaders of the model city : magistrates who know enough to direct research and to supervise the application of scientific method to all the problems of civic life in a community of 5,040 families.[130] Scientific form and literary form are thus two kinds of civic activity which are rooted in biology on the one hand, and in idealism on the other. As used for educational purposes, they co-operate and play into each other's hands ; and the reviser and writer of the new literature keeps the balance true ; so that, when he swings toward science, his literary and biosocial training keep him from over-balancing, and, when he swings toward literature, his scientific training keeps him from an overswing into subjectivity, into the futility of the idle dream.

[1]Rep. 376e–377c, 378de, Prtg. 325c f., cf. Laws 653b.   [2]Cf. Laws 653de, Laws 672cd, cf. 673cd. Laws 791e, cf. Laws 815e f. [3]Laws 788e f., 789d f. 790c f., Tim. 88b–89c, 47cd. [4]Laws 791ab, Tim. 89a, 70a, 73cd, 75c, cf. Tim. 42a–c, 43b ff., Phaedr. 245c f. For difficulties in connection with self-mastery when drink interferes with the unifying and ordering function of the central self-motion, cf. Symp. 215a (Alcibiades). [5]Laws 653c f., 672c f., 673cd, Tim. 29e f., 47b f., 53a–c, 69bc. [6]Cf. Laws 653c f., 655d f., 656d f. [7]Laws 793d–794c. [8]Laws 653 d f., 672c f., 673c f. [9]Laws 659d f., cf. Rep. 425a, cf. Rep. 422e, Theaet. 180e f., Laws 813 d f. [10]Laws 797b ff. Rep. 424b f. [11]Cf. Laws 643b f. Cf. Laws 771 de. [12]Laws 808de f., Lysis 207e ff., Prtg. 325d f., Rep. 590d f. [13]Cf. Rep. 395b f., 401, 522ab. Laws 793e ff. Cf. Laws 828 ff. [14]Laws 782e f. 793a–d, cf. Rep. 458c f. Rep. 571b f. Cf. Laws 835d ff. Cf. Phaedr. 250e f. Soc. is

the Virtues, but can't define. *Phileb.* 43b. [15]*Rep.* 558e ff. Cf. *Gorg.* 491e f., cf. *Symp.* 211c f., *Rep.* 571d f., *Phileb.* 31c f. [16]*Rep.* 399a–c, e–402a, *Laws* 654 ff., 672cd, 673cd, 796b f., 813d f., 814e ff. [17]*Tim.* 29e f., 47b f., 53a–c, 69bc. [18]*Tim.* 53c ff. [19]42e f., 30d ff., 39e f. [20]Cf. *Symp.* 186d f., 188a f., cf. *Crat.* 419bc, cf. *Prtg.* 353cd, cf. *Gorg.* 518cd, *Rep.* 556e, *Tim.* 82–86a, 87c, *Phileb.* 31cd, *Laws* 691c. *Soph.* 228a. [21]*Laws* 643b f., 794 ff. *Rep.* 425a, 444d. [22]*Laws* 797, 839a, 423e f. *Rep.* 443b f., 540d, 591c f. [23]*Crat.* 421d f., 424b ff., 431b, [24]*Crat.* 387b–d, 388bc, 422d f. Cf. *Theaet.* 206d. Naming is differentiated from such a " gesture " as onomatopoesis in such names as " cock-a-doodle-do," but this is later taken back *re* primitive names. [25]*Crat.* 423d, 426b f., *Rep.* 399e f., cf. 404de, *Laws* 816cd, 672e, cf. 656c ff., 669b f., 812d f., cf. *Theaet.* 206b. [26]*Crat.* 812d f. *Rep.* 398cd. [27]*Laws* 669c ff., 812 (with England's notes) de. *Rep.* 397cd, 398a, *Laws* 658 f., cf. 700 f. Cf. Aristot. *Problem.* XIX 18. Cf. *Tim.* 80ab. [28]*Laws* 812e, 660b–c ; *Soph.* 253b. Cf. *Rep.* 397b f. [29]*Laws* 653d f., 672b f., 673c f., 812e f., 790d f., 791e f., [30]*Laws* 810e f., 814d ff. *Rep.* 603c ff. [31]*Rep.* 386 ff. [32]*Laws* 802d f., *Tim.* 47cd, *Prtg.* 326b. [33]*Ion* 535b f. condensed, cf. *Prtg.* 326a, *Laws* 810c, 811a. [34]*Ion* 533d ff. *Phaedr.* 245a, 265ab, *Laws* 682a, 719c, cf. *Theaet.* 201e ff. *Prtg.* 326b. [35]*Crat.* 387b f. 423e f. *Rep.* 393, 597e ff., *Tim.* 19de, *Laws* 719c, *Tim.* 47cd. [36]*Crat.* 424a, 426c f., 427c, 434cd, 422ff. 425d. The words in the text are rough equivalents of the Greek words used as examples by Plato. Such a name as " cock-a-doodle-do " is not regarded by P. as legitimate (*Crat.* 423c). [37]*Crat.* 425d, 428e, 430ab, 431cd, slightly condensed. [38]*Rep.* 411ab. [39]Lucian, *Vera Historia*, Pt. II *ad init.* [40]*Crat.* 391, 393d f., 397c f. [41]*Crat.* 391e f., 398a–c, 425c, 432c ff. Cf. *Rep.* 514–614b ff., for a celebrated example, and also *Phaedo* 109 ff. [42]Adam's *Plato's Republic*, notes on 382d, 414b, J. A. Stewart *The Myths of Plato*, 1905 pp. 20–51, cf. 451–456.[43]*Laws* 644c f., 803b f. cf. *Rep.* 514 f. Cf. *Apol.* 42a, cf. *Gorg.* 492d f. 526d f. [44]*Crat.* 414 d, 424e f., 431, 432d ff., Large numbers of examples are given in the etymologies (409c ff.) *Phaedr.* 266d f. [45]*Phaedr.* 267a f., 269a f. [46]*Phaedr.* 264. [47]*Phaedr.* 266c f., 268c 269c. [48]Cf. *Phaedr.* 245a f., 264c, 269d, 271 f., 275e f.–278b, *Menex.* 234c f. [49]Cf. *Menex.* 235a f. 236e f–249c. *Laws* 663e ff., 803d f., 810e f., 812b f., *Rep.* 377a ff. [50]*Rep.* 400d f.–402a. [51]*Rep.* 400e 492a–c. *Laws* 663e ff. Cf. *Laws* 659a f., cf. 393c. [52]*Laws* 738b–d, 828a–829d, cf. *Rep.* 394e f. Cf. *Laws* 625c f. [53]*Laws* 793a f., 798a f., 802a f., 810e f., *Rep.* 401 f. [54]*Prtg.* 325e f. *Laws* 858c f., cf. *Menex.* 235d, 239b, cf. *Rep.* 561 ff. [55]Cf. *Laws* 629 ff., 666c f. *Rep.* 501a–c. *Rep.* 470e, 500e f. (Philosophers—artists who imitate the heavenly pattern—will begin by taking the State and the manners of men, from which, as from a tablet, they will rub out the picture, and leave a clean surface. They will have nothing to do with either individual or State, and will inscribe no laws, until they have either found or made a clean surface.) [56]Cf. *Laws* 736c f. [57]*Laws* 654e f., 669 f., 800 f.–803a, *Phaedr.* 270e ff. *Rep.* 398c f–402a. [58]*Crat.* 431a f., *Rep.* 377c ff., *Laws* 802d f., cf. 801b f. [59]*Rep.* 377bc, 378b, 381e, 387bc, 388d, *Laws* 655d ff., 811b, 812bc, 390b, 391e, cf. 595a, 605ab. [60]*Crat.* 423bcd. *Rep.* 396b, 397ab. [61]Virtuosity : cf. *Phaedr.* 235a, *Rep.* 397cd, 398a, *Laws* 658 f., 667b ff., 669 ff., 700 f. [62]*Rep.* 378b f., 381d f., 386 f., 388d, 390 f., 395c f., 397d f., 603c ff., *Laws* 801b f. [63]*Rep.* 376e, 382c, *Laws* 793a, 798a f., 838d f. *Critias* 107b f., *Menex.* 237 ff., cf. *Laws* 713, 926e f. cf. *Polit.* 271 ff. *Prtg.* 325c ff. [64]*Rep.* 377b ff. *Laws* 817, 810d f., 802a f. [65]*Crat.* 390c f., *Laws* 802bc, 829d, 858de. [66]*Laws* 800a, 801a f., 811b f., 817b f., 957a f., *Rep.* 379a ff. [67]*Rep.* 398d, *Laws* 700, 657b f. cf. 799a f. [68]*Rep.* 399a f. *Laws* 814e–816d. [69]*Ion* 534d. [70]*Laws* 660a f., 802b f., 957c f., 811b f., *Rep.* 399 f. [71]*Crat.* 388d f. cf. *Laws* 701. [72]*Tim.* 35 ff., 46e f., *Rep.* 617b, on which Adam writes " A choir of eight Neo-Pythagoreans would have had no difficulty in rendering the music of the spheres on a small scale." [73]*Tim.* 35c f. Cf. E. Frank : *Plato u.d.s–g. Pythagoreer*, p. 155. [74]*Laws* 818c f., 821b f., *Tim.* 47b f., cf. *Laws* 903b ff. Cf. *Phaedr.* 245c f. [75]*Rep.* 508e f., *Sym.* 210–212, cf. *Laws* 719b, 802ab, 811b. Cf. *Crat.* 423d f. *Ion* 533d, ff., *Phaedr.* 245a, 265b, *Meno* 99cd, *Apol.* 22a–c. [76]*Phaedr.* 2 68c – 270b ; cf. *Laws* 682a. [77]Sir R. Blackmore. The reference in the original is to Dryden, not to Homer. See Johnson's *Life of Dryden* (Lives of the Poets, Chandos Classics Edition, p. 158). [78]That is to say, it is definitely rewritten in the spirit of Platonism. *Laws* 802a f., 810e f. Cf. *Phaedo.* 109 f., *Phaedrus* 247b f. 248b, *Rep.* 509ab, 531 ff., *Sym.* 211b f., 903b ff. cf. *Laws* 682a, 964c, 967d f. [79]Cf. *Phaedr.* 269d, 270a. *Laws* 802bc. [80]*Laws* 811c f. The reference is tasteful and delicate, and shades off (in other passages) into phrases like " writings which agree with the writings of the legislators " (i.e., with Plato's *Laws*). The *Laws* ends with a hint that Plato's Academy will have to be copied in the Model City. *Symp.* 209a, 210c f., 215a f., 216d f., 222a, *Apol.* 33ab, *Theaet* 149–151c, cf. *Phaedr.* 275e f., 278a f.

⁸¹Cf. Friedländer, p. 51 ff. ⁸²*Phaedr.* 275de, 276c. ⁸³*Laws* 810e f–812a, *Phaedr.* 276a. ⁸⁴Cf. *Phaedr.* 275a–278b, *Laws* 811e f., 964c f. ⁸⁵*Laws* 802b f., 811, 817b f. ⁸⁶*Laws*, 794c ff. While stories are told to the children, and they take part in action-songs and choruses, which partly involve the principle of the new literature, reading and writing are not taught before the age of ten. (*Laws* 810a). ⁸⁷*Laws*. The assembly which revises the laws consists of older men, and also of younger men, co-opted for the purpose by their seniors. These younger men are " between the ages of thirty and forty " (*Laws* 951d f.), i.e., are of the same age as the students of dialectic in *Rep.* They discuss laws, and " learn with all diligence " kinds of knowledge approved for throwing light upon the subject (presumably including a study of Plato's *Laws*, and *Republic*, and *Politicus*). *Laws* 956e f. states that younger legislators supply all omissions of the older legislator in minor matters, studying, revising, and giving local application to the laws of actual communities ; and " studying writings about them," using as his test " the one sure test " of conversation and literature " the writings of the legislator," i.e., Plato's *Laws* and kindred writings (*Laws* 811df).

Laws 961 refers to the same council of old and young men (not less than thirty) as being highly educated (964) in dialectic ; and the special training in idealism prescribed in 965–968 with its applications to theology, astronomy and civics, appears to correspond to the higher education of the *Republic* Bk. VII—i.e., is presumably the kind of training given in Plato's own Academy.

⁸⁸*Laws* 810e–811a, d–812a. Cf. *Prtg.* 325df. ⁸⁹*Prtg.* 32–6d, 347cf. cf. *Phaedr.* 268c, *Phaedr.* 271d f., 277e–278b, *Theaet.* 150b f. Cf. *Symp.* 207e f., 209a f. ⁹⁰*Crat.* 414c f. 424b f. 431 ff. cf. *Crat.* 398 f., 402e f., 410a f., 412e. *Laws* 810b, 812a, cf. *Crat.* 386de f., 389df., 394b f. *Laws* 656d f. ⁹¹*Phaedr.* 271bf, 277bc. *Laws* 800 f. 802d f. *Rep.* 392d ff. ⁹²Cf. *Laws* 656d f., 660e f., 799a f., 802b, *Rep.* 397de. ⁹³Cf. Jowett : *Tr. Plato*, Vol. III, pp. clxiii, clxv, ccix, ccxiii. ⁹⁴*Crat.* Cf. Jowett, Vol. I, pp. 293–298. ⁹⁵Cf. Jowett, *Op. Cit.*, Vol. IV, pp. 283, 285, 411, f., 521, 524, 533. ⁹⁶*Phileb.* 30b f. ⁹⁷*Parm.* 135 f. Cf. A. E. Taylor. *Plato.* Wilamowitz, *Platon*, pp. 106–116. ⁹⁸*Phaedr.* 266b. ⁹⁹*Tim.* 52d f. 30a–c, 28 f., 69b, *Phileb.* 16c f. ¹⁰⁰*Phaedr.* 265d f–266c cf. *Rep.* 420d, *Phileb.* 17b f., *Laws* 668de, 669b f., 903c. *Prtg.* 325e f., *Laws* 810e f. 956e f., 961, 964–968. ¹⁰¹*Crat.* 389d f. 393 f. 394a. *Prtg.* 326b. ¹⁰²*Laws* 802, 809e ff., cf. *Rep.* 377b f., 379 ff. ¹⁰³*Crat.* 394a–b–c. *Laws* 660bc, 669b f., 812d f. Cf. *Soph.* 253b, ¹⁰⁴The reference is to " Isocrates the fair " (*Phaedr.* 279ab). (He did not accept the invitation). ¹⁰⁵*Laws* 801d, 802a f., 811b f. 817cd, 951 f. ¹⁰⁶Cf. *Crat.* 390c f. ¹⁰⁷*Rep.* 395b f., 590e f., 592, Cf. *Phaedr.* 245a, 277e ff. *Tim.* 52d f., 41 f., 29e f., *Laws* 739d f., 801b f, 967d f. ¹⁰⁸*Laws* 903b ff. ¹⁰⁹Cf. *Laws* 811b f., cf. 951d f., 956e f. Cf. Note 87, *supra.* ¹¹⁰*Laws* 802e f. 956e f., cf. *Rep.* 592, 540a–c. ¹¹¹*Rep.* 395c f., 397f., 605 f., *Laws.* 811, 817d. ¹¹²*Rep.* 377, 381c, ¹¹³*Rep.* 378cd, *Laws* 657f, 664d. ¹¹⁴*Laws* 653c f., 657c f., 772de, 775a, 799, 809c, 816c, 828 f., 834e, f. *Rep.* 413e f., 465e, 468 d f., 540bc, *Laws* 947. ¹¹⁵*Laws* 664 f., 810e f. ¹¹⁶*Laws* 659d f., 665c, 802c, 816e, cf. *Rep.* 424bc. ¹¹⁷*Crat.* 389d f. *Laws* 802ab, 811b f ¹¹⁸*Crat.* 397b. Cf. *Laws* 816ab, *Phileb.* 39c f. Cf. Soph, *Ajax* 550–1 ; *Iliad Z* 476–480. ¹¹⁹*Theaet.* 176a f. *Prtg.* 326a f. Cf. *Phaedr.* 252d f. *Rep.* 591c f., 540ab. ¹²⁰*Phaedo* 98b f., *Tim.* 46de, 53c f., 61d f., 73b f. 81b f., 89b f., ¹²¹*Gorg.* 502c, *Rep.* 399e f., 601b, 529b f. *Phaedr.* 245a, 719b, *Rep.*, 602f. *Prtg.* 356c f. *Polit* 284a. *Phileb.* 26a, 55d ff., 64d f. ¹²²*Rep.* 595a f., 607c f., 603 f. ¹²³*Rep.* 376e f., 476b, 533b f. ff. *Phaedr.* 269e f., 276e f. *Soph.* 266c f. *Phileb.* 55d ff. *Laws* 967d f. ¹²⁴*Rep.* 531e, f., 608a f. *Polit.* 257a, *Prtg.* 316e, *Laws* 967cd. 811b f. ¹²⁵*Rep.* 522 ff. 533b–d. *Polit.* 258d, *Phileb.* 55d–59b. *Parm.* 143 ff., cf. *Laws* 746e f. *Crat.* 432ab, 435a f. *Gorg.* 450d f., 453e. ¹²⁶*Rep.* 376e f., 522a f. ¹²⁷*Rep.* 395b f., 402a, 485b ff. 401b f. *Tim.* 39bc, 47a, *Phileb.* 55d–57d, *Laws* 747bc, 771b, 809d. ¹²⁸*Rep.* 525c–527d, *Laws* 817e–820d. ¹²⁹*Rep.* 412de, 413c f (esp. 413e), 522a f, 536c–537c, Cf. *Laws* 818a, 967 f. ¹³⁰*Rep.* 524d–540b, cf. 591–2, *Laws* 737b f., 745b, 746d f., 771, 877d, 965–968a.

CHAPTER IX

THE PUPILS AND LEARNING

As background for the present study, let us survey rapidly the general features of Plato's educational theory, in so far as these have been established. The world is best regarded, Plato thinks, as a balanced, self-maintaining texture of motions. In themselves, these motion-tendencies are thought of as nonlogical, merely factual, chaotic. The balance, which asserts itself in this motion-welter and becomes self-maintaining, is thought of as " divine " in origin and ideal in significance. It is the work of a transcendental creative Agent, who " animates " the world by bestowing upon it the principle of selfmotion. This operates by moving in a circle ; and the circular movement of an all-containing sphere gradually superinduces upon its chaotic contents the forms appropriate to regular solids of the types which can be inscribed within a sphere. So far as thus formalized, the original motions become patterned and take on structural form : the elementary forms of fire, water, earth and air.

And further : certain large balanced structures, composed of these elements mingled according to a principle of proportion which makes them self-maintaining in quasi-circular movement, develop patterning and regularizing tendencies of their own, which they impress upon the world around them. That is to say, such bodies as the sun moon and stars superinduce upon our earth and its environment, the rhythms of day and night, month and year, the seasons, the winds and tides, and the other rhythmic patterns which we regard collectively as " nature." These, in turn, influence the rhythms of life and growth of the lesser animate structures of our earth : the animals and human beings.

Human beings are also composed of the four elements, mingled according to a principle of proportion which makes their characteristic motion-tendency self-maintaining. Their selfmotion, located primarily within the brain, interacts with the environment in such a way as to impress itself and its characteristically human patterns of living upon that environment. The chief phases of the human life-cycle, which is self-perpetuating, are birth, growth to maturity, love and reproduction, a longish period devoted to group self-government, associated with the gradual decay and final death of individuals, their places being taken by members of the rising generation.

Group self-government is similarly an example of self-maintaining motion, patterning itself, roughly, upon the example of the self-maintaining system of the stars in their courses. Both systems are, in diverse ways, examples of the ideal principle of maximal value-development. The best conceivable system for human beings is thought out for us in the *Republic* and *Laws*.

The problem of education, as Plato sees it, is how, starting with human babies, with their instinctive motion-tendencies, their complete ignorance, and their complete helplessness, to assist them to develop themselves into self-maintaining citizens of his model city : able and willing to take their places in carrying on and indeed improving upon its traditions. The problem can be solved, be believes, only if all the citizens, and every one of the social institutions characteristic of the ideal community, co-operate and bring to bear their efforts.

That is to say : every childish potentiality must be encouraged to pattern itself upon the model of the ideal community. Childish motion-tendencies become dances : folk-dances, civic dances, stylized upon ideal civic principles. Childish games become gymnastics : folk-gymnastics and folk-games, military gymnastics and community festivals : preparation for adult life in the ideal community. The expressive cries of infancy are taught to shape themselves into music and language stylized into literature : folk-language, folk-music, folk-literature, revised and rewritten so that their rhythms prepare participants for life in the model city. The playful curiosity of childhood, associated with practical mathematical techniques, leads to science and philosophy : community science and community philosophy. So too with the army, the law-courts, the political assemblies, and the churches : all these institutions can be made to work toward the same end. And love also, that nonlogical but intensely human passion in which the original chaos is never far below the surface, can become through participation in song and dance, solemn festival and long community supervision, sublimated into a most powerful agent of community idealism.

Among these institutions, one is associated with the growth-to-maturity phase : the school. What is its function ? During the maturing period, children play games out of school hours. They participate in community festivals, both gymnastic and musical. They share in the fortunes of the community, and associate with its members in their artistic and economic activities. All are subjected to the same influences ; the seasons, the food-supply, the contingencies of war and peace. Interacting with such extra-scholastic extracurricular influences, the growing children learn a number of lessons : community lessons, all of them. Within the school things are much the same. What the child learns is largely what we should call extracurricular : dancing, singing, marching, military games, all connecting up with the monthly gymnastic festivals and the daily temple-services. Reading and writing are taught, it is true. But the method is as extracurricular, as like life in the family, as possible. Reading and writing are taught as games. The children read and write their own names. Taking these as starting-points, they compare their names with the names of other children. Only very gradually, as an extension of this activity, do they acquire a more systematic and logical grasp of the significance of syllables and letters, grammar and language.[1]

The school, that is to say, is simply a more specialized kind of home : something half-way between the original, family home, and the future home, the community. In this intermediate home the place of mother and nurse is taken by the teacher (as later by the magistrate). The teacher is trained, partly indeed, in the technical side of reading, writing, and music : but trained especially in teaching children, teaching community children to become community men and women. He assists his pupils to develop community spirit : so that they move, speak, think, write, and otherwise express themselves more and more in accordance with the approved community patterns.

Education and learning can be understood in two senses. You can take a child, much as you might take almost any young animal, and train him in the details of his movements : so that his actions follow a pattern which you prescribe *ab extra*. You drill him until his responses to your imperatives become automatic : reproducing the outlines of your pattern with mechanical fidelity. You concentrate upon accurate space-time movements until you get the result for which you are looking. In this way you produce *Wunderkinder* and professionals : flute-girls, copperplate writers, *virtuosi* of one sort or another. But that is not the way in which you get educated men and women. In fact, Plato is disposed to deny to such methods the name of education or learning altogether.[2]

Why so ? Because, in the interaction between the child's self-motion and the environment, you have taken sides with the environment. You have fòrced upon the brain and nervous system of the child an alien pattern : a mechanical system which can maintain itself only at the expense of the child's original self-motion. A child so trained becomes more and more a bit of what you have made him : a technician, a robot, a useful slave, perhaps. He becomes less and less of a man : less and less competent to develop his own self, to become a free self-determining citizen of an ideal community. You have taught a subject. You have failed to educate a child.

Education and learning, in the only sense which Plato is willing to recognize as genuinely educative, stimulate the self-development of the child as a whole. The environment, or it may be the environment as deliberately modified by some teaching *persona*, stimulates by furnishing potential problems : problems which appeal to something within the growing child—his hunger, his need for movement, his love of play. Such problems should be within the capacity of a growing child to solve for himself. It is by meeting the environment half-way, selecting the problems which it offers and adopting them as his own, and solving them to his own satisfaction, that the child gradually makes his way toward personal maturity.[3]

This is true of physical, social, moral, æsthetical, and intellectual self-development. In each and every field, the education which really educates is self-education : education of a self by a self. Whether the self accepts as its own, problems furnished ready-made by the environment, or whether it sets itself its own problems and largely creates its own environment (as in the case of creative artists) : it learns in the only sense in which learning is genuinely educative, by growing from within, acting as a whole and developing, step by step, as it solves one problem after another, always as a whole. Learning is always an extension of the organism's original selfmotion, an inner growth of selfmastery, from control over its own organism to control over its environment, physical, social, moral, aesthetical, and intellectual.[4]

Let us consider a few examples. At the age of three " the childish nature craves sports." The urge to play develops spontaneously from within. The community provides a suitable environment : community playgrounds, with a supervising matron in charge. Brought together by their nurses, the children do not have to be trained or drilled or ordered to amuse themselves. The attendance, indeed, may be regarded as compulsory. But once there, nothing in the environment forces them to play. They play spontaneously. All that the nurses do is to keep an eye on their charges and see that nothing harmful takes place. No child is permitted to injure itself or the other children. The matron is indeed armed with authority, and uses it. But it is against adults, slaves or foreigners whose influence is undesirable, that her power is directed : not against the children. The children in this sheltered and entirely suitable environment live their own lives. They set themselves to play their own games : the games human children play the world over. They manipulate the sand and other features of the physical environment. They run, skip, and jump. They play ball ; and as they grow toward the age of six, they play more together, in more organized groups. This involves taking sides and following leaders. In this way they develop a selfmastery and selfcontrol which are moral and social as well as physical. They are playing as free children with free children : acquiring the rudiments of give and take ; learning to be little citizens in a community which has a place for every-one.[5]

Or take the six-year-olds in their sport schools. Here they learn to play their parts in a variety of military sports : including in Ancient Hellas, the accurate use of the slingshot, the javelin, and the bow. The professional shows them how, and assists their first spasmodic efforts with suggestions on points of detail. But mastery over such weapons, i.e., the attainment of genuine accuracy in their use, is something that the children have to learn for themselves. They learn by doing. By trying this and that, projecting themselves into what they are doing, they gradually get the feel of things into their own hands : and they can co-ordinate their various activities so as to produce, with a fair degree of certainty, the desired result. To each individual child, learning presents itself as a series of individual problems. These he has to tackle in his own way and solve for himself. There is no other way in which he can learn. There are no substitutes.[6]

We can realize this if we take a more modern example which falls within our own experience. Children in our more modern sports-clubs are taught fancy skating, swimming, and a variety of other games. What the professional actually tells them, and actually shows them, is helpful : well worth while. But no child learns the outside edge and the various skating figures and jumps by merely watching and listening. He has to do something for himself, something which comes from within. He has to get the feel of the various curves and movements into his own limbs and body ; and his balance is not something external ; it is *his*, a balance which he himself exercises and controls. Every new twist and leap that he learns, he learns in the same way : by trying, throwing himself into it until he can do it. And he does it as an extension of his own self-balance and self-movement.

Or take the teen-age children learning to read, write and make music. Again the professional indicates how the thing is done. Again he gives all sorts of useful advice on points of detail. And in proportion as the subject-matter grows more complicated, there is more for him to explain—far more. But as far as the pupils are concerned, their procedure is exactly the same as in the early phases. They learn, not by mechanical mimicry of the professional's spacetime movements, but by trying, by projecting themselves into the activities concerned, until here too they get the feel into their throats, hands, and bodies generally ; until the gestures which are *their* gestures succeed in giving satisfaction. What the Greek child learns is to perform : to express himself before an audience. The words of his recitation are borrowed from this or that national poet : a man perhaps long since dead. But what the child acts out, what lend life and meaning to his portrayal, are his own feelings, his own aspirations, his own hopes and fears. In all such learning, it is the self which expresses itself, and in expressing itself expands and grows towards maturity.[7]

So too when the school period is over and the graduate projects himself into the life of the adult community. In the army, in business, in social and civic life, he gradually learns to find his own place : not by following mechanically rules which are conventional, merely formal ; but by living his own way into community life. He tries out this and that activity, following up the lines along which he proves successful and finds satisfaction. In so doing, he learns to educate himself as a whole : continuing to develop and grow in usefulness. If he shows aptitude for success in administration, he is picked out by his superiors and is given special opportunities : e.g., the opportunities involved in junior membership on the great Nocturnal Council. But whether he learns or not depends, finally, upon himself. No one can take him and turn him willy-nilly, *ab extra*, into a good administrator. He has to have the root of the matter in him.

The growth has to be vital : from within outwards. Only so does learning, genuine growth, come. In every phase of life, in farming or fighting, in money-making or love-making, in advising or carrying out policies and orders : his life and growth are in his own hands. The judgment which he develops, whether well balanced or ill-balanced, is his own judgment : an extension of his original selfmotion. It is by his own acts that he learns and goes forward ; or fails to learn and—makes way for others. [8]

Of intellectual learning, Plato himself provides almost perfect examples. In the *Meno* an intelligent but untutored man is stimulated to tackle a fairly complicated geometrical problem. Socrates " tells " him nothing, but merely brings up cases and presents problems for his judgment. These Socrates presents simply, drawing lines and pointing to the relevant parts of the diagram, so as to make it possible for the pupil, by concentrating his attention, to grasp what is meant. By making these problems his own and projecting himself eagerly into their solution, the pupil finally succeeds ; and, as Socrates points out, if a man continues along such lines he will eventually learn, by teaching himself, to become a mathematician. Of this (Socratic) method of learning, there are in the Dialogues innumerable examples ; and in each case it is by his own efforts that the pupil eventually succeeds in learning. [9]

We can experience this directly for ourselves. For we too, when we read the dialogues, find the problems challenging and arresting. By thinking our way through them we too develop, grow, and learn for ourselves. Part of what is known as the vitality of Platonism consists in this. It is almost impossible for an intelligent reader not to project himself into these problems and participate in the discussions : taking sides and suggesting to himself a multiplicity of hypotheses for further research. There is in these works something of the original magic which conjures up the thrill of self-initiated investigation and discovery, as we learn by growing into insights which represent a genuine advance upon our starting-point.

We learn always as " wholes." Just what does this mean ? The pathway of human education, as Plato describes it, does not run straight. It zigzags. When we are engaged upon intensely intellectual work, the muscles of the body are not receiving their normal amount of exercise. Mathematicians sometimes suffer from dyspepsia. On the other hand, in the physical life of military encampments, there is little opportunity for philosophical speculation. Consequently, the line of development which he proposes for his citizens as they grow toward leadership-positions points now toward gymnastic, now toward music ; now toward field-work, and now toward the study. Each new direction excludes, at least for the time being, the preceding direction. From this, it might well look as though we learn by parts, and not at all as wholes. Yet this is not Plato's meaning. As he sees the matter, we learn as growing wholes : as wholes turned now in this direction, now in that ; but always as wholes.[10]

Let us look at his position more closely. The human body is composite. It is made up of the four elements, water, fire, earth, and air, in accordance with a certain formula. What makes it a " whole " ? The central selfmotion developing itself within the brain. If this controls the elements in accordance with their proper formula, preserving them in a balance which is self-maintaining : the body is a " whole." This balanced condition is called " health." If the balance is upset, so that the central selfmotion is unable to maintain control over the proper proportion : excess or deficiency of one of the elements establishes itself ; and dropsies, fevers, or other forms of disease, ensue. If the physician attempts to restore the balance by merely local and external applications, as by surgery, cautery, or powerful drugs : he may succeed as far as the mechanical proportion of elements is concerned, and may yet leave the control of the vital selfmotion (which might make the balance self-maintaining) permanently weakened. In this case the symptoms disappear, but the patient does not recover. To cure the patient it is necessary, not so much to attack outlying symptoms, as to strike at the centre : to change radically the patient's whole way of living, so that the central control may extend its principle of self-maintaining balance over all the organs and health may again become established—health which is a growth from within outwards.[12]

The educational situation is precisely analogous to this. Spiritual health depends upon selfmastery : upon a well-rounded development of all the normal human interests in such a way as to produce well-balanced judgment, competent to organize all human powers, to integrate and direct them along the lines of membership in Plato's model city. Gymnastics and physical hygiene, for instance, affect more than the body. They affect the whole person. Muscle development *per se*, especially if accompanied by persistent over-eating (as with professional Greek wrestlers), makes a man sleepy, useless for an alert civic life.[13]

Military exercises, on the other hand, can and do help us to develop military spirit, the spirit suitable for citizens who are preparing themselves to defend their country at any time. Undertaken in the proper spirit, growing from within outwards, military exercises do not interfere with, but express, selfmastery ; and the future leader can throw himself wholeheartedly into such exercises, in full confidence that they will help to fit him for leadership, and will not make him narrow-minded, overbalanced in the direction of athletics.[14]

So also on the other hand. Persons who devote themselves to sedentary pursuits, to music, literature, science and philosophy, may allow these to escape from their selfcontrol and to obscure the central purpose of developing good citizenship. If so, such persons become narrow-minded, " quite eccentric " ; unfit for useful membership in the ideal community. But if such studies are directed from within and are not allowed to escape the control of a selfmastery which is well aware of the kind of self it intends to develop into : such studies are helpful to the citizen and indispensable to the leader. So too of biosocial interests. Sex-passion and even family love, fondness for one's wife and children, can become excessive. They may upset the balanced judgment of the citizen and give rise to the development of a private spirit opposed to public spiritedness, and so may entirely unfit a man for civic usefulness. On the other hand, if the responsibilities and joys of family life are undertaken in the spirit of a well-rounded life in the ideal community, a wife and family may be of the greatest spiritual assistance to selfmastery, and may be indispensable to the supreme magistrate, the minister of education.[15]

It is all a matter of the right spirit. If selfmastery in the spirit of a member of the ideal community is maintained, as it is by education, all the details of life, physical, social, economic, and intellectual, fall into their proper places, as parts of a well-rounded human development. Education concentrates on one at a time, mastering field after field of life. But the breadth and strength of the central self-mastery prevent any *one* from taking charge and upsetting the balance ; and spiritual health is maintained throughout. We learn, not in part, but as wholes : directed now to the acquisition of this excellence, and now of that ; but always to the maintenance of the central balanced selfmastery.[16]

With this general background in mind, let us proceed to investigate how, in their school environment, the pupils actually learn, i.e., educate themselves into social selfmastery and so grow into fuller capacity for membership in the ideal community. The general rule is that they learn by doing, doing for themselves, not by being passive and having something done for them, but by active self-expression.   How are we to understand this ?

The tendency to be active, to be doing something, to be making gestures of some sort, gestures with the hands, feet, tongue, head, and whole body, is fundamental in the life of organisms.   As the adult sees it, this tendency furnishes the raw material upon which may be superimposed the orderly rhythms and patterns which give us dancing and singing, gymnastic and music, art, literature and written law.

No animal at birth is mature or perfect in intelligence.   In the intermediate period, in which he has not yet acquired his own proper sense, he rages and roars without rhyme or reason ; when he has once got upon his legs he jumps about without rhyme or reason.   This tendency to rapid motion which exists in all animals is the origin of music and gymnastic.   Having attained the sense of rhythm, man created and invented dancing ; and melody arousing and awakening rhythm, both united formed the choral art : including song (the rhythmic movement of the voice), dancing (the rhythmic movement of the body), and gymnastic (the scientific training of the body).   This choral art is in our view the whole of education.[17]

For the adult, interested in educating the young human animal into a useful citizen, the problem is (1) to determine what rhythmic patterns are natural to human beings (2) to determine what military exercises, ceremonial dances, and literary patterns are most suitable for the purposes of the model city, and (3) to surround the growing animal with an environment calculated to stimulate him to form himself upon the approved patterns.   For the pupil, the problem of learning, of forming himself, is a little different.   Surrounded by the approved patterns, and always in contact with the approved teachers, he has as guides, three very strong inner impulses : (1) his pleasure-pain sense (2) his feeling for social approbation, and (3) his feeling for unity and self-mastery.[18]   In a few cases there may develop a degree of philosophic insight : reflective understanding of the nature, functions, and limitations of the three inner impulses, such as we find in Plato himself, in his philosopher-kings, and in very few other persons.   But, apart from the rather special education of Plato's own Academy, the development of philosophic insight is regarded in the dialogues as rare : a *lusus naturae,* a happy accident, or a miracle requiring the direct intervention of Providence.[19]

(1) The pleasure-pain sense is primitive, universal, and non-logical. It is connected with the tendency to be active, to be doing something, to be interacting with the environment in ways which are characteristic of the organism. In so far as environmental stimulation enables the organism to realize its own motion-patterns, a heightened sense of reality results. This is " pleasure." In so far as powerful environmental motions thwart and perhaps overwhelm the expressive tendencies characteristic of the organism, unpleasantness or pain results.[20]

For instance : the sensory organs of the body have very definite structures and functions. The eye is formed to assist us in seeing, the ear to assist in hearing. These organs have characteristic inner motions of their own, related to the central selfmotion of the brain, with which they are connected. It is a certain interactivity of these inner motions with specific external motions which makes seeing or hearing possible ; and the same is true of all sensory experience. Excessive environmental stimulation, as when the unprotected eye subjected to strong sunlight, is directly painful. Deficient stimulation, as when the light-adapted eye is plunged suddenly into darkness, is confusing and unpleasant. Moreover, there is a sense in which every effective stimulation of our sense-organs constitutes a disturbance, a violence which interrupts the even flow of their inner motions. But where the degree of stimulation merely calls forth an outflow of energy which is well within the capacity of the organ, so that its interaction represents a recovery of balance and the attainment of a new equilibrium, this characteristic reaction is always experienced as pleasure.[21]

In this way we may take pleasure in simple sensations, in bright colours or pure tones : without any reference to order, system, or aesthetical or logical arrangement, such as is found in the more complex experiences associated with pictures and symphonies. So also touching, tasting, and smelling, of themselves may be accompanied by simple but undeniable pleasures : quite independently of the complicating social or antisocial settings in which these and other sensory pleasures may be experienced.[22]

So too with the organs of digestion. The assimilation of material which fills up the gaps left by the wear and tear of life, in the digestive processes which restore the due proportion of the bodily elements and thus renew our physical equilibrium, is accompanied by pleasure. And somewhat similarly : the recovery from disease, which has further disturbed the proportion of earth, water, fire, and air in the body, to a healthy condition in which the balanced equilibrium of the natural self-motion is completely restored, is universally regarded as extremely pleasant.[23]

Such pleasures are simple, direct, quasi-instinctive : certainly non-logical. Many other activities which are complex and systematic, remote from direct and instinctive experiences, may also furnish occasions of pleasure. Human beings sometimes take an especial delight in the ordered movements of the dance, in the systematic rhythmic patterns of music, poetry, and literature : possibly also in the abstract thought-patterns of science and philosophy. They may take both pride and pleasure in the well-regulated patterns of an ethical or religious life such as that devised by the Athenian Visitor for the dwellers in his model city. To a few highly cultivated men and women the almost excessively well-regulated life of a philosopher-king may be extremely pleasant.[24] It must, however, be admitted that the majority of mankind believe otherwise ; and that, on the whole, it is the simple, direct and quasi-instinctive pleasures, such as those asociated with satisfying the natural human appetites of hunger, thirst and sex, which are typical and definitely heighten the sense of being alive. As to the value of the more complex pleasures, whose appreciation seems to require a more sophisticated education, there exist serious differences of opinion.[25]

What kind of guidance is afforded by this primitive, simple and direct pleasure-pain sense to the schoolboy or schoolgirl who is trying to learn to be a useful citizen, seeking to form himself or herself somehow upon the community-approved patterns ? Let us consider a few examples.

In the first place, the community-approved patterns for children of school age call for punctuality and docility. Attendance at school is compulsory, and classes open at dawn or thereabouts. The family (in the model city) rises very early and gets most of its work done before noon.[26] How does the simple pleasure-pain sense guide the schoolchild in respect of early rising and willing obedience to parents, tutors, and schoolteachers ? Plato describes the schoolboy as largely nonlogical : childish, foolish, ill-regulated, insidious, sharp-witted, insubordinate ; apt to misbehave on the street and in public ; so incapable of self-direction that practically every adult citizen has to keep an eye upon him. This description indicates that a schoolchild, if left to himself and the guidance afforded by his own simple pleasure-pain sense, will continue to behave—nonlogically. As far as permitted, he will live according to nature. That is to say, he will go native : snatching at the simple pleasures of life as they come, and developing no farsighted plans or elaborate self-control.[27]

In the teen-age schools, it will be much the same, except that he is now somewhat habituated to school routine. He studies music and literature. In music, if his taste is left to itself, he will be attracted, not by the set rhythms and carefully regulated patterns of the " classical " music, but by the easy melodies and exciting rhythms of the " popular " music. In literature he will respond to what entertains him : thrillers and love-stories. Serious social studies like Plato's *Laws*, and technical philosophy like the last half of the *Parmenides*, will be voted dull and a bore. As far as his self-directed efforts are concerned, such books will remain unread. As a simple-minded hedonist, he is out, not to improve his mind, but to amuse himself.

To sports, on the whole, he may be expected to react kindly. Throwing things, learning to shoot accurately, riding, running, and racing, are simple and amusing in themselves. And there is something in his nature which responds easily to their appeal. The camping and defence exercises, especially where there is a strong *esprit de corps*, also provide an outlet to his restless energy which is, on the whole, pleasant. As we see in our modern sports clubs, such activities are attractive in themselves, and do not need to appeal to the organized force of the community to induce the boys and girls to devote themselves to them.

In the *Laws*, however, it is made clear that military sports, like everything else in the educational programme, while playful in manner, are strictly compulsory. It is anticipated that there will be some reluctance ;[29] and we may well wonder, at the present day, whether military discipline, however " playful," will prove entirely attractive, for long, to the pleasure-seeking motive, in so far as that remains simple and unsophisticated. It may well be that regard for social approval will be required to lend its power-ful assistance, at least as an auxiliary motive. This, however, will be considered later.

On the whole, the guidance of the pleasure-pain sense must be regarded as insufficient for the attainment of useful citizenship. The growing schoolchild, if he has no other motive, cannot but interact with his environment as it impinges upon him, both at school and at home. In so interacting, he will gradually come to some sort of *modus vivendi* with it : dodging trouble as well as he can, hitting back blindly when he gets the chance, and dragged reluctantly toward the assumption of such civic responsibilities as cannot be evaded. Army service, marriage, and the maintenance of a home are, in the end, practically forced upon him ; and he makes some sort of a soldier, some sort of a husband and father, and some sort of a citizen. But intelligent, purposive co-operation with the principle of model citizenship is too much to expect of a simple, instinctive hedonist ; and as a member of the model community, he will never be of much use either to others or to himself. The motive of hedonism alone will be insufficient.[30]

(2) The second guide to self-education is furnished by the child's social sense ; and in particular by his desire for social approbation. This motive is powerful : more powerful, as a rule, than the primitive sense of pleasure-pain. In the typical Hellenic city, it is ih operation almost twenty-four hours a day. As soon as the child is able to understand at all what is being said to him, he finds himself perpetually in the presence of admonition, approbation, or it may be disapprobation, from everyone with whom he comes into contact. Relatives, servants, family friends, schoolteachers, adult citizens, community officials of every sort are at him all the time. By bearing, word, and deed, they are perpetually impressing upon him the desirability and importance of making the best of himself—from their adult point of view. He is urged to be a credit to his family, to his school, to his community ; and he plays the family game, the school game, and the community game, as best he can : seeking always to win the approbation of his elders and betters.[31]

And it is not only his elders whose approbation he desires and actively seeks. His fellows and contemporaries, the schoolboys with whom he plays both in and out of school, the fellow clubmen with whom he plays the game of politics, his fellow demes-men, his fellow soldiers, his colleagues, in every field of activity in which he interests himself : all these exercise an immense influence over him. He finds himself trying always to be one of them, to be an accepted member of the group, one of the gang : to act as they act, to speak as they speak, to dress as they dress, and to think as they think.[32]

All this is both natural and indeed inevitable. The effect upon him of such influences, their appeal to him to form himself upon their pattern, if they converge and point in the same direction, is very great. If reinforced by mass-psychology, as it usually is, the effect upon him is simply overwhelming. Subjected to the nonlogical power of the clamour and imperatives of large bodies of fellow-citizens assembled in the theatre, the courts, or the field, while the walls, rocks, or other features of the environment re-echo the noise and redouble the force of the social pressure upon him, no young man can stand out against these influences. Social fashion completely overpowers his half-developed critical sense, and he accepts the group as his group : taking over their problems as his problems, their ideas as his ideas, their ways as his ways. In this manner he necessarily develops for himself a group mentality and a group personality. He ceases to think of the men he knows as Tom, Dick, and Harry. In convention assembled, they become " Fellow-citizens ! "—and so does he.[33]

It is under the influence of this sense of group-membership and its desirability that the young man learns to turn himself into an Athenian, a Spartan, a Cretan : not merely to think of himself in that way, but to be, in thought, word, and deed, precisely that. So with ourselves at the present day. Many of us have been in the habit of thinking of ourselves as *our* selves : independent personalities, selfcreated and selfcreating, living our own lives in our own way. But let there come a social catastrophe, a great war : and we suddenly discover that we are not so much self-dependent individual selves as Americans, Englishmen, Germans, Frenchmen, or what not. We are not men without a country, but emphatically and with a reality far beyond expatriation, fellow-countrymen.

What Plato seeks to do with this nonlogical but powerful tendency to identify ourselves with some group and educate ourselves into membership therein, is to turn it to account for ideal purposes. Properly environed, there is no reason, as he sees the matter, why children should not learn, should not educate themselves, to be members, not so much of an actual, as of an ideal group. If idealism rather than nationalism, tribalism, or localism, is the constant theme of the social environment, he cannot see why children of selected parents should not develop an *esprit de corps* as members of a (mythical) " silver " or " golden " class : an order educating itself and dedicating itself to the highest ideals of service, rather than to the simple pursuit of pleasure, power, or wealth. The instinctive desire for social activity, for doing things along with others, acting and feeling always as members of a group which accepts us and our identification of ourselves with it, can attach itself (Plato believes) not only to concrete biosocial groups and communities whose interests are in the commonplace goods of life. It can attach itself to groups whose interests and even associations are almost wholly ideal.[34]

This is especially likely to take place where the particular group which devotes itself to ideal interests possesses a local habitation and a certain prestige : as was the case with the Pythagorean Order in the ancient world, and as is the case with innumerable orders and associations in our own time. But if the environment is right, and the process of learning or self-education is thorough, this instinctive desire can find complete satisfaction in a group-membership whose interests altogether transcend local and even temporal considerations. Plato is doubtless here thinking of his own Academy, which was a community of Friends of Ideas, as such : a group whose idealism appealed to Syracusans, Macedonians, and Thebans, quite as much as to native Athenians, Their sense of belonging persisted, long after they were separated by spatial and temporal considerations from the Athens where other representatives of the Friends continued to live together.[35]

In the modern world, the sort of thing Plato has in mind is exemplified not only by churches and universities, and the orders and brotherhoods associated with these institutions. It is exemplified also by an immense variety of associations which have no direct connection with church or college work : the service clubs, the sport clubs, the professional and business associations, the political, local, national, and international associations, of which we have so many.

With us, as with Plato's contemporaries, such associations are highly stimulating to self-education. In order to maintain membership and good standing in these which we regard as important for our purposes, we learn to develop ourselves far beyond family and local influences. We prepare ourselves to enter a realm in which ideal interests colour and permeate nearly everything which the members think, say, and do. And this is almost as true of informal, as of formal association. Plato expects those to whom his plans appeal, to live always in the spirit of membership in the Ideal Republic which is the City of God ; much as Kant expects his disciples to fit themselves for membership in the Kingdom of Ends by becoming self-determining rational personalities whose idealism altogether transcends space and time ; or as the Church expects us to prepare ourselves for membership in the *communio bonorum* whose existence is (humanly speaking) almost wholly transcendental.[36]

In what ways does the learner benefit by following the guidance of this social sense ? In the first place, in assimilating himself to his group, he accepts and imitates or forms himself upon its problems and ideals. He merges his personality with the *persona* of the group, and becomes, no longer an isolated individual, but an embodiment of the whole group. This develops and strengthens his morale. His self-confidence increases in almost exact proportion to the enlargement of the self which membership in his group gives him. We see this in the case of the college boy, the army man, and the big corporation executive : not to mention the citizens who succeed in getting themselves elected to important positions more than once. In ancient Greece this increase in morale was especially noticeable in the case of the Spartiates, the ruling class of Sparta's fighting men.[37]

In the second place, in assimilating himself to an established group, the learner benefits by acquiring its cultural heritage. The literature, art, and music of the community become his literature,his art, and his music. This means that his imagination becomes stimulated, enlarged, refined, and humanized to an extent which is almost miraculous : as we see in the case of some of the brightest products of our modern educational system. In the ancient world, it was among the citizens of Athens that this cultural development was especially noticeable.

Plato supposes that membership in the ideal republic or model city will combine the benefits associated with both Sparta and Athens ; and that his regulations in the way of improving the military gymnastic and rewriting the traditional literature will give to the citizens of his " Cretan or Cnossian colony " the greatest possible human benefits : so that, from every point of view, his new citizens will realize the very best that they have in them : physically, morally, socially, intellectually, and spiritually. Only a very small group will be able to live continuously upon the heights. But the rest will be helped, by their active membership in the institutions of the ideal republic, to advance as far as it is possible for them to advance, following always the leadership of their philosopher-guardians.[38]

Learning then, as Plato understands it in his theory of education, is not a matter of building up mechanical associations by intensity, recency, and frequency, as our modern textbooks of educational psychology declare. Rather it is a matter of projecting the self wholeheartedly into the spirit of membership in the ideal republic, and being permeated by its spirit, its morale, and its culture, in return. This is not mechanical, but vital, part of the atmosphere of life in a city in which play, sports, dances, and processions and other civic social functions are taking place all the time. Such self-development is helped by the satisfaction which it gives to the instinctive desire for social approbation. But it is throughout a matter, less of nature, than of nurture : of nature guided to ends determined by philosophy. Nature left to itself would (Plato thinks) never develop anything so excellent as his ideal republic. It takes the full force of philosophy to conceive and plan the main outlines of such a city. The result is, not what is natural for humanity, but what is best, ideally best, for humanity. The instinctive desire for membership in a group is not, of itself, capable of furnishing guidance as to *which* group it is wisest to join. *That* demands something more than instinct, namely, wisdom or philosophic insight. The motive of craving social approbation is thus a help to the learner ; but while he projects himself into the supporting environment which is provided for him : it is not his social sense, but the insight of a Plato which guides his choice and furnishes for him an environment in which that choice will find itself ideally satisfied.[39]

(3) The third motive of self-education, and perhaps the most important of all, is the child's growing feeling for self-mastery. In part this is nonlogical : unconscious urge, biological unrest, as the selfmotion located within the cerebrum seeks to extend its unifying control over the organs of the body and to bring about the balanced equilibrium in which bodily health consists. The struggle at this level persists throughout life. The child, the adolescent, the adult, and the senescent, have here problems of their own. Each is engaged, willy-nilly and often unconsciously, in trying to achieve and maintain control over the organs of his body : to dominate, rather than to be dominated and succumb. Unwise eating and drinking, the first effects of gymnastic exercise, sexual indulgence, overwork of any kind, especially when associated with a sedentary life ; all produce upsets of one sort or another, disturbances of the bodily equilibrium, whose effects may temporarily or permanently weaken the central self-control.[40]

But while the struggle at this level is unending, and its significance for self-education is never to be regarded lightly : it can be taken care of, to a considerable extent, by a prudent and well-organized way of living. The manner of life developed in the model city, with its round of sports, processions, and festivals for everyone, has matters so arranged that it is not too difficult for the average citizen to follow the community customs, to keep himself in a healthy condition ; and that, too, without taking much thought about the matter. Self-habituation to the *mores* of the ideal republic will do the business. As long as he goes through the regular civic routine, rising early, doing his work chiefly before noon, taking his part in open-air sports and ceremonies in the afternoon and in social life and relaxation in the evening— nothing too much and everything in a well-balanced way : health, strength, and physical selfcontrol will be the natural consequences. He does not have to bother about this, because it is all arranged for him on the best and wisest principles by those responsible for the maintenance of well-balanced life in the model city. The rules are well-considered and sound ; and as long as he conforms to them, nature can be trusted to take the course marked out for it. [41]

It is, however, when we look at the social level, that we begin to discover the especial importance for self-education, of this feeling for a unified life and for selfmastery. Selfcontrol, with the young and immature, is a fluctuating affair. They live largely by impulse and respond to short-time attractions. They are easily elevated and easily cast down. When cast down, they easily give up, and try something else : following any strong lead that is given them. Social life is a whirlpool of claims and counter-claims, and a child or adolescent finds himself sucked in willy-nilly. He is drawn hither and yon, and feels almost torn asunder as he responds impulsively to every strong claim upon him. In the deliberately sheltered environment of home and school, the background and outlook of his life may be so arranged for him by older and wiser heads that he has a fair chance to acquire a certain stable equilibrium, a balanced judgment of definite char-acter which will respond as a self-maintaining whole to the social stimuli which impinge upon him in the home town. But the strength of that character will be severely tried if he has occasion to leave the relatively closed circle of home town life and meet without protection the social forces of the great world outside. [42]

In Homer's *Telemachus* we have an adolescent wrestling with his environment and feeling keenly the weaknesses inherent in his still immature self, as he endeavours to win through to the social selfcontrol which characterizes the adult ; and in Cleinias, Hippocrates, and a number of youths in the *Dialogues*, we have Plato's depiction of the same struggle. In Homer, protection and help come from the father, the wise Odysseus. In Plato, they come rather from the teacher, the wise Socrates. In both cases we note a certain loosening of the ties which bound together the somewhat narrow circle of childish interests, and a reforming and reconstituting of the weakened personality upon a firmer basis, in a way which involves a certain merger of personality with the father or teacher.[43]

Not all fathers are as wise and competent as Odysseus ; and as the growing youth passes from the home-phase to the adult phase, the father is not always able to meet his son half-way and facilitate the merger of personality which furnishes just the assistance required. What of the teacher ? Some teachers are like the Sophists. As Plato sees them, Sophists, if carefully selected for the needs of this son or that, may be able to furnish precisely the assistance needed. But in other cases a teacher more like Socrates seems, on the evidence, to be required.[44] The ideal teacher, in any case, stands midway between the home and the world. Like Eros, the spirit which mediates between the human and the divine, he leads the youth toward the fulness of mature life, in which he is able to mingle freely with others : first with one; then with two, and finally with all.[45]

Before full maturity is reached, parents retain control ; and to some extent also teachers, who stand partly in *loco parentis*, partly in *in loco civitatis*. While they are in their school years, and even later, Plato provides for the inhabitants of his model city further shelter. He forbids them to travel, to withdraw themselves from the guidance and control of the community authorities, until civic as well as personal maturity may be presumed to have been attained.[46]

The importance of social selfmastery, of the development of a stable civic character and balanced judgment on the part of the citizens, is obvious from the adult point of view. What is it from the point of view of the child and adolescent, who have not yet sufficient experience to pass final judgment upon its value ?

In the case of the child, playing under the guidance of parent and sports teacher and living in a milieu constituted chiefly by similar children similarly guided, there is very little selfconsciousness. There is very little sense of the adult phase of life, which is still in the future, and almost no intimation of the importance of developing a socially unified quasi-civic existence. The child busies himself with his play. He develops skill in shooting, in horse-riding, and in other sports : taking them one at a time, and concentrating upon each to the exclusion of all other interests for the time being. His social relations with his fellows, his relatives, and the general public, such as they are, do not run altogether smoothly. If he plays the part of spoilt child on the street, he is liable to be corrected, with unexpected severity, by the first civic passer-by.[47] But such relations are, in the main, largely arranged for him by the older generation. He thus does not have to face the problem of arranging his own social life as a whole, but his central self-motion is able to concentrate upon this and that aspect of a child's social life ; and by taking them separately and in detail, he is enabled to solve the social problems of childhood fairly well.

That is to say, the overarching unity of his life, so far as there *is* any such unity, comes, not from himself, but from others : the older and wiser persons who arrange the routine of his life for him. What the child does for himself, socially, is to respond to the stimulii of his social life, as they occur, one at a time. He makes friends with this or that parent, this or that brother or sister. He makes friends with this or that teacher, and this or that schoolfellow. He also makes enemies, of a sort ; and he learns to conduct himself toward friends, enemies, and indifferent persons of his age or social circle, in ways which give satisfaction. He merges his personality with those whom he loves, and withdraws it, not without pain, from those who love him not : acquiring in the process, something of the quality of courage, of self-control, and of justice, as well as of friendship. By such mergings, his personality grows rapidly on its social side. It grows in breadth. It grows in depth. And above all, it grows in strength.[48] The Greeks expressed this in the Homeric proverb so frequently cited by Plato, " Two going together " and the power of their feeling for it comes out in their development, in the forms of their language in daily use, of the dual number, in addition to the singular and plural numbers found in most developed languages.

In pre-school play, children are only intermittently conscious of the support which comes to their efforts to unify their forces and to concentrate upon the solution of their problems, namely when their unsupported efforts fail, and they seek assistance from parent, nurse or family friend. In school life, they are still only intermittently aware of the support which can be furnished by teacher or comrade. Their strong feeling is for doing things themselves : growing into stronger selves by solving their own problems without assistance, or at any rate without home assistance. But the feeling for attaining success by making concentrated effort combines rather easily with the feeling for social approbation discussed above : and thus arises a distinct feeling that the self which has merged into the family, the school, or the friend is a more powerful self, better able to concentrate its (larger) forces, and so more likely to overcome obstacles and win through to success.[49]

The adolescent faces rather special problems, partly of physical, partly of moral, and partly of intellectual character, which threaten to overwhelm the relatively stable self achieved in the latest years of childhood. To these problems Plato refers occasionally, and with sympathy, although he has written no lengthy treatise on the subject. The adolescent far more than the child, feels his own weakness, and the need of leaning on some leader, whether a stronger comrade, a teacher or superior officer, or (occasionally) a parent. Those to whom the adolescent looks for leadership and personal assistance in winning through to adult selfhood are, in point of fact, usually outside the immediate family.[50]

The adolescent definitely feels the need of making an effort to adjust himself, to unify his life, with its multiplicity of loosely integrated and unevenly growing interests. He tries to build up a personality with an organized constitution, analogous to the constitution of a good city. He is much helped by his association with older and stronger friends. But he also looks to the school and its opportunities for self-education, to assist him in learning to be the captain of his own soul. He finds himself strengthened, on the one hand, by the continuing discipline afforded by the organized gymnastic of the teen-age schools, and its culmination in the regular sports festivals of the community. All this, as well as the preparatory relation to army life, helps him to develop his spirit, his morale, as well as his muscles and his physical health.[51] But, with his growing emotions and intelligence, he finds even greater stimulus and support from the other side of school life : especially from its preoccupation with good literature.

At this period his nature is somewhat dreamy and romantic ; and in literature he finds his counterpart. It is personal, and yet not too aggressive ; for he can take it or leave it, and can study it almost at his own pace. He can project himself imaginatively into its situations and can effect a kind of personality-merger with its hero : a young man of promise, unstable like himself and subject to misunderstandings and misfortunes, but eventually overcoming all obstacles and winning through to romantic satisfaction. In so projecting himself, he not only experiences directly the subjective satisfactions associated with such imaginary mergers of personality. He also feels himself to be going through a period of initiation, which is preparing him for the wider emotional and personal interests and insights of adult life. His judgment is still largely undeveloped, and his growth is still uneven ; but he feels directly a certain guidance and support in his efforts to develop selfmastery.[52]

He is further supported by his study of science, which equips him with techniques, especially mechanical techniques, which strengthen his intelligence in solving the problems which he accepts as his own. He finds he can rely on these techniques in controlling and mastering some of the uncertainties of emotion.[53]

But science raises nearly as many problems as it solves, and he finds himself looking further, and seeking support in some kind of philosophy. In the intellectual currents of contemporary life, he finds himself swept somewhat helplessly hither and yon. He feels baffled, bewildered, and discouraged, and easily develops a tendency toward scepticism and cynicism. Community usages and the wisdom of traditional outlooks in religion somehow have lost all authority. They seem to have cut loose from their moorings and to have gone adrift. As a child, he found them strengthening. As an adolescent, he feels that he has gone adrift with them. He has discovered that he does not know ; and the discovery is anything but reassuring. From philosophy he hopes to learn, not only method : a dialectical technique which will give firmness and direction to his inquiries ; but also to acquire a *punctum stans*, a basis which rests, not upon " authority " but on reason. As such, it will not fluctuate with every romantic change of mood, but can be trusted to remain, to stay put, and to lend adequate support to everything he can build upon it.[54]

Finally, as adolescence passes over gradually into adult life, he finds himself stimulated and confirmed in his efforts to build upon this basis, by reading books which deal, not with emotions and personal life-problems, but with community life and the rationale of the principles which guide law-givers in building up what are universally regarded as good civic constitutions. He finds himself, that is to say, particularly assisted by reading such books as Plato's own *Republic* and *Laws*. Such reading is not *in vacuo*, but is particularly helpful if theory and practice go along together. The life so stimulated is the best life for man.[55]

When Plato considers the needs of the adolescent, he finds certain points at which it is possible to improve the kind of support for which youth is looking. The gymnastic training in the schools, for instance, can be more directly inspired by civic spirit than is usually the case if the matter is left to the trainers themselves to train their pupils at will. It becomes less a matter of muscle-building, and more definitely a matter of strengthening the morale : definitely co-operating with the adolescent in his effort to acquire disciplined self-mastery in the service of the community.[56]

So too with the literature. The actual literature available for school purposes is poetry like the *Iliad* and *Odyssey*, and the dramatic *rifacimenti* of Homeric themes which, given a local setting and a little patriotic and sophistic eloquence, achieve the crowning success of being acclaimed as prizewinners at this or that musical festival. Such literature appeals powerfully to the imagination and the emotions. Too powerfully. It is indeed the perfect counterpart of the adolescent mind. It is dreamy and romantic, on the one hand ; and on the other, it exalts violence and direct action, and is entirely devoid of wisdom and the balanced judgment of civic common sense.[51]

Such literature does not do for the adolescent what he hopes it will. He is looking for something to cure his malady : to help him integrate his life, to acquire mastery over his uncertainties and fluctuating emotions, to develop the clearsighted rational judgment and the cool, sure, decisiveness of the adult. And this is precisely what he does not find. The heroes of Hellenic literature are only too ready to lament and wail, to shed romantic tears as they pace in frenzy the shore of the vast untamable ocean. They roll on the ground and pour dust on their heads, and call upon their goddess-mothers to help them out of difficulties into which they have got themselves. So far is an undiluted diet of romantic poetry and crime thrillers from curing the maladies of adolescence, that it aggravates the disease and renders it chronic, carrying it over into adult life.[58]

That is why Plato insists upon having imaginative literature revised and rewritten *in usum scholarum*. He intends to ensure that what the adolescent reads shall give him what he needs and shall strengthen, as well as broaden, his character. The thrills and chills, the coarse laughter and unmanly howls of Homeric literature must go. On the other hand, the passages which depict manliness and endurance, resourcefulness and initiative, comradeship and friendship, selfcontrol, discipline, and love of honour, wisdom in counsel, joy in community enterprise, and reverence for the great powers that guide and direct human destiny, may well be put into the hands of the young. Literary tradition on such points furnishes examples which are a pattern to all creators of imaginative literature ; and the adolescent, entrusting himself to the guidance of what the best wisdom of the community has approved, will find what he seeks : the support and direction which will strengthen and assist in integrating his character, and will thus prepare him to play a man's part in a man's world.[59]

And science too. Rightly understood, the study of science can do more for the adolescent than provide him with useful techniques, and an antidote to moodiness. It not only banishes the blues, but furnishes a vision of its own : the vision of Truth. This vision is as attractive as the sister-visions suggested by (revised) imaginative literature : the dream-pictures of Manliness, Self-control, Friendship, Piety, and the like. But it appeals more to the depths of character. It is more austere, and its votaries find their whole outlook upon life radically transformed. They find themselves withdrawn from the surface of life, with its sensuous colourings and tonal harmonies, its fluctuating beauties and kaleidoscopic charm. From somewhere deep within them they find developing an eye which envisages, beneath the surface of things, a texture of law, a tissue of abstract Forms, colourless, shapeless, intangible to sense, but apprehensible by mind. In this developing mind their souls find their true pilot. As they learn gradually to identify themselves with this scientific attitude, the fever and fret of adolescence subside. Their characters take on depth as well as strength. They become serene with the serenity of objectivity. And their growing familiarity with the realm of law and order gradually fits them to enter the life, not merely of biosocial adults, but of those leaders whose insight into the ultimate essence of value enables them to guide and direct the community of men and women to their highest fulfilment.[60]

For this higher development of science into philosophy, with its ultimate apprehension of the principle of ideality itself, with its careful study of the principles behind human law-making, and its final application of those principles to every detail of personal and communal life, Plato has written, to assist the growing mind, his Dialogues : especially the *Republic* and the *Laws*. Doubtless he anticipates a growing stream of philosophic literature inspired with the same thoughts and issuing from his own Academy : written, not only by his own students, but by independent thinkers, themselves also friends of ideas. By studying this new literature, the adolescent and youthful adult learns, not merely to integrate his character upon a new principle : i.e., upon idealism rather than the pursuit of a maximum of power, pleasure, and wealth ; but also to co-operate with God in realizing the Divine plan for humanity. Higher than this, the force of human reason cannot go.[61] The learner has now learnt all that the schools can teach him. The rest is life : with its vitality enlightened by reason and its rationality vitalized by intimate personal contact with every phase of human life, biological and social, as well as intellectual.

[1]*Theat.* 206a b, 207d f., *Charm.* 161d, Cf. *Polit.* 277b. [2]*Gorg.* 485a–c, *Soph.* 229d, *Laws* 643d f., 666d f., 810ab, *Rep.* 536d f., 659c f. [3]*Laws* 653 ff., 819b f. *Rep.* 425a, 485b ff. 537a, 529d f. [4]Cf. J. Stenzel : *Platon der Erzieher*, 1928, p, 77. *Rep.* 443c f., 590e f. *Laws* 653d f., 665c, 669b f. 764e f., 790b f. [5]*Laws* 791b f., 793d f. [6]*Laws* 794c f., 643b f., 645ab, *Laws* 815a f. [7]*Symp.* 187d, cf. *Rep.* 399a f., e f. Cf. Stenzel : *Op. Cit.* pp. 62–3, 401d f., *Gorg.* 503a f. *Laws* 659d f. 795d. *Laws* 790c–791c, cf. 802d f. Thus he acquires the civic virtues, temperance, Cf. 656a f., 664b, 812b, (*Rep.* 399bc, *Laws* 814d ff.), Courage (*Laws* 814d f.), Dignity (*Laws* 795d), Freedom, 395bc, Grace (*Rep.* 401d f.), and the beginnings of wisdom (*ibid* 402a)., as well as health, agility, beauty (*Laws* 795d). Cf. *Laws* 643c, *Rep.* 466e f. Play., *Prtg.* 327b f. [8]*Laws* 957, 961b, 964d f., 966b f., 951d f. For tests of self-control cf. *Laws* 648c., 829, 830d f. [9]*Meno* 82b ff., 84c, ff., 98a., cf. *Polit.* 277b. *Theaet.* 150b, 157cd, *Phaedo* 73a. [10]*Rep.* 521c f., 485b–487a, 490ab, 411–412a. Cf. *Tim.* 88. *Polit.* 309 ff. [11]*Symp.* 186de, 188ab., cf. *Crat.* 419bc, *Tim.* 82–86a, 87c, 88b (*Laws* 720d, cf. *Rep.* 857de), 591d, 444cd, cf. *Gorg.* 505a., *Phileb.* 31cd, 25c. [12]*Charm.* 156e f., *Tim.* 88e f. *Rep.* 406d–e. [13]*Rep.* 443e, 404ab, 410b f. *Tim.* 86b f., *Soph.* 228–230, *Polit.* 310a, *Phileb.* 26 (Spiritual doctoring is analogous to physical doctoring, refutation taking the place of cathartics—except that refutation affects the whole, and cathartics the part—and appreciation of law and order taking the place of the proportion of the 4 elements). [14]*Rep.* 466e f. *Polit.* 306b ff. *Laws* 813b f. 830c f. 832b f., 942 f. [15]Cf. *Rep.* 464d, 487d ff. 548ab, 549c f., *Laws* 644b, 765d f. All higher officials in the *Laws* will have been married, and most of them will have been fathers as well. *Laws* 721, 772de, 774 f., 784b, f., 785b. [16]Imagine a tripod with its feet firmly planted in (a) music (b) gymnastic, and (c) biosocial interests. From its apex imagine a pendulum swinging freely. This represents a man being educated. When he studies mathematics or philosophy, the pendulum swings in the direction of music (a). It is prevented from overbalancing by the counter-pull of the other two limbs of the tripod. So when he receives military training (b). He is prevented from becoming an extreme militarist or an uneducated boot by the counter-pull of philosophy (a) and family love (c). So too when he falls in love (c). He is assisted against an overbalance in the direction of sex by his philosophical education (a) and his pride in keeping his body in training. Thus at all times he acts as a whole, retaining his balancing selfmastery, and becoming a well-rounded individual, a useful citizen (*Laws* 783a, 835d ff.). The typical German scholar's insistence upon the importance of *Knabenliebe* in Plato's philosophy is—at least in relation to the model city of the *Laws*—exaggerated. [17]*Laws* 672–673d, condensed ; cf. also 653d f. The significance of this nonlogical tendency to be active, is as fundamental in Plato's theory as in the more modern views of the sociologist Pareto (cf. Pareto's *Mind and Society*, E.T., sects, 1089, 1092). [18]*Laws* 653a, 836a, 838a f., 839d f.,

841a f. ¹⁹*Meno* 99–100, *Ion* 533d ff,, 542, *Phaedr.* 245a, 265b, *Apol.* 22a, *Laws* 682a, 719bc. ²⁰*Rep.* 357bc, 515cf., cf. 403a, *Tim.* 44d f., 47b f., *Laws* 732e ff. La Fontaine : *Le plaisir d'après Platon et Aristote*, pp. 1–53. *Laws* 815d f. cf. 653d f. ²¹*Rep.* 475d, 476b, 515de, 516e f. *Tim.* 64–68d, *Phileb.* 52bc. ²²*Rep.* 559ab, 584b. *Phileb.* 51a f. ²³*Tim.* 81a f., 82–86–89c. *Rep.* 558e f., 444c f., 585a f. *Phileb.* 25e, 31c f., *Sep.* 591d. *Symp.* 186de, 188ab., cf. *Gorg.* 505a. ²⁴*Rep.* 401d f., 588e f., *Laws* 667b f., *Rep.* 582e f., 586e f. 587d f. *Prtg.* 353cf–357b. ²⁵Cf. *Rep.* 439d f. *Phdo.* 66b f. *Laws* 782e. *Gorg.* 491d ff. *Phileb.* 12c f. ²⁶*Laws* 807d f., 804d, 814c, 810a. ²⁷*Laws* 808d f., cf. 668d, 766a, 793de, *Lysis* 207d–209, *Rep.* 590e f. ²⁸*Laws* 802b f. Rep. 397d, *Parm.* 135d ff. Cf. *Laws* 829b f., which indicates that correct sentiments are more important, if the outcome of noble character, than technical artistry (cf. *Lach.* 182d f.). ²⁹*Laws* 942 f., 813d f., 830e f. ³⁰*Rep.* 439cd, 571b ff., 580d ff–586c, *Theaet.* 172e f., *Prtg.* 356d, *Gorg.* 513c f., 515 ff. *Phdo.* 66b f., *Apol.* 31e f., *Laws* 732e ff., 791d f., 668a, 700d f., 658e ff., 840ab, 835d f. Cf. Lodge : *Plato's Theory of Ethics*, pp. 343–354. ³¹*Prtg.* 325c f. *Soph.* 229e f., *Euthyd.* 275a f., 278d f–283b, 288c ff. *Laws* 729b, 719e, 723a, *Rep.* 492b–493e, 519, 413c f. 412de, 429e f, 715b f., 942a f. ³²*Rep.* 520b, 416b f., 521a, 423e f., 462 ff. *Laws* 945e f. ³³*Rep.* 492a f. Cf. Menex., *passim.* Cf. *Prtg.* 342cd, (cf. 347c f.). ³⁴*Rep.* 520d7, 519c5–6, 535b f., 416e f., 413e f., 462 ff., 458b f. ³⁵Cf. Jäger : *Aristoteles*, pp. 105–116. ³⁶*Rep.* 540a, 591b f. *Laws* 903b ff. Cf. T. N. Whitehead, *Leadership*, pp. 11, 21, 30 etc. ³⁷*Crito* 52, f., *Rep.* 412d, 492b f., 494cd. (cf. *Alc.* I 105 b f.). *Prtg.* 324d f., 322ab, e f. *Laws* 633b–d. Cf. *Gorg.* 485d f. ³⁸*Rep.* 519c f., 521b ff., 421bc, 540ab, *Polit.* 297b, *Laws* 735a, 818a, 964bc, 965a, 967d f. ³⁹*Rep.* 462 f., 492 ff. 497cd, 517d, 520f., 533 f., 586 f., *Laws* 942bc, 969b. ⁴⁰*Tim.* 82–86a, 87c, *Soph.* 228a, *Symp.* 188a, *Gorg.* 518b–d, *Prtg.* 353cd, *Rep* 405cd, 556de, 559bc, *Phileb.* 31cf. *Laws* 691c, 797d f. ⁴¹Cf. *Symp.* 186d f., *Rep* 403c f. 590d f., *Phileb.* 26ab, *Polit.* 308d ff., cf. *Rep.* 443b f. *Tim.* 88 f., *Laws* 808d f., 942. ⁴²*Laws* 949e f., *Rep.* 538 f. cf. 492 ff., 358c, 362e f., 365a f., 366e f. ⁴³*Rep.* 431, 538c, 590d f., *Phaedr.* 276f, 278a, *Epist.* 341c f, *Euthyd.* 277d ff., 285ab, 288b–291a, *Meno.* 80a–c, 84a f., cf. *Theaet.* 150d f. cf. *Symp.* 206c f. ⁴⁴*Theaet.* 151b, *Lach.* 200c f. ⁴⁵*Symp.* 202d f., 204a f., 209, ff. *Rep.* 402bc, *Phaedr.* 252df., 256bc, *Laws* 837c. ⁴⁶*Laws* 950 de., *Rep.* 590e f., *Lysis* 207d ff. ⁴⁷*Laws* 808e f. ⁴⁸*Laws* 681b, *Lysis* 207b ff *Prtg.* 324e–328a, *Rep.* 462f. 590e f. cf. *Laws* 790e f., 793d f. 653 ff. *Symp.* 209 f. *Laws* 942a f. Cf. Lodge : *Plato's Theory of Ethics*, pp. 93–97, 110–111. ⁴⁹*Prtg.* 310e, 312d, *Lysis* 207c (cf. *Rep.* 337d, *Apol.* 38b, *Crito* 44c, *Laws* 739c). ⁵⁰*Prtg.* 310e f., 325e ff. *Lach.* 179e f., *Euthyd.* 274 f. *Sym.* 209 f. *Laws* 809d–812a, 813e, *Rep.* 492b f. ⁵¹*Rep.* 403e f–408, 410bf., 466c ff. *Polit.* 309 ff. *Laws* 813 ff., 942 f. ⁵²*Rep.* 397d, 399 f. *Prtg.* 325e f. *Laws* 810e f., 658c ff. *Ion* 535, cf. *Laws* 903b ff. Cf. *Euthyd.* 277d f., 285ab. ⁵³*Rep.* 533b f., 521c ff. ⁵⁴*Rep.* 538 ff. Cf. *Meno* 80ab., *Laws* 885c f., 886d, 888b ff. ⁵⁵*Laws* 957c f., 964c f., 967d f., cf. 811b f., 817c f. *Rep.* 586d f. Cf. Lodge : *Plato's Theory of Ethics*, ch. XV. ⁵⁶*Rep.* 410b ff., *Gorg.* 506e f. *Polit.* 308e, 309b ff., *Laws* 773, c. f., 802e. ⁵⁷*Rep.* 604d f., 608ab, 475cd., 476b f. *Ion* 535 f. *Laws* 719ab, 801b f., *Apol.* 22a, *Meno* 99cd., *Phaedr.* 245a, 265b. ⁵⁸*Rep.* 377 ff. 600b ff. 443c f. ⁵⁹*Rep.* 390d, 389e, 395bc, 400c ff. *Laws* 682a, 802, 810d f., 817. ⁶⁰*Rep.* 500c f., 502e f–506b, 507b ff. 479d f. 523d ff. ⁶¹*Rep.* 443c f., 497cd, 540a f., 590e ff. 533a, 534e, cf. *Laws* 968d f. 811b f., 957c f.

CHAPTER X

MIND

Modern writers who apply philosophy to educational problems are wont to construct, as an essential part of their task, distinctive and contrasting theories of " mind," and to insist that it is of vital importance for educational practice to select and adopt as our guide—the one in which the author appears to believe.[1] If we are to take seriously—and there can be no doubt that it is intended that we should—the competing theories presented for our information and deliberate choice : all we can say at a first glance is that the great tradition of European philosophy seems to sponsor some very queer accounts indeed of the nature, structure, and functions of the processes popularly regarded as " mental."

Thus, somewhere in the tradition a dreadful theory known as Faculty Psychology seems to have come to birth and to have been widely adopted. This theory attempts to classify and systematize the functions indicated by such popular terms as Seeing, Touching, Imagining, Remembering, Hoping, Desiring, Willing, etc. Terms like these are simply lifted from ordinary everyday language : that is to say, from popular usage which never dreamt or imagined that persons of trained logical intelligence might some day try to fit them into the rigid framework of a scientific or pseudo-scientific system.[2]

We distinguish such terms informally, for this or that concrete and specific purpose. Of course. Why not ? But if we seriously attempt by logical devices to draw formal distinctions between such terms as Desiring, Wishing, Choosing, Willing, etc., or such terms as Sensation, Perception, Imagination, Rote Memory, Intellectual Memory, and the like : we soon discover that, the neater and the more distinctive we make our definitions, the further we seem to be getting away from the actual phenomena of which we are proposing to set forth the formulas.

In our theory, Seeing is sharply distinguished from Imagining, Remembering, and Reasoning. But in practice, who is there who does not know that we simply cannot " see " without—at the same time and as an integral part of the experience of " seeing "—imagining, remembering, and reasoning ? And *vice-versa*. These alleged distinct processes all run into one another. So much so, that if we insist upon putting asunder what nature presents as a complex tissue, presently we find our theory compelled to invent additional mechanisms for bringing the pieces together again. Faculty Psychologists are apparently equal to the demands made upon their inventive powers. But the further they develop their theories, the more abstract they become ; the more remote from the facts.

Again, can any one seriously suppose that it really helps us to understand and explain how " the mind " works, to say that we remember by means of, or because of, our " faculty " of Memory? And further, as educational theorists insist : Is it not positively misleading to treat each individual " faculty " as a kind of self-subsistent substance, capable of being trained in isolation from the rest ? Is it sound or wise to believe that we can take a course in Memory-training, or in Logical-thinking—or, for the matter of that, in Aesthetical or Religious training, or, even more generally, in Discipline and Selfcontrol ?[4]

And finally, how in the world is such a group of alleged entities, conceived as isolable if not isolated, not merely to be joined together *inter se*, but to be related to " the mind " itself—whatever that may be ? Yet further mechanisms have to be invented ; and the further the theory proceeds along the road paved with its own inventions, the worse things get.

Suppose we ask : Who is the parent of this monstrosity ? We come upon a mystery. Everyone knows all about the theory. But everyone we approach disclaims responsibility and hints darkly that it was—some other fellow. Suppose we ask : Which other fellow ? Someone says, " Oh, it goes back to the XVIII Century and John Locke, the founder of modern psychology." But if we look up the *Essay on Human Understanding*, we find Locke repudiating, with virtuous indignation, any such idea.[5] In fact, his language is remarkably like the language used in the XIX Century by psychologists putting this theory, once for all, in its place.[6] So it wasn't Locke, then. " Oh, well (we are told), it goes back to the Greeks. You'll find it in Plato and Aristotle."

H'm. Is that so ? True enough, we find the Greek term *dynamis* used now and then, in both Plato's and Aristotle's writings, in ways which might lead a careless reader to suppose that here at last he had run to earth the wicked parent of this unwanted child. But if we look more carefully, we find pretty much what

we found in Locke's *Essay* : namely, an unqualified rejection—
expressed, however, with urbanity and humour rather than with
virtuous indignation. " No one can suppose (we are told) that in
each of us, as in some sort of Trojan horse, there are perched a
number of uncounted senses." And we are frequently warned
against pushing too far the metaphors involved in " the free use
of words and phrases," and treating the result as scientific
theory.[7]

Plato is writing in the pre-textbook stage of psychological
reflection, and it is doubtful whether he has any hard and fast
theory of mind. Nevertheless, wherever the context seems to
require that a definite attitude should be taken towards this or
that mental process, referred to loosely in popular language, we
find evidence of a critical reflection which has penetrated rather
far beneath the surface of the free and easy metaphors of Plato's
contemporaries, and more than a suggestion that if we persist in
such reflective inquiries, we shall succeed at least in freeing ourselves from the commoner prejudices and sources of error. Let
us therefore follow up the suggestions and indications of the
chief contexts in which mental processes are dialectically discussed,
and discover at least toward what they lead us.[8]

Greek linguistic usage does not say, " My head aches, and a
drowsy numbness fills my brain," or anything of that sort. On
the contrary, it normally makes the self central. The Greek
says " I am in pain, in respect of my head (in respect of my eyes,
limbs, etc.) ." He does not ordinarily find this linguistic usage
significant, suggestive of problems or theories. Plato, however,
deliberately emphasizes the unity, the dominance, and the
central significance of the self. So much so that his theory of
" mind, or whatever we please to call it " can hardly be distinguished from his theory of the self, i.e., of the central selfmotion,
the animating principle usually translated " soul," which forms
the constant background of his discussions of this or that mental
process.

Thus, when Plato refers to mental processes, he uses inter-
changeably the terms which faculty psychology is concerned to
keep distinct. The Hellenic equivalents of Understanding,
Intelligence, Mind, etc., are used in one and the same context,
as if they were synonyms. They pass over, without any felt transition, into terms expressive of Cleverness, Insight, Prudence, and
Wisdom, in ways which include a goodly number of verbs as well
as adverbial phrases and nouns. In connection with the verbs

there is usually some reference, unobtrusive or obtrusive, to the " self." And at some point in the discussion there is usually a slightly obtrusive introduction of the "soul," the central animating principle. It is made quite definite that it is " we " ourselves who are active, and that it is self-initiated activity which makes our various experiences " ours."

Thus, in our interaction with the environment, we experience whatever we do experience through the instrumentality of the body. But, whatever the physical mechanisms employed as instruments, the experience, when we get it, is ours. It is not physical, but mental. For example, the eye is a complex optic mechanism for focussing, reducing to unity, certain light-vibrations, and passing them on to the brain, of which the optic mechanism is largely an outgrowth. Mechanically speaking, vision is mediated by an interactivity of *two* kinds of vibration, (1) vibratory motions coming from the visible object, and (2) vibratory motions whose source is intra-ocular, controlled by the central selfmotion issuing from the brain and animating the optic mechanism. The intra-ocular motions correspond to what is nowadays called the *Eigenlicht* : the " cortical gray " or " quasi-phosphorescence " which is associated with the visual experience even in the absence of external stimulation, and which presumably mingles its own characteristics with the qualities which come from the light-waves reflected from the physical objects. What is generated by this intermingling of central and external vibrations is a fluctuating experience which we call visual. A variety of colours, in process of constant change, and with no fixity or permanence of any sort, makes its appearance. [9]

Parallel experiences account for audition and for other specific kinds of sensation. The combination of central and external stimulations gives rise to rapidly changing, obscure and indeterminate experiences which we can hardly call " ours " at first. It is in fact, not until the central selfmotion has mastered and captured and brought within the central organ (the brain) these external vibrations, that it succeeds in superimposing upon them its own patterns and thus reduces them to determinate and specific form, as " red " or " green," " middle C " or " E in alt," etc.[10]

Let us make this a little clearer. Objective vibratory processes, viewed by the mathematical methods of the Pythagorean scientist, are practically infinite in number. With a vibrating string you can produce, as a matter of everyday demonstration, not merely the waves which underlie the tones, half-tones, and quarter-tones recognized by musicians. You can produce tones whose intervals are yet more fractional, as small and as many as you please. Any and every vibration-frequency has its tonal aspect, and, mathematically regarded, is precisely as legitimate as any other. Thus in terms of abstract theory, you could have n tones, n scales, and n patterns, with no reason whatever (as far as abstract theory goes) to prefer any group of tones, scales, or patterns, to any other. And yet, as we all know, when the central self-motion characteristic of the living organism has interacted with these vibrations and has mastered them, it reduces them to a few types which have significance for a given organic species, and it shows marked preference for a select number of those types.[11]

So too in the field of colours. It is possible to construct a light-reflecting surface which will provide the physical stimulus, not merely for the three or four " simple " colours, but for any and all of their various compounds and shadings to infinity. If we arrange these in a series, on the colour-scale thus produced, any colour-variation you please, viewed mathematically in terms of physical light-waves, is precisely as legitimate as any other. There is no reason whatever why any given three or four should be picked out as in any sense " primary " or as in any way preferable to any others. To the Pythagorean scientist, all this is obvious. And yet, here again, as we all know, when the central selfmotion characteristic of the human organism has interacted with these and has made them its own, by reducing them to a few types which have significance for the human organism, we apprehend these types as " primary," and we feel marked preference for certain colours and colour-combinations.[12]

How are we to account for this ? Consider the parallel case of bodily movement. The motions of the limbs and body, interacting with the environment, eventually settle down to certain rhythmic patterns which are characeristic of the self-activity of this species or that. Birds hop and fly. Fishes swim. Human beings walk, run, and dance. These are their specific motion-patterns, and their significance is primarily biological. Thus each organism has its own specific motion-patterns out of which it builds up balanced systems which it finds satisfactory : helpful for its own purposes. Human beings, for example, gradually come to construct rhythmic war-dances, processional peace-dances, and mating dances of one sort or another. These are generally of biological, and specifically of human, social significance.[13] The rhythms involved can be studied by the Pythagorean scientist and formulated in mathematical terms. Indeed, it may be possible to go further and to relate the mathematics of these patterns to the secret formula of the species, i.e., the formula which expresses the proportionate relationship of the bodily elements characteristic of the particular species, the balanced rhythm or *logos* of the central selfmotion which holds together, guides, and animates the organism. If of a more speculative turn of mind, we can even go further and attempt to relate the secret formula of each species to the secret formula of nature as a whole, the principle which holds together, guides and animates the entire world. In so far as we fancy ourselves capable of establishing such a relationship, we can eventually imagine that we see, in the human preference for a few, rigidly selected march and dance rhythms, a divinely guided reproduction of the regular patterns followed by the stars in their courses, the courses marked out for them by the Creator.[14]

Expressive sounds are precisely parallel to these expressive gestures and movements. Birds twitter and sing in ways characteristic of their species. Animal cries—hunger-cries, danger-cries, mating-cries—are equally characteristic for the different species of land-animals. Human sounds, whether spoken or sung, are equally characteristic of their species, and are limited in range and intensity to what human beings find satisfactory for their purposes. They serve to communicate the typical emotions of fear, anger, sorrow, and joy ; and are thus primarily of biosocial significance. The vocal ranges characteristic of a baby, a child, a woman, a young man, a mature man, and an old man, are even more limited. They are definitely expressive of certain phases of the human life-cycle. Naturally (and properly) associated with the corresponding gestures and rhythmic motions characteristic of the species in its age and sex groups, the outstanding tones which have meaning for human beings are determined by preference-patterns which are instinctive, innate in the organism. The clear, pure tones in which we tend to take pleasure are determined, not by reason, but by the ear ; although doubtless science is right in suggesting that there is some relation between their mathematical basis and the secret formula of the species, and indeed of cosmic nature. Be that as it may, there can be no doubt that the various scales and harmonies which have become standardized in musical theory and practice are based primarily upon nonlogical preference-patterns and are to be regarded as racial, characteristically human.[15]

For his own special purpose of educating human beings, preparing them for membership in his ideal community, Plato makes a narrower selection here, just as he does in the field of rhythmic movements generally. Instead of permitting his citizens to skip, run, and jump at will, he selects for their education two types of motion-pattern. They are taught either (1) to go marching as to war, with forceful, purposive rhythmic swing, or (2) to proceed in time of peace with dignity, with stately ceremonial tread. So also in the field of tonal preference-patterns. He restricts the musical expressiveness of his citizens to the tonal ranges characteristic of (1) manly feeling, and (2) dignified civic attitudes : i.e., to the Dorian and Phrygian modes or scales. Other types of musical expressions, such as the dithyrambic dance-movements, though natural to humanity, are rejected : because they have no direct relation to the military and civic needs of his ideal community.[16]

So too in the field of colours. The reason why, out of all the innumerable vibration-frequencies, only some ten or a dozen become, as a result of our interacting intra-ocular vibrations, especially selected and enhanced—those we mark with particular names such as red, yellow, green, blue, and a few intermixtures and shadings of these—is clearly due to something in the structure of our visual mechanism. The outstanding colours, those which become especially amplified in our perceptual interactivity with the environment, areprimarily, no doubt, of biological significance for the organism. They are useful to us as indications of food, danger, or sex : as with their help we appreciate motions akin to our own in the environment, or motions which are distinct and alien. Viewed mathematically, as the Pythagorean scientist views them, the basis of their fundamental rhythms or vibration-frequencies is doubtless related to the secret formula of balanced selfmotion, the principle which holds together, animates, and controls the body as a whole and every one of its organs, including the visual organs, in particular. This in turn can presumably be compared in speculative fancy with the secret formula which, it is supposed, controls the planets and the whole cosmic system of motion-patterns.[17]

It is not difficult to realize that if an organism is to fly in the air, to swim under water, or to walk upon the land, it will require in each case a structural equipment of wings, fins, or legs, and sensory and other organs which, in the case of each species and indeed of each individual, will have to be balanced against each other and against the shape of the body as a whole. The matter becomes even more clear, if we compare such organisms which neither fly, swim, nor walk, but are rooted in the soil, and obtain the necessary water, air, earth, and sunlight by a very different system of organs —roots and leaves—and live a very different species of life. In each case, the way of life necessitates a certain balance of the organic structures involved, and the vital principle realizes itself by preserving and maintaining the specific and indeed individual balance appropriate to the organism's way of life. The fundamental rhythms of this balance can doubtless be expressed in a mathematical formula ; and it is the business of the scientists to investigate and establish the formulas which operate in nature and are primarily of biological significance.[18]

It is the further business of *social* scientists to make use of a smaller number of formulas of balance, and to establish a balanced system suitable for guiding and controlling social life so as to realize the optimal values of human living. Plato speaks enthusiastically of discovering and applying the secret formula of civic Eros, the central self-motion which will ensure the adequate reproduction of his guardian class, and which is positively related to the precise numbers of farmers, merchants, artisans, and officials of his model city. The formula of civic life is thought of as positively related, not only to the formula of cosmic life, but also to the formula which governs every detail of biological existence, including the functioning of the human organs of sense.[19]

Let us pause to consider the situation which we have before us. Apart from the minded organism we have a number of motions taking place, flitting in and out of spacetime without any inner principle of unity, law and order. Plato thinks of them as essentially irregular and chaotic : not quite apprehensible by mind. But he also believes that the Divine Artist who created the orderliness of the world has superinduced upon their irregular motions certain geometric patterns, whose regular forms can very well be grasped by the mind. That is to say, the original motions remain, in their essence, if we can speak of essence in this case, nonlogical ; but the geometric patterns which control the direction of those motions can quite well be grasped by the Pythagorean scientist.[20]

Let us now add to this situation the minded organism. Like the macrocosm to which we are now adding it, the organism is the seat of a number of motion-tendencies which are not inherently regular. But they are, to some extent, controlled by the inner principle of selfmotion located in the brain, and their motion tendencies are thus reduced to certain rhythmic forms and patterns, characteristic in type for this species and that. Interacting with the patterned motions of the environment, the central selfmotion finds its efforts to acquire selfmastery, control over its own organism, partly assisted, and partly impeded. A lifelong conflict ensues, the organism seeking to develop its own life-patterns in an environment which is partly alien and, in combination with its fellows, to bring into existence the balanced kind of civic life which Plato depicts in the *Republic* and *Laws*.[21]

Let us observe a human organism succeeding in this process of interaction. At first its control is inadequate. It is almost like one of Leibniz's monads, with no windows opening upon the objective world. Its experiences are at first all confused, with only a very few enhanced and recognizable sensations. For awhile it lives in a very narrow circle of distinct colours, tones, odours, tastes, and touches : the environment in general being so fluctuating as to belong entirely to the margin, rather than to the focus, of its attention. The boundaries of its little world are set by instinct, inherited organic tendencies characteristic of its species ; and its interests and experiences are all biological and social.[22]

With most of us, however much we may eventually expand the circle of our interactive experiences, the biosocial pattern remains predominant. " First a house, then a wife, then an ox for the plough " (as Hesiod writes) circumscribe our interests. To things outside we remain, until the end, a little blind. Why not ? We have *our* home-life, *our* wife and family, *our* farm or other way of earning *our* living. If we succeed in wresting from the world enough to support us in *our* way of living, that is all we ask of it.

What are " we," and how do experiences becomes " ours " ? There is the baby self, the child self, the adolescent self, the mature self, the senescent self : each a definitely biosocial self, and each with a very definite circle of interests. Out of the interactive process, the self and its world come into existence *pari passu*. The baby self develops in relation to a father, a mother, and a nurse. The schoolboy self develops in relations to teachers, examiners, and a school system. The civic self comes into existence in relation to judicial, electoral, and deliberative assemblies which have a local habitation and local names. That is to say, the innate tendency toward selfmastery, on the part of the central selfmotion, develops in association and interaction with the patterned tendencies of the environment : especially in so far as the environmental patterns correspond to and amplify and support the tendencies of the organism which are seeking self-expression.[23]

Is there any way of extending the self beyond this narrow circle of biosocial interests ? Yes. In two directions especially. In the first place, while we undoubtedly select a few colours, tones, and odours chiefly because of their biosocial appeal : we find ourselves doing something more. We take pleasure in the *purity* of the chief colours, tones, and shades. This is an *aesthetic* pleasure, and is quite distinct from the ordinary biological or social appeal of our experiences. Thus human beauty may, it is true, have a pronounced sex-appeal : to an adolescent or mature adult, very much so. But in general, we can distinguish aesthetic from biosocial interest. It is not that the one is merely contemplative, leaving us inactive, while the other calls forth an intensely active response. We are active in both, though in different ways. The aesthetic pleasure, like all pleasures, demands our active co-operation. We search actively for such pleasures : following them up and reorganizing the environment so as to increase its capacity for providing us with aesthetic satisfactions.[24]

Aesthetic experience is far wider than an experience which is immediate and merely instinctive, biosocial. By means of the representative arts we enlarge the horizon of human experience. The results are by no means opposed to biosocial interest, and may even be regarded as a mediate and indirect expansion of that interest. Eros, for Plato, is always a mediator, a guide who leads from the instinctive toward wider and more spiritual reaches of experience. The new widening of our horizons sets the centre of human experience a little differently, and so brings into being a different kind of self : a self whose interests, while still biosocial, are biosocial in a different way from those of the self which remains narrow, untouched by beauty.[25]

Thus Homer's world of pictured gods, demigods, and heroes expands enormously the circle of human interests. But in a way his *personae* can be regarded as human beings writ large. The biosocial interest is still there. Zeus and Here are a glorified " Mr. and Mrs." ; Athene is definitely "Daddy's daughter." The wily Odysseus is gloriously human ; and the charm of the young

people, while doubtless of divine origin, is such as we could wish
for our own sons and daughters. But in thus expanding the circle,
Homer has displaced the instinctive centre. By adding the heroic
and the celestial overtones, he has given us an attitude which is
new. The centre of his world-picture is more near the heroic than
we should find in a picture which left out the heroic and the divine
and confined itself to a merely instinctive humanity. In this
way we realize that art enhances and ennobles human experience,
raising it from the merely actual to a more nearly ideal level.[26]

Literature, music, architecture, and kindred arts thus furnish
the learner with one of the two great roads to freedom. By letting
ourselves go and following their guidance, we pass beyond the
stage of the instinctive self. We broaden and deepen our experience, in proportion as the new picture-thinking develops an imagination and an intelligence in which the aesthetic motive displaces
the centre of interest from the merely biosocial and establishes it in
the region of the beautiful which for Hellenic feeling is already
halfway toward the good : the *kalokagathia* or civic excellence
which in its highest form is the direct offspring of the ultimate
principle of ideality and value, the idea of good. By means of
art we habituate ourselves to living freely and easily amid ideal
values : pictured indeed in forms which our relative immaturity
can appreciate and enjoy, as we follow our guide in the imaginary
worlds depicted by Homer, Aeschylus, and the rest.[27]

" As we follow our guide "—what does this mean ? It means
that literature and art are not of themselves sufficient to guide and
teach the learner. They furnish the subject-matter of this branch
of education. But the subject-matter requires something further :
a rather special sort of teacher. Left to itself, literature would
turn us into *littérateurs*, technical authors. Left to itself, music
would turn us into *virtuosi*, technical musicians. Precisely as
wholehearted devotion to carpentry would turn us into carpenters, or shoemaking into cobblers. Our study of the arts must
thus be, not professional in spirit, but amateur. If we are to derive
from our study of them their full value for general education, our
teachers must be real educators : men who teach learners rather
than subjects, and are so imbued with an understanding and
appreciation of community spirit that they can pass on to us, as
we work with them, something of that community idealism which
is essential to the learner who is to develop into a good citizen.
Whatever the technical equipment of our teachers, they must also
have studied, and studied deeply, such works as Plato's *Laws*, in

which the civic and educational theories of which he approves have received adequate expression.[28]

So much for literature and art as a way of passing beyond the merely instinctive attitude toward life and its values. What is the second road to freedom ? It is furnished by science and by everything which we regard as intellectual, leading toward knowledge and the ideal truth. Like the arts, the sciences also habituate us to feel at home in the realm of ideal values. To pursue truth is quite as inspiring as to pursue beauty. But the mathematical techniques in which science is so rich do for us what art (as Plato understands it) can never quite accomplish : something different.[29]

Pictorial thinking, however excellent in its own way, has its limitations. Its function is to enhance, rather than to transcend, the world perceived through the senses. Art selects, unifies, emphasizes, and systematizes—images. It provides imaginary haloes for the things and persons of our ordinary, everyday world. It refines, ennobles, and idealizes the facts of life, " taming and soothing its wildness by harmony and rhythm." By its aid, our nonlogical feeling becomes inspired, almost transmuted into pure idealism. We sense, behind the veils of beauty, a world of wonder and magic : with its crudities disguised and forgotten, its biological necessities transformed somehow into the radiance of utter glory. And this is all to the good. In glimpsing the ideal, rather than seeing the everyday, side of life, it may well be that we approach more nearly to its fundamental, essentially real nature. It may be. But—and this is the point—pictorial thinking, as such, can never tell. The images of art are fleeting and unsubstantial. You can do with them what you will. You can construct images whose suggestions are of transcendent beauty. You call the result " idealism." You can construct (if you will) images whose suggestions are mean and sordid. You call the result " realism." You can (if you insist) depict the merely actual, patiently creating mirror-images which might be mistaken for the actualities of this world : without interpretation of any sort, whether " idealistic " or " realistic."[30]

How are you to choose between these different uses of imagery ? Is the one " truer " than the other, or merely more " useful " ? You cannot tell. You may appeal to feeling. " Inspiration " may inform you that this or that powerful image is a depiction of essential truth, and that you are making yourself the channel for the delivery of a divine message. But suppose your message is challenged and rejected. Suppose your " divine mission " is denied. What can you do about it ? Construct more images ? Yes, indeed. But if they too are coolly rejected, what then ? You are estopped. Thus Protagoras, when permitted to speak in the form of a myth, is impressive enough. But when his picture is challenged, he proves utterly unable to maintain his position. Homeric pictures are at least equally impressive. But they prove entirely unable to defend themselves against criticism, or even against alternative pictures. So too Socrates himself constructs picture after picture, in his endeavour to work upon the mental processes of Callicles in the *Gorgias*. But his pictures are coolly and deliberately rejected, or are even used with a reverse interpretation ; and as so treated, they prove entirely futile. Something new in the way of method has to be introduced, if Socrates is not to give up the attempt to convince. Pictorial thinking thus has its limitations.[31]

Science provides the " something new." " The little matter of one, two, and three," and the logically constructed concepts, take us to a field in which proof and disproof in a dialectical sense become possible. Mathematical physics and dialectical reasoning make us at home in a realm which transcends the fluctuations of sensuous perception and the plausibilities of pictorial imaginings. And here too, just as the artists need the interpretation of an idealist-minded teacher to make their work educative : the scientists need to be supplemented by the interpretation of the philosopher, before their work can be regarded as educative, in the sense of fitting the student for civic leadership. Left to itself, the study of science would turn the student into a technical scientist : a geometrician, an astronomer, an expert in the field of physical acoustics. But for *general* education, to develop and strengthen the mental processes needed by the philosopher-king, the assumptions of science need to be transcended, and its techniques used for their effect upon the self : building up a personality devoted to truth rather than to the things of this world and everyday biosocial interests.[32]

The true lover of knowledge will not rest in the multiplicity of individuals which is appearance only. He will go on until he attains knowledge of the true nature of every essence by a sympathetic and kindred power in the soul : drawing near and becoming incorporate with very being, having begotten mind and truth. Then he will have knowledge and will live and grow truly. His mind is fixed upon true being, his eye directed toward things fixed and immutable, all in order moving according to reason; to these he will conform his self imitating that with which he holds reverential converse.[33]

Thus guided and directed by philosophic teachers, the study of science can be used to turn students, not into scientists, but into philosophers. As soon as the current of their desires sets strongly toward the discovery of truth, the other, instinctive and biological desires become correspondingly weakened, and the student becomes something of an intellectual. There is, indeed, a certain danger here. If left to himself, the student who has once tasted the delights involved in the pursuit of knowledge for its own sake may become fixated in the academic life. He may develop a certain reluctance to re-enter the world of practical men and women, once he has learned to regard it as inferior. He may feel that he has somehow earned the right to remain forever in the realms open to the spectator of all time and existence.[34] As we know, the greatest student who issued from Plato's Academy, Aristotle, deliberately concluded that the life of a community leader or practising statesman was definitely inferior to the life of the philosophic scientist, the remote theoretician who devoted himself to " pure thought thinking itself." For himself, Aristotle preferred, " not to do, but to be."[35]

There is danger, that is to say, that the two roads to freedom, roads designed to liberate those who follow them, from the narrowing influence of exclusively biosocial interests, may succeed only too well. Art and science may educate the student out of all natural feeling for the affairs of everyday humanity. The painter or musician devoted to creative virtuosity, the scientist fascinated by the problem of discovering and formulating technical laws in some field remote from concrete human interests, the philosopher unwilling to do anything but go into his study and think, develop into quite eccentric persons. From the standpoint of civic philosophy and the ideal community, their lives, however fascinating to themselves, are wasted. The "freedom" into which they have led their followers is negative, entirely futile.[36]

For himself, Plato does not accept the gospel of Art for Art's sake or Science for Science's sake. He recognizes the fascination, but is as inflexible with the scientist as with the poet. At the gates of his model city no intellectuals, men without a country, will be encouraged to knock. Whatever their gifts, they will not be granted the *entrée*. For, as Plato sees it, freedom is not bare freedom, *freedom-from*. It is positive, *freedom-to* : freedom to live an ideal community life, the life of citizen-guardians, of men

devoted, as Socrates was devoted, to his community, in its
actuality no less than in its ideality. To it they owe all they are,
and all they have. In it they enjoy the fullest possible freedom
to live the best conceivable human life : the life of free men,
members of a free city, each making his own special contribution,
the contribution for which his nature is best fitted, to civic life,
and each sharing fully in all the joys and sorrows, the interests
and achievements, of his fellows.[37]

Both roads to freedom are therefore pursued, not blindly, but
under the guidance of a teacher who is himself an example of
community spirit. Thus pursued, art and science both alike lead
toward a freedom which consists in the wholehearted pursuit of
civic duty and civic happiness : the richest and most satisfactory
sort of life for human beings.

In what ways is this life satisfactory ? In the first place, it is a
life in which the goods of the body : health, strength, and that
physical beauty which is the outward expression of a well-regulated
way of living, are developed to the full. Developed not, *bien
entendu*, for their own sake, as with those muscle-bound athletes
whom most Hellenic cities released from civic life so that they
might keep in training for the Olympic championships—but
developed always as an element in the life of citizens. This
feeling of civic healthiness, of a physique which is not one-sided
and narrow but plays its parts in the full life of the community,
is thoroughly satisfactory from the standpoint of physical self-
feeling. The healthy citizen rejoices in his health and strength.
He feels good.[38]

In the second place, it is a life in which the goods of character :
courage, justice, temperance, friendship, and religious feeling, are
developed to the full. Here too, always as elements in civic living.
The courage of the citizen-soldier is a shared courage. It is the
expression, not so much of the individual's personal pugnacity, as
of the resolute purpose of the whole community of which he is
the trained representative when he takes his place in the ranks.
The citizen develops a group-self which is wider and deeper than
his individual self and helps him to become a public-spirited
member of the community. He feels himself a member of a Hellenic city-state, with all that this implies ; and his *morale* expands
accordingly. The life of civic virtue is especially satisfactory from
the standpoint of social self-feeling.[39]

In the third place, it is a way of living in which the intellectual
life, with its " goods " such as sense-perception, memory, opinion

and reason, receives a well-rounded development, with the fullest opportunities for exercise of which the citizen, as such, is capable. In considering, however, whether such a life would be satisfying to an intellectual, we must look a little more closely at what is offered him.   How does the life of the model city differ, in respect of intellectual opportunities, from the actual cities of *Hellas* ? These, as is well known, differed enormously from one another. In Sparta, somewhat as in Cretan cities, opportunities for any sort of intellectual life were extremely narrow.   This narrowness is accentuated by the *jeu d'esprit* which suggests that possibly at special times, when all foreigners have withdrawn, Spartan citizens get together for the practice of philosophy.   At the other extreme, namely in the city of Athens, intellectual life was conspicuous, and it is doubtful whether its intellectual opportunities have ever been surpassed.[40]   The stimulus was great, and the range of opportunity was very wide.   It is hard to imagine any modern community whose citizens would be able to appreciate, at first reading, anything so brilliant as the best Aristophanic comedies.   Yet they were entirely successful at Athens.   The standards of the best Attic literature, in every form that has come down to us, were so high that even yet many of these works are accepted as models. Yet at Athens they were thoroughly appreciated.   In fact, if we include among institutions which offered intellectual stimulation to Athenian citizens, not only the courts, the assembly, the dramatic festivals, and the exhibitions and lectures of distinguished visiting authorities, but Plato's own Academy, with its overwhelming attraction for the *crème de la crème* of the world's intellectuals, it is hard to see how Plato's imaginary constructions can have been intended to surpass in intellectual stimulus and opportunity, the possibilities of his own native city.

And as soon as we look at the matter in this way, we see at once that there was no such intention.   In Athens, intellectually gifted visitors of all sorts were welcomed and highly esteemed. They were given every facility to display their gifts to all and sundry.   In Plato's ideal republic, on the contrary, visiting poets, dramatists, and lecturers, however undoubted their intellectual attainments, especially if they have something to offer which is exciting, stimulating and new, are rigidly excluded.   The traditional Hellenic literature is revised and enormously reduced both in bulk and in range.   As for new poems, not only are the patterns of form and sentiment all prescribed beforehand, but the actual composition is restricted, for the most part, to men of action rather than to professional authors. It is entirely understood that such amateurish performances will not reach a high standard, and Plato is quite complacent about this. Technical excellence is not considered desirable in the model city ; which is a city, not of artists, nor even of scientists, but of—citizens. [41]

Again : in Athens there was no restriction upon the creative artist in any and every field of art. In fact, he was encouraged and stimulated to outdo both the classics and his contemporaries. But in Plato's ideal republic matters are far otherwise. Experimentation and novelty are, in principle at any rate, almost entirely excluded ; and the range of imitative art is deliberately narrowed in a spirit of civic utilitarianism. Music, for instance, is restricted to military marches and processional hymns. And in the model city of the *Laws* something similar is attempted. [42]

Consideration of this sort of evidence makes it plain that Plato's ideal constructions are intended to come in respect of interest and opportunity afforded to intellectuals, somewhere between Sparta and Athens. Life in the model city would be, intellectually speaking, more stimulating than life in Sparta, but considerably less stimulating than life in Athens. It is thus quite clear that Plato is not making a bid for intellectuals to take up civic building lots in his model city. They are not wanted, and their desires and requirements are deliberately left unsatisfied. [43]

What precisely, then, is Plato trying to achieve, intellectually, in the life of his model city ? He is trying to satisfy, not the intellectual, but—the citizen. The citizen is not a man set apart from the general life of the community : to cultivate his talents *in abstracto*. His learning is not book-learning : to be written down on paper, kept on shelves and passed around from hand to hand. His knowledge is not the science of the specialist : the technical expert who knows everything about some one thing, and nothing about civic life in general. His wisdom is not the wisdom of the great scholar : a professor whose profundity in his own field is an object of admiration to the simple, but who does not himself remember his own street address. [44] The citizen's learning is a part of the citizen's life : as he learns by action each day to be more of a citizen. His literature is civic literature : the poems which celebrate civic heroes, the hymns which adore civic divinities, the public addresses which formulate civic policies and commemorate civic achievements, the records which educate in the rationale of civic legislation. Such literature has as its concrete setting, its stimulus, and its theme, the life of the community itself. It is lived rather than written, acted out rather than read. It is actual civic living, enhancing, by reflecting upon, itself : a fundamental note generating the overtones which give it its own characteristic *timbre*.[45]

This is true, not only of the mass of the citizens, but also of the select few who prepare themselves for civic leadership. It might be supposed that, during the years of study, while they " toil " at what they are learning and are becoming familiar with general principles rather than with detailed facts, they are withdrawn from civic living and are, in actual reality, turning themselves into intellectuals. But this is not Plato's intention. While they are doing their service in the army, they are doubtless withdrawn from other sides of civic life ; yet it is the community army in which their service is done, and its spirit is the community spirit. In precisely the same way, during the years of their intensive devotion to dialectic, their background is the community background, their outlook is the community outlook, and their spirit is, on the whole, the selfsame community spirit. Their intellectual studies are in addition to, not instead of, the regular civic excellences, and make them not less, but more civic in quality.[46]

To citizens with this civic background and outlook, the intellectual opportunities of the model city are not less, but more satisfying than the detached footloose studies of the mere intellectual. In their civic literature, art, science, and philosophy they feel more genuinely at home than they would do in an intellectual life which existed somehow in a sphere of its own cut off from the old home town. To their civic-intellectual self-feeling, life in the model city, providing them, as it does, with all the stimulation and support which they can, while remaining what they are, enjoy, is to be regarded as entirely satisfactory.[47]

So far, we have traced the biological self of the baby gradually becoming the neighbourhood child, the schoolboy, the adolescent, the mature citizen, and to a certain extent the official, in the ideal republic or the model city. We have watched him passing beyond the merely biological phases of life and taking on civic attributes ; and we have considered how these are related to literature, science and philosophy. In all this we have clearly been dealing with life and growth. But what—it may be asked—has all this to do with *mind*, the subject of our investigation ?

The answer, from Plato's standpoint, is—everything. Life, in its growth from the biological to the ideal-civic phase, *is* mind. It is precisely in such life and such growth that mind manifests itself. Education, learning, schooling (if you will) are not something abstract and technical, something you can set aside from general social development in a civic group. On the contrary, it is only in so far as the civic background and outlook permeate the family, the school, and each and every social institution, from the army and the law-courts to the music festival and lecture room, that anything recognizable as the life of the mind comes into existence.

The life of the mind is, in fact, identical with the Hellenic way of living. To build up, here and there on the surface of the habitable earth, centres of co-operative civilization, in which every member participates along with the rest, and in the process becomes a deliberative, policy-determining and policy-executing citizen, is to live the rational life : the rational life, that is, for beings who remain human. As developing to the maximum the social potentialities of human living, it is the application, to civic life, of the idea of good, the principle of maximal value.[48]

For the idea of good, the principle of ideality and value, is never, with Plato, regarded as a merely abstract principle, which could exist in some absolute vacuum, in an isolation which would render it meaningless and deprive it of vitality. It is always thought of in relation to the concrete living processes, which, already partially organized in accordance with its pattern and design, become more fully organized, so that the pattern and design become more dominant and recognizable.[49]

For instance : the end-organs of sensation, considered as mere mechanisms, are instruments : instruments for selecting and focussing light-vibrations, air-vibrations, and those watery and earthy stimuli which, when thus concentrated and amplified, have significance for the organism as tastes and touches. But these organs are never mere mechanisms. They participate in the life, the full life, of the organism. Physically, eye and ear are the terminals of the cerebro-spinal " marrow " which grows out from the brain into all parts of the body and serve to unify, control, and direct the organism in its relations with the external world. They convey their messages, fluctuating and uncertain as these are, to the central selfmotion within the brain. But that is not the whole truth. Their messages are not merely received by the central principle. They are co-ordinated, transformed into memories, opinions, and theories. Eventually they furnish forth the content of logical concepts and ideas : ideas which not merely condense but re-orient their concentrated meaning-essence in its value for the social, civic, and intellectual life of the organism.[50]

All this work of selecting, concentrating, co-ordinating, and re-orienting, so as to bring out the full meaning-value of sensory experience for human organisms engaged in the co-operative venture of building up an ideal civic life on earth, represents the functioning of the idea of good, operating, as it does, always in the concrete. It is operative in our experience from the first, in sensation, in memory, in imagination, in the formation of opinions, beliefs, and hopes ; that is to say in our experiences which are oriented toward the external world.[51] It is operative also in " pure " experience : i.e., when we turn our attention away from the directly receiving end of experience, namely, sensation, and toward the reflective activity called by Plato " dialectic, the conversation of the soul with itself," and confine our activities to concepts on their conceptual side. In this activity, analyzing and classifying conceptual systems such as mathematics, physics, and harmonics, so as to discover their common forms, the categories which run through and organize them all upon identical principles, we eventually discover the final principle which has been at work throughout our development : the principle of ideality and value itself. Once clearly discovered, this is never treated as a barren abstraction, but is used for the deliberate and more efficient reorganization of every side of our experience, so as to co-operate with God in realizing the ideal plan for humanity in the universe.[52]

The universal light which lightens all things, the absolute good, is the pattern according to which they (the philosopher-kings) are to order the State and the lives of individuals, and the remainder of their own lives also ; making philosophy their chief pursuit, but toiling also at politics and ruling for the public good ; bringing up also in each generation others like themselves, whom they will leave in their place when they depart to the Islands of the Blest.[53]

That is to say : Sensation, Imagination, Memory, Opinion, Reason, etc., are not, for Plato, so many distinct " faculties "— like the individual and distinct men shut up in the Trojan horse of Homeric legend. These words, taken from the ordinary use of language, are intended to indicate certain phases of our living. It is *we* who sense, imagine, remember, opine, and reason ; in so behaving, we set in action and express our whole selves. When three persons, John Doe, Sir Isaac Newton, and Plato, open their eyes and see an apple falling from a tree : John Doe sees the apple, a possible luncheon. Sir Isaac sees the whole Law of Gravitation, together with all its consequences (in principle) for the science of physics. Plato sees the need for a tissue of laws concerning agriculture and property rights in his model city ; together with a system of local and central magistrates, all suitably educated and the highest of them like the best pupils of his Academy, namely, with insight into the supreme principles of philosophy ; and everyone with an eye to the proper behaviour of small boys on the public highway, and a certain pride in his own model citizenship.[54]

In other words : the infinitesimal prick of sensation awakens the whole life of the self : the whole self of the plain man, the whole self of the great scientist, the whole self of the great philosopher. The functioning of the sense-organs, the terminals of the nervous system of this man or that, is already shot through with the interests, hopes and beliefs of the person who, by their instrumentality, sees—whatever his education, his background and outlook enable him to see. It is age and wisdom, the experience of a long life of noble citizenship, which gives to Cephalus the eye to see rightly : to see his way clearly through the superstitious fears which beset a man on the threshold of old age, when he comes face to face with the thought that he must surely die. It is youth and inexperience which lead Glaucon, Cleinias, and so many of the charming young Athenians depicted in Plato's pages to formulate boldly opinions which they shortly find reason to change. It is the mature experience of the professional teacher of public speaking, with his one-sided technique, his crowd-psychology, his tested and approved commonplaces, and his almost complete lack of dialectical training, which makes Protagoras, Gorgias, and so many of Plato's sophists fall easy victims to the picture-thinking, the sly questions, and the logical traps set them by Socrates. What Socrates really does by means of these devices, is to appeal from their technique, their commonplaces, and their theses, to their own self, their full and complete self ; and it is this, the complete self of Protagoras, of Gorgias, of Thrasymachus and the rest which finally sits in judgment upon the theses at first maintained, and either rejects them or accepts amendments which are more adequate expressions of the full experience, not only of the individual participants in the discussion, but of the whole group, including the readers of the Dialogues.[55]

If, then, we ask, what is Plato's theory of " mind," we discover that it is identical with the life of the self : or rather, of selves interacting and developing themselves in a social tissue of civic life. This tissue is partly nonlogical, that is to say, biological and social ; partly it is Hellenic, a co-operative venture in rational guidance of instinct toward a more ideal living ; and partly it is philosophic, a co-operative venture in academic discussion with an eye towards improving, in principle and in detail, every phase of human life. " Mind " is thus a name designating social behaviour, especially when mediated by language, by the arts, by the sciences, and by philosophy. It is thus especially in evidence in the life of culture, e.g., in Plato's Academy and similar institutions. But the life of culture is always conceived as arising out of, and intimately related to, the ordinary, biosocial life of humanity ; and however abstract and remote the techniques of mathematics and dialectic may at times appear, when viewed from the outside : they are essentially, for Plato, the intellectual skeleton of the arts which animate human life and make it more human, more alive.

" Mind " is thus not a substance, or a nexus of quasi-substantial " faculties." It is intelligent social behaviour, a cultural inter-activity of men, women, and children, as they build up a life which is more life, more in quality as well as in quantity : a life more worth living, the good life which is the biosocial expression of the idea of good.

[1]E.g., B. H. Bode : *How we Learn*, 1940, Chs. II–IV, VII–IX, XIV. Cf. also R. C. Lodge : *Philosophy of Education*, 1937, Chs. VII–IX. Cf. also C. W. Morris : *Six Theories of Mind*, 1932. [2]Cf. B. Jowett : " On the Nature and Limits of Psychology " (in *The Dialogues of Plato*, E.T., 1892, Vol. IV, pp. 175–191). [3]Cf. E.g., William James : *Principles of Psychology*. [4]Cf. Bode : *Op. Cit.*, Ch. VII, for a discussion of the evidence which has led theorists to reject the theory of " faculties " as a guide to educational practice. [5]*Essay*, Bk. II, Ch. xxi, Sects. 17–20. [6]Cf. e.g., G. F. Stout : *Manual of Psychology*, 1899, Bk. I, Ch. III. [7]*Theaet.* 184b f. ; cf. *Crat.* 453d ff. [8]The pre-textbook stage of writing about such subjects did not last long, if we can regard Aristotle's *De Anima* and *Parva Naturalia* as of the nature of systematic textbooks. Upon a student like Jowett, the Platonic discussions apparently have a negative effect. He is convinced that psychology can never be a science. Upon a student like Aristotle, the effect was apparently the precise reverse. [9]Cf. I. Beare : *Greek Theories of Elementary Cognition*, p. 8. Cf. R. C. Lodge : *Plato's Theory of Ethics*, pp. 34–36, 294–8, *Tim.* 43b f., 64b f. *Theaet.* 156 f., 182, 184c ff., cf. 191d, *Phileb.* 33c f., 35c f. with Bury's notes. [10]*Tim.* 44a f., 45b f., 64b ff., *Theaet.* 153d f. 186c. [11]*Tim.* 44b, 67a f., *Theaet.* 154a, 159 f. *Rep.* 531, *Phileb.* 17b f. cf. 24a ff., 51d. The simple sensations are given at birth by nature) *Phileb.* 35c f. 51b, d. [12]*Tim.* 43bc, 56bc, *Rep.* 67c f. *Theaet.* 182, (Since whiteness is a flux or change which is passing into another colour, and is never to be caught standing still, can the name of any colour be rightly used at all ?). [13]*Theaet. Tim.* 91c f. *Laws* 653c ff., 672c f.,

771e, 795d f., 814d ff., 823b f. 942c. ¹⁴*Tim.* 47, 53b ff. ¹⁵*Tim.* 80ab, *Rep.* 397–399, 531a f., *Phileb.* 17b f., 25d f., 51b d. Cf. *Symp.* 187 f., *Laws* 802d f., 669b f., 670d. ¹⁶*Rep.* 398d f. *Laws* 812d f., 814d f. ¹⁷*Tim.* 43c, 45b f. 67c f. *Theaet.* 153d f. 156 f. *Phileb.* 51b f. ¹⁸*Tim.* 40a, 42a f., 77, 91d f., Cf. *Phaedo* 81e f. *Soph.* 220ab, *Polit.* 264c ff. Cf. *Symp.* 188a, Rep. 491d, *Laws* 845c Cf. *Hipparch.* 225c, cf. *Critias* 111c f. Cf. *Laws* 680d f., 765e f. *Prtg.* 334ab, (Cf. *Rep.* 611d f). ¹⁹*Rep.* 531d, 546, *Tim.* 35f, 43b ff., 53b ff., *Laws* 737b f., 740 f., 746d f. 771, 847d f., 848d f., 877d, 967d f. ²⁰*Tim.* 28 ff. 35a ff., 38a, 43 f., 52 ff. 68b, 69a f., cf. *Rep.* 531 ff., *Laws* 967d f. ²¹*Symp.* 208e ff. *Rep.* 484b f., 501, 540, *Tim.* 42a ff., 48a., *Theaet.* 176e f., *Polit.* 308d ff. *Laws* 729d f., 730e, 840c, 895 ff. ²²*Phaedo* 65 f., 69, *Rep.* 442cd, 521c, 523d f., 533b ff., 560, 603d. *Tim.* 43b f., 64a f. 69c f., 90a f. *Laws* 653a *Symp.* 206b ff. ²³*Rep.* 484b ff., 540a f., 590e ff. cf. *Theaet.* 153d 160c, 176a f. *Laws* 664 f., 764a, 766a f., 782e f., 790c f., 793e f., 804c f., 810 e f., 957, 964e f., 967d f. *Prtg.* 325c f. ²⁴*Rep.* 400e ff., cf. 411ab. *Symp.* 209–212a. *Phileb.* 51b ff. ²⁵*Symp.* 208e ff. *Phaedr.* 249d ff. ²⁶*Rep.* 400b ff. *Polit.* 308c f. *Laws* 653b ff., 664, 672d f., 682a, 719bc, 811. ²⁷*Laws* 659c f., 664b f., 670d f. *Rep.* 377 ff. 395a f., 401 f., 522ab. *Phaedr.* 245a. ²⁸*Symp.* 209b ff. *Phaedr.* 275–277, *Laws* 811b, f., 957b f., 964b f., 967d f. ²⁹*Rep.* 522a ff. ³⁰*Rep.* 377d f., 379d f., 386b ff., 401b, 596c f., 598 ff. *Ion* 533e f., *Laws* 682a, 719bc, 811. *Phaedr.* 245a. ³¹*Prtg.* 329a, *Rep.* 601–602, *Phaedr.* 275c f., *Laws* 719bc, *Gorg.* 490 f., 492e ff. ³²*Prtg.* 356e f., *Rep.* 522c ff. 525d, 526d f., 527d f. 529d f, 531–537. *Laws* 967d f. ³³*Rep.* 490ab, 500bc, condensed, cf. *485d.* cf. *Symp.* 210d f. ³⁴*Rep.* 537d ff., 519c ff. ³⁵Arist. *Politics,* 1324a 25–33, 1325b, 14–23, 1337b 33–1338c, 12. ³⁶*Rep.* 487c f., 489b, 495c f., 595–608b. *Laws* 656c f., 811. ³⁷*Crito* 50–54, *Rep.* 433f., 462–466, 612, 614. ³⁸*Laws* 661a f., cf. *Eryx,* 397e f. *Rep.* 410b–412a, *Polit.* 309e ff. Cf. Lodge : *Plato's Theory of Ethics,* pp. 356–360. ³⁹*Rep.* 395b f., 462–5, 467–471c, *Tim.* 25bc, *Menex.* 242c–245e *Laws* 942 f. Cf. 808e f. ⁴⁰*Laws* 625e f., 633, 780b f., 942b, *Prtg.* 338d, 342, *Lach.* 183ab. ⁴¹*Rep.* 398a, 568b 595 ff., 605a, 607a. *Laws* 802, 810e f., 817b f., 829c f., cf. *Lach.* 188c f. ⁴²*Rep.* 395–402, 424 f. *Laws* 657f., 660a, 789ef., 801, 812d, 815 f. ⁴³*Rep.* 395bc, 398a, *Laws* 817. Cf. *Laws* 803de, 806d, ff., 817e f., 822e f., 835de. The higher magistrates are educated (*Laws* 967d f.), but are not " intellectuals." ⁴⁴*Theaet.* 173c f., 175a f. *Phaedo* 64 ff., 79cd, 96–99, *Rep.* 487c ff., 517a, e f. *Symp.* 218a, cf. *Gorg.* 485, 487c. *Soph.* 254a. *Phileb.* 62a f. ⁴⁵*Rep.* 423d f., 444c, f., 590e f. *Laws* 664, 689, 801c f., 806d f., 811, 817, 957, cf. *Phaedr.* 276 ff. ⁴⁶*Rep.* 374 f., 522d f., 525b f., 526d, f., 536b, 537–540, *Laws* 760 ff., 942 f., 957, 961, 964b f., –968. ⁴⁷*Laws* 809b–823a. 663 ff., 667b, f., 802, 806d f. ⁴⁸*Prtg.* 322cd, 323a,c, 324e f. *Crat.* 412c f., *Symp.* 210d f. *Rep.* 331d ff., 419–421c, 443c f., 462–464b., 465e f., 505 ff, 517c, 519e f. 540ab. Cf. Lodge : *Plato's Theory of Ethics,* pp. 43–45, 47–50. *Laws* 757b f. ⁴⁹*Rep.* 505 ff., 540cb. Wilamowitz–Moellendorff : *Platon I* pp. 420–424 points out that the " idea " (" form ") of good is, for a Greek, not different from, but identical with " the good." In Plato, the term is always used with the understanding that it is not a mere abstraction, but enters into the concrete nature of everything, without exception, which we call " good." ⁵⁰*Rep.* 517bc, 540ab., *Tim.* 64a f., 67a f. 69b ff. *Phileb.* 38b ff. Polit. 309a f. Natorp : *Plato's Ideenlehre,* pp. 140 ff. ⁵¹Cf. Lodge : *Op. Cit.,* pp. 31–38, 184–187, 290–367. ⁵²*Rep.* 511, 517b f., 532 ff., 537c f., ⁵³*Rep.* 540ab, slightly condensed. ⁵⁴Cf. *Laws* 845b f. (and the whole context), cf. 808e f., 822e f., 957, 967d f. ⁵⁵*Rep.* 539cd, 582a, *Laws* 658e, 715de, 765d f., 802b, 951, *Prtg.* 352a, 361c f., *Gorg.* 453a, 457c f., *Rep.* 354, 358b f., 449a f. 358a, 486e f. 505b f.

CHAPTER XI

EDUCATION AND DEMOCRACY : PLATO AND THE MODERNS

On the subject of this chapter there are, broadly speaking, two schools of thought. On the one hand, we have the classical scholars. On the other the authorities on present-day pedagogy. Practising schoolteachers stand somewhere between these two extremes : drawn now to the one side, and now to the other : not a little bewildered by what they hear maintained.

The classical scholars, intimate with the details of Socratic and Platonic teaching, for the most part really believe that, on matters of educational theory, the last word was spoken, and well spoken, between 428 and 348 B.C. They are not unacquainted with the writings of Rousseau, Pestalozzi, Froebel, and John Dewey. They read educational controversy, so far as this gets into the magazines. They have friends among present-day schoolteachers ; and they send their children to present-day schools. In general they are strongly in sympathy with present-day practices ; and with many of the criticisms currently passed upon the severely formal methods of the past, they heartily concur. But—to put the matter quite simply—the enthusiastic conviction of present-day educationists ; their undisguised belief that what they are doing or proposing to have done is startlingly novel and indeed revolutionary ; their readiness to advertise their views by calling them " The *New* Education,"[1] and their classroom practices by calling them " progressive " and referring to their institutions as " Schools of *Tomorrow* " ;[2] to classical scholars all this seems (at least when they are speaking among themselves) naive : amazingly so.

Their reason for so thinking is a simple one. The conflict between the old and the new in education—between a heavy-handed formalism which proposes to impress upon the rising generation the behaviour and opinions which the wisdom of the fathers has decreed should be so impressed, and a sympathetic stimulation of initiative and growth through play and sweet reasonableness : leading to a development of character and insight which will help our children to become good citizens in the brave new world—is not something which made its first appearance in the 1900s. Or, for the matter of that, in the 1800s ; or the 1700s, the 1600s, and so on. And so on : as far back as you like. For instance, in Homeric literature we find the hero Diomede stoutly maintaining the superiority of the men of his own generation to their predecessors ; and we find the hero Achilles being educated (after a shot at co-education which misfired) in a distinctly " advanced " and novel school, where he learned, by doing, under an instructor whose methods were, at least for the times, regarded as revolutionary.[3]

But it is especially when scholars read the Dialogues of Plato that they seem (to themselves) to find clear and unmistakable expression of almost all the beliefs, practices, emphases, and even slogans which present-day educationists acclaim as ultra-modern. This is partly, no doubt, a matter of words. When scholars come to translate the Hellenic phrases, they find themseves naturally using words which turn out to be almost identical with the terminology of our modern pedagogic manuals. Classical scholars would themselves be the first to insist that the industrial, social, and civic context in which the Hellenic terms received their characteristic fringe of meaning are in many respects different from the modern context : yet they still believe that there is some correspondence between words and things ;[4] and in particular, that the pedagogic situation then and the pedagogic situation now are not so different, in essentials, as present-day authorities would like to believe.

For example : there is apparent in the Dialogues a conflict between the old and the new in education. The older methods were more formal, more literary, more restrictive of physical movement. Schoolboys sat on benches and learned by heart approved texts. Discipline and obedience were enforced by the stick. Schooling was regarded as a kind of slavery, in which the pupils exercised neither choice nor initiative, and from which they escaped as soon as they could.[5] Many teachers, even in dealing with adolescents who had passed beyond this elementary stage, are represented as incapable of conceiving and applying less dictatorial methods. They regarded the pupil as essentially passive, a recipient of the superior wisdom which it was their function to pour into him, if necessary, by force.[6]

In contrast with this kind of method, we have the method of Socrates : informal, doubtful of the value of literary training, and with freedom of physical movement. His pupils sit, stand, or walk as they please. There are no approved texts to be learnt by heart. *Memoriter* methods and literary criticism are alike viewed askance.[7] Interest takes the place of discipline, and Socratic discussions are essentially a school of freedom. Scholars come or go as they will ; and when present, their participation in the question-and-answer method is entirely voluntary. The appeal throughout is to their initiative, their choice, and their judgment ; and when they feel that they have attained to maturity, they go their ways ;[8] prepared to play their part, as reflective citizens, in the life of their times.

Scholars believe that this general conflict between the old and the new in education corresponds, in principle, to the general conflict between the old and the new characteristic of our own times. And they believe further that the detailed techniques of educational practice approved of in the Dialogues correspond, almost point by point, to the detailed techniques approved of in our most " advanced " present-day schools. To make the matter more precise : they believe it would be perfectly feasible to construct, without going outside the text of the Platonic Dialogues, except for purposes of application to the present day, a manual of educational techniques suitable for study and adoption by beginning teachers, covering about the same ground as almost any of our present-day manuals. For example : if a Plato-scholar took the chapter-headings, and even the section-headings, from beginning to end, of a widely-used recent textbook for Normal School students, [9] he would experience no serious difficulty in paralleling the chapters and sections ; and, in the very few cases where there would be a difference between Plato's suggestions and the modern doctrines, it would be hard to convince the scholar that the advantage (even for the present day) was always with the modern authority.

To make the matter more concrete : there is plenty of material in the *Dialogues* on all the following topics : The telling exercise or lecture method ; the study of ideas in relation ; inductive and deductive lessons ; the exercise to arouse appreciation ; the formation of habits and the increase of skill ; training pupils to study ; the recitation lesson ; the review lesson ; the socializing phases of school work. There is plenty of material on story-telling, on playing games in connection with education, on the art of questioning, and similar topics. There is even, if one is willing to look sympathetically as well as carefully, a good deal of material on industrial education. Socrates, himself an artisan's son, has a respect for the social, as well as the pedagogic value of industrial experience ; and while it is true that Hellenic industry is of the type which is found before modern science and the industrial revolution had ushered in the machine age, it is surprising to discover how much, how very much of what is regarded as of value on this point in our present-day manuals is already formulated and emphasized in the *Dialogues*.[10]

And further : everything in connection with the schoolwork in Plato's scheme is socialized, as well as vitalized : from beginning to end. Not only is the bookwork always acted out, somewhat as in the acting which was—and is—so conspicuous in the " Messenger's Speech " of the typical Greek tragedy ; but every phrase and every sentence of the revised literature adopted by Plato for the schools of his model city is instinct with community feeling, aglow with community idealism. It is not old stuff, fit only for the museum shelves, but is entirely reprocessed : tailored to measure in accordance with the needs of the very latest generation in his model city.[11]

And the games played and practised in the sports schools too. These are no archaic make-believe, like our modern falconry and archery, but are the real thing : up to the last minute drill, shooting, commando-practice, and battle-manoeuvres in full mechanized equipment and with live weapons. Games ? Yes, in a way ; but socialized and vitalized ; with dangers which are genuine, and with a sense of reality which is complete. It is hardly possible to conceive of anything more efficient, more thoroughly attuned to the needs and the life of the time.[12] Life in the school, and life outside the school, are not, in the model city, two distinct kinds of life. The community is a larger school. The school is a smaller community, with methods adapted to the young. But they are parts of one and the same life : the life of model citizenship ; and the one melts imperceptibly into the other.[13]

Glance over the whole of this evidence (says the scholar). Look well at Plato's state-supported schools, with their teacheries. Consider the highly socialized, state-appointed staff of teaching experts. Observe the arrangements for the efficient administration of the whole system by a specialized and highly competent minister of education, whose office is acclaimed as the most important of all the great offices of state. In principle and in detail the whole system of education is plainly designed to do as much as can be done (humanly speaking) for the rising generation in its growth toward full citizenship. Considering all this, how is it possible (the scholar asks himself) for our modern educationists to take toward Plato the highly critical attitude that so many of them do ? Why is it that they seem unable to recognize their true friends, their spiritual kin who fight under the same banners as themselves ?

Is not Socrates everywhere acclaimed as the model teacher for all time? Was not Plato the first in the great tradition of European education to formulate the principles still followed by those who believe in vocational education, in education for the professions, in education for citizenship, and in education for leadership ? And did not Plato, in addition to formulating the theory which has become an integral part of our tradition, also establish, in the field of higher education, an academic institution of the greatest practical as well as theoretical value : an institution which he administered himself with distinguished success, and which persisted after the death of its founder for some eight and a half centuries ? Do not his literary remains, the *Dialogues*, still furnish inspiration to almost every one except, perhaps, our most characteristic modern educationists ?   How are we to account for this ?

The conversation of the soul with itself (remarks the modern educationist) does tend to result in that baffled feeling. If the classical scholar would direct his question, not to himself and those like him, but to one of *us* he would soon receive an answer. He might not like it. But at any rate it would be clear and decisive. When we say (as we indeed do) that for us Plato has an interest which is *only historical*, and that we are convinced that, if we are to do justice to the needs of our own times in this twentieth century A.D., *we have to scrap completely the educational tradition of which Plato is a conspicuous part*, we mean precisely what we say. Just as Plato scraps Homer, we scrap Plato, and for the same reason. His ideas don't fit our civilization.[14]

So long as we confine our attention to the fourth century B.C., or thereabouts, we do not attempt to deny Plato's significance, both as a theorist and as a practitioner in the field of education. The facts to which the scholar appeals are beyond doubt. We recognize the social and vital values in Plato's work. Of course. We also admire a number of things (not everything) in Plato's hero, Socrates. As far as Plato himself is concerned, and the times in which he lived, the scholar's appreciation and admiration are almost entirely justified.

But when we look at the Platonic tradition, the tradition starting after Plato's death and carried down to our own times—well, really. It overdoes things. It goes far beyond what the evidence will support. The scholarly tradition which attempts to interpret Plato to each new generation as though Plato were still a sort of inspired contemporary : a Christian priest speaking the language of the King James version of the Bible ;[15] a missionary of the modern democratic, Victorian style, à la John Stuart Mill ;[16] a technical idealist of the Marburg School ;[17] a scholarly, quasi-Teutonic *Gelehrter* ;[18] or a kind of empirical idealist (save the mark !) hardly to be distinguished from our present-day pragmatists except in the greater breadth and depth of his sympathies ;[19] really, you know. It won't do. It's as bad as Plotinus treating him as an other-wordly mystic.

The evidence of the tradition is entirely convincing of one thing. Scholars see in Plato a full-length mirror-image of themselves : a little idealized, no doubt ; a little etherialized, showing them not as they are, but as they would like to be, or perhaps would like to be thought to be. But really, the facts are far too simple for us to believe what the scholar tells himself and other scholars, and would apparently like us to accept as gospel truth. It won't do at all.

For what are the simple facts ? Plato was not a Christian, but a definitely pre-Christian type. To translate his *Dialogues* into biblical English is to give them a twist and a bias which are simply misleading ; and every scholar knows it.[20] Plato was not a Victorian democrat, or any other sort of democrat. He hated democracy and all its works. He was an aristocrat, and didn't care who knew it. Tradespeople, " little bald tinkers " and the like, excited in him nothing but contempt—the same kind of contempt with which the aristocratic bully Odysseus treated the radical Thersites in the *Iliad*. He had an almost equal contempt for women, and indeed for all persons weaker than the aristocrat's standard demands.[21] In the technical difficulties of idealism he does, it is true, show a certain interest—but it is demonstrably not the interest of the Marburg School.[22] As to the *Gelehrter*-interpretation, its most distinguished exponent was himself aware that Plato-students would smile and raise their eyebrows at his fancy picture of the great Academic settling down after his futile attempts to enter the world of action, as *nur noch Lehrer*. And as to the quasi-pragmatist interpretation : well, does not the evidence show that Plato personally supposed himself to have disposed of pragmatism—at least in its fifth century B.C. form—for all time ?[24] So much for the tradition.[25]

The fact is, ancient civilization rested upon the institution of slavery, with all that this involves. It is this which, more than anything, constitutes the great difference between Plato's world and ours. Plato's educational system is intended to apply to a very small group of aristocratic rulers and supervisors : to (1) the " golden " class of higher magistrates ; to (2) the " silver " class of military men (and women) ; but not at all to the great majority. Not at all to the business men and industrial firms with their methods of exchanging goods and services, thus making ancient civilization tolerable to the master-class. Not at all to the farmers and other primary producers, whose quasi-serflike efforts made it possible for the masters to eat, drink, and be (relatively) merry. In both these enormous groups of under-privileged persons there was, indeed, a kind of home training which fitted them for their life-work : a kind of apprenticeship system ; but this Plato steadily refuses to regard as real education[26] And below these was the class of the completely dispossessed : the slaves. The slaves outnumbered the possessing classes many times over, but did not participate in their life and education, except in a purely ministerial capacity.[27] Plato's educational system is thus narrowly aristocratic and applies to a mere fraction of the people. It is therefore completely out of date, and completely out of place in our modern democratic world.

This, then, is our answer to the classical scholar. He may not like it ; but at least he must admit its clearness and its cogency. Is it too much to hope that he will let by-gones be by-gones, and will join us in solving the problems of the present, with methods adapted to the present age ? As Callicles *almost* says :

Leave to others these niceties, whether they are to be described as follies or absurdities ; for they will only give you poverty for the inmate of your dwelling. Cease emulating these paltry splitters of words. Be up to date. Study the philosophy of business. Acquire the reputation of real wisdom. Emulate the modern man, the man of substance and honour, who achieves success.[28]

The classical scholar at once admits the clearness and the cogency. You reason well, he says. You ring the changes cleverly

and forcibly upon aristocracy and democracy, slavery and freedom, the many and the few. You are entirely right in supposing
that there is nothing amiss with your logic. But, my dear sir, is
there not a further question ? Must we not inquire whether your
premises are factually correct? Is your use of terms, perhaps, intro-
spective rather than objectively documented ? Is it possibly
so unrelated to the Platonic text as to make your reasoning (excellent as this is) miss the mark ? If so, you will have given an
exhibition of shadow-boxing (will you not ?) or possibly of how
well you can thrash a man of straw. But you will not have reached
Plato at all.

For consider. Is Plato really an " aristocrat " in your sense of
the term : a Colonel Blimp whose blood is excessively blue ?
It is true that Plato was born and brought up in a noble and well-
to-do family and that he mixed in good society. It is true that, to
point a simile for a particular audience, he does let his Socrates
(surely, no " aristocrat ") use that unfortunate phrase about the
" little bald tinker." It is also true that he criticizes, very severely,
something which he calls *demokratia*. But let us look more closely
into his meaning. Should not we, ourselves, criticize what he
criticizes, and with equal severity ? Only with this difference :
that we should call it, not " democracy " but *the abuses of democracy* ?
We should then assert that he is himself criticizing the abuses of
democracy, not criticizing what we nowadays understand as
democracy itself.[29]

And if we look more closely at the text : we at once discover
that his ideal constitution is not, emphatically not, an *aristokratia*
wherein rule is determined by nobility of birth. On the contrary,
this is one of the forms of constitution which he explicitly rejects.
Biology is not equal to the demands made of candidates for leadership, not even when helped out by scientific eugenics.[30] In the
ideal community of the *Republic*, it is not blue blood that is the
chief factor, but physical, moral, and intellectual excellence.
The problems of government are complicated and difficult ; and
for their solution, nothing less than the finest characters and the
best brains will do. " Until philosophers are kings, until political
greatness and wisdom meet in one, cities will never have rest from
their evils." Science, wisdom, philosophy : these are the
desiderata for leadership ; and these are the fruits of education
bestowed upon persons of ability. The selection of candidates
is determined, by Plato as with us, by tests : tests of character,
tests of intelligence, and the broad test of experience, both

practical and theoretical.[31] Everyone is given as much education as he can take : with the idea of preparing him to function in whatever position in the community life suits his abilities *plus* his training. Is not this precisely *la carrière ouverte aux talents* : equality of opportunity ? Is Plato, on this point, at all different from ourselves ?[32]

May we assume (continues the scholar) that, in the light of this evidence, the charge of " aristocracy "—i.e., of maintaining that privilege, place, and power should be determined by birth, rather than by ability and education for service—is withdrawn ? Withdrawn, not merely graciously, or with a touch of condescension toward a gifted writer who apparently meant well, but lived a long time ago and was thus not in a position to appreciate our modern democratic spirit : but entirely withdrawn—not without an apology for the unnecessarily harsh things that were said in error ?

Let us proceed to the second charge. The ancient world, we are told, rested upon slavery : *de jure* as well as *de facto*. It was an accepted theory that the few should profit by the toil of the many, and that the many should forever toil for the advantage of the few. Whereas in our modern world things are different. With us, slavery is abolished : abolished forever *de jure*, and becoming increasingly abolished *de facto*. We still have with us certain attitudes and tendencies which are relics of an indefensible past. But our underprivileged individuals and submerged masses are not cut off from hope. For difference of privilege is not with us an institution tolerated and accepted in theory ; and we work for a freedom which is recognized as a human birthright : a freedom which is positive, an equality which is not merely political and legal, but economic and social, part of the fabric of our being.

On this point, Plato's dreamings, however idealistic, did not succeed in emancipating themselves from what was the universal practice of the ancient world. As soon as you look closely, you see that his ideal republic and his model city rest upon the institution of slavery : a slavery which exists *de jure* as well as *de facto*. The difference between his views and ours is thus absolute : so different that there is really nothing to be said. The only wise course is to put his volumes back upon the shelf : to stay there forever, unless perhaps some historian of the past should desire to take them down.[33]

What rejoinder can the classical scholar make to this charge ? As before, he admits the cogency of the critic's logic. As concepts, freedom and slavery are opposed. Their contrasts furnish a theme for Fourth of July orators : a theme upon which the critic works his will without let or hindrance. But can these sharp contrasts really be shown to apply to Plato's world and to ours ? Is the difference between Plato and ourselves as abolute as the critic maintains ? The scholar meets the charge by whittling down the alleged difference : starting first from the Platonic, and secondly from the modern situation.

As we all know, there are, in what is called slavery, a number of type-forms which vary greatly in severity. The Hellenic type, especially the type found at Athens in Plato's time, is regarded as one of the less severe. According to the tradition, accepted by present-day scholars, Plato himself was for a time a slave, with the status of a captured enemy alien.[34] He condemns the Greek practice of holding Greeks as slaves, although, like Aristotle, he registers no objection if the servants used on the farms, in industrial establishments, or for personal service in the homes, are Barbarians.[35] He finds the institution itself a little embarrassing to his principles, and accordingly in the *Laws* has his young men on military service in the home country observe the principle of justice by " doing their own work " themselves. They decide to wait upon themselves and to make no use of compulsory labour :

> Let them meet together and determine that they will be their own servants, and, like servants, will not have other slaves and servants for their own use, neither will they use those of the villagers and husbandmen for their private advantage, but for the public service only ; and in general they should make up their minds to live independently by themselves, servants of each other and of themselves.[36]

That is to say, if we may assume, on the basis of this evidence, that slavery in the sense of personal service is discouraged in the model city on principle, and considerably reduced in practice : it still remains true that the labour necessary on the farm, in industry, and in the home is furnished, not by the free and joyous self-dedication of citizens to a life of honest toil in a civic Garden of Eden ; but by underprivileged classes of foreign extraction. They toil because they must : either because they have nothing to offer in exchange for food and shelter but their physical strength,[37] or else because they are—well, yes—slaves.[38] The charge that Platonic civilization rests upon slavery is mitigated. We point to the fact that the resident aliens who carry on the operations of industry and commerce, while far from being citizens, enjoy a legal status which is definitely above the status of slaves.[39] We point to the fact that the labourers who sell their thews and muscles in exchange for food and shelter, while under-privileged, are also (apparently) no more slaves than their counterparts in the present-day world. We can even draw atten-tion to the ancient slave's *peculium*, his savings account, as it were, by diligent attention to which he could ultimately purchase his freedom. But it remains true that a certain proportion of the labourers in the model city are thought of and spoken of as slaves : slaves *de jure* as well as *de facto*, although the *de jure* side is nowhere emphasized by Plato. And to this extent the charge is—ad-mitted.

What do we find when we turn to the modern situation ? With us, much of the hard work of the world is done by machines. And this is increasingly the case. But agriculture and industry, in spite of being largely mechanized, still require a great deal of labour : men to push and pull, to lower and hoist, to open and close, to fetch and carry, to grub around and to do—what they are told to do. So too around our offices and homes. In spite of the labour-saving devices, there is still much work, plain uninteresting work, to be done. How do we handle this in our modern age ? Have we succeeded in overcoming what the *Encyclopaedia* calls " the anti-pathy to regular and sustained labour which is deeply rooted in human nature " ?[40] Have we developed labourers to whom work is pure joy : charming gnome-like figures who " whistle while they work " and sing together while off to work they go, in har-mony as well as in step with the needs of the brave new world ? In our era of co-operative enterprise, do our working classes accept freely, gladly, and intelligently their place in the industrial scheme? Do they in some fundamental sense love the life which is theirs ?

The answer is not entirely simple. It is influenced by a number of factors which may vary enormously within a single generation. One and the same group of workers may in one year be proud of themselves and satisfied with their place in the scheme of things : co-operating enthusiastically with their executives. In the next year, if conditions change, they may be in open revolt, out on strike. In the next year, if the strike is broken, they may be back at work : submitting to discipline and driven by need and the hunger of their families ; but with bitterness and hatred in their hearts. Skilled craftsmen and men of the artistic type normally take pride in their workmanship. They enjoy their independent creativity. Some of them enjoy repetitive exactitude. But they will work well only when their importance receives reasonable recognition. If driven rather than led, the quality goes out of their work ; and formality in their relations with their executives takes the place of the former easy understanding.

In the case of unskilled labour, the situation is not essentially different : except in so far as the workers, not feeling themselves to be indispensable as individuals, trust less to individual workmanship and more to group action to enforce their claims to consideration. Relations with executives tend to be formalized, and there is a good deal of mutual mistrust and dislike.[41]

Our modern sociological writers draw attention to " the proletariate " whose ranks are swollen by immigrant labour with low living standards : what Plato would call " foreigners attracted by pay." It is true that members of this class are not technically " slaves." They are not captured enemy aliens retained in a position of servitude. They have not been kidnapped by traders in human flesh and sold to purchasers who own plantations or factories. They are not serfs *adscripti glebae*, or anything of the sort. And yet : in spite of our oratorical vaunts of liberty and the rights of man, the literature written by workers who have lived this life of labour on our farms, in our mines, and in our factories, as well as the reports of trained social workers, indicates that we have still a long way to go before we achieve complete economic democracy. The new Jerusalem has not yet been completely built in England's green and pleasant land, and something less than the American standard is the lot of our underprivileged classes in the new world.

In the new world. And what of the old world ? It is only in Abyssinia that slavery exists as an institution so interwoven with social customs as to be almost inextricable ? For some years now we hear of war-prisoners, of labour camps, of slave-labour, and of slave-armies ; and in many parts of the world there is no thought that these conditions will be merely temporary. On the contrary : the declared policy of large and strongly organized racial groups is to make these conditions permanent. The labour of captured enemy aliens is a feature of our times as of Plato's ; and the place of private kidnapper-traders is taken by the organized demands of conquering states. And when we consider the modern harshness and ultra-ruthlessness, it looks as though the advantage, morally speaking, is with the comparatively easy conditions depicted by Plato. How long this state of things will con-

tinue is at present undecided.   But in the meantime, the charge
that Plato's civilization is utterly different from ours because its
labour is slave-labour, while our labour is something else, is a
charge which must be dropped because it is not in accord with the
facts of present-day life.

The third charge is that Plato's education is only for the few :
i.e., for the members of his " golden " and " silver " classes, and
not at all for the bulk of the populace ; not at all, that is to say,
for the traders, the artisans, the labouring classes, and the slaves.
Its principles have therefore little or no application to modern
conditions, and it must be regarded as out of date.

What can the scholar say to this charge ?   He can begin by
drawing a distinction between certain types of education.   In
our modern world we have different kinds of education, and of
these not all are intended for Tom, Dick, and Harry.   Not by any
means.   For example, we have what we call " higher " education,
such as is pursued in the graduate schools of our universities.
This necessarily rests upon certain pre-requisites, and, in the
nature of the case, is not thrown open to all and sundry.   It is
available only to those students who have demonstrated, normally
in their undergraduate courses, that they have the capacity,
both of character and of intelligence to profit by such training
for superior service.   And such students constitute only a small
fraction of the population.

On the North American continent, something less than one-
hundredth of the population attains to the status of the Bachelor
of Arts degree ; and in Europe the percentage is still smaller.
Out of this group again less than one-fifth of the students prepare
themselves, by postgraduate studies, for the professions of law,
teaching, religious ministration, and other advanced forms of
social and governmental service.   It is at once obvious that, with
us, this " higher " education is designed and suited only for the
few.   It is certainly not intended for the masses of traders, artisans,
and labourers of one sort or another, who constitute the great
bulk of the population.

The education given to members of Plato's " golden " class
corresponds precisely to this postgraduate education of ours.   It
is offered only to those students who have demonstrated, by passing appropriate tests, including tests of character as well as tests of
intelligence, that they have the capacity to profit by it.   And it is

offered precisely in the intention of preparing the best students for positions in the professions of law, teaching, religious ministration, and other forms of advanced social and governmental service.[42]

In fact, education for leadership can be given wisely only to students who have demonstrated that they possess the capacity for leadership. This is recognized as true in our time ; and it is only reasonable to recognize it as equally true in Plato's time. The fraction of the population in any age of the world's history, which is competent to apply itself with advantage to such education, is necessarily small ; and even today, with all our educational facilities, the world is not exactly overrun with great statesmen of the kind called by Plato philosopher-kings.

In so far then as the charge means that Plato's *higher* education is only for the few, and not for the bulk of the population, the scholar admits this to be a fact, He shows, however (1) that the same is true of our own system of higher education, and (2) that this is necessarily the case, and should be regarded as a matter, not for blame, but for praise.

And further : in our modern world we have a type of education which we offer in " secondary " schools such as High Schools and Junior Colleges, and call " general " education. Such institutions are frequently referred to as " The *People's* University," and it is contended that their graduates are prepared for " citizenship." They offer education in the literature, the traditions, and the techniques characteristic of our civilization. For the great majority of the graduates this constitutes a finishing school. They have gone as far as formal education can take them, and are now " prepared for life." This means that they are prepared gradually to take their place in industrial and civic life, and generally to function as adult citizens. For the especially gifted few, that is to say, roughly speaking, for the upper third of the graduating class, these schools further provide the general knowledge which is regarded as a basic pre-requisite to the " higher " type of education discussed above.

These schools are themselves by no means attended by all and sundry. They build upon the product of the " primary " schools ; and not all graduates of the primary schools receive a High School or College education. And of those who do enter upon a High School course, many fall by the way : precisely as is the case with the freshman class of a Junior College.

The " general " education of these secondary schools corresponds pretty closely to the education prescribed by Plato for the members of his " silver " class. This too furnishes preparation for " citizenship " ; and it is offered to all who show, by passing the entrance and continuation tests, that they have the capacity to take it with advantage to themselves and the community. As in our modern High Schools and Colleges, many fall by the way ; but considerable numbers persist to graduation at the age of eighteen to twenty. [43]

That is to say, with Plato as with ourselves, general education in the literature, traditions, and techniques of the group is offered to all who show that they can take it with advantage to the community and themselves. It should perhaps be added that, with the exception of military training, the Platonic community does not make formal, institutional provision for vocational and technical training ; and that thus our secondary schools, to the precise extent to which they provide for such training, appeal to a wider group of students than those who attend Plato's schools for citizenship. But apart from this, the resemblance between Plato's schools and ours is very close. In particular, attendance up to a certain period is compulsory for all prospective citizens. There is no intention to be exclusive and to limit this kind of education to the few : with Plato any more than with ourselves. [44]

Finally, let us consider the field of what we call " elementary " training in the " primary " schools : that is to say, training in the elements, the three Rs, and in early physical and social education. Plato's system differs here from ours. The formal training in reading, writing, arithmetic (and, with Plato music), comes in the 'teens. The earlier period (from six to ten) is devoted to " sport " : that is to say, to acquiring proficiency in the military dances, games, and field-sports which have a community *raison d'être*, as well as a certain appeal to the activity-impulses of child-hood. What we nowadays leave largely to private or semi-private initiative : to the Y.M.C.A., the Y.W.C.A., and the various sport-clubs, Plato has taught, by state-appointed professional teachers, to all prospective citizens, and the training is compulsory. The scope of such training in the model city is at least as wide as the scope of the secondary education offered to the members of the " silver " class ; and it is clearly intended, not for the few, but for the many. [45]

And now the time has come to face directly what is undoubtedly intended to be the main point of the modern criticism of Plato, namely, that Plato ignores vocational education. It is admitted— the facts being beyond dispute—that in the ancient world technical and vocational education existed. This education was given in a kind of apprenticeship system which had grown up naturally and had become traditional. The rising generation learnt in the family, by doing what it saw its elders doing. The potter's children and young apprentices learnt their trade by looking on and helping, by being shown and doing. This traditional system was followed in all training for vocations and technical pursuits : much as in the modern world until very recent times. In many parts of the world this system is still followed.

The point of the criticism is, not that this kind of thing did not exist in Plato's world, and not that it was not reasonably efficient. The criticism is, that Plato did nothing for it. He refused to regard it as " real education," and left it to unprogressive tradition, unaffected by his educational principles.[46] Platonic education, that is to say, concerns itself primarily with developing the upper classes of society : the leaders and the military. For those who devote themselves to the trades and crafts and to industrial and agricultural labour : in a word, for the vast majority of the population, Plato does nothing. His system is thus, not for the many but for the few ; and therefore it is out of place in our modern world.

When the point of the criticism is thus sharpened, what can the classical scholar urge in reply ? As before, admitting always the clearness and cogency of the critic's reasoning, he can only plead for a closer attention to the textual facts on which the premises for such reasoning, if this is really intended to apply to Plato, should be firmly based. He directs attention to the considerable amount of material in the *Dialogues* which bears upon this subject of technical and vocational education. Socrates, speaking no doubt with first-hand knowledge, is perpetually bringing up the analogy of the arts and crafts ; and in connection with his theory of education, it is at once plain that he speaks of the practice of the artisan classes with respect ; and also that he derives from that practice a good deal of what is usually regarded as characteristically " Platonic " in the education prescribed for the " silver " and " golden " classes. Here, it may be said, Plato appears to receive more than he gives.[47]

The working family whose members live together in biosocial unity : associating in the performance of tasks in which the labour of each makes for the welfare of all, and where the younger learn by helping, watching, and imitating their elders until they can themselves do what their elders do : is itself a school for citizenship. And this is true whether the economic activity in which the members of the family co-operatively engage is the making of pots, the weaving of garments, or the building of houses. Plato's " silver " class of military auxiliaries learns its main business of fighting in precisely this sort of way ; and Plato points the analogy by explicit reference to artisan practice.[48] Moreover, in spite of the fact that in the *Republic* (not in the *Laws*) *private* family life disappears, its place is taken by *group* family life ; and this is intended by Plato to share in all the natural, biological feelings which make for unity in the individual family. The " silver " class as a whole is intended to live as one big family. Members of the parent group are expected to feel towards *all* members of the child group somewhat as Mr. Chips felt towards " his children," his pupils in the school. Members of the child group are expected to turn to *all* members of the older generation in the community for assistance and affection, somewhat as our children do to a few " uncles " and " aunties " among the friends of the family.[49] Members of the same age-group are expected to feel a genuinely brotherly and sisterly intimate confidence, such as with us exists only upon a limited scale.

So too in the model city. The attitude of the neighbourhood children toward the playground matron, of the schoolchildren toward their successive teachers, of the festival-candidates toward their adjudicators, of the adults toward their magistrates and guardians, follows always the same plan. Adults assisting informally in watching over the children's safety and orderly behaviour on the streets, old men telling moral stories to the young, officials of all sorts watching over the welfare of the community, whether in their daily round of duties or in the deliberations of the Nocturnal Council : all alike do their special work against a continuous background of extended family feeling. Plato's own Academy exemplifies the same thing, and so do our modern schools and colleges.

It is in a continuous milieu of this biosocial kind, that the specific activities of individuals are developed. To the association of growing children with their elders in the typical artisan's family, there corresponds precisely the association of schoolchildren with their teachers, of soldiers with their officers, of citizens with their " guardian "-magistrates. Each projects himself imaginatively into the position of his elder-brother or parent, as it were. He assimilates himself to his teacher, operating as he imagines his teacher would operate. In such imagination-mediated co-operation there is effected a kind of personality-merger between him and his leader. In fact, almost all the characteristics usually regarded as specifically Platonic, and found in the *Symposium* and *Phaedrus* as well as in the *Republic* and *Laws*, are closely analogous to the educational situation in the artisan family, and the analogy is deliberately drawn by Plato.[50]

It would appear, then, that from the practice of artisans Plato derives a good deal of what he finds useful for the education which he prescribes for his silver and golden classes in the ideal community. Are we to say that in this relation his position is that of receiver rather than giver ? Or does the relation work both ways ? Does he give as well as receive ?

The answer is not entirely simple. In a Platonic dialogue, the writer does not always adorn the tale by pointing the moral. On the contrary, he tends to leave that to his reader. But the evidence is there, and he who reads, if he is willing to do his part, can find, understand, and apply the evidence for himself.

So here Plato's system of education for his higher classes can be regarded as largely an idealization of the learning by doing, in a socialized and vitalized family milieu, which he finds to be characteristic of the families of potters, weavers, and carpenters. The learning by doing, the socialization and the vitalization, are extended forwards. But as soon as we look closely, we discover that something of the idealization extends backwards. The resident aliens who carry on most of the commercial activities of the community, the artisans who carry on most of the industrial activities essential to the community, the labourers and the slaves are not, of course, citizens. They do not own lots, elect magistrates[51] act as members of the armed forces, or carry on any of the other functions of full citizens. But they are not simply left to themselves, to do their own work as long as they are useful, and then to be flung upon the scrap-heap. They function always under the guidance of the magistrates. Their positions, duties, and privileges are prescribed by law ; and in their way they are as much members of the community as anyone else. Consequently something of the community idealism, the tendency to do one's work in the spirit of service and loyalty to the group, may enter into their lives and may inspire them to act somewhat beyond their station. In such cases if younger members of the " copper " class prove capable of passing the tests of character and intelligence which

control membership in the "silver" class, such members are
taken up into the higher class, and are given the education
which qualifies them for full citizenship.[52] If older members of
this class perform some signal public service, Plato indicates that
the magistrates may extend indefinitely the twenty-year residence-
permit.[53]

In such ways the community really does something for its under-
privileged classes. And it also furnishes guidance and assistance
in the way of education. In the first place, a certain degree of
education is involved in the law itself, insofar as the law takes
cognizance of their activities. Written law is always regarded by
Plato as a highly educative factor,[54] and there is a large mass of
legal regulation covering commerical, agricultural, and industrial
activities : all of which has to be understood by those engaged in
such activities.[55] Living in a well-regulated community is also,
of itself, an educative factor.

But this is not all. In the second place, we find direct education provided for certain groups within this general non-civic
class. It is provided under the authority of the minister of education, and is paid for by the state. For example : the state appoints
and employs a considerable group of teachers. These teach the
various military sports. They teach reading, writing, arithmetic,
and music. They teach the approved literature. Teachers of these
various subjects are all foreigners, not citizens. Under the direction of the minister of education they are trained for the business
of teaching. Not trained in the practice of their specific arts :
but trained to be teachers, teachers of children, teachers of the
community children. Amongst other things they are trained and
examined in the philosophy of education required in the model
city. They have to show that they understand, as well as approve,
the content of such books as Plato's *Laws* (and similar writings),
before they receive their licenses to teach.[56]

This training offered to experts who are being invited to teach
in the model city is analogous to the training given to all higher
officials (who are not foreigners, but full citizens). All higher
magistrates are given " higher " education : presumably in some
such institution as Plato's Academy, directed by the minister of
education. This fits them for functioning as magistrates, officials
who really represent the community spirit in action. Unlike the
general education offered to all prospective citizens, this is not
amateurish, but strictly professional. Students do not take a
gentlemanly interest in it. They " toil at " the higher studies

(much as in the *Republic*) until they really arrive at the desired level of insight.[57]

The professional training which makes a musician a technical expert on his instrument, and makes a literary man a technical master of words and rhythms, like the professional training which makes a carpenter an efficient carpenter, a weaver an efficient weaver, a potter an efficient potter, and the prospective teachers of such subjects experts in the specific subject-matter which they propose to use in teaching young citizen-amateurs, is not provided directly by the state. It is left, indeed, to the usual apprentice-ship system. But this is not left to itself. The state, which employs musicians and literary men to carry out the technical side of the revision of the traditional literature, and employs teachers of this or that subject-matter, indirectly, by insisting upon proficiency in its employees, encourages the existing apprenticeship system, and indeed demands that it shall be efficient. By holding before would-be teachers and other experts the prospect of state appointment and state employment, Plato's model city does a great deal toward maintaining standards of *expertise* and developing an *amour-propre*, as well as efficiency, in the establishments of its artisans and other non-citizens. There is little, if anything, of an educational character going on within the precincts of the model city, whether among citizens or among non-citizens, which remains uninfluenced by the minister of education.[58]

Finally, there is a good deal of education which, always under the direct authority of the minister and provided directly by the state, is given, not merely to young citizens and prospective citizens, but to *all* children, and indeed to all persons, including explicitly the slaves. This is the education of character which comes from participating in the approved community processional singing, in which children and adults submit themselves to the spell, the magical charm of the model city and its ways of living. *Every* member of the model city, whether full citizen or not, " young and old, bond and free," never ceases to charm himself in choral song : which is regarded as the essence of education.[59]

Our conclusion, on the basis of this evidence, is that the criti-cism which insists that Plato's education applies only to the few, and not to the many, is not in accordance with the textual facts. While Plato does not work out in detail a complete educational system for his non-civic classes : the classes which perform the agricultural, industrial, commercial, and educational work which has to be done if the citizens of the model city are to be enabled to live their beautiful, ideal-human life : he does do something for their education. Partly directly and partly indirectly, he ensures that for each class there shall be a type of training which will fit it for the performance of its specific function in the community : and also a kind of general education, identical with that given to prospective citizens, which will " charm " it into living in the spirit of loyalty to the model city.

That is to say,: Plato's intention is plainly to give to each person living within the city precincts as much education as that person requires to enable him to " do his own work " : to make his own characteristic contribution to the life of the community. This is true whether the resident is a member of the servant class, an expert in the useful arts and crafts, a professor of the fine arts, an organizer of industry, or a professional engaged to teach this and that to " the children of well-conditioned parents." All such persons are under-privileged, non-civic. Many of them, e.g., the commercials, the teachers, and, where possible the servants, are outsiders : foreigners who will never be confused by either young or old with the regular citizens.[60]

From this evidence we realize that the charges that Plato's educational views are excessively " aristocratic," that his ideal community rests upon an unmodern institution, namely, slavery, and that his theories apply only to the few members of the master-class : so that his ideas are completely out of touch with our modern kind of democratic civilization : are not in accord with the textual facts, and should thus be withdrawn.

In fact, we can go further, and can compare Plato's educational ideal with the educational ideal of the most modern authority on democracy and education. John Dewey defines democracy as primarily " associated living, conjoint communicated experience." That is to say, his model city functions as a kind of melting-pot, in which groups and individuals communicate and share in each other's experiences. The difference which he believes distinguishes his views from Plato's, is primarily the difference between groups and individuals. He believes that Plato's individuals are stratified into three hard-and-fast classes : the " golden," " silver," and " copper " classes mentioned in the *Republic* ; and that these are kept as distinct as is humanly possible. Within each group there is intercommunication of experiences. But there are far too few groups to enable the individual to realize a full human personality. Individuals are unique, and cannot wisely be stratified in a few set, unprogressive classes. They should be enabled to participate freely in a great variety of group experiences as in our present-day world.

There is here a neat conceptual contrast. We get the idea that in Plato's world you become some one thing. You become a worker of some sort, or a soldier of some sort, quite distinct from any worker, and obligated to function as an auxiliary to the rulers. In the third place, if you show unusual intellectual ability, you become a member of the ruling class, entirely distinct from the workers, and also rather sharply distinct from the military group. You don't mix with the other groups, and so, your experiences are rather sharply limited. You have these three possible lines of development, and no others. This view is attributed to Plato, and it is criticized on the ground that there are far too few groups recognized by Plato to do justice to the facts of the human situation, and that there is no recognition of individual differences in their really very great variety.[61]

The classical scholar does not find, in the Platonic text, any justification for attributing to Plato any such hard and fast " stratification." As *he* reads the *Dialogues*, the distinction between the three classes seems quite general : just as we might, in a general way, distinguish post-graduate students from military men and from hand-workers today. It is a general distinction which helps to make Plato's views clear. But there is no evidence that the individual has to be forced into one of three moulds, whatever his individual tastes and capacities, in any sense in which the same is not true today. There are plenty of passages which recognize individual differences ; and there are, in the model city, quite a number of governing committees on which representatives of different cultural groups work together, pooling their information and abilities : all in the interest of the community as a whole. Professional writers, musicians, and other technicians co-operate in this way with law-lords, members of the " guardian " class, to the benefit of both sides.[62] Young men on military service decide to wait on themselves, without using slaves, and thus participate in the experiences associated with the more " servile " side of camping : doing " their own work " in a very literal sense.[63] It is true that there is not much fraternization, outside of the natural group-associations.[64] But there is an immense amount of participation in community life, especially at the monthly festivals and field meets : which make modern melting-pot ideals seem pale and weak by comparison.

And we have further to remember that Plato's community is very small : so that everyone knows pretty well how the other fellow lives. People are thrown together—far more so than at the present day—and there is not, in Plato's plan, much possibility of factions, cliques, or anything which could be called *strata* in any final, unchanging sense.[65]   Finally, we have to remember the institutions which, in spite of the logical persuasiveness of Dewey's views, are explicitly demanded by Plato as recognizing the possibility and desirability of progress, as contrasted with the fixity of written constitutions : institutions such as the Visitor or Travelling Spectator in the *Laws*,[66] and as Plato himself, the original lawgiver, in the *Republic*.

Our conclusion is that this factual evidence, sympathetically understood, makes the criticism of " stratification " pointless, as applied to Plato. There is no difficulty in paralleling, from the *Dialogues*, such phrases of Dewey's as that " social organization means utilization of the specific and variable qualities of individuals, not stratification by classes."[67] And to say that Plato's " aim was to construct a state in which change would subsequently have no place ; not even minor details are to be altered " is simply not in accord with a complete reading of the text.[68] Plato's education is in fact, quite as much as Dewey's, education for what Dewey considers to be " democracy "—at least, in principle. For some difference in details as to what constituted "democracy" in Plato's time and what constitutes " democracy " in ours, certain allowances will of course have to be made.[69]

---

[1]Cf. The important volume, written by many teachers, under the editorship of (Sir) John Adams, entitled *The New Teaching* (4th edition, n.d., Hodder and Stoughton).   [2]Cf. the charmingly written book with this title, written by John and Evelyn Dewey (1915, Dutton). It is partly theoretical, and partly informative as to current practices of " progressive " schools. [3]Cf. *Iliad*, IV, 405. For the school taught by Chiron, cf. Apollodorus, *Bibliotheke* III, 10. 13, (Teubner). [4]Cf. Plato : *Crat.* 422–439. Cf. J. Stenzel : *Platon der Erzieher*, pp. 283–285. [5]*Prtg.* 318d, 325d f. ; *Lys.* 208d ff. ; *Rep.* 518bc. [6]*Rep.* 337d, 345b, 518bc ; cf. *Prtg.* 320c. [7]*Prtg.* 329a, 347b f. ; *Rep.* 595b ff. ; *Phaedr.* 275b–276d, 277e f. ; *Laws* 810e f. [8]*Apol.* 32e f. ; *Lach.* 187d f. ; *Gorg.* 509ab ; *Theaet.* 148e–151d. [9]I have in mind Lida B. Earhart's *Types of Teaching*, 1915. A more recent manual, such as George E. Freeland's *Modern Elementary School Practice*, 1920, while full of present day examples, could be pretty well paralleled without going outside the Platonic text. These deal with the elementary school. For secondary school work, a book such as H. H. Foster's *Principles of Teaching in Secondary Education*, 1921, will be found to contain little if anything in the way of " principles " which cannot be paralleled from Plato. That is to say, these books, while full of wise saws and modern instances, are entirely in the spirit of the great educational tradition which is usually considered (H. L. Nettleship : *The Theory of Education in Plato's Republic*, 1935, Introduction, p. 1 (by Spencer Leeson), as having originated with Plato.

In a number of other widely-read books, such as Francis B. Pearson's *The Vitalized School*, 1917, and Herman Harrell Horne's *Story-telling, Questioning and Studying*, 1917, the spirit in which the work is conceived and written is quite closely analogous to the spirit of Platonism. In the case of Horne's book, this is undoubtedly entirely clear to the author. [10]I would suggest a comparison of the evidence from the *Dialogues* (considered *supra*, Ch. II) with a recent book such as Herman Schneider's *Education for Industrial Workers*, 1915. [11]*Laws* 802ab, 811 ; cf. Kenneth J. Freeman : *Schools of Hellas*, 1908, p. 97. [12]*Rep.* 537a ; *Laws* 794c–796d, 813–816, 829–831, 832d–834d, 942. Cf. Becher : *Op. Cit.*, pp. 169 ff. [13]*Prtg.* 326c f. ; *Rep.* 368c f., 423d ff., 434d f., 466e f. ; *Laws* 659c f., 719e, 722 f., 772e, 811c f., 880d f., 887a, 907d–909a, 964bc, 965 ff. [14]The precise grounds on which it is claimed that Plato's educational ideas should be rejected, differ from writer to writer. Thus, in Frank M. McMurry, *How to Study*, 1909, pp. 198–9, we read " To Plato, the use of the intellect for practical purposes was subordinate and almost disgraceful. The summation (*sic*) of existence was to be found in reflection, and the ambition of the educated man was to escape from the concrete world, in order to live in the world of abstract truth. Reflection, contemplation was an end in itself, and the thinker or dreamer, rather than the efficient man, was the ideally educated person. That goal is now condemned for its extreme selfishness. . . ." Cf. also B. H. Bode, *How we Learn*, 1940, pp. 57, 59, 68. (On the other hand, see *Rep.* 519c f., 539d–540b, not to mention 413c f., and *Laws* 770). Cf. Otto Neurath and J. A. Lauwerys, " Nazi Textbooks and the Future—II," *Journal of Education*, 1944, esp. p. 575, where we read " A German philosopher characterized Hitler's advent as the victory of Platonism. It would be a mistake to say he was falsifying the views of Plato. Plato was a totalitarian reformer. In the *Republic*, the main purpose of the State is to preserve the purity of the race and to organize the people for war against foreign barbarians, who are to be looked upon as natural enemies. The *elite* classes must be specially trained to fight, and must be brought, as young children, to scenes of slaughter and battle, so that they may develop a proper blood lust. The State must control all marriages, literature, and music." (condensed). Cf. also " Plato's ' Republic ' and German Education " *J. of E.*, 1945, pp. 57 ff. " The *Republic* could be used . . . to promote the ideals of Nazism . . . without falsifying the views of Plato." (Slightly transposed). The resulting controversy in the pages of the *J. of E.* brings out sharply conflicting views of how Plato's textual statements should be interpreted. [15]Illustrated by B. Jowett's translation of the *Dialogues*. [16]Illustrated by G. Grote : *Plato and the other Companions of Socrates*, 1888. [17]Illustrated by P. Natorp : *Platos Ideenlehre, Eine Einfuhrung in den Idealismus*, 1903. [18]Illustrated by U. v. Wilamowitz-Moellendorff : *Platon²*, 1920, and very many others. (Cf. Neurath and Lauwerys, *loc. cit.*, *J. of Education*, 1945, p. 57, " Scholars may be pleased by the idea of philosopher-kings, which brings to mind a vision of learned gentlemen of quiet and benevolent disposition—somewhat like university professors— enthroned in the seats of power.") [19]Illustrated by R. C. Lodge : *Plato's Theory of Ethics*, 1928, and also the present volume. [20]Thus Wilamowitz refuses to take *any* translation of Plato seriously, including both Jowett's and his own. *Dafür verstehe ich sein Griechisch zu gut* (*Platon²*, Vol. I, pp. 5, 55). [21]*Rep.* 455c f., 549d ; *Tim.* 42b ; *Laws* 694e, 675b, 781, 814a. Cf. Wilamowitz, *op. cit.*, Vol. I, pp. 49, 57–8. Cf. also Neurath and Lauwerys, *loc. cit.*, p. 58 (" looking on the people as a mass which has no authority, distinguished Plato's republic from Western communities. . . . Brutal inhumanity characterizes Plato's treatment of the seriously sick and mental defectives "—condensed). [22]The interpretation of the *Parmenides* (in which these difficulties are especially discussed) is still a matter of dispute among the commentators. Natorp's voice (Marburg School), while philosophically impressive, is only one among many ; and of those of us who still try to interpret the evidence seriously, it is still true that there is not one scholar who succeeds in getting his interpretation accepted by the others. [23]Wilamowitz, *op. cit.*, Vol. I, p. 459, and Ch. 14 " *Gleichviel*," says Wilamowitz. [24]This is the position usually taken by commentators who interpret the *Theaetetus* (e.g. H. Bonitz, *Platonische Studien*, 1875, H. Credé, *Die Kritik der Lehre des Protagoras in Platons Theätet*, 1880 ; and apparently A. E. Taylor, *Plato, The man and His Work*, 1927, pp. 326-339 ; and many others). Other students of great authority either take the side of Protagoras (Grote), or even go further and suggest—perhaps playfully ?—that Plato was becoming converted to Protagoras' version of " humanism " in his old age (F. C. S. Schiller). I do not myself suppose that Plato regarded himself as having refuted *any* philosophical position, as such, for all time). [25]Cf. Warner Fite, *The Platonic Legend*, 1934. Neurath and Lauwerys, " Nazi Text-books and the Future," *J. of Education*, 1944, p. 575, refer also to Wieland's *Aristipp*, and R. H. S. Crossman's *Plato Today*, as showing that " Plato was a totalitarian reformer." As far as the controversy in the *J. of Education* (1944-45) is concerned, I have no doubt that Neurath and Lauwerys are right in their contention that Nazi teachers would find many a passage in the *Republic* which they could use, reasonably enough from their standpoint, to confirm the views characteristic of Hitlerite Germany. I have also no doubt whatever that students working under Professor G. C. Field (" Plato's ' Republic ' and its Use in Education," *J. of E.*, 1945, pp. 161-2, cf. pp. 290-4) would develop in dialectical technique and philosophical insight, without falling into any onesidedness of interpretation of the text. In studying these ancient texts, while it is undoubted that a biassed teacher *can* select and distort evidence, surely we should not discourage those who see more, rather than those who see less, of value in them. My own attitude toward the modern attempt to " debunk " the tradition which sees more rather than less in Plato's work, is expressed in my review of Fite's book (*Ethics*, XLV, 1935, pp. 361-3). [26]B. H. Bode *op. cit.*, pp. 55 ff. This is in accord with the evidence of *Laws* 643d f. But it by no means follows that what Plato refuses to regard as " real " education *for full citizens* (which, as Nettleship, *op. cit.*, p. 19, says is " non-technical ; it teaches no knowledge or mental accomplishment having a direct bearing upon the functions eventually to be exercised by those who receive it "), is not regarded as perfectly " real " education *for professionals* who are *not* citizens. [27]*Rep.* 578c f. ; *Laws* 776c-778a. [28]*Gorg.* 486c, slightly transposed. The " pragmatism " of the modern critics is quite generally recognized (cf. John Pilley, *J. of Education*, 1945, pp. 342-44). [29]Cf. H. L. Nettleship : *Lectures on Plato's Republic*, p. 309, cf. p. 296. Cf. Wilamowitz : *Op. Cit.*, Vol. I, pp. 427, 436. [30]*Rep.* 415ab, 546-553. Cf. R. C. Lodge : *Plato's Theory of Ethics*, p. 482, n. 77. As W. Becher : *Platon und Fichte : Die königliche Erziehungskunst*, 1937 insists, over and over (e.g., pp. 26-8, 33), the position of *Herrscher* or *Führer* in Plato rests on *Leistungsfähigkeit.* In fact *every* member of the State is *Leistungsträger des ganzen.* [31]*Gorg.* 486d-488b ; *Rep.* 413c f., 415ab, 503a, e, 537ab, d, 539e ; *Laws* 649d f., 653df., 735, 751cd, 831a, 966b. [32]Cf. Correspondence in *J. of Education*, 1945, pp. 120, 163-4, 226, 292. It is easier to formulate this demand in an imaginary Utopia (as Plato does) than to realize it in practice. In the present-day world State assistance is increasingly forthcoming to encourage underprivileged children to receive as much education as they can effectively take ; but we have not yet quite reached Plato's ideal. [33]B. H. Bode : *How We Learn*, pp. 55, 57, 59, 68, 74. [34]J. Stenzel : *Platon der Erzieher*, 1928, p. 93 : *Sicher ist der Verkauf Platons auf dem Sklavenmarkt zu Aigina* . . . Interpretations of this incident differ, and many scholars hesitate to express positive opinions as to the facts of the situation. [35]*Rep.* 469bc, 471a, d ; *Laws* 777d ; cf. Aristot. ; *Pol.* vii 10, sect. 13. There is here, it must be confessed, a slight confirmation of the " racial superiority " attitude which Messrs. Neurath and Lauwerys find in Plato (see *Jour. of Educ.*, 1944, p. 575, 1945, pp. 57, 58 and 394). [36]*Laws* 763a. [37]*Rep.* 371d, 547d ; cf. *Phil.* 55d f. [38]*Laws* 742a, 760e, 763a, 848. The laws concerning farming seem, in general, to assume that there will be slaves working on the land. [39]Resident aliens who wish to enter business pay no foreigners' tax, business tax, or customs duties. Their residence permit is normally for 20 years, and depends on good behaviour. They obey numbers of regulations. *Laws* 745a, 847b, 850, 914c, 915d, 920a, 925e. [40]The quotation is from the article on " Slavery " in the *Encyclopaedia Britannica*, fourteenth edition, p. 773. The whole article is relevant to the present discussion. [41]Cf. T. N. Whitehead : *Leadership in a Free Society*, 1937, pp. 57, 59, 62, etc. Cf. also R. C. Lodge : *Philosophy of Business*, 1946, pp. 331-333. [42]*Rep.* 412d-414b, 520b ff., 535 f., 537cd, 539d f. ; *Laws* 951d f., 957, 962b f., 964 ff. This higher education is offered (I take it) to approximately 1 per cent of the population— i.e., to about 10 per cent of those who are destined for " full " citizenship. The remaining 9 per cent of these latter are given only what we should call a high school (and junior college) education. The remaining 90 per cent of the population (noncivic) are given technical and vocational education, on the quasi-apprenticeship plan. The charge against Plato amounts to saying that the vocational group are given only a vocational education, with no opportunity to enter high school or university. (This is, however, not in accordance with the evidence of *Rep.* 415b, 423cd). [43]*Rep.* 413d f., 415b, 537bc. [44]*Laws* 809e f., 817e f., 819b f. [45]*Laws* 794, 804c f. [46]*Laws* 643d f. Cf. Bode : *Op. Cit.*, pp. 4, 55, 59, 68. [47]For instance : when I originally set out to investigate Plato's account of education for citizenship and leadership, I found it impossible to do so adequately without first bringing together and investigating the evidence on the subject of technical, vocational, and professional education contained in the *Dialogues*. This evidence furnished a good part of the background necessary for understanding the education of the " silver " and " golden " classes. It was helpful especially in understanding the part played by association, imitation, and assimilation, as well as in appreciating the importance of mathematical techniques. Cf. *Phil.* 55d f. [48]*Rep.* 466c f. [49]*Rep.* 463b f. When a small child detaches itself from its mother in a public place, and flings itself around the leg of a total stranger with joyous cries of " Daddy ! Daddy ! " the benevolent looking stranger may, with us, be seriously embarrassed, and may find it difficult to live down the incident. In the *Republic*, the response would have been dignified approval. In academic institutions, especially when small, this sort of feeling exists today. [50]For discussion of the evidence in detail, cf. *supra*, Ch. II. [51]*Laws* 741 f., 743cd, 846d f., 919c f. Only those who bear arms have a vote at election time (*Laws* 753) ; although adjudicators at the music festivals (who have to be experts) are apparently nominated by what we should call members of the music-teachers' association—who (as teachers) would be professionals, and not citizens (*Laws* 765). Apparently the expert adjudicator would report to a representative of the magistrates (who *are* citizens), and the appropriate committee of magistrates would make the award of the adjudicators " official." (*Laws* 835a.) But the matter is not very clearly worked out in the actual text. In so far as the working classes fulfil their function, they are *Leistungsträger des ganzen*, ennobled by their functional membership in the model city (Becher : *Op. Cit.*, p. 33). [52]*Rep.* 413c f., 415a f., 546d ff. [53]*Laws* 850b f. [54]*Apol.* 24 ; *Crito* 50 ff. ; *Prtg.* 326d ; *Laws* 811c f., 880de, 890c f., 951b–957d, 964b f., 967d f. [55]*Laws* 842 ff., 915 ff. [56]*Laws* 764c f., 804c f., 811d f., 817e ff. Cf. *Lach.* 185 c. [57]*Rep.* 536d ff. ; *Laws* 818a, 951e f., 957, 964 ff., 967d ff. W. Becher : *Platon und Fichte* ; *Die königliche Erziehungskunst*, 1937, pp. 98–99, thinks that, in the *Laws* " philosophy " is not taught at all (*gänzlich abgesehen*), and that arithmetic, geometry, and astronmy are the highest *Unterrichtsfächer*. To my mind, the evidence referred to in this note indicates otherwise. [58]*Laws* 765d f., 801d, 809, 811de, 812e, 813c, 829d, 835a, 936a, 951e, 953d, 964b ff. [59]*Laws* 663d–665c. [60]*Laws* 777d, 804d, 850, 920. [61]John Dewey : *Democracy and Education*, pp. 102–105. Cf. also B. H. Bode : *Op. Cit.*, p. 74. On the other hand Paul Monroe : *Textbook in the History of Education*, 1915, p. 133, considers the criticism exaggerated in practice. [62]*Prtg.* 319d ; *Rep.* 377b f., 401 ; *Laws* 657a f., 659d f., 660a, 738b f., 764c f., 772a f., 799a, 801c f., 802a f., 809, 811b f., 812c f., 816bc, 817d, 828ab, 829c f., 848d f., 934b. This evidence does not agree with the wide belief that it is the magistrates who make the laws, and that Plato's ideal government is " totalitarian " (Cf. *J. of Educ.*, 1945, pp. 58, 164, 224). [63]*Laws* 763a. [64]That is to say, of neighbourhood children, schoolboys (or girls) attending the same school, and similar local groups : especially where there is some family or occupational connection. [65]*Rep.* 422-3, 462 ff., 551d ; *Laws* 739. This is a spiritual unity, no way incompatible with diversity of function (*Rep.* 369b f. Cf. Nettleship : *Theory of Education*, p. 18). [66]*Rep.* 497cd ; *Laws* 951 f., 961ab, and the conclusion of the *Laws*. [67] " We order our guardians to degrade the offspring of the guardians when inferior, and to elevate into the rank of guardians the offspring of the lower classes, when naturally superior. The intention is that, in the case of the citizens generally, each individual shall be put to the use for which nature intended him, and then every man will do his own business " (*Rep.* 423cd, cf. 415ab). [68]For discussion of the detailed evidence, cf. R. C. Lodge : " Plato and Progress," *Philos. Review*, 1946, pp. 651–67. For the evidence of *directed* progress, see this book, pp. 85, 176. [69]I desire to draw attention to the fact that my text does *not*, at any place, state or (intentionally) imply that, in my opinion, Plato was a " democrat "— any more than he was a " Fascist " of the Nazi type, or a " Communist " of the Russian type. Neither do I really believe that textual study supports the view that he was " anti-democratic " in any especially sinister sense. My opinion is that he advocated a complex constitution, balanced against going to extremes in *any* direction that could be classified as one-sided (cf. *Laws* 832b–d. Cf. also *Meno* 99bc ; *Polit.* 292c f., 301e f. ; *Laws* 712e f., 715b f). The " balance " is due to the living wisdom embodied, not merely in the ruling class, but also in the other classes which agree that the ruling shall be in the hands of those whose natural gifts, including loyalty to the community ideal, and also their excellent education, qualify them for taking the lead (*Rep.* 431b f.).

CHAPTER XII

PLATO AND PRESENT-DAY EDUCATION

The charge of anti-democratic tendencies being withdrawn, can it be taken as admitted that Platonic and modern conditions are sufficiently alike for us to apply directly to our present-day school systems the principles which we derive from the *Dialogues* ? Well, hardly. There *are* certain differences between Plato's time and ours : differences insisted upon quite as much by the classical scholar as by the modern educational authority ; and before we can apply Plato's ideas to our own times, these differences must be stated and evaluated.

The differences between Plato's world and ours are partly expressible in terms of number, space, and time. They are largely due to the changes which have come about in science and industry : changes so great that it may well seem to a thinker like John Dewey that *any* speculative reflection which antedates the industrial revolution, not to mention American democracy and the modern pragmatic movement in philosophy, can have only a remote, historical interest.[1]

In the first place, our political, economic, and social world is immensely bigger than Plato's. Where Plato's mind boggles at numbers much higher than five thousand, we are quite at home with the thought of model communities of fifty thousand, five hundred thousand, or even five million families. Indeed, we have little difficulty in conceiving of states ten times, or a hundred times that size. Why should we ? When we read Plato's *Laws*, we are at once impressed with the minuteness of the scale to which his thinking is geared. How puny, how tiny, how narrowly local, for all its proud boast of universal humanity and rationality, is the Hellenic type of city-state !

A small, relatively isolated fragment of land on the island of Crete, gives Plato all he cares to ask for in the way of local habitation : room to construct yet one more detached experiment in civic living under narrowly controlled conditions. So far as possible, the customs, habits, background, and outlook of his five or six thousand citizens are to develop in their own little back-wash : in deliberate detachment, so far as the great majority of his puppets are concerned, from the ways and institutions of other civic communities. The local boys are to be kept local. It is all small-town stuff. What of the world outside the city gates? Conceived in terms of social atomism, its sprawly and unwieldy aggregations, largely fortuitous, are to be regarded as necessarily devoid of inner unity, necessarily tending toward social chaos. Keep away from them ! Keep them away from us ![2]

This is so remote, not only in direct experience, but in idea, from our modern ways of living (except in isolated small towns), that at first we hardly know how to take it. With our system of arterial roads bypassing, rather than connecting, all the little communities in our modern countries, we tend to think nationally rather than locally. With us the nation, rather than the small town, is the unit.

In fact, many of us go further. We find it both natural and proper to think internationally. Plato was afraid of the sea. Its brackish waters facilitated intercommunication and thus endangered the isolation which he hoped would prove protective to the moral standards of his five thousand and forty families.[3] He wished to keep the world many rather than one. He would have been even more afraid of the air, could he have seen, in the story of Daedalus, anything more than a myth and a warning against aviation. *We* welcome both the sea and the air. In spite of the various sources of friction between nations, sources linguistic, economic, political, and local : we believe that the tendency of progress in every sort of intercourse, in trade and commerce, in science, art, social culture, and education, is all in the direction of making the world, not many, but one. We conceive of this, for the most part, not as dominated by a single national group, but as a loose federation, wherein each national group makes its characteristic contribution to the life of the whole, and receives in return more than it gives.

Thus the numbers, which with Plato are small, with us are large; and the space, which with Plato separates, with us unites. The differences between Plato's polished miniature and our vast social cosmos, are thus immense ; and it may turn out to be true that they affect to some extent the application, to our world, of his educational theories and plans.

In the second place, while Plato's world is in space rather than in time, we moderns live in time rather than in space. Plato's

Laws, for all their localism, are intended, not for this time or that, but for eternity. His reflection definitely seeks to transcend time altogether. His dialectician, the philosopher-king, spectator of all time and existence, envisages a perfect pattern of a perfect social order. The blueprint of his ideal republic, the blueprint of his model city, once constructed in outline, are there, once and for all time. They await only appropriate empirical conditions : the emergence of some dictator or king's son inspired by a love of philosophy, or of some philosopher adequately trained and entrusted with power, for the pattern to be applied and realized in the concrete. Plato's philosophy is *philosophia perennis*.[4]

With us, however, matters are far otherwise. We live in the dimension of time. Change, incessant and rapid change, is of the essence of our world. We look before and after, but we do not attempt to step out of the picture and construct some eternal-now which transcends the past and controls the future. A timeless present which embraces the whole of eternity and is conceived, like the vision attributed to God, as containing all truth for ever and ever, seems to us a somewhat formidable idea : an idea for which there is, in our experience, not much evidence. We are empirical creatures : human, all-too-human.[5]

We live forward, with a background which inevitably conditions our outlook. When we sit in judgment, we do not expect to achieve an ideally absolute truth. Far otherwise. " Our " thoughts (as we call them) are only in a very limited sense ours. They are a function of the historical conditions of which we are the outcome. Our best thinking merely focuses a given problem sharply, and permits the significant and relevant conditions to come through somewhat more adequately. We are indeed the spearbearers of the human tradition. But it is the tradition which makes us, not we who make the tradition.

Plato's aim is to step outside history altogether : to enter an ideal realm, a realm of absolutely perfect patterns, and to see as God sees. God creates by selecting the best and most beautiful patterns in this realm, and applying them to an otherwise chaotic empirical world. Plato's philosopher-king, like God, selects the best and most beautiful pattern : namely, the pattern set forth in the *Republic*. Armed with this, he steps back into the picture again : into the " cave " of human history. For the rest of his earthly life he applies this pattern to actual men and women, as far as this can be done : thus co-operating with God in creating, out of relative chaos, a new world of beauty and goodness.

When filling in the outline, he will often turn his eyes now upwards, now downwards. He will look first at absolute justice and beauty and temperance, and then at the human copy. He will mingle and temper the various elements of life into the image of a man : conceiving this image according to that other image which Homer calls the form and likeness of God. One feature he will erase. Another he will put in : until he has made the ways of men, as far as possible, agreeable to the ways of God.[6]

At the present day, we do not find it at all difficult to construct Utopias. In fact, we find it hard not to. But we have lost faith in pipe-dreams. We regard all such constructions as fancy pictures, produced by the imagination without too much regard for the empirical conditions of their realizability. We believe them all to be expressions of their own times : permeated with temporality, historical through and through. We believe that Plato's ideal republic and model city, Campanella's City of the Sun, More's Utopia, and the rest, are one and all equally products of wishful thinking, influenced by the conditions of their times. Why not ?

We too can construct social ideals : better adapted to a world which we believe to be in process of rapid change. Even John Dewey, modern as he is, has a social ideal, which represents *his* (wishful) interpretation of American Democracy ; no less than Josiah Royce, with his Beloved Community. We all do it. But whereas some of the earlier constructors of such Utopias apparently believed themselves to be achieving absolute truth, something that would hold good for all time : we are under no such illusion, either about their efforts or about our own. We are well aware that they are all equally functions of the historical conditions which are in process of making us what we are coming to be. Their significance is essentially transient, not " eternal."

Between the eternal and the temporal point of view there is thus a very considerable difference ; and it may be that the difference here between Plato and ourselves will prove considerable enough to make certain features of his educational theories inapplicable to the present-day education of schoolchildren.

These differences are due largely to changes in science and industry. Plato's world is largely pre-scientific, as we understand science. Cultivated men could doubtless talk plausibly about atoms, and the application of mathematics to life. They could construct rival hypotheses and discuss the difference to everyday life and thought made by the adoption of this rather than that. It was all very stimulating to the imagination, and a pleasant time was had by the intellectuals. Medical men found such hypotheses helpful in giving to their patient observations a certain unity which these might otherwise have lacked. Every now and then some bright spirit actually thought out ingenious ways of understanding and predicting the course of celestial events. The ancient precursors of Sir James Jeans explained the rationale of eclipses and the long-standing puzzle about the evening and morning star. And mathematics advanced by leaps and bounds.

But of the patient co-operative observation and experimentation in which the real *work* of science consists, there was in Plato's day only the merest beginning ; and that, not at Athens. And especially of the enormous body of physical, chemical, biological and geological knowledge, upon which our thought rests as a matter of course, so that our lives are pervaded by science and its applications : there was not even a trace.

It is amusing to find a man like Aristotle writing in all seriousness that it is only after all the necessities and conveniences of life had been discovered, that men directed their attention to theoretical investigations : to science and philosophy.[7] He was writing in an Athens which was without hot and cold water, without gas and electricity, without automobiles and airplanes, without telephones and radios, and with only the most primitive substitutes for movies. Manpower and mulepower are almost the only kinds of power contemplated ; and there is not even a suggestion of the mechanized surroundings which we take almost for granted. With Plato and Aristotle science is chiefly a matter of pure theory : knowing for knowing's sake, pursued by a few choice spirits in Academe, discussing the solution of problems propounded by a master-intellectual.

Plato's world is so different from ours, that it is hard for us to realize the difference. Science has almost completely transformed the world into which we are born, so that we grow up along different lines. It is not only a matter of things : a matter of locomotives and steam-shovels, mass-production and the assembly-line, air-liners and diamond drills. It is a question of differences in the human mind.

We are almost *born* gadget-minded. Modern science is at the service of anyone who knows enough to throw a switch or turn a wheel ; and scientific method is universally accepted as the standard way of atacking almost any sort of problem. Nearly every kind of organized business has its research department : to which technical and fact-finding problems are referred as a matter of course, before final decisions are made. In Plato's world, this question or that is referred to a committee of experts : expert builders, expert engineers, expert musicians, expert poets or theologians.[8] But with us almost every question of any importance is so handled, and is so handled as standard procedure.

With us the influence of science is universal. It is no longer regarded as concerned with pure theory. Science is concerned directly with practice : controlling the environment to suit the convenience of everyman. Our age is thus not merely the age of gadgets. It is the age of the gadget mind : and of the mind which confidently applies scientific method to the solution of all problems, theoretical and practical.

A difference so great, so all-pervasive, will of course affect to some extent the educational systems suited to two such different worlds. We shall thus expect to find it necessary to make considerable alterations in Plato's curriculum, if indeed we are able to adapt it at all to the needs of our modern scientific age. For example, it will be necessary to provide room, even in general education, for the study of science : in ways and to extents not even remotely contemplated by the founder of the Academy.

And finally we turn to industry. In Plato's time there were factories—of sorts. The manufacture of bricks and the preparation of materials used in the building trades ; the manufacture of cloth and its preparation for use in the garment industry ; the mining of ore and its preparation for use in the manufacture of tools and weapons : in all such cases the work was carried on, not by individuals as such, but by co-operative organization. The technical operations involved were carried on, partly by skilled craftsmen, partly by relatively unskilled labour : the whole being organized and directed by a manager, *entrepreneur*, or owner who found his account partly in the resulting profits, partly in the prestige and power associated with his position, and partly in the successful carrying through of the work itself.

In Plato's model city, the workers in such industries are always considered as belonging to the non-civic, underprivileged classes. Unskilled labourers are mostly slaves. Skilled workers may be slaves, or may belong to the artisan class. The *entrepreneur*, whether manager or owner, belongs, in Plato's scheme, to the commercial class of aliens permitted to do business in the city for a limited period only. It is forbidden that any citizen should have any direct connection with trade or industry, whether as worker, as manager, or as owner. [9]

The reason for this is well known. The factory worker, held down to his task and obeying orders given him from above, becomes formalized, mechanized and dehumanized : physically warped and one-sided, an instrument capable of obeying orders, and nothing more. He becomes progressively less and less able to express himself as a free self-determining citizen : in deed, in word, and in thought. He is a slave in name and a slave in nature ; and where the only power is manpower, it is inherent in factory work that this should be so. [10]

As far as the manager or owner is concerned, Plato is doubtful whether the business of directing the lives of other men and women primarily for one's own profit or prestige is compatible with the kind of morality which he expects of his model citizens. The simplicity of attitude which insists upon each citizen doing his own work himself, and doing it always in the spirit of community service, seems to exclude the pursuit of wealth or power ; and that is why, while recognizing the importance of this motive in getting the work of the world done, Plato determines that it shall be done by outsiders operating on a limited residence-permit. [11]

If we turn to consider modern times, we find the factory-principle of organized industry almost infinitely extended. But there is a certain difference. The growth of science has made possible the harnessing, not only of manpower, but of steam-power, electrical power, and power from a variety of sources. " Plants and firms have increased in the number of men employed ; but still more in the capital invested in them. Between 1923 and 1929, in the United States, the ratio of horse-power to the number of wage-earners increased from 3.76 to 4.86." [12] That is to say, each worker, instead of releasing the power of one man (as in Plato's time), now releases the power of almost five horses : and that is true of each and every worker in the plant.

This has brought about immense differences. Where Plato's model city rested upon an agricultural economy (like Russia before the first five-year plan), modern communities have become increasingly industrialized. The production of goods has been multiplied many times over ; and the status of the working classes has undergone a corresponding change.

As John Dewey sees it :[13]

> The peculiar thing is not the enslavement of masses of mankind to the necessities of making a hardly-won precarious livelihood ; that has existed at all times and places. The distinctive thing is increased consciousness of this state of affairs and discontent with it ; the belief that it is unjust and unnatural ; the conviction that it is a monster to be extirpated. Such an attitude could not have arisen until industrial civilization had sufficiently advanced to bring with it the perception of the possibility of a free life upon a higher level for all mankind ; until command of natural energies by means of machinery had enabled imagination to conceive of leisure for all.

Not only has the production of material goods reached such a point that we can all dream dreams of an economic millennium just around the corner. A very large percentage of the present-day community lives and moves and has its social life in an atmosphere permeated by industry. In some communities the whole social atmosphere of the place is dominated by the coal industry, the steel industry, the packing industry, the watch industry ; much as the social atmosphere of some medieval community which has not been drawn into the modern industrial stream may be dominated by its cathedral, its castle, or its university. Thus we have a number of mining towns, railroad towns, shoemaking towns, and the like.

And further : just as in a college the young people who come together ostensibly to study, of themselves develop a whole collegiate life, of which life study is, in many cases, merely the background ; so any large industrial plant furnishes its employees with a kind of nucleus : around which there develop friendships, rivalries, sport interests, and indeed a whole quasi-collegiate way of living, both in and out of business hours.

This means that whereas, in Plato's model city, it was expected that the tone would be set by the 5,040 families of full citizens, the " upper five thousand," as we might call them : the modern industrialized community is far too large for anything of the kind. The tone is set by the industrial masses ; and it is changes in industry that furnish the dominant interests. The upper ten thousand, if they could be separated from the development of modern industry (which they can not), would soon perish of boredom. To keep themselves interested, they keep in touch with the latest industrial gadgets. Take up any popular magazine or digest

of literature. You will find that the stories, as well as the advertise-
ments, have industry and industrial progress as their background,
if not as their foreground.[14]

Thus where Plato expected his citizens to live a life in which
industry is never even mentioned : a life in which military sports,
dances with a military flavour, daily processions to the community deities, and almost perpetual chanting of the praises of
the community, as the citizens " charm themselves " into the
community spirit, are the outstanding features :[15] the modern
citizen finds it hard to take Plato seriously. Work is real, life is
earnest, and the game is not the goal.

So great is the difference, that we should expect it to affect our
educational institutions : to such an extent that, while retaining
doubtless something of Plato's liberal education and even his
interest in quasi-Etonian playing fields, we should welcome into
our curriculum much which to Plato would seem merely technical.
We should endeavour to make of the vocational and professional
the nucleus of our real culture.

So far we have established certain very great differences between Plato's world and ours. Plato's world is small, in self-
contained localized units :   each of which is engaged in pursuing
life, liberty, and happiness in ways which transcend empirical,
industrial, and temporal interests. Plato's ideal is an agricultural
community, interested chiefly in moral and religious self-culture.
It maintains itself in competition with alien groups by military
fitness ensured by devotion to community-approved sports. And,
while not utterly disallowing progress, it proposes to remain without essential change forever and forever.

Our modern world is large, with its units (if they can really be
considered such) closely interrelated and interwoven. Its pursuits
are not transcendental, but one hundred per cent empirical. As
Dewey puts it :[16]

Only a blind man would deny that characteristic traits of present
life are a mad scramble for material commodities, a devotion to
attainment of external power, and an insensate love of foolish luxuries
and idle display.

The modern ideal is an industrialized community on the largest
possible scale : competing with the rest of the world for ever
greater power, wealth, and luxury ; and proposing to change

and keep on changing : in so far as new discoveries in science and corresponding developments in industry make such change add to the wealth and power of its citizens.

Granted these differences, how much of Platonic education remains usable, in principle, at the present day ? Let us answer this question with reference to (1) infant education, (2) primary education, (3) secondary education, and (4) post-graduate adult education.

(1) Infant education. Babies are not modern at all. They come innocent of everything in our modern world : its science, its art, its industry, and its worship of material success : calling only for mother-love and very simple, but very complete attention. Mother-love is a very ancient institution ; and there is no evidence that it has changed in fundamentals from Plato's time to the present.

The modern sophisticated mother, with her medical attendant, her nurses and nursery, with its up-to-the-last-minute gadgets, with her prenatal and postnatal hygiene, living by the book—may be inclined to question this. She may be inclined to think that modern science has made of infant education something very different from what it was in Plato's philosophy. What did Plato know about modern children, anyway ?

Yet on this point the evidence of the *Republic* and *Laws* is entirely convincing. In Plato's ideal community and model city sophisticated mothers are depicted as provided with doctors and nurses, and with reasonably well equipped nurseries too. Mothers are shown as living in accordance with the approved manual. They have their prenatal and postnatal hygiene ; and—this is the point—it is almost word for word what we find in our own latest authoritative guidebooks for young mothers.

The daily walks for expectant mothers, the swathing band for infants, the open-air outings in which children are " carried by their nurses somewhere or other : into the country, to their relations' houses, or to the temples," the care that children shall not try to walk too early : all this is the same in Plato as in our modern manuals. The function of crying and tossing the limbs about as forms of exercise important for developing healthy self-control ; the rocking of children in their nurses' arms to help them get over their little upsets and to go to sleep again : all this seems to be understood quite adequately, and with a sound scientific background, in the *Laws*.

So too when the child can walk, it is taken to the local open-air playground, with nurses and a playground matron in attendance. There it learns by playing : playing partly by itself and partly with other small children ; and what it plays is much the same in Plato's time as in our own.

To this elementary physical education there is added throughout the beginning of moral and social education. Courage, self-reliance in meeting childish problems ; docility, obedience to parents and nurses and a willingness to play with others ; such attitudes are carefully fostered. The child-psychology and infant-pedagogy of our day do not change, but endorse the traditional lessons inculcated by Plato. Now as then, then as now : young children learn by doing ; and they grow up in an atmosphere of teaching which has been vitalized and socialized by the best community insight.

Very young children are conservative, and so is the tradition which watches over their early upbringing. The toys with which they most readily play—ropes and balls, dolls and animals, and the ways in which they play : running, skipping, jumping, uttering cries and manipulating things : have all become a part of the tradition. They have remained without fundamental change throughout the centuries ; and the ancient philosopher is as well contented as we are ourselves, that this should be so.

As far as infant education is concerned, then, there is no fundamental difference in principle between what Plato teaches and what we find in our most modern theory and practice. Both Plato and we formulate and follow the almost universal human tradition ; and it justifies itself both in scientific theory and in everyday experience.

(2) Let us proceed to consider primary education : in connection with schools attended from the age of six to the age of ten. Here we note, first of all, a great difference between Plato's ideas and our practice. The three Rs are taught in our elementary schools, and they are taught very thoroughly. We do not go so far as to subscribe to the Victorian prescription that " A child of *five* should be able to read, write, and parse a simple sentence." We do not expect a child of pre-school age to be able to tell time

by the clock (with its Roman numerals), to locate the hymns in church, to add and subtract, and to tell the story of the infant Samuel, of Moses in the bulrushes, of King Alfred and the burning cakes—although there *are* a few children of that age who can do all these things. But we do, in our elementary schools which take children up to the age of ten, teach most of these techniques, together with a great deal of what is called " book-learning " : including, not only poetry and traditional stories which are sure-fire stuff with children, but the beginnings of general science.

Incidentally, in out-of-school time, many of us expect our young children to read with avidity the traditional fairy tales and adventure stories ; ard the expectation is entirely justified. In families where reading is a matter of course, we find the modern child insisting, not unlike Alfred the Great, on being taught to read and write : at least its own name and a few simple words, before it goes to school.

In Plato's theory of education there is none of this for young children—except possibly in connection with the Hellenic equivalent of Bible stories. Mothers and nurses in the *Republic* use a kind of authorized collection of such stories ; and in the *Laws* old men are represented as narrating tales with a moral tendency. But reading, writing, music, and presumably arithmetic are deliberately postponed, as far as school study is concerned, until the teens.

The Hellenic method of learning to read was somewhat formal and slow. The child (of ten) was taught to identify, first the individual letters, then the individual syllables, then certain combinations of syllables (such as occurred in names, starting with the child's own name and the names of friends), and so eventually verbs, nouns, and sentences with all their further complications. In Victorian times the method was not entirely dissimilar. It was still formal ; but the texts used provided far more assistance than fell to the lot of the (older) Greek child. A,T : At ; B,A,T : Bat ; C,A,T : Cat ; F,A,T : Fat ; M,A,T : Mat ; etc., was followed immediately by such sentences as *A Fat Cat Sat on A Mat*, accompanied by a suitable illustration which appealed directly to the child.

With such help from the carefully graded textbook, the Victorian mother somehow managed to teach her children to read pretty well before they went to school ; and even, after a while, to read silently—an achievement apparently unknown to the Greeks of Plato's day. The present-day teacher is helped yet further by phonetic methods ; so that there is no occasion for our children to wait until their teens before attempting successfully both reading and writing.[17]

On the other hand, the Greeks paid more attention than we do to physical training. Plato's schoolchildren, girls as well as boys, spent most of their school time up to the age of ten in acquiring proficiency in riding, shooting (with bow, javelin and sling), running, dancing (both with and without arms), and in what we should call military drill : particular attention being paid to the development of ambidexterity. The physical education which with us is given partly in school hours, but even more out of school (in connection with our sport clubs and open-air playgrounds), is with Plato given in school. The training is given by professionals, and it is compulsory. Considerable attention is given to deportment and manners : especially to ensuring quiet and modest behaviour in the streets, on the way to and from school.

During this period, the children of artisans, who are not intended, for the most part, to develop into full citizens, receive in the home circle, or in the factory which is an extension of the home circle, the kind of training which will fit them, naturally and step by step, to pursue the family trade professionally when they are old enough. At first they play with the instruments of the parental trade (hammer, rule, and saw, if they are to be carpenters), using tools of suitable size and weight for their childish strength. Then gradually they learn to assist their parents in this, that, and the other phase of the parents' work : until in the end they are sufficiently developed to carry on for themselves.

What theory they study comes in connection with practice, especially in the later phases of practice in the teens : such as the mathematics involved in calculating the correct distribution of materials, the proper proportions of utensils and buildings, etc., together with enough practical economics to enable them to carry on successfully with the financial side of their profession.

In Plato's *Dialogues*, the education offered to future citizens, and the training offered to future artisans, while from some points of view sharply distinguished, are not really two distinct kinds of education. As far as children of the ages of six to ten are concerned, they are in principle one and the same kind of education applied in two different fields. Playing with javelins and slingshots until a certain proficiency is acquired in their use, and gradually learning to assist the parents in this, that, and the other phase of the parents' work in guard duty and on the field of battle, is explicitly identical in principle with playing with the tools of the artisan.

In both cases, the child learns by doing, in association with older professional teachers, against a general family background. In both cases, he is learning, along with his parents, to take his part in carrying on a serious activity which is important to the welfare of the community. In both cases, he enjoys his play, while it is play ; and he feels conscious of the serious value of what he is learning. In both cases, nothing trivial or useless, either to himself or to the social group, is being learned.

Is there, in Plato's primary school education, anything which in principle is unmodern, formal and traditional, of interest only to the student of the archaic and out-of-date ? Or are his principles the same as those on which our most modern and progressive schools pride themselves ?

Let us look at a widely used modern manual : produced by an authority whose " educational leaders " appear to be "Dewey, Hall, Judd, Cubberley, and others." In a section on *The Trend of Modern Practice* we are informed that

The modern school is developing its practice along four special lines :
1. The development of a new methodology which works through the use of problems, projects, motives, and interests.
2. The selection of subject matter that is worthy of the time and the efforts of pupils.
3. Teaching in a way which will conserve rather than injure the health of children.
4. The realization of an individual-social balance which will adjust itself to the needs of individuals and at the same time employ the social motive and satisfy the demands of the community.

No. 1 means that the child is taught to " think," i.e., to " organize, evaluate, and judge," instead of merely memorizing subject-matter. No. 2 is a plea for functional English, functional spelling, functional arithmetic, functional writing, rather than formal and mechanical efficiency. Nos. 3 and 4 mean exactly what they say, and are opposed to class formalism. All are worked out in detail, in relation to actual and typical teaching situations.

If we inquire how far (if at all) such modern tendencies differ from what we find in Plato's *Dialogues*, it must at once be admitted that these efforts in the way of modern reform of practice are precisely in a line with the whole traditional theory which derives from Plato. Every one of them could be paralleled, without the slightest difficulty, even to the " functional " reading, writing, spelling, and arithmetic (although these, with Plato, come in the teens rather than in the earlier schools).[19]

As to No. 1, the Socratic method, as expounded in the *Meno* and the *Theaetetus*, is the classical example of what is meant. As to No. 2, while Plato's estimate of what is most worthy of the time and efforts of children from six to ten (namely, physical training with a military twist) differs from the modern (peace-time) estimate : the principle involved is in both cases one and the same. As to Nos. 3 and 4, there is no difference whatever in principle,[20] although it must be admitted that the modern textbook applies the principle in a more thorough-going way to the details of schoolroom practice, and does it very well indeed.

In fact, with children of the ages of six to ten, there appears to be no occasion for making very much difference in their education merely because they are born in the A.D. 1900s rather than in the B.C. 350s. Riding, shooting, dancing, and other activities in the way of physical education, may have changed a little in detail. But they are much the same in principle ; and to give them a slightly military twist is really—almost ultra-modern. As to ambidexterity, there are differences of opinion as to its value at the present day. But many authorities still believe in it, and the idea still has something of a modern ring.

As far as grounding in the three Rs is concerned, there is a great difference. We really do teach reading, writing, and arithmetic in our elementary schools. But—and this is the point—this is not, in itself, what we regard as characteristically " modern." What our authorities do claim as modern, is *the way in which we teach* these simple, but important tool-subjects. We teach them by dramatizations, by a number of technical devices which make the learning easy and connect it with the child's interests on the one hand, and his social future on the other. But this—which we regard as characteristically modern—is precisely the spirit in which Plato desires these subjects to be taught, when they *are* taught ; and as to the techniques of smart teaching, it is surprising to the modern student to discover that they are *all*—including not merely the spelling-book dodges, but also the dramatization, and the making use of group interests and community needs—

paralleled, not merely in Platonic theory, but also in the practice of schools which Plato regards as advanced.

We conclude then that, as in the pre-school play, so also in the elementary school-training urged by Plato, there is no essential difference between the attitude which Plato considers desirable, and the attitude which *we* consider desirable. The modern world, in spite of its great size, its immense advance in science, and its all-pervasive developments in industry, does not come into the focus of the young child's mind. From six to ten, he is conscious of it only in a vague and remote way. It is there, on his horizon, waiting till he has grown older and has developed sufficiently to come into effective contact with it. *Then*, indeed, perhaps. But not now. Not till he has advanced beyond the age of ten.

(3) Let us now consider the education which is offered in the secondary schools, to boys and girls from ten to sixteen or eighteen. In these years, Plato prescribes compulsory education in reading, writing, music, and presumably arithmetic, followed by a study of the laws of the community. Military sports and music festivals continue on the side, and this phase of education leads naturally, for the vast majority, to service in the armed forces. The literary and musical training is not formal and confined to the elements. It is definitely functional. The student learns to express himself readily in speaking before others, in writing, and in singing. His course includes dramatic study of the greater works of literature, revised so as to bring out their vital and social significance. These works include, not merely selections from Homer, Aeschylus, Sophocles, and the rest, but also Plato's *Laws* and similar publications ; and the aim of this secondary education is to fit the rising generation to take its place in the life of the adult community.

Independently of this education for full citizenship, there is a continuation of the usual industrial education for those classes of non-citizens who are being prepared to earn their living by the practice of the industrial arts or by commercial pursuits. This is a relatively informal system of education : something like what later ages know as the apprenticeship system. As farming is learnt on the farm, by quasi-members of the farmer's family : so factory-work is learnt in the factories. Based upon the proficiency acquired in play by the children of industrial families, it is now serious work, and leads by gradual steps to full professional participation in industry or commerce.

Let us compare with this the education offered in our modern high schools and junior colleges. These fall into two relatively distinct groups. On the one hand, we have the " classical " high schools, which provide a training partly literary and partly scientific ; and on the other we have the " technical " high schools, which prepare more definitely for industrial or commercial life. In many cases these two types are merged, and there are also a number of more specialized types still in the experimental stage : well adapted, apparently, to the needs of particular groups of students and particular localities.

How does the education provided in our " classical " high schools and colleges compare with Plato's education for full citizenship ? The subject-matter differs considerably. Plato's students make no study whatever of foreign language and foreign literatures. They prepare themselves for adult life in the home town by studying Greek literary masterpieces, and no others. In our modern institutions, in Victorian times at least two foreign languages used to be compulsory. These were, as a rule, Latin and (frequently) Greek ; and they were studied intensively. French and German might also be studied, although with less intensity. English (the mother-tongue) was acquired chiefly in connection with studying other languages ; although a few literary masterpieces were " prepared for examination."

This would seem to constitute a departure from the principles of Platonic education. And yet, the intention was to be true to those principles. The literary studies were intended (precisely as with Plato) to broaden and deepen the imaginative sympathies, and so to prepare the student culturally to enter the adult life of the community : a community in which quotations from Latin and even Greek authors were still made in public life. The study of history took (roughly speaking) the place occupied in the Platonic scheme by learning local laws and reading books on law ; and if a little science did at one point creep into the modern curriculum, it remains true, on the whole, that the Victorian graduate was nearly as innocent of the message, the methods, and the techniques of science as his Hellenic prototype.

In recent years, however, a great change has come over our high schools and junior colleges. Gone is the old, simple, compulsory curriculum. For High School students, Latin is no longer compulsory, and can be regarded as academically moribund. Greek is practically defunct. Even French and German are no longer studied as they used to be ; and in many parts of the present day world, it is perfectly possible to pass successfully through high school (and so to prepare oneself for present-day adult living), without having studied any foreign language at all.

That is to say : as far as foreign language study is concerned, the modern high school has gradually come closer to the Platonic ideal than was the case in Victorian times. The greater emphasis upon social studies is entirely in a line with Plato's insistence upon the study of law, especially local law.

In another respect, however, there is a great and increasing difference between Plato's secondary schools and ours. We really include a good deal of what may be called " general science " in our present-day education of youth from the age of ten to sixteen or eighteen. We actually teach a good deal about birds, beasts, and flowers ; about climate and the physical environment. And many of our high schools and colleges teach something, not merely of the imagination-stirring wonders of physics and chemistry, but of their exact reasoning and of their laboratory techniques. Just how these sciences should be studied is, at present, a matter of dispute. Should we regard man as made for science, or science as made for man ?

Some authorities treat science as the way, the truth, and the life. They teach that we should form ourselves upon science as upon Truth. We are to endeavour to rise above the biosocial, all-too-human point of view, with its " instinctive fever and fret," and are " to see as a God might see," impartially, impassively, objectively.[21] Others, no less authoritative in the field of education, maintain that " science " results from applying a number of useful techniques and abstract methods developed by human organisms interacting with and trying to control their environment. The high school student should study science and should learn to master some of these techniques : not with the idea of prostrating himself humbly before what he takes to be eternal verities, but purely in order to make use of them for his convenience and for the purposes of his social group. His chief aim should be, to learn to apply scientific methods to social problems, and to move easily in a world in which facility in applying such methods is rapidly taking the place once occupied by facility in quoting some honoured tag from the Classics : the *Eheu fugaces* ! of Horace, the *O tempore, O mores* ! of Cicero.[22]

Neither of these authoritative groups desires high school youngsters to turn themselves into scientists. That stage of development comes later. The idea is rather, to study science for its effect in developing the scientific attitude of mind. Where opinions differ is as to how this attitude is to be understood. Is it an attitude of acquiescence in objectivity, or is it an attitude of interactivity with objects, of bending nature to our purposes by first mastering some of the dodges which have proved successful ?

What does Plato teach on these points ? The study of science, with him, is postponed to a later period. Even then, his aim is not to develop his students into scientists, but to produce a certain effect upon their minds : to induce serenity and develop a love of Truth. During the secondary period, the only science that is studied by the majority of his citizens, namely, mathematics, is studied, not so much for its possible effect in awakening transcendental idealism, as for its practical usefulness in enabling the average citizen to carry on his regular pursuits in the community. There are few activities in which a little mathematics is not helpful.[23]

That is to say : Plato's attitude toward the use of scientific subject-matter in educating youths of ten to sixteen or eighteen, is not seriously different in principle and in general tendency from the modern use of such subject-matter. There is, however, a very great difference in the amount of time given to science in the curriculum.   For the would-be *general* citizen, the amount of time prescribed for mathematical study in Plato's ideal republic and model city, is deliberately quite brief.   And no place in the curriculum whatever is allotted for studying the methods and results of the biological and physical sciences.

In our modern high schools there has recently been a pronounced tendency to reduce, for the *general* student, the amount of time spent upon mathematics, especially pure mathematics. But there has been an equally pronounced tendency to increase the amount of time spent upon natural and social science. It is therefore fair to conclude that, while the general spirit of scientific study is not demonstrably different in principle, the present-day high school graduate may be expected, in practice, to be considerably more science-conscious than the Platonic general student.

In the field of industrial training for youths of the ages from ten to sixteen or eighteen, the present-day school system does far more than was attempted in Plato's time. The informal apprenticeship system was doubtless adequate for the purposes of Plato's world, and contained elements of biosocial as well as of technical value for the trainees.   But with the relatively vast increase in modern times of scientific knowledge and specialized techniques as applied to industry, it has proved entirely unwise to leave to informal, quasi-family associations the function of passing on to the rising generation the information and the skills requisite to put the present-day student abreast of his subject.

That is why, with us, technical high schools and institutes of one sort and another have come into being. Their aim is to give " manual training which will make for mental development and sound physical health " on the part of trainees, and will at the same time assist in " the material and moral advancement of the whole group of citizens." The present-day tendency is to discourage trade-schools as such, and to give a pre-vocational training in general shopwork, together with continuation-school training, partly of a general, partly of a specific character.[24] This is not contrary, in principle, to Platonic principles. But the provision of specific schools acting under public authority and largely paid for by public funds, goes far beyond anything even remotely contemplated by any ancient educationist.

(4) Let us now compare Plato's *higher* education with what the modern world offers to advanced students. Plato's system is partly theoretical, partly practical. On the side of theory, it includes (1) prolonged study of the principles of morals and politics, and (2) severe study of the exact (mathematical-physical) sciences, with especial reference to their inter-connections and presuppositions, leading to apprehension of " the unhypothetical first principle."[25] On the practical side, it includes the holding of a succession of minor positions of military and civil leadership. The aim is, not to turn the students into scientists or generals or lawyers, but to fit them for positions of administrative leadership when they attain to full maturity : so that they will be able to apply scientific method to social problems with sureness and decision, in a spirit of service and loyalty to the community.[26]

Apart from this education of expert " philosopher-kings," we understand that specialists who devote themselves to science and medicine, art and letters, education and religion, law and industry, continue their professional studies along the lines indicated earlier.[27] They co-operate with the philosopher-kings : working with them on appropriate committees, in accordance with the general principles of the model city and ideal republic.[28] Their higher education comes to them partly from this co-operative activity, and partly from the practice of their respective professions. There is also a vague reference to membership in something like Plato's Academy.[29]

So much for Plato. What does the present-day world have to offer its advanced students : those who (like Plato's select students) have demonstrated by examination and by character-tests that they are fit for higher education ? In our advanced schools, men and women prepare themselves for life in the professions, along all the lines which we find in the Platonic community, and in much the same ways : certainly in the same spirit.

Is there any difference ? In detail, yes. Owing to the vast increase in scientific knowledge, equipment, and techniques, we have had to develop a large number of professional schools : colleges of agriculture, architecture, engineering, education ; institutes of art, of music, of applied science ; graduate schools of research in a number of fields. Of all these we can detect little more than the germ in Plato's theories. This is to be expected. But the germ is there ; and the point is, that the principle is the same now as it was then : namely, to fit the advanced student, not for withdrawal from the world into abstract contemplation, but for a life-work of social service in the here-and-now world.[30] And it must be admitted that our most modern developments are along these very lines. We simply carry forward the torch handed down by Plato.

There is one point at which many critics maintain that there is a fundamental difference of principle. The ancient outlook, it is asserted, was transcendental ; and this is especially true of the realm of " ideas " toward which Plato endeavours to lead us. The present-day outlook, on the other hand, is strictly empirical, biosocial, confining itself deliberately to the world of the here-and-now. So immense is the difference separating the present-day outlook from the Platonic point of view, that there does not exist, and there cannot be built, any bridge of understanding, along which a student can safely pass from our world to Plato's, or from Plato's world to ours.

These criticisms are characteristic of the modern pragmatist school of philosophy. And it is indeed primarily this school whose representatives assert that Plato's views are out of date and belong properly on the museum shelves : locked away behind plate glass, where they can be viewed by the curious, who have an idle hour to pass, away from the actual world. And if it were factually correct that idealism is antiquated, and that pragmatism is the only modern view held widely and effectively at the present day : there would doubtless be something in the pragmatist contention.

But what are the facts ? In Plato's *Dialogues* we find reflections of a conflict between idealism on the one hand, and pragmatism and naturalism or materialism on the other :[31] a conflict as to whose grounds and significance Plato appears to be very well informed. In the present-day world we find the same conflict of the same schools still proceeding. Their difference corresponds, roughly, to the difference between those who, in Aristotle's time, attempted to reduce all causal explanation to a single type : the type of the formal cause (idealism), of the efficient cause (pragmatism), or the material cause (realism, naturalism). It is therefore hardly permissible for the representatives of any *one* school to arrogate to themselves the title " modern," and to claim that their views, and their views only, are suited to present-day ways. There are plenty of idealists, both theoretical and practical, and plenty of realists, both theoretical and practical, at the present day : all ready and eager to dispute the premises upon which the pragmatists rely.[32]

The claim, therefore, that

Whatever is transcendental, is out of date ;
Idealism is transcendental ;
Therefore, idealism is out of date.

can hardly be taken for granted. To suppose that it *is* granted, is simply not to be in accord with the factual evidence. And the further claim, resting upon this, that Plato's views, because idealist and transcendental in background and outlook, are *ipso facto* to be dismissed as out of date and essentially unmodern, thus falls to the ground.

In fact, we might do well to apply to this situation the *general* statement of John Dewey, usually regarded as the leader of the pragmatist school. He tells us that[33]

A philosopher who would relate his thinking to present civilization . . . cannot . . dispense with consideration of the underlying classic tradition. If he ignores traditions, his thoughts become thin and empty. Traditions are something to be employed.

Our conclusion thus is, that present-day educational theory does not have to scrap the past while it sets out to create the brave new world of the future. It is all the stronger if it retains its continuity with what is of value in the great philosophic tradition which bears us powerfully forward. In that tradition, sympathetic and accurate study reveals Plato as still among our leaders He is not just another figure of the remote past, whose ideas may be taken as read, on the ground that they were all wrong and unmodern anyway. On the contrary : his ideas, looked at closely, are seen to be our ideas ; and his inspiration is still vital and useful to us in our task of creating a humanly worthwhile educational system.[34]

[1]See Dewey's Chapter on " Philosophy " in *Whither Mankind?* ed. Beard, 1930, pp. 323–331. [2]*Rep.* 422d f., 462 ff. ; *Laws* 704b f., 739b f., 742ab, 817b f., 850b f., 949e f., 964c. In a community with 5,040 full citizens, Warner Fite, after considering the suggestions of scholars, comes to the conclusion that, if we include the slaves as well as the metics and other non-citizens, the total population would be about 70,000. (*The Platonic Legend*, 1934, pp. 10–11.). [3]*Laws* 704d f. [4]*Rep.* 472c f., 592 ; *Laws* 709e f., 739. (This statement is not to be taken as final.) [5]Cf. O. Spengler : *Decline of the West*, tr. Atkinson, 1939, pp. 9 ff., 172 ff., etc. [6]*Rep.* 501b f., slightly condensed. [7]*Metaphysica*, 982b 22–27. [8]*Prtg.* 319b f. ; *Rep.* 401 ; *Laws* 656d f., 659d f., 738b f., 764c f., 772a f., 799a, 801c f., 802a f., 809, 811b f., 812c f., 816bc, 817d, 828ab, 829c f., 848d ff., cf. 934b. Cf. Warner Fite : *Op. Cit.*, pp. 201 ff. [9]*Laws* 741e f., 846d, 919d f. [10]*Lysis* 207d ; *Gorg.* 483b ; *Rep.* 577c f., 590c ; *Laws* 720, 776cd, 777–78, 793e f., 808de, 848de, 917c f. [11]*Rep.* 556 ff. ; *Laws* 741e, 832, 846d f., 849b f., 918c ff, [12]P. Sargant Florence : *The Logic of Industrial Organization*, 1933, pp. 92–93. [13] In *Whither Mankind?* (ed. Beard), 1930, p. 323. [14]I have in mind especially the *Saturday Evening Post* and *Yachting*. I do not doubt that *Good Housekeeping* and the *Ladies' Home Journal* would tell the same story. Cf. also T. N. Whitehead : *Leadership in a Free Society*, 1937, pp. 11, 21, 29–30. [15]*Laws* 653 ff., 664 f., 670c f., 770c f., 803d f., 813b ff. [16]*Whither Mankind?* p. 324. [17]The modern techniques are not, however, different in principle from the techniques used in teaching reading and spelling in Plato's time and even earlier. Athenaeus : *Deipnosoph.* 453c–d tells of the spelling-drama of Kallias, in which BA, BE, BI, BO, BU, GA, GE, GI, GO, GU, etc., were acted out by the members of the Chorus, dressed to represent the letters ; and the actions were set to music. " After this choric song came a lecture on the vowels (in iambic verse), the Chorus being told to repeat them, one by one, after the speaker." There has also been found at Athens a terracotta fragment (conjectured to have belonged either to some spelling-book or to the wall of a schoolroom), which reads *ar bar gar dar* ; *er ber ger der.* (See Kenneth J. Freeman : *Schools of Hellas*, 1908, pp. 88 ff. [18]G. E. Freeland : *Elementary School Practice*, 1920, p. 5. In showing that the modern tendencies are in accord with the Platonic prescriptions, I do not intend to criticize adversely this modern authority. Nor do I suggest that he and his " educational leaders " are unaware that the theory they are championing is not an absolutely new discovery of theirs. (P. 97 implies the contrary.) My purpose is rather to suggest that those who (like Professor Bode) state that their interest in Plato is *only* historical, and apparently do believe that they have scrapped the past, and are creating a school-world *de novo*, might well revise their opinions in the light of the evidence. [19]Cf. e.g., *Laws* 747b, 809c ff., 818c–819c. There is no noticeable " transcendentalism " about the *elementary* schoolwork (military sports) in Plato. [20]It might be supposed that Plato's " ideas " deal with the type rather than with the individual, and so make no allowance for individual differences (cf. Dewey : *Democracy and Education*, pp. 104–105). But see *Phaedr.* 271d f., 277c ; *Theaet.* 150d f. And could anyone have been more obviously an " individual " than Socrates himself—not to mention the other chief *personae* in the *Dialogues* ? Cf. also *Laws* 739, 746, etc. [21]This is, in general, the attitude of modern " realists," and it is exemplified in Bertrand Russell : *Problems of Philosophy*, 1912, pp. 244–250. [22]This is, in general, the attitude of modern " pragmatists," and it is exemplified in John Dewey : *Democracy and Education*, 1921, pp. 261–270. The difference from Plato is considerable. Yet it would still be

possible, relying on the Platonic text alone, to write a manual for high school teachers-in-training which would parallel closely such a text as H. H. Foster's *Principles of Teaching in Secondary Education*, 1921. [23]*Rep.* 525cd ; *Phil.* 55d f. ; *Laws* 747ab, 809c, 819c ; cf. 737c f. This applies only to the *average* citizen. The members of the specially selected *leadership* class are expected to study their mathematics in a very different spirit. Partly, they " toil " at it, instead of learning it " in play," or (as we should say) " without tears." Partly, they are stimulated to develop transcendental idealism. [24]Cf. Herman Schneider : *Education for Industrial Workers*, 1915. We do much the same in our Colleges of Engineering. [25]*Rep.* 510b f., 521c ff., 538c ff. ; *Laws* 818a, 951e f., 957, 963b f., 964b–969. [26]Cf. R. C. Lodge : *Plato's Theory of Ethics*, pp. 109–122, and Ch. IX (Private and Public Spirit). [27]*Supra*, Chs. II–III. [28]*Rep.* 377, 386 ff., 401, 595 ff. ; *Laws* 656d f., 660, 764c f., 799–803a, 811b f., 816c f., 817b f., 828a f., 829d, 847d, 848d f., 920b f. [29]*Laws* 964b–969. [30]*Rep.* 519c f. Cf. Lodge : *Op. Cit.*, pp. 110–122, 181–184, 260–270, for discussion of the detailed evidence. [31]E. Frank : *Plato u.d.s–g. Pythagoreer*, 1923, maintains (p. 119) that " Plato's entire thought is, in a sense, one long Dialogue with materialism." Most readers believe they find this conflict in the *Crito, Phaedo. Gorgias, Protagoras* and *Republic.* It is more technically and demonstrably present in *Theaet.* 176, cf. 155d f., 184b ff. ; *Soph.* 246–248 ; *Laws* 903b ff. Warner Fite : *The Platonic Legend*, roundly challenges the degree of " idealism " usually seen in Plato, and indeed largely denies its existence in the objective text. But see W. Becher : *Platon und die königliche Erziehungskunst*, 1937, pp. 15–16. [32]Cf. *Essays in Honor of James Edwin Creighton, The New Realism, Critical Realism*, and the personal statements of idealists and realists in *Contemporary American Philosophy* (2 vols.). [33]In *Whither Mankind ?* (ed. Beard), p. 330. [34]I desire to draw attention to the fact that it is Plato's ideas, his general principles, not the particular social institutions in which he endeavoured to apply those principles to his own age, which for me, as for most Piato students, are of fundamental importance. I am in sympathy with the position of Professor G .C. Field (*Jour. of Education*, 1945, pp. 161–2), although I can readily see that a " naïve " reading of the text of the *Republic*, with an eye to Plato's actual institutions rather than to his principles (as advocated by Messrs. Neurath and Lauwerys (*Ibid.* pp. 57–8, 224, 394)) might, and probably would, lead readers whose background and outlook were Nazist, to find support for these views in certain parts of the text.

APPENDIX I

NUMBERS IN THE MODEL CITY

That a thinker so completely convinced as was Plato of the importance of arithmetic in determining administrative questions had before him some scheme, some background of definite figures to which he could refer in drawing up the outlines of his " model city " is, from the internal evidence of the *Laws*, reasonably certain. If we could recover the main features of that scheme, it would doubtless be of assistance in rendering precise for the modern reader at least the numerical proportion of school-children, teen-agers, men liable for military service, men available for parenthood, for the higher magistracies, etc. We should thus be able to substitute, for the vague and fluctuating images with which many a reader closes Plato's volumes, concrete and mathematically exact outlines : with a resulting gain in clearness and certainty.

It has occurred to me that we could make use of modern mortality tables. With their aid we could calculate, for a community of 5,040 heads of families, which would be distributed somewhere between the ages of twenty-five and eighty, the normal distribution over those years, and indeed over the years preceding the age of twenty-five. We could find out (1) the precise number of births requisite to provide for a community of 5,040 males so distributed ; (2) the precise number of school-age children at each stage of the educational system ; (3) the precise number of men available for military service ; (4) the precise number of men available for marriage and parenthood, and, if desired, for a number of the higher magistracies.

It is obvious that figures derived from " English Life Tables, No. 8," deduced from experience in modern England and Wales,[1] can hardly be expected to be identical with the ancient Hellenic figures (such as they were) which it is to be presumed that Plato had before him. That is to say, the absolute figures will differ. But it is not unreasonable to expect that the relative proportions of the different age-groups will present a close analogy : entirely close enough to clarify and render precise the numerical relations of the different groups in the Model City.

Thus, from the modern mortality tables, it appears that, in order to keep up the numbers of a group of 5,040 males from 25 to 79 inclusive, there would have to be between 164 and 165 births each year. Of schoolchildren from six to sixteen inclusive, there would have to be 1,471 males. If we include females, there would presumably be 2,942 schoolchildren under the direction of the minister of education in any given year. In the sports schools (ages 6 to 10 inclusive), there would be 673 males. If we include females, there would be 1,346 schoolchildren in the sports schools. In the literary and music schools (taken together), there would be something like 800 teen-age males in any given year. If we inquire how many would go on and receive " higher " education, which is given to all members of the " nocturnal council," we find the numbers suddenly become very small. At the age of 30, when young men of distinguished ability are co-opted into the Council, there are only 125 males from whom to choose, and of these the greater number would be engaged in military or other duties. Only a very few of the 30–40 age group would be sufficiently promising ; and they would be the recipients of higher education. Not more than 100, and not less than 60 would be engaged in these higher studies in any one year.

In military service, to which men are liable from the twentieth to the sixtieth year, the extreme number of males available would be 4,689. As some of these would be needed for the various magistracies, and not all would be absolutely fit physically (in spite of their education in gymnastic), this means that the total armed forces of the Model City would seldom exceed 4,500 effectives. In extreme cases, women past the official age of child-bearing could be called upon : which would conceivably add about 1,000 effectives to the citizen-army, making an absolute total of 5,500.

For the purposes of parenthood, males of the ages of 30–40 would be available. The number of such males would be 1,193. As Plato expects one marriage in seven to be fruitful in each year, that means that he anticipates something like 170 births in each year. This is slightly in excess of the calculation of 164–5 births which we find in modern population statistics. But (1) the ancient mortality may well have been slightly heavier, and (2) Plato contemplates a waiting list for his citizenships, i.e., he anticipates something more than the number of births required to keep up the number of 5,040 males.

Older men in the Model City (*emeriti*) are regarded as gradually dropping off the active list, although an exceptional man may still be asked to serve as " priest." By the time the age of 79 is reached, there would only be twenty-two persons left alive. As they gradually retire, their places are taken by the younger men reaching the age of about twenty-five.

¹For details as to the precise figures, I am indebted to my colleague, Professor L. A. H. Warren, of the Department of Actuarial Science in the University of Manitoba. Without his kindness in responding to my request. I should not have been able to discover the precise figures discussed.

EDUCATION OF WOMEN ACCORDING TO PLATO

RABBI SOLOMON FRANK, PH.D.

The usual account of Plato's theory of education rests upon the *Republic* rather than upon the *Laws*. It studies the development of idealism, to the neglect of the nonlogical sides of education. In particular, it regards the education of women as substantially the same as the education given to men. This, however, presents a distorted and misleading account of Plato's views. Independent investigation of the *complete* evidence contained within the *Dialogues* indicates that education is conceived by him primarily as nonlogical ; and that the logical or dialectical training, when actually given, is given only to candidates already educated more fundamentally by the methods developed by artisans and artists. If we examine the different stages of the education given to women, this will become clear.

(*a*) Nonlogical.—The planned community, whether ideal republic or model city, is to be founded upon the basic concept of Justice. As applied to women, this means that women's unique and positive capacities, which can be utilized in making definite contributions to the life of the planned community, are to be developed by all the social institutions—home, school, church, army, lawcourts, community festivals, etc.—which are regarded in the *Dialogues* as of directly educational significance.[1]

What are the positive functions of women, from the standpoint of the planned community ? First come the biological and social functions, connected with the different stages of the life-cycle. Each of these should receive, if it is to be developed adequately for the life of the planned community, especial educational care. Consideration of the life-cycle starts, in the *Dialogues*, with the period before the child is born. It deals with prenatal care, commencing with the marriage and conduct of the parents under eugenic conditions approved by the community and enforced by public opinion and the oversight of women magistrates with wide powers.

In the *Republic*, the general aim of the regulations which surround the process of conception is the perfection of the coming generation, by no means as an end in itself, but primarily as a means to the continuance of the planned community ; that is to say, as a means toward its preservation and maintenance in a condition approximating to perfection, as far as this is possible with human material. The coming generation is to be, if possible, not only more excellent physically than its parents ; but also more excellent as material for civic life, more useful and of greater all-round value to the community, than the preceding generation. That is why only adults who excel both morally and physically are especially encouraged to undertake for the State the service of parenthood.[2] What flows from this source to the infant, and is of significance for its education from the very beginning, is not only physical strength, with a corresponding tendency toward the natural good temper which is a concomitant of general health and strength, but also, as Plato believes, a certain moral disposition. The moral atmosphere of parenthood in a soundly planned community has of itself a certain pervasive influence[3] ; and in addition there is the more especial atmosphere of service to the community, which is the characteristic attitude of Plato's " silver class." Finally, there is (Plato believes) a direct tendency to inherit the moral, as well as the physical, nature of the parents. That is largely why the ancient equivalent of V.C.'s are especially encouraged to reproduce their kind.[4]

In the *Laws*, details are different. There is here no attempt, by mating like with like, to increase with each new generation the civic and military usefulness of the citizens. There is less thought of biological progress, and more determination to maintain in equilibrium a state which is already about as excellent as can be expected of humanity.[5] Some attention is paid to the possibility of institutional progress[6] ; but the intention is, explicitly, to maintain the *status quo* rather than to introduce novelty, as such. The aim is, accordingly, not to grow in any new, one-sided direction, but to keep as close to the approved norm, the " mean," as possible. Mating is to be, not between likes, but between unlikes, with the deliberate intention of producing " equability of the children's disposition."[7]

Again, there is, in the *Laws*, no selection of especially virtuous citizens for the function of parenthood. Every one of the 5,040 citizens of the model community is induced, partly by public opinion and partly by explicit pains and penalties for the reluctant,

to marry and to produce, under direction of the women controllers of marriage, an appropriate number of children. Particular care is taken to see that the conditions surrounding conception, and indeed the whole antenatal conduct of the parents-
to-be shall be as beneficial as possible to the physical and moral
well-being of the expected infant. [8]

But although the details differ considerably, the all-pervasive
influence of the community, and the especial attitude of community service in parenthood, are the same in both Dialogues.
There is also the same faith that moral, as well as physical characteristics, are inherited. What is passed on to the coming generation in the *Laws* is, in addition to physical health and strength,
an equable disposition, and all the general values which attach
to legitimacy and community approval.

Once born, the first three years of the child's life are devoted,
in the *Laws*, primarily to physical development. The babies
develop by nutrition and physical growth, and gradually acquire
mastery over the simpler movements and physical adjustments to
the environment. The nutrition is provided, partly by the
mothers, and partly by especially suitable nurses, who relieve the
biological mothers—at least in the higher classes—of much of
the trouble which, in less well-planned communities, all too
frequently falls to their lot in looking after very young children. [9]
The nurses carry the children until it is quite certain that the
children are able to stand without distorting their limbs ; and
regulations are made to ensure that the children receive as much
fresh air and exercise (while carried) as is good for them. [10]

But the training received during this period is not exclusively
physical. The general moral atmosphere, and the attitude toward
perfecting the young for their future life of citizenship in the
model community, continue to exercise a pervasive influence.
And in addition, certain tendencies begin to show themselves at
this early period which clearly require moral direction and
guidance. Very young children exhibit a certain restlessness.
During the first three years, they tend to express their uneasinesses
by crying : so as to attract the attention and assistance of parents
and other attendants. This tendency to cry whenever the child
is afraid or is in want of anything may easily, Plato thinks, lay the
physical foundation for dispositions which, if further developed,
will become the vicious habits of querulousness, excessive timidity,
tantrums, and bad temper : dispositions and habits to which the
female sex is peculiarly liable. [11] If indulged and encouraged,

the infant develops the beginnings of self-will, and may easily turn out to be a " spoilt " child.

The proper educational procedure in such situations is twofold. On the one hand, the infant should be neither unduly indulged, nor unduly repressed. All children have to learn " neither to seek after pleasures, nor to shrink from pains, but to embrace the middle state, which is gentle, benign, and godlike." This is of especial importance in infancy, for " it is then especially that character becomes engrained by habit."[12] But infants are too weak to acquire self-control by themselves, and there is a second, more technical, way in which they can be assisted, by parents and nurses, toward the desirable attitude of selfmastery. The principle of selfmotion, located within the brain, is at first easily hindered from functioning : whether by sudden sensations, by the powerful incoming stream of nutrition, or by a variety of stimuli which, in the young child, produce "fears and terrors." Such invasions from the external world cannot entirely be controlled ; but their power over the central self-motion principle can be mitigated, and the central principle can be reinforced, by a very simple technique : the technique of shaking the child, rocking it in the arms.[13]

Medical experience prescribes for adults who habitually overeat or in other ways live not wisely, but too well, so that they become dyspeptic and unable to control their own health, a decorous substitute for a good shaking. A course of gymnastic, open-air riding and driving, or an ocean voyage, does the trick. The central selfmotion is reinforced, and the balanced equilibrium in which health consists, is restored.[14] So also dancing and a rather special kind of music produce in adult women, in the Corybantic rites, an abatement of their fears and frenzy, and a restoration of their normal self-control. In the case of young children, rocking them in the arms, while singing a lullaby to them, produces the same beneficent effect ; and Plato accordingly recommends that infants should live, if possible, " as if always rocking at sea." " Thus does the use of exercise and motion in the earliest years of life greatly contribute to create a part of virtue in the soul."[15]

We do not ordinarily realize that formal education begins at so young an age. Yet in truth everything which is done for the infant makes a lasting impression upon it. Such education helps to determine the type of citizen that the child will eventually become, and also the manner of service which, as citizen, it will thereafter contribute to society. By careful planning, by adherence to the " middle state "—giving the child, in keeping with the needs of the individual, state, and society, a maximum of sensory happiness, and limiting it to a minimum of necessary pain—we shall arrive at a positive answer to Plato's question concerning early education : " If during these three years every possible care were taken that our nursling should have as little of sorrow and fear, and in general of pain, as was possible, might we not expect at this age to make his soul more gentle and cheerful ? "[16]

If a state has chosen as its goal the healthy growth of society inspired by a desire for the happy development of the individual citizen, then the child from earliest infancy must receive such care, guidance and training as will produce eventual spiritual, as well as physical health and adequate development. This training is not to be left entirely to the parent. It must be undertaken by skilled nurses who are themselves under constant supervision and direction by the appropriate magistrates. " Man is a tame or civilized animal ; nevertheless he requires proper instruction and a fortunate nature, and then of all animals he becomes the most divine and most civilized ; but if insufficiently or ill educated, he becomes the savagest of earthly creatures. Wherefore the legislator ought not to allow the education of children to become a secondary or accidental matter."[17]

It is to be seen from this that Plato recognizes the importance of applying the principles of education at the earliest possible moment in the life of the child. It is often overlooked that education envisages *all* the human faculties for learning, the nonlogical, antelogical, or " derivatives "[18] as well as the logical. It is with an understanding of this most fundamental educational principle that Plato provides for the commencement of the educational process long before any logical education can be given the child.

In fact, with the great masses of Plato's citizens, what logical education *is* given (a little practical mathematics and a little— very little—general science) is so slight as to be almost negligible. Almost the whole of their training comes from gymnastic and music, from the nonlogical arts which appeal to the imagination and develop the habitual docility of the plain citizen and fit him for happiness rather than for leadership.[19]

Hence it is essential to place before the mind of the child, while it is constantly open to impressions and while memories and habits are definitely in the formative stage, those nonlogical elements of education which serve as the foundation upon which the entire educational superstructure which fits the growing child for citizenship can safely rest.[20]

After the infant has learned to walk and balance itself, a second stage in the life-cycle is reached. Accordingly the next three or four years (approximately from the age of 3 to the age of 6) are spent largely in open-air play in supervised community playgrounds. " All children between the ages of three and six ought to meet at the village temples, the several families of each village uniting on one spot. The nurses are to see that the children behave properly and orderly : each group of children and nurses being under the control of a playground matron, selected from among the women controllers of marriage, and clothed with all necessary power."[21]

The play of the children is largely spontaneous. The instinctive urge to play develops from within, but the children's games to which it gives rise have become somewhat standardized, the world over, and are to be regarded as racial, a part of the human tradition, not lightly to be altered in the smallest detail. Young children of themselves take kindly to rules in their games, and indeed in their whole social life. They learn, during these three or four pre-school years to play together, to be neighbourhood children, to take a first step away from a purely family life toward group life, with a forward glance toward schooldays and eventual citizenship.[22]

At this stage, Plato thinks the nurses have an opportunity to provide quite a little in the way of moral education, preparing their charges for some of the restraints of community life. They see that the children play " properly and orderly " ; and sports and games provide an especial opportunity of educating the child out of the disposition toward being self-willed. He learns, not only to overcome obstacles, but to play with older children, who take the lead. Thus a certain docility is acquired ; and also there are penalties for breaking the rules in games, penalties whose enforcement does not involve breaking the spirit of the freeborn child (as punishment on a more serious occasion might do), and yet guides the child toward acquiring a greater measure of self-control. By thus associating with his equals on competitive terms, and by imitating what he sees the other children doing, the child himself learns by doing. What he learns is not only the techniques involved in playing ball or the ancient equivalent of Prisoner's

Base ; he also learns to assimilate the norms involved in group living.[23]

The next stage of the life-cycle is the period from six to ten years of age. The sexes are now separated and are sent to separate schools. Here the young girl learns to be a schoolgirl, associating exclusively with schoolgirls, and being taught all she learns by schoolmistresses. What she learns, while superficially not unlike what her brothers are learning in their boys' school, is acquired in a very different spirit. Her voice, carriage, manners, and outlook become definitely feminine, suited to the capacities of her sex and expressive of its nature. All roughness and violence are discouraged. Emphasis, in all she says and does, is upon gracefulness, propriety, gentleness, and docility. When she competes, it is always with other girls, never against boys. The conditions of competition are always adapted to the capacities of her sex ; and while she is taught to develop a healthy and vigorous physique, there is never the slightest suggestion that she is any sort of boy—that mischievous, gawky, insubordinate creature almost perpetually calling for management, control, and chastisement.[24]

The school attended during this period is not like a modern school. It is more like what we nowadays regard as a sports' club, in which *extra*curricular activities are indulged in outside of school hours. In a present-day " Winter Club," young girls come in after school hours : to learn, partly by imitating each other and partly by receiving professional instruction, to swim, skate, and play Badminton. In the Platonic school, the girls learn dancing, horsemanship, and the use of the bow, javelin, and sling—" if they do not object "—or at any rate until they know how to handle these weapons and heavy armour, with the left as well as with the right hand.[25] In the regular monthly sports-meets, the girls compete with one another publicly in footraces (with and without armour), in horse-races, and in shooting-matches and military drill. But they are emphatically *not* forced by law " to do everything the boys do."[26]

Superficially, it looks as though the girls, because they learn to do some of the things that the boys are learning to do, are after all learning to be almost-boys. But this is not Plato's intention. They learn " if they do not object "—a proviso inserted a number of times in the *Laws*. And further : they learn in an almost entirely different spirit. The boys learn to handle arms as a prelude to army life. The boys' school is a kind of military school, where military sports and military gymnastics are studied in a spirit of professional *expertise*. Again and again in the Dialogues it is emphasized that the boys are to be athletes trained for the actualities of warfare—trained, that is to say, in something like the modern spirit of commando practice. In the *mêlée* and similar features of the monthly field-days, it is expected that there will be real dangers and real casualties ; and it is in precisely such field-days that the training of the boys' schools receives its regular tests.[27] The girls, however, are not being trained with any such direct eventualities in mind. In the *Laws*, they do not take part in *mêlée* and similar contests. Indeed, they do not go into the army, as the boys do. They can be used for military purposes only in later life, " after the period of child-bearing is over," and even then only in genuine emergencies.[28]

The military drill of the girls, then, is undertaken in a more amateurish spirit ; for in the *Laws* the girls are really being prepared, not so much for military, as for domestic life. Their dancing in armour, for instance, is in honour of the virgin goddess Athene, and is quite different from the boys' *expertise* with heavy arms. Generally speaking, it is the boys who participate in the " Pyrrhic " or war dance and in the numerous marches and processions on horseback and under arms which are a feature of pre-war life in the model city. The girls participate rather in the " Emmeleiai," the more moderate peace-dances.[29]

The next stage of the life-cycle is from the age of ten to the age of thirteen or perhaps to sixteen. The girls now go to a different kind of school, where they are taught to read and write and, after acquiring these accomplishments, to spend three years learning to make music. This education in letters and music is compulsory, and the secondary schools, like the first school, are State schools, taught by expert teachers who are State appointees, thoroughly trained in the spirit of Plato's Dialogue, the *Laws* as well as in their fields of especial competence.[30]

The content of this six years' work is contained in authorized textbooks, consisting chiefly of the national literature re-written by experts *in usum scholarum*, and of a similarly censored series of dances and music-accompaniments.[31] The purpose of this secondary education is to develop the whole personality of the girls so that they take on, in rhythms, melodies, and sentiments attitudes peculiarly suited to their sex,[32] the attitudes characteristic of women citizens of the model community. Just as the military schooling received reinforcement in the monthly fieldmeets, so the musical schooling prepares for the monthly musical festivals, and indeed for the regular processional chants in honour of the various civic deities : of whom at least one is honoured for each of the 365 days of the calendar year. It is to be presumed that it is especially in honour of the female deities that the young women are trained to chant their hymns : in honour of Athene, Artemis, and the like.[33]

And here we must pause briefly from pursuing the further development of women in their biological life-cycle. So far we have considered the influence of the home, of the neighbourhood, and of the school, upon the growing girl. In the *Laws*, the influence of the home continues throughout her life. As maid, wife, mother, and matron, her life is definitely centred in the home : a home permeated by community spirit. The influence of the school persists, after her sixteenth year, only indirectly : namely, in the monthly gymnastic and music festivals which continue to keep alive in her the spirit of her education. What is that spirit ?

As far as we have studied it, it is intensely, narrowly, local. Her interests are concentrated upon the community into which she has been born, in which she has progressively immersed her growing self. All that she is, all that she has become, she owes to that community : a community which she has never left, and indeed has never thought of leaving.[34] The influences with which she has been surrounded from birth, the voices she hears on every side, the travellers' tales repeated by the few older persons who have had occasion to travel and visit other communities : everything tells her that the community into which she has been born and in which she had been educated, is the best conceivable form of human association. With every fibre of her being she believes that she is indeed fortunate to be a member of this happy city, this heaven upon earth. And in the few influences which (for contrast effect, and to make her more fully realize her wonderful good fortune) have given a hint of other places and other views, she has learnt to regard everything not seriously idealistic as " foreign," " low," and altogether despicable.

For example : the entertainments of Classical Greece, in the form of tragedy and comedy, whose popularity is due, Plato thinks, largely to their emotionalism and vulgarity, are excluded from the model city as from the ideal republic. Not for Plato's citizens their ranting lamentations and cheap, crime-story thrills ! Citizens whose whole life is a serious drama cannot waste their time and imperil their strength of character by filling their imaginations with make-believe fears and desires, and by giving way to a senseless love of revelry. Casual poets, with their troupes of hired actors, will be treated as illegitimate competitors of the State *ethos*, with spurious and probably injurious wares for sale. The magistrates can be trusted to handle them suitably.[35] Comedy is particularly dangerous. It produces an inconsistent mixture of pleasure and pain in the spectator,[36] accustoms the mind to vulgarity, is the amusement of slaves, and—to tell the truth—is actually liked by children, whose judgment is so little developed that they even love puppet-shows ![37]

At the same time, something of this sort must be shown to the citizens ; but under conditions which will definitely prevent their ever letting themselves go and identifying themselves with anything so foolish and indeed dangerous to their idealism :

It is necessary also to consider and know uncomely persons and thoughts, and those which are intended to produce laughter in comedy, and have a comic character in respect of style, song, and dance, and of the imitations which these afford. For serious things cannot be understood without laughable things, nor opposites without opposites, if a man is really to have intelligence of either ; but he cannot carry out both in action, if he is to have any degree of virtue. And for this very reason he should learn to know both, that he may not in ignorance do or say anything ridiculous and out of place. He should command slaves and hired foreigners to imitate such things ; but he should never take serious interest in them himself ; nor should any freeman or freewomen be discovered taking pains to learn them.[38]

This example illustrates one way in which Plato's citizens are expected to overcome the weaknesses incident to localism, while retaining and indeed strengthening the virtues inherent in it. The authorized literature will broaden, as well as deepen, a stay-at-home girl's horizon. Like the philosopher Kant who only once left his native Königsberg, she will take her walks abroad vicariously, and will find within the borders of her home town all that she needs for the most satisfactory of lives, a sheltered life of unwavering idealism.[39] The traditional literature, wisely and properly selected for her by older and more experienced authorities, will give her the feeling of belonging to a community which is not simply local and out of the great world, but is a Hellenic community, a community universally Hellenic, the *beau-idéal* of the inner spirit of Hellenism, and indeed of humanity.[40]

So much for the influence of literature. But there is, throughout her life, a further influence, more universal, more ideal, as well as more definitely pervasive : namely, the influence of religion. From her earliest years, she is exposed to its power ; and it must at once be admitted that no educational influence which she ever encounters in her life equals or even approaches the power of religion. It is indeed religion which gives to the home, to the school, to art and literature, the power for good which these have. All alike shine by borrowed light. They are the lanterns by which the human puppets attempt to illumine the darkness of their world. But the light itself comes from a higher source. " The soul of man has come out of that brighter life, and is at first unable to see in the unaccustomed darkness."[41] The power which the eye possesses, and which enables it to see its way, is a sort of effluence of rhythmic rituals which make the whole soul rhythmic and harmonious. It is by taking part in the festivals of the Gods, " and with their help," that in appropriate dances and expressive chants maid and matron, boy and man, become truly educated, attuned to a mystical sense of their divine origin and destiny.[42]

Religion exerts powerful nonlogical influences. There are powers felt to be beyond us. These must be propitiated, we feel, by sacrifice, prayer, ritual, and symbol.[43] The sacred and the profane, the approved and the taboo or forbidden, exert a mighty influence. With the development of the religious spirit, the desire for friendship with the Gods leads men to endeavour to assimilate his nature to what he takes to be divine. In this way a community of feeling is formed.[44] Thus the power of religion is not primarily intellectual or logical. It makes a direct appeal to something deep and fundamental within us. It seeks to answer the first questions born of awe.[45] It seems the best way to enter into fellowship with the powers beyond us, so that success may be attained both here and hereafter.[46]

Hence religion as a nonlogical influence becomes a most potent factor in the girl's life. She is constantly exposed to its influence. From the age of three to six, the children meet daily at the temple. At the earliest age mothers, nurses and old men tell stories of the Gods. Delight is taken in the daily festival.[47] The Gods are invoked in every vicissitude of life, and at the beginning of every enterprise. Prayers are offered at daily sacrifice, and there is a constant atmosphere of propitiation. The girl also learns much in the special festivals for women.[48]

The basis of all Platonic education is music for the soul and gymnastics for both soul and body. Music is an important part of the curriculum. It is associated directly with religion, because good music is like good company. Only that person is educated who is well trained in choral singing and who can both sing and dance.[50] For the Hellenic type of dance is an imitation of that which is represented. It symbolizes religion. As movement is natural to the young, the rhythm and harmony of dance and song are raised to a religious level. Therefore the approved and established forms of song and dance are consistently taught as parts of the educational curriculum.[51] The educational system is shot through and through with religion. At every step in the learning process, religion with all its nonlogical implications is constantly brought before the girl's mind. The symbolism of dance and processional, of sacrifice and vestments, the intensely religious atmosphere pervading home and school carry over the influence of the first and earliest attendance at the temples, an integral part of the child's life the moment it learns to walk. But the nonlogical carry-over is not left to the school and the home. It pervades the free periods as well. Free times are largely to be spent at the temples. Festivals are times of rest when opportunity is given to attend service. As religion is part of the State law, attendance is mandatory.[52]

There is an additional reason for this. Plato reminds us that temple attendance improves education. When children are thus in constant attendance, listening and participating in the service by song and dance, their souls are charmed into harmony with the established law. We begin to look upon the Gods as companions, leaders and friends.[53] These nonlogical elements are of themselves sufficient to influence the mind. No appeal to reason is necessary. The influences extending from earliest infancy, from dusk to dawn, are sufficient to permeate the being of the girl with a profoundly religious spirit. Thus is brought about the passage of God from heaven to earth : i.e., the actualization of the spirit of goodness in human affairs. The girl dances, for example, in honour of Athene. She dons shield and helmet, and carries in her hand a spear : in imitation of the outward garb of the statued form before which she dances. But this is merely external. Inwardly she learns, as she dances, to identify her life with the life of the Goddess. In the ritual dance she experiences identity, and assimilates directly something of the divine virtue of Athene, the warrior-maid.[54]

So too with the music in which she participates. It is especially suited to bring out the characteristic excellences of her sex. Its rhythms, harmonies, and melodies make for moderation and temperance, because these are the especially characteristic womanly qualities.[55] As she moves in procession or dance, she chants the sacred formula, telling that the Gods of the State are good only and the givers of all good. Her prayers are prayers for divinely sent good, and never for evil ; and the entire State in which she lives, dances, and prays, embodies the idea of good.[56]

As a maid, she worships at the shrine of Athene ; as a young wife, at the shrine of Artemis.[57] She learns to look forward with solemn acceptance to " weaving the web of life " and conditions herself to her destined place in the life of the planned community : a life which every voice that she has heard from birth assures her is the best for woman as well as for man ; a life whose praises she has herself chanted every day since she learned to sing.[58]

She knows that for a ten-year period duty requires that her functions as wife and mother belong to the State ; and she therefore goes to the mating-dance and the sacred vows of the marriage festival, with their tremendous nonlogical influences for education in the service of the community, secure that in faithful obedience to the matron-magistrates and the community deities she is filling that place in life to which destiny and the divine plan, no less than human wisdom, call her.[59]

After this period is over, as a matron she worships at the shrine of Here, goddess of wedded life ; and if she becomes one of the matron-magistrates who partly direct and control the pro-creative activities of young married couples, and partly act as experts who give social advice as well as admonition in biosocial matters, her chief daily work centres at the temple of the goddess Eileithyia, one of the daughters of Here, as whose servant she now regards herself.[60] In later life she may be appointed priestess of any one of the female deities of the community, either for a single year, or for life. In this case, her chief function as priestess is to offer to her goddess gifts from the women worshippers, in the form of acceptable sacrifices and to pray on behalf of the community for blessings in return : in accordance with the ceremonial forms prescribed by rule or traditional usage. Her further function as curatress of the temple buildings and superintendent of the temple ritual includes certain other powers, such as the power of excommunication, the exclusion from participation in the sacred rites, of impure persons whose presence would otherwise have polluted the prayers and sacrifices.[61] She is also entrusted with the duty of dispensing hospitality to certain types of visitor from other communities, such as priestesses of her particular deity, or female theological experts making inquiries concerning her deity ; and in this capacity she acts as a magistrate, dispensing judgment in the case of minor offences committed by or against her official guests.[62]

If, now, we glance over the whole of woman's life in the planned community, we see that it is permeated throughout with the influence of sincere and simple religious feeling, especially suited to her nature and social destiny in the community. The influence of this religion is not a matter of logical definition and deliberation. It is rather a matter of acting, dancing, singing, and following the prescriptions of a community cult in all her thoughts, words, and deeds. The influence of religion upon her is thus nonlogical, and fits her for her life and destiny as a woman, as a freewoman in the planned community. It conditions her for the acceptance of her changing phases as maid, wife, mother, matron, and possibly priestess : always in the service, and always under the protection, of a goddess who represents in idealized form the particular phase of the life-cycle through which she is herself passing at the time.

So conditioned, she walks through life with a sweet seriousness, devoting herself to the domestic and religious duties of a peaceful life : sacrificing, chanting, performing the ceremonial dances, and thus propitiating the goddesses and living according to the appointment of nature : entering into companionship with the beings whom she worships, and thus, in her simple happiness, participating in reality, as far as a woman may.[63]

We now leave the subject of religion, and resume our study of education in the model city, in connection with the phases of the life-cycle which come after the period of formal schooling is over. Formal education for girls ceases at about the age of sixteen. They then leave school and are considered as of marriageable age.[64] This is one of the most important phases in a woman's life-cycle, and women are educated for it, partly by life itself, and partly by public opinion and by the instructions and admonitions of matron-magistrates. These matrons are the same as the play-grounds matrons who supervised the years of pre-school play in the temple precincts. They represent authority, community protection, mature experience, safe guidance, and wise counselling in intimate matters.[65] They teach the young women that marriage is a sacred mystery, in which women weave the web of life and co-operate with God in the work of creation.[66] They teach them also that marriage is of profound concern to the State, and that it is their civic as well as their religious duty to marry and bear children[67] according to the laws of the planned community. The young women become acquainted with young men—from whom during the period of formal education they have been kept separate—at the mating dances,[68] and while their choice is always partly left to natural inclination,[69] they are guided, by persuasion and by consideration of their overarching duty to God and the community, to select marriage-partners who are not, for the most part, like themselves in taste and disposition, but unlike. The idea is that a union of opposite qualities will produce offspring who are close to the human norm and illustrate the principle of the mean.[70]

For ten years after marriage, the young wife is taught to place her function as a mother at the service of the State, in obedience to the intimate advice and indeed direction of the matron-magistrates.[71] Throughout this period she is being educated by those with whom she associates, namely, the other young wives and the matron-magistrates ; and the public opinion which they represent enters into her nature partly by association and social assimilation, partly by the processes of exhortation. These processes of admonition and exhortation are not regarded by Plato as logical, as processes in which intellectual considerations of an abstract, economic, mathematical, or philosophical nature play an important part. On the contrary, he regards them as definitely nonlogical. They are of the precise nature of the " preambles " attached to his individual laws. They act " like preludes of music." Their function is, to prepare the minds of the young, " to conciliate goodwill, so that they will readily accept the prescriptions of the law." This is said with especial reference to one of the fundamental laws concerning marriage.[72]

After this ten-year period of service to the State is over, the young mother becomes a matron. She is now, so far as her intimmate associations with men are concerned, entirely her own mistress : free to follow her own inclination for the rest of her life. There are, however, certain provisos which Plato treats as obvious. She must practice birth-control. And her *liaisons* are not to be flagrantly public. Provided she behaves quietly and with discretion, the State is not interested in her private life. " Concealment shall be honourable."[73] This phase of her life is not logical, but biological ; and its educative influences are respect for public opinion, the preambles of law, law itself, and music and gymnastic exercise : influences which fall definitely into the category of the non-logical.[74]

The final phase of a woman's life in the planned community begins with the age of forty. She can now begin to hold office. The kind of office for which she is peculiarly fitted by her nature and experience, is the office of matron-magistrate. In this office she is one of the " controllers of marriage " and also assists in supervising the pre-school community games of young children. This gives full play to her womanly nature in its maturity. Her natural feeling for enjoying gossip is directed to noble and useful purposes ; and her protective interest in young children is encouraged and provided with an official outlet, and also with a certain measure of power and recognition in the community life.[75] In addition, her genuine control over the personnel and numbers of the next generation gives her a position of very great power and importance. If, in later life, she becomes a priestess of one of the community cults, this too is a position of prominence and importance.[76]

In these positions, as in all higher magistracies, there is much which calls for higher education, of a definitely mathematical and logical type. The women who preside over marriage and the new generation of citizens, will have to know something of Plato's " nuptial number," which has become almost a bye-word for its mathematical obscurity ;[77] and they will also have to have made an especial study of law—a duty enjoined on all magistrates.[78] In addition to this, both types of woman magistrate will have to have made an especial study of the matters dealt with in the Timaeus, namely the mathematical and philosophical principles involved in the creation of the cosmos. " They will have to have contemplated the mind of nature which is said to exist in the stars, and seen the connection of music with these things, and harmonized them all with laws and institutions."[79]

But the further study of the logical side of woman's education can be postponed. Meanwhile we can see that even in these exalted magisterial positions, nonlogical elements, not only of civic and religious responsibility and service, but of personal pride and social importance, are clearly present. We thus conclude that the education which prepares woman, in the planned community, for the performance of her particular tasks as woman, is predominantly nonlogical in its methods, as well as in the material of an instinctive, emotional, and habitual nature to which it is applied.

The educative process, if we leave in the background the eugenic and pre-school provisions, began with the age of six, when the girl was first separated from the boys of her own age. It continued throughout her school career, emphasizing the feminine and domestic aspects of her nature and destiny. It conditioned her for her duties to the State and the Gods as wife and mother—and possibly also as magistrate in domestic relations and as priestess. Both in school and out of school she learns the lessons of life by association, by imitation, and by assimilation : by living in social surroundings which influence her through feelings which are primarily biosocial, in a word, nonlogical.

Most citizens, because of their limited capacity, will receive only such a degree of education as will enable them to live at the level of " right opinion." Some few, an almost infinitely small selection of the population, can be educated to complete human maturity. These alone can be given the opportunity to attain to the beatific vision of the principle of ideality and value.[80] This vision will come only to those who, during the years assigned to nonlogical education, have evidenced a capacity to enter upon a radically new kind of study. Thus " one woman has the temper of a philosopher and the temper of a guardian." Such women will be permitted to enter upon a course of definitely higher studies.[81]

When will this period devoted to higher studies be undertaken by women ? According to the *Laws*, a woman may marry at sixteen, though normally it will be a little later.[82] Ten years are now given over to childbearing. Hence we may infer that women, as a general rule, will hardly be in a position to enter upon the higher course of studies until they have reached the age of thirty. At that time, the women who have received and have excelled in the basic education, and have given (in their mathematical games) proof of the possession of altogether special gifts of nature, will embark upon the course of studies which qualifies them for leadership.

As we consider the process of higher education, we understand the difficulties involved. Most of us live at the level of " right opinion." We have accustomed ourselves to accept what is universally regarded as right. Hence we are like habitués of the shadow-plays which with the ancients occupied the place taken in our life by the Talkies.[83] What we have always accepted as reality is but a man-made shadow. When we come out into the light of day again, it is hard to adjust ourselves to the real world.

Once we have become thoroughly conditioned and indoctrinated, it is difficult for us to adopt an objective attitude : to scrutinize critically and to evaluate what we have come so utterly to accept.

There is involved a change in nonlogical point of view, a change which it is difficult to acquire and difficult to maintain. The difficulty is only increased if the full light of reason is thrown upon the twilight belief, upon the presuppositions which still have power over us. It takes a lengthy period of education before our minds become capable of coping with the flood of light. At first we turn, groping for support, toward convictions which, although mere " opinions," are guaranteed by community belief as opinions which are " right." This support assists us in not altogether losing our bearings. Very gradually, like men long blindfolded, we accustom ourselves to the light of reason which is being thrown mercilessly upon our cherished ideas.[84] It is because our minds have been deeply rooted in opinions which are " right," that we are enabled first to endure and then to use the new illumination to see beyond " opinion " to genuine truth ; and, in the end, to achieve understanding of the ultimate principle, the idea of good.[85]

This is the path which the women aspirants for leadership will tread. Only the very best minds, namely, those which have acquired a secure foundation of nonlogical training, in addition to being blessed with especial gifts, are to ascend to the top rung of the ladder of learning. Having such minds, such women, when they have finally achieved insight into the idea of good, are to return to the cave where those who dwell on the plane of opinion are still to be found, and are to train the masses nonlogically.[86] As matrons, magistrates, and priestesses, it is then their duty to direct and supervise the environmental conditions of the citizens. The new philosopher-queens guide the procreation, birth, and early education of the citizens, as well as the general promotion of the spirit of good citizenship. In the benefactions which they thereby bestow, as well as in the increased dignity and public esteem that falls to their lot, they take especial joy. They also realize an especial kind of happiness in the intellectual satisfaction which comes to those who see everything in the clearest conceivable light.[87]

The details of the higher education are known to every reader of the *Republic*. The subjects studied are mathematics, astronomy, harmonics, and dialectic ; and they are studied in such a way as to develop the students' powers of philosophical insight to the utmost.   In the *Laws*, the same subjects are indicated for study, and there is also a good deal of emphasis upon the importance of studying " the writings of the legislator," i.e., treatises upon law, and also the detailed laws of different communities.   In addition to training in abstract thought, such studies are of specific assistance to the philosopher-queens in the performance of their magisterial duties.

The women " guardians " are assigned, in the *Laws*, certain specific functions.   They are to be known as " controllers of marriage," and their practical duties are formulated as follows : They are (1) to see that the marriage-laws are obeyed, and to bring and press charges where necessary ; (2) to supervise the pre-school training of children, with right of appeal to the police authorities to enforce their directions ; (3) to assist (like modern social workers) in settling disputes between husband and wife, between parents and children, and generally, between relatives.[88]

How does the rather special training in mathematics and astronomy which the women guardians have received, help them toward the fulfilment of these rather simple-appearing duties ? In mathematics, the women guardians have " attained to problems," i.e., have learnt to deal with ultimates, with the mathematical why of things.   Where most women appreciate colour, for instance, as an experience of a sensuous sort, the trained mind apprehends a " law of proportion," or mathematical equation.   Where most women appreciate words and musical sounds for their sensuous and social values, the trained mind perceives, underlying the air-vibrations which produce vowels, a definitely mathematical equation.   In investigating why some numbers are harmonious, and others not, the trained mind is looking for the ideal principle behind this constant recurrence of mathematics in all things.[89]

So also in the *Timaeus*.   Plato there finds that while being, space, and generation existed before the creation, there was chaos. There was lack of balance or proportion.   When, however, God created the world, he desired that all things should be good and beautiful.   He therefore bestowed upon them proportion.   He " created in each thing in relation to itself, and in all things in relation to each other, all the measures and harmonies which they could possibly receive."   He fashioned " all things by form and number."[90]

What are the measures and harmonies, the form and number, in the life of the State ?   These must deal with that which is most important to the life of the State, namely, its population, as well as the relative numbers of artisans, business men, farmers, teachers, priests, and magistrates. [91]

Plato thought out a definite number which would constitute the population of the State.   In the *Laws* this is stated to be 5,040. How was the population to be maintained at its proper level, taking both deaths and births into consideration ?   The *Republic* gives an enigmatic answer : indicating, however, that it is related somehow to the seasons and to the revolutions of the planet. [92]

It will therefore be the duty of the matrons meeting at the temple of Eileithyia, having before them the mortality tables and the number of marriageable young women, and being possessed of their own determination that at least one marriage in seven shall be fruitful each year, to calculate the number of children which must be born in order that the population level may be maintained.   Thus we see that to the matrons is given the supremely important task of acting, not only as controllers of marriage, as such, but also as controllers of population.   It is their especial function to maintain the biological and biosocial continuity of the planned community. [93]

Finally it should be realized that, in investigating and applying the principle of the " nuptial number," the matrons are in administrative charge of the mysterious secret of life itself, so far as this is humanly possible.   At their humanly directive level, they are co-operating with the Creator and his celestial satellites in " weaving the web of life," in a way which almost elevates them to the position of the Three Fates of Hellenic mythology.   The Demiurge created the vital principle of the soul, whose mathematical proportions are set out in the *Timaeus*. [94] The celestial beings whose solar and sidereal influences control the seasons and the climatic conditions upon earth, made possible a physical environment suitable for embodied human existence— also on definitely geometric principles set forth in the *Timaeus*. [95] " The principles which are yet prior to these, God only knows, and he of men who is the friend of God "—that is to say, presumably, the Pythagorean scientist and the Platonic philosopher.   The matrons play their part in directing, also on mathematical principles, the human actions involved in passing on the torch of life. It is vital, if the human community is to be a reflex of the divine plan, [96] that the mathematical pattern involved in human generation should be in harmony with the mathematics of the celestial motions ; as these in turn are in harmony with the divine principle followed by the creative Demiurge. For only so can the continuity of the planned community be preserved.[97] Thus we realize that the very small number of women whose innate capacity fits them to occupy such a position, are given the higher, mathematical and dialectical, training ; and that this, superimposed upon the firm base of nonlogical education which has fitted them for citizenship, and always operating in a nonlogical setting of a mythological and religious nature, eventually prepares them for their especial function. This function is exceedingly important, and indeed is indispensable, in connection with the guidance, maintenance, and direction of the planned community which Plato regards as the earthly application and completion of the divine plan laid up in heaven.

[1]In the *Republic*, the private home is eliminated for members of the " silver " and " golden " classes—i.e., for all who are recognized as full citizens. Its place is taken by the group home or state nursery. But in the *Laws*, the private home is reinstated as part of the constant educational background of *all* citizens ; and the appointment of women magistrates to direct and control the married life of all citizens for ten years, " entering into their homes and applying admonitions and threats," indicates how important this institution, under community direction, may be.—I desire, throughout, to acknowledge the assistance afforded to me by the advice and suggestions of Professor R. C. Lodge, of the University of Manitoba. [2]*Rep.* 459–461. [3]Cf. *Menex.* 238c. [4]*Rep.* 460, 468. [5]Contrast *Rep.* 424 " The State, once well started, moves with accumulating force. Good nurture implants good constitutions, and these improve more and more ; and *this improvement affects the breed in man* " (ital. mine) with *Laws* 656–7, 772, 797–9. [6]Cf. The appointment of a travelling inspector of foreign social institutions, *Laws* 951–2. [7]*Laws* 773, cf. *Statesman* 306 ff. [8]*Laws* 774–6, 873–4, 792. [9]*Laws* 789 ff., cf. *Rep.* 460 f. In the *Laws* it is the biological mothers who supply nutrition. In the *Republic* it is group mothers, nurses furnished by the State. [10]*Laws* 790. [11]*Laws* 694–5, 792–4 ; cf. *Rep.* 605–6. [12]*Laws* 792. [13]*Laws* 790–1 ; cf. *Phaedrus* 245, *Timaeus* 43–4. [14]*Tim.* 88–9 ; *Charmides* 156–7. [15]*Laws* 790–1. [16]*Laws* 792. [17]*Laws* 795–6. [18]For the meaning and extension of the term " derivative," and its immense importance in present-day sociological theory, see V. Pareto : *The Mind and Society*, esp. vols. I and III. Its importance is adequately recognized by Plato himself, though not (as a general rule) by most of the scholarly interpreters of the *Dialogues*. [19]*Laws* 817–9, 967–8 ; cf. *Rep.* 521–2, 525cd, 533. [20]*Laws* 663–4, 793 ; cf. *Rep.* 377 ff. [21]*Laws* 794, condensed. [22]*Laws* 793 f., 797–8 ; cf. *Rep.* 424. [23]*Laws* 793 ; cf. *Lysis* 207 ff., *Rep.* 590. Most of the actual games mentioned in the *Dialogues* (e.g., like " the old man's game of draughts ") require a good deal of skill, and belong chiefly to a later period of life than the one we are considering. [24]*Laws* 794, 808, 820. Generally speaking, girls are brought up on the model of the goddess Athene. [25]*Laws* 794–5. [26]*Laws* 796, 829, 833–4. [27]*Laws* 829, 830, 831 ; cf. *Rep.* 431, 503, 537, 539. [28]*Laws* 785, 813–4. In the *Republic*, it is indeed stated that women of the silver class are to function as warriors on the battlefield (453) ; but it is also stated that " one woman has a turn for military exercises and is warlike, while another is unwarlike and hates gymnastics " (456). It is thus only the women with a natural turn for warlike pursuits who are to be selected and educated for this function ; and at that, they are alloted the less heavy duties of military life (457), and are " never to violate, but always to preserve, the natural relation of the sexes "(466). [29]*Laws* 796, 802, 815–6. [30]*Laws* 809–11. [31]*Laws* 802 f. ; cf. *Rep.* 377 ff. [32]*Laws* 802 ; cf. *Rep.* 466cd. [33]*Laws* 745, 806, 848 ; cf. *Crit.* 109, *Theaet.* 149. [34]*Laws.* 950. [35]*Laws* 817 ; cf. *Rep.* 395–6, 595. [36]*Phileb.* 48. [37]*Laws* 658, 816 ; cf. *Rep.* 397, 514, 606. [38]*Laws* 816. [39]*Laws* 951 ; cf. *Rep.* 409. [40]*Rep.* 470. [41]*Rep.* 518. [42]*Laws* 653 ff., 903 ff. ; cf. *Rep.* 508, *Phaedr.* 245 ff. [43]*Laws* 644, 713, 803, 902, 906–7, 930 ; cf. *Phaedo* 62, 80, *Statesm.* 271, *Tim.* 42. [44]*Laws* 653–4 ; cf. *Euthyphr.* 14, *Lys.* 214, *Phaedr.* 255.

⁴⁵*Laws* 821, 855, 886–7 ; cf. *Cratyl.* 397. ⁴⁶*Laws* 887 ; cf. *Apol.* 41, *Phaedo* 63, 81, *Rep.* 612. ⁴⁷*Laws* 794, 828. ⁴⁸*Laws* 801, 804, 828, 887 ; cf. *Tim.* 27. ⁴⁹*Laws* 643, 794 ; cf. *Rep.* 466–7. ⁵⁰*Laws* 654, 656, 672–3, 795 ; cf. *Crito* 50, *Rep.* 376, 403. ⁵¹*Laws* 654, 799, 815–6. ⁵²*Laws* 653, 800. ⁵³*Laws* 653, 659. ⁵⁴*Laws* 796, 814. ⁵⁵*Laws* 802–3. ⁵⁶*Laws* 801–3, 817 ; cf. *Rep.* 379, 540, 592. ⁵⁷*Laws* 796 ; cf. *Protag.* 321, *Theaet.* 149. ⁵⁸*Laws* 659, 660, 665. ⁵⁹*Laws* 772, 775, 784, 903, 930, 932 ; cf. *Rep.* 459. ⁶⁰*Laws* 774, 784. ⁶¹*Laws* 799, 800, 868, 871. ⁶²*Laws* 953. ⁶³*Laws* 663–4, 803–4, 903 ff. ⁶⁴*Laws* 785 ; cf.*Rep.* 458. ⁶⁵*Laws* 784, 794. ⁶⁶*Laws* 721 ; cf. *Rep.* 458, 460, *Tim.* 41–2, 92. ⁶⁷*Laws* 721, 773, 774 ; cf. *Rep.* 461. ⁶⁸*Laws* 772 ; cf. *Rep.* 460. ⁶⁹*Laws* 772, 776 ; cf. *Rep.* 458. ⁷⁰*Laws* 773. In the *Republic*, courageous natures mate with courageous natures, so as to produce yet more courageous offspring. In the *Statesman* (309 ff.) and *Laws*, however, Plato has changed his mind. He now regards approximation to the human norm, the mean between extremes, as of greater importance in preserving the race and in ensuring the unity of the planned community. ⁷¹*Laws* 784. ⁷²*Laws* 721–3. ⁷³*Laws* 784–5. The matron still retains her position of mistress in her own husband's home, on its domestic side. ⁷⁴*Laws* 783, 835–6 ; cf. *Rep.* 458. ⁷⁵*Laws*784–5, 794, 930, 932. ⁷⁶*Laws* 759, 799, 800 ; cf. *Statesman* 290. ⁷⁷*Rep.* 546. ⁷⁸*Laws* 957. ⁷⁹*Laws* 967. ⁸⁰*Laws* 793, 838 ; cf. *Rep.* 414, 429–30, 475–6, 517, 533, *Sympos.* 202, *Statesm.* 309, *Phileb.* 66. ⁸¹*Laws* 957; cf. *Rep.* 456,540. ⁸²*Laws* 784, 785. In the *Republic* (460), twenty is the age indicated. ⁸³*Rep.* 514, ⁸⁴*Rep.*515–6, cf. 538. ⁸⁵*Rep.* 517. ⁸⁶*Rep.* 519. ⁸⁷*Rep.* 484. ⁸⁸*Laws* 784, 794, 802, 829, 930, 932. ⁸⁹*Laws* 657 ; cf. *Cratyl.* 424–6, *Rep.* 525, *Tim.* 68. ⁹⁰*Tim.* 29–30, 52–53, 69. ⁹¹*Laws* 745–7. ⁹²*Laws* 967–8 : esp. "He who has not contemplated the mind of nature which is said to exist in the stars, and gone through the previous training, and seen the connexion of music with these things, and harmonized them all with laws and institutions, is not able to give a reason of such things as have a reason. He who is unable to acquire this in addition to the ordinary virtues of a citizen can hardly be a good ruler." Cf. also *Rep.* 546. To put the matter simply : Plato expects such magistrates as the matrons who preside over marriage and young children to have studied thoroughly, not only his own *Laws* and similar writings (*Laws* 811, cf. 967), but also the *Timaeus*, and probably also the *Statesman* and *Republic*. ⁹³*Laws* 785. ⁹⁴*Tim.* 35–37, with A. E. Taylor's notes (in his *Commentary*). ⁹⁵*Tim.* 53 ff., with A. E. Taylor's notes. ⁹⁶*Laws* 903 f. ; cf. *Rep.* 592. ⁹⁷*Rep.* 546, *Laws* 967–8.

BIBLIOGRAPHY

For complete bibliography of works on Plato, consult the latest edition of Ueberweg's *Grundriss*. The partial bibliography which follows consists of books referred to for specific reasons.

ADAM (JAMES).—*The Republic of Plato*, edited with critical notes, commentary, and appendices. Cambridge University Press, 1905.

ADAMS (GEORGE PLIMPTON) and MONTAGUE.—*Contemporary American Philosophy*, 2 vols. The MacMillan Company, New York, 1930.

ADAMS (SIR JOHN).—*The New Teaching*, 4th Edition. Hodder and Stoughton, London, n.d.

APOLLODORUS (GRAMMATICUS).—*Bibliotheca*, ed. Frazer, Loeb Library, Heinemann, London, 1921.

ARISTOTELES.—*De Anima, Metaphysica, Parva Naturalia, Politica.* Berlin Edition, 1831–1870.

ATHENAEUS.—*Deipnosophistae*, ed. Gulick, 4 vols. Loeb Library. Heinemann, London, 127–30.

BARNARD (CHESTER I.).—*The Functions of the Executive.* Harvard University Press, Cambridge. Mass., 1940.

BEARD (CHARLES A.).—*Whither Mankind?* Longmans, New York, 1930.

BEARE (JOHN I.).—*Greek Theories of Elementary Cognition from Alcmaeon to Aristotle.* Clarendon Press, Oxford, 1906.

BECHER (WALTER).—*Platon und Fichte : die königliche Erziehungskunst.* G. Fischer, Jena, 1937.

BLACKMORE (SIR R.).—See under JOHNSON.

BODE (BOYD H.).—*How We Learn.* D. C. Heath and Co., Boston, 1940.

BONITZ (HERMANN).—*Platonische Studien.* Berlin, 1875.

CREDÉ (HARTMANN).—*Die Kritik der Lehre des Protagoras in Platons Theätet.* Offenbach a. M., 1880.

DEWEY (JOHN).—*Democracy and Education.* The MacMillan Company, New York, 1921.

DEWEY (JOHN).—Philosophy. In *Whither Mankind?* ed. Beard (*q.v.*).

DEWEY (JOHN and EVELYN).—*Schools of Tomorrow.* E. P. Dutton and Co., New York, 1915.

EARHART (LIDA B.).—*Types of Teaching.* Houghton Mifflin Co., Boston, 1915.

ENCYCLOPEDIA BRITANNICA.—14th Edition. London and New York, 1929.

ENGLAND (EDWIN B.).—*The Laws of Plato.* Text, Introduction, Notes, 2 vols. University of Manchester Press, 1921.

FITE (WARNER).—*The Platonic Legend.* Charles Scribner's Sons, New York, 1934.

FLORENCE (P. SARGANT).—*The Logic of Industrial Organisation.* Kegan Paul, London, 1933.

FOSTER (HERBERT H.).—*Principles of Teaching in Secondary Education.* Charles Scribner's Sons, New York, 1921.

FOUILLEE (ALFRED).—*La Philosophie de Platon : exposition, histoire, et critique de la théorie des idées.* 2 vols. Alcan, Paris, 1869.

FRANK (ERICH).—*Plato und die sogenannten Pythagoreer : ein Kapitel aus der Geschichte des griechischen Geistes.* Halle, 1923.

FREELAND (GEORGE E.).—*Modern Elementary School Practice.* The MacMillan Company, New York, 1920

FREEMAN (KENNETH J.).—*Schools of Hellas.* MacMillan and Co., London, 1908.

FRIEDLÄNDER (PAUL).—*Platon* I (Eidos, Paideia, Dialogos), II (Die platonischen Schriften). W. de Gruyter and Co., Berlin and Leipzig, 1928–30.

GOODELL (T. D.).—Plato's Hedonism. In *American Journal of Philology,* Vol. XLII, 1921.

GROTE (GEORGE).—*Plato and the Other Companions of Socrates.* Vols. I–II, London, 1888. Vols. II–III, Longmans, London, 1892.

HOBBES (THOMAS).—*Leviathan,* 1651. Reprinted by E. P. Dutton and Co., New York, n.d.

HOMER.—*Iliad,* ed. T. W. Allen, 3 vols. Clarendon Press, Oxford, 1931.

HORNE (HERMAN HARRELL).—*Philosophy of Education.* The MacMillan Company, New York, 1930.

HORNE (HERMAN HARRELL).—*Story-Telling, Questioning, and Studying. Three School Arts.* The MacMillan Company, New York, 1917.

HUME (DAVID).—Enquiry concerning Human Understanding. In *Essays,* ed. Green and Grose, Vol. II, Longmans, Green and Co., London, 1898.

JAEGER (WERNER).—*Aristoteles.* Berlin, 1923.

JAMES (WILLIAM).—*Principles of Psychology,* 2 vols. Henry Holt and Co., New York, 1890.

JOHNSON (SAMUEL).—*Lives of the Poets.* Chandos Classics edition. Frederick Warne and Co., London and New York, n.d.

KAFKA (GUSTAV).—*Sokrates, Platon, und der sokratische Kreis.* Reinhardt, München, 1921.

LOCKE (JOHN).—*An Essay Concerning Human Understanding* (ed. Frazer). Clarendon Press, Oxford, 1894.

LODGE (RUPERT CLENDON).—On a recent Hypothesis concerning the Platonic Socrates. In *Proceedings of the Sixth International Congress of Philosophy,* New York, 1927.

LODGE (RUPERT CLENDON).—*Philosophy of Education.* Harper and Brothers, New York, 1937.

LODGE (RUPERT CLENDON).—*Plato's Theory of Ethics : The Moral Criterion and the Highest Good.* Harcourt, Brace and Company, New York, 1928.

LUCIAN.—Vera Historia. In *Luciani Samosatensis Opera,* Vol. II, ed. Jakobwitz (Teubner Series), Leipzig, 1877.

MCMURRY (FRANK M.).—*How to Study, and Teaching How to Study.* Houghton Mifflin Co., Boston, 1909.

MORE (PAUL ELMER).—*Platonism.* Princeton University Press, 1917.

MORRIS (CHARLES W.).—*Six Theories of Mind.* University of Chicago Press, 1932.

NATORP (PAUL).—*Platos Ideenlehre. Eine Einführung in den Idealismus.* Leipzig, 1903.

NETTLESHIP (RICHARD LEWIS).—The Theory of Education in Plato's *Republic.* Originally an essay in *Hellenica* (Longmans, 1880), now reprinted by Clarendon Press, Oxford, 1935.

NETTLESHIP (RICHARD LEWIS).—*Philosophical Lectures and Remains,* edited with a Biographical Sketch, by A. C. Bradley and G. R. Benson. MacMillan and Company, London, 1897.

NUNN (T. PERCY).—*In the New Teaching,* ed. Adams (q.v.).

PARETO (VILFREDO).—Trattato di sociologia generale. E.T., *The Mind and Society,* 4 vols., Harcourt, Brace, and Co., New York, c. 1935.

PEARSON (FRANCIS B.).—*The Vitalised School.* The MacMillan Company, New York, 1917.

PERRY (ARTHUR C).—*The Status of the Teacher.* Houghton Mifflin Co., Boston, 1912.

PIAGET (JEAN).—*The Moral Judgment of the Child.* Kegan Paul, London, 1932.

PLATO.—*Opera*, ed. Burnet. 5 (? 6) vols. Clarendon Press, Oxford, n.d.
RAND (BENJAMIN).—*Modern Classical Philosophers :* Selections Illustrating Modern Philosophy. Houghton Mifflin Co., Boston, 1908.
RITTER (CONSTANTIN).—*Platon*, 2 vols. München, 1910.
RITZER (FRANZ).—Fichte's *Idee einer Nationalerziehung und Platons Pädagogisches Ideal.* Beyer and Söhne, Langensalza, 1913.
RUSSELL (BERTRAND).—*Problems of Philosophy.* Thornton Butterworth, London, 1912.
SABINE (G. H.).—*Philosophical Essays in Honor of James Edwin Creighton* (ed.). MacMillan, New York, 1917.
SCHILLER (F. C. S.).—Plato or Protagoras ? In *Mind*, Vol. XVII, p. 518—526, 1908. Also book, pub. Blackwell, Oxford, 1908.
SCHNEIDER (HERMANN).—*Education for Industrial Workers.* A Constructive Study applied to New York City. World Book Co., Yonkers-on-Hudson, 1915.
SOMBART (WERNER).—*The Jews and Modern Capitalism* (E. T. Epstein). Unwin, London, 1915.
STENZEL (JULIUS).—*Platon der Erzieher.* Felix Meiner, Leipzig, 1928.
STEWART (J. A.).—*The Myths of Plato.* Macmillan and Company, London, 1905.
STEWART (J. A.).—*Plato's Doctrine of Ideas.* Clarendon Press, Oxford, 1909.
STOUT (GEORGE FREDERICK).—*Manual of Psychology*, University Tutorial Press, London, 1899.
TAYLOR (A. E.).—*A Commentary on Plato's Timaeus.* Clarendon Press, Oxford, 1928.
TAYLOR (A. E.).—*Plato the Man and His Work.* Dial Press, New York, 1927.
THORNDIKE (E. L.).—*Educational Psychology*, 3 vols. Teachers' College, Columbia University 1921.
WALDEN (J. W. H.).—*The Universities of Ancient Greece.* Charles Scribner's Sons, New York, 1912.
WHITEHEAD (T. N.).—*Leadership in a Free Society.* Harvard University Press, Cambridge, Mass., 1937.
WILAMOWITZ-MOELLENDORFF (ULRICH VON).—*Platon*, 2 vols. Second edition. Weidmann, Berlin, 1920.
WINDELBAND (WILHELM).—*Platon.* Sixth Edition. Frommann, Stuttgart, 1920.
WOOLDRIDGE (H. E.).—*Oxford History of Music*, Vol. I. Clarendon Press, Oxford, 1901.

INDEX OF NAMES

INDEX OF SUBJECTS